# HOW AMERICANS ENFORCE THE LAW

# HOW AMERICANS ENFORCE THE LAW

*DIEGO A. ZAMBRANO*

STANFORD UNIVERSITY PRESS
Stanford, California

Stanford University Press
Stanford, California



Library of Congress Cataloging-in-Publication Data

Names: Zambrano, Diego A. author
Title: How Americans enforce the law / Diego A. Zambrano.
Description: Stanford, California : Stanford University Press, 2026. | Includes bibliographical references and index.
Identifiers: LCCN 2026022594 (print) | LCCN 2026022595 (ebook) | ISBN 9781503647824 cloth | ISBN 9781503648395 paperback | ISBN 9781503648401 ebook
Subjects: LCSH: Citizen suits (Civil procedure)—United States | Actions and defenses—United States | Law—Political aspects—United States
Classification: LCC KF8896.5 .Z36 2026 (print) | LCC KF8896.5 (ebook)
LC record available at https://lccn.loc.gov/2026022594
LC ebook record available at https://lccn.loc.gov/2026022595

Cover art and design: Jason Anscomb

Typeset by Newgen in Adobe Garamond Pro 10.75/14.75 pt

The authorized representative in the EU for product safety and compliance is: Mare Nostrum Group B.V. | Doelen 72 | 4831 GR Breda | The Netherlands | Email address: gpsr@mare-nostrum.co.uk | KVK chamber of commerce number: 96249943

Printed and bound by CPI Group (UK) Ltd, Croydon, CR0 4YY

## CONTENTS

# Introduction

Volkswagen's doomsday announcement came at the end of summer 2015. Michael Horn, the President and CEO of Volkswagen Group of America ("VW"), strutted to applause in front of a large audience of VW investors gathered in Manhattan. Instead of delivering the usual CEO pablum and rosy description of VW's performance, he came with bad news: an admission that millions of VW cars were in violation of emissions standards across the world and that VW had "screwed up." This was no selfless act of contrition. Horn was forced to disclose the company's misconduct by the US Environmental Protection Agency's recently issued "Notice of Violation of the Clean Air Act,"[1] along with a detailed description of the cheating software the agency had found in VW cars. Soon after, VW admitted it had installed "defeat device" software designed to evade emissions testing in over 10 million cars. The company, in other words, had created an elaborate scheme to defraud authorities.

The announcement unleashed a torrent of lawsuits in the United States. American lawyers went immediately to work, filing thousands of claims in California (where testing of many affected vehicles took place), Tennessee (home to a large VW manufacturing plant), Virginia (host to relevant documents, witnesses, and key executives), and elsewhere. A major plaintiffs' firm, Hagens Berman, filed a nationwide class action and individual lawsuits across twenty states. Lawyers were flooded with calls from angry consumers duped by VW cars that had been marketed as environmentally friendly.

Within a few months, the Judicial Panel on Multidistrict Litigation consolidated all claims against VW in a multidistrict litigation ("MDL") before Judge Charles Breyer in San Francisco.[2] The consolidated complaints asserted violations of the Racketeer Influenced and Corrupt Organizations Act ("RICO"), the Magnuson-Moss Warranty Act, state fraud, breach of contract, unjust enrichment laws, and state consumer protection laws. Every one of these claims, statutory or common law, allowed private consumers to file individual lawsuits.

In less than a year, Judge Breyer blessed a settlement agreement that gave consumers cash and forced VW to buy back their vehicles at their full pre-disclosure value (or offer a fix for the problem). Most consumers could expect to collect between $5,000 and $10,000. The lawyers also received a handsome payment of about $324 million in fees and costs. VW agreed to provide billions of dollars to support environmental initiatives, too. All in all, VW spent around $11.2 billion in consumer payments and nearly $3 billion in other settlement costs. The settlement reflected Judge Breyer's efficient management, speed, and competence. He spent the entire year organizing the litigation; selecting lead counsel (Lieff Cabraser Heimann & Bernstein); appointing former FBI Director Robert Mueller as settlement master; holding hearings with government officials, counsel, and consumers; crafting a "common benefit" fund for plaintiffs' lawyers to share expenses; overseeing settlement negotiations; and developing complex theories of remediation.

But in VW's home country, Germany, the company's fraud unleashed only a trickle of consumer lawsuits with no consolidated resolution in sight. Consumers filed claims either against VW dealerships or against Volkswagen AG directly. But claims against dealerships were geographically scattered and there was no procedure for bringing them all together. As for claims against Volkswagen AG, German consumers could rely on individual tort claims, but there has been no quick or consistent resolution in favor of consumers. At most, VW offered German consumers rebates if they bought new cars.

The contrast between the experiences of US and German litigants generated anger among German consumer groups. German legislators responded with a draft bill that would allow consumer groups to file group claims. But a German attorney told *The Wall Street Journal* "[t]his law is a sham," because it empowered only some organizations to file lawsuits and not individual consumers.[3] Not only did Germany lack a class action device, but it also didn't have the web of statutory claims that exist in the United States, nor punitive damages. German consumers were instead left to rely on German regulators and judges, who, perhaps, were friendly to VW and too aware of its status as a German corporate champion.

---

While most countries rely on administrative schemes and robust bureaucracies to regulate the health and safety of their citizens, Americans like to do things differently. In place of bureaucratic governance, the United States relies on a constellation of private rights of action embedded in most significant statutes. Just like RICO, the Magnuson-Moss Warranty Act, and consumer protection statutes empowered consumers to sue VW, statutes on antitrust, employment, civil rights, and the environment allow private parties to enforce the law via lawsuits. Many Americans intuitively know this, but they have no idea how important private lawsuits are in enforcing the law.

Across the major areas of federal regulation, private parties are typically the *main* enforcers, filing 98% of civil rights claims, around 90% of antitrust claims, and a significant chunk of employment, environmental, and securities claims.[4] In these enforcement cases, "private lawsuits become a regulatory tool and the legal system transforms from one where 'one citizen can seek redress from another in an orderly fashion' into one where citizens or groups of citizens can enforce the law for systemic regulatory purposes."[5] That, in short, is what this book calls private enforcement.

But private enforcement is not just reserved for significant areas of economic activity. It is *everywhere.* If you happen to be in Salt Lake City and encounter an issue with a particular drug dealer—say, a family member buys meth and lands in rehab, or the dealer pockets your money and vanishes—a Utah law allows you to file a civil lawsuit against the dealer "for injury resulting from an individual's use of an illegal drug."[6] In New Mexico, you can sue to prevent an unlicensed veterinarian "from engaging in the practice of veterinary medicine."[7] A New Jersey law allows private claims against pet dealers who offer agreements that transfer "ownership of a cat or dog at the end of the lease term."[8] (For example, a dealer who leases out a French bulldog puppy like a car and then threatens to repossess it when the family misses a payment.) In South Carolina, a statute lets you sue someone who may have "damaged" your family member's grave.[9] Again and again, states create private rights of action to prevent or regulate conduct that is otherwise policed by the government. And these examples represent only a tiny fraction of the thousands of federal and state private rights of action on the books.

This is how governance happens in America. Whenever faced with a major social problem, legislators mobilize private attorneys and plaintiffs to enforce the law, not just to pursue private aims. This kind of legislative scheme is more powerful when private rights of action are paired with a broader procedural infrastructure: multiple damages provisions, attorney fee-shifting, class actions, contingency fees, jury trials, and expansive discovery.

Once you realize that litigation is often a deliberately designed form of regulation, other features of our legal system start to make more sense. Consider, for instance, the common observation that America has far more lawyers and lawsuits per capita than other developed countries. While the United States has about 400 lawyers per 100,000 people, Germany comes in at around half of that number with 200 per 100,000 people.[10] Journalists and even scholars sometimes express either amazement or dismay at this statistic. But they have it all wrong. Comparing the number of lawyers in America and Germany is not an apples-to-apples exercise. Germany channels most regulatory enforcement into an extensive *ex ante* administrative state staffed by career civil servants. The United States, by contrast, relies heavily on both public and private enforcement, letting lawyers act *ex post* as roving bureaucrats, enforcing the law wherever litigation makes economic sense. An appropriate cross-country comparison, then, would look at the size of the entire enforcement apparatus, lawyers plus bureaucrats, public and private. While there is no clean comparative data on the number of bureaucrats, Germany appears to employ far more bureaucrats than the United States.[11] Taking the full regulatory apparatus together shows that American and German regulatory schemes are more comparable than at first blush.

Twenty years ago, Robert Kagan called this system "adversarial legalism," defined as "policymaking, policy implementation, and dispute resolution by means of party-and-lawyer-dominated legal contestation."[12] He distinguished it from "bureaucratic administration" and "the judge-dominated style of litigation common in many other countries."[13] The United States, Kagan argued, "employs these other methods too," but "adversarial legalism is far more prominent."[14] Kagan evaluated some costs and benefits of adversarial legalism and explored its appearance in both the criminal and civil justice systems. Sean Farhang then built on this in *The Litigation State*, exploring the growth of private enforcement in the 1960s and 70s.[15] Unlike Kagan, Farhang was concerned with causal origins. Much of Farhang's book defends what he terms the "separation of powers" theory that private enforcement is a legislative choice. When Congress and the Presidency are controlled by different political parties, legislators prefer to delegate enforcement to private parties rather than an ideologically distant bureaucracy. Farhang focused entirely on the federal code and mostly on the Civil Rights Act of 1964, finding some quantitative and qualitative support for the separation of powers theory.

But neither Farhang nor Kagan examined the full historical and institutional scope of private enforcement in American law. By focusing on "adversarial legalism" as a "legal style," Kagan devoted less attention to the legislative mechanism that drives private enforcement: ubiquitous private rights of action. This distinction is important because a country could embrace adversarial legalism—as many common law countries do—with or without private enforcement. In other words, what distinguishes the United States is not just a "legal style" per se, but the repeated legislative reliance on private enforcement provisions. Farhang, meanwhile, built an elegant theory about the separation of powers driving private enforcement at the federal level in the 1960s and 70s. His focus on federal legislation and divided government during the civil rights era proved valuable for understanding that specific historical moment. However, as this book demonstrates through empirical analysis of state legislation, this theory has limited explanatory power beyond the federal context. When you look at the states, there appears to be no uptick in legislative embrace of private enforcement during periods of divided governance. Nor do Democratic or Republican control of state legislatures explain its popularity. Even other features of a state, like lawyers per capita or tax receipts, are uncorrelated with the adoption of private enforcement. In short, the separation of powers theory does not provide a complete explanation of American private enforcement. More fundamentally, a comprehensive understanding of private enforcement requires exploring the history of rights to sue and developments across the fifty states.

This book tells the full story of how Americans enforce the law. It does so with four main goals. The first is to document the phenomenon of private enforcement with empirical depth. Drawing on machine learning analysis of state and federal codes, the book reveals more than 10,000 private rights of action across the fifty states—a vast regulatory system hiding in plain sight. Through detailed comparisons with France and Canada, the book also shows how this approach to regulation is uniquely American. While French authorities control environmental and consumer protection laws through administrative enforcement, and even common law countries like Canada rely more heavily on bureaucratic oversight, the United States uniquely empowers private parties as regulatory enforcers.

The second goal is to uncover private enforcement's deep historical roots. The book digs into colonial and Early Republic history to expose the foundations of private enforcement and its relationship to the Constitution and American governance. Some scholars traced its origins to the 1960s civil rights movement, while others focused only on a narrow set of provisions called qui tam. But these narratives overlook centuries of American legal development. This book explains how colonial and early American lawmakers routinely passed "penal statutes" that allowed private citizens to sue for violations of regulatory law. This tradition of private enforcement, including both informer actions and qui tam bounties, shaped American governance from its earliest days.

The book's third aim is to replace familiar explanations about why the United States embraced private enforcement with a more historically and empirically grounded account, one that I call "layered path dependence." Private enforcement first took root because early lawmakers inherited English penal statutes and, lacking bureaucratic capacity, defaulted to that template. That default then became self-reinforcing as Congress and state legislatures repeatedly grafted private rights of action onto new statutes to hedge against bureaucratic monopoly of enforcement, even while expanding agencies. Finally, the twentieth-century growth of a powerful lawyers' lobby alongside procedural innovations—liberal discovery and class actions—transformed those rights into a durable mass-litigation engine. These layers knit together over time, locking the United States into a system where private suits and public regulators complement rather than replace each other. America's reliance on private enforcement, therefore, is not a simple cultural preference or a congressional tactic but the cumulative product of historical inheritance, the lawyers' lobby, structural incentives, and civil procedure rules.

The final goal is to examine how private enforcement sometimes fails, producing rent-seeking litigation that is especially destructive in environmental law. The book first distills the political theory for private enforcement into three key elements: making up for limited state capacity, avoiding regulatory dysfunction, and surfacing hidden information through litigation. These elements provide clear criteria for evaluating when private enforcement is justified. Applied to specific domains, these criteria reveal why private enforcement works well in employment law—where workers have unique access to information about violations and regulators lack resources for oversight—but fails dramatically in environmental law, where it has enabled rent-seeking litigation that blocks housing construction and infrastructure development. The book concludes by proposing reforms to limit private enforcement where it undermines rather than serves the public interest.

In addressing these four goals, the book offers a mixed-methods approach, combining original work conducted for this book and related papers: empirical quantitative studies, comparative studies of the US and France, a historical investigation of Founding era documents, and so on. And the book tackles key comparative and normative questions: When does private enforcement succeed or fail? What are its costs in areas like environmental law and housing construction? Why did the United States respond to oil spills with private rights of action while France did not? And how might we reform it for the twenty-first century?

---

The book comes packed with implications for current social and political debates. Consider some examples of private enforcement regimes in the news:

**Democratic Instability and Trump**. The Trump administration is teaching us the important role of private enforcement during periods of democratic instability. Litigation rights advocates have long highlighted that private plaintiffs serve as a failsafe when governments are unresponsive. That is true here: Even if the Trump administration refuses to enforce critical laws against corruption or regulations on foreign platforms, private enforcement could fill this gap, ensuring that the law remains independent of politically motivated governance. If the Department of Justice (DOJ) risks becoming a political instrument of the executive, private litigants become vital for enforcing regulatory statutes. In this way, private suits provide stability in legal enforcement regardless of which political administration holds power. Moreover, private enforcement empowers victims of unlawful, politically destructive actions. For example, the Department of Government Efficiency (DOGE) and the Trump administration conducted an unlawful campaign of unilateral defunding of multiple agencies, mass terminations of civil servants, and unauthorized access to confidential databases. Private enforcement through statutes like the Privacy Act—which enables individuals to sue federal agencies for failing to comply with personal records handling regulations—proved to be one of the few recourses against these violations.

**Environmental Law and Construction**. Private enforcement of environmental law has been weaponized against housing construction, green energy, and mass transit projects. It turns out that America faces extraordinarily expensive infrastructure development compared to other countries. From transit systems to residential construction, and roads to basic public facilities, building costs in the US consistently outpace international norms. Some of these stories have become well known among a burgeoning "abundance" movement: New York's Second Avenue subway extension required $2.5 billion for what became known as the world's costliest subway mile. California's high-speed rail project between Los Angeles and San Francisco ballooned into a $113 billion debacle. Even modest projects like a single public restroom in San Francisco carried a $1.7 million price tag. Highway construction tells a similar story of increasing costs over time. This pattern stands in stark contrast to other developed nations like Japan or France, which achieve far more cost-effective construction. The housing sector presents perhaps the most dramatic example, with mounting evidence showing that American urban housing prices have reached extreme levels, primarily driven by zoning restrictions and regulatory barriers.

Key to this massive problem are more than 700 private rights of action in state environmental laws that allow nearly anyone to file lawsuits against proposed construction projects. These lawsuits both produce economic rents for "not in my backyard" advocates ("NIMBYs") and unions and increase costs for most projects. Wealthy DC residents, including a country club, have held up construction of a metro line to the Maryland suburbs planned in 1989 over concerns for an "invertebrate known as an amphipod."[16] Legacy environmental groups routinely file claims against wind farms, clean energy transmission lines, and solar projects. Fit for a bizarro world, the Sierra Club filed a claim to stop construction of a large solar farm in the Mojave Desert because a few bikers enjoy desert views, they prefer the land "unspoiled," and a group of turtles may be affected.[17] It is no exaggeration to say that private enforcement has weakened American dynamism and increased the costs of construction. It does this by allowing anyone (labor unions, homeowners, misguided environmental organizations) to oppose housing, mass transit, and clean energy projects through rent-seeking lawsuits.

**Partisan Battles over Guns and Abortion.** States are currently battling to regulate politically contentious areas via private enforcement. The most prominent example is Texas's SB 8, a bill that banned abortions in the state of Texas and allowed "anyone" to enforce its provisions via private lawsuits against abortion providers. The statute was deliberately designed to empower only private parties to avoid pre-enforcement challenges in federal court. This was not a one-off. California's SB 1327 copied the strategy, empowering any citizen to sue gun manufacturers in some circumstances. Governor Newsom challenged the Supreme Court: "The question is whether they are complete and abject hypocrites and frauds if they reject our bill that's modeled after that abortion bill as it relates to [a] private right of action to go after assault weapons."[18] Judge Roger Benitez of the Southern District of California issued an immediate injunction against enforcement of SB 1327, quoting statements by other government officials that both SB 8 and SB 1327 were "cynical . . . an abomination . . . outrageous and objectionable."[19] States will continue to push these boundaries to promote politically contentious regulation.

**Antitrust Enforcement.** Some of the most contentious regulatory actions by the Biden administration came from the Federal Trade Commission and its former chair, Lina Khan. Khan came to prominence after writing a law review article that criticized the lack of post-1980s antitrust enforcement by the DOJ and Federal Trade Commission (FTC). But her article demonstrated a misunderstanding of our regulatory system. As this book discusses, not only are 90 percent of federal antitrust actions filed by private parties but also every state has a robust private right of action for antitrust claims. If you truly care about antitrust law, the main actor was never Lina Khan, nor the FTC, nor even the DOJ. This ecosystem is instead dominated by an antitrust plaintiffs' bar that represents millions of consumers and business competitors in thousands of lawsuits every year. These attorneys even creatively draw on foreign regulators, sometimes filing antitrust cases in the US after a company has been penalized by European antitrust regulators. This means that recent court cases that have cut down on private enforcement of antitrust law are more important than any decision by Lina Khan. Again, for good or ill.

Given these examples (and others), this book argues that we need to move beyond wholesale embrace or rejection of private enforcement toward more discriminating analysis of when and how it serves the public interest. The framework I develop below provides important tools for making these judgments. But applying this framework effectively will require careful attention to how private enforcement performs in practice.

---

The book's central focus is how the law mobilizes lawyers and everyday Americans to enforce regulatory policy via private lawsuits. Part I lays out the basics of this system, some data on its prevalence, its colonial history, and its modern version.

Chapter 1 explains that when legislators craft new laws to address social issues—pollution, business competition, or minimum wages—they have a choice. They can empower public employees, salaried and subject to government control, to issue rules, regulations, licenses, and, if appropriate, file enforcement claims. Or legislators can craft a private right of action that allows any party to file a lawsuit. When they choose private enforcement, they rally plaintiffs' attorneys to act as substitutes for bureaucrats. Of course, legislators often do both. But the distinctive thing about the United States is how common it is for legislators to include a private right of action and to rely on the private lawsuits it creates as the main vehicle of enforcement actions.

To contrast private and public enforcement, this chapter explores how the French bureaucracy—the quintessential administrative state—enforces the most important French statutes. Unlike the United States, private litigation in France is not a pillar of regulatory enforcement but merely a side player in larger bureaucratic schemes. To make this point, the book contrasts the divergent reactions in France and the United States to major oil spills. Specifically, the 1999 *Erika* oil spill disaster, in which a major oil tanker caused massive pollution off the coast of France, provoked significant regulatory and criminal enforcement. But a similar disaster in the United States, the 1989 *Exxon Valdez* oil spill, instead provoked a mixed set of cases by class action attorneys, individual victims, states and localities, and, yes, the DOJ. Unlike in France, however, private claims were on an equal footing with government enforcement actions. And Congress responded to the disaster by creating a new private right of action for oil spills, a provision that came to play a prominent role after the BP oil disaster of 2010.

Chapter 2 documents the appearance of private enforcement in state and federal codes. Building on previous work using machine learning and large language models, the chapter explores the more than 10,000 private rights of action in state and federal law. It shows how these provisions appear in statutes governing banking, labor, taxes, the environment, and, well, everywhere else. California and Texas lead the way, with nearly 200 private rights of action, while most states average between fifty and one hundred. The federal government has adopted about 350 of them. Surprisingly, private rights of action have been expanding in small states that aren't ideologically homogeneous, including Utah, New Hampshire, Connecticut, Nebraska, and Wisconsin. More recently, private rights of action appear in statutes on privacy or lawsuits against police. But environmental statutes have long been among the most prominent examples. Consider the 1974 New Jersey Environmental Rights Act, which allows "[a]ny person" to enforce dozens of other environmental regulations and ordinances. A New Jersey legislator argued that the statute "will enable citizens to have ready access to the courts to resolve environmental disputes."[20] And the New Jersey State Bar Association praised the statute as an "effective[] grant to interested citizens the right to sue polluters without having to prove special injury to the plaintiffs."[21]

Still, the sheer number of private rights of action doesn't tell us how often these provisions are deployed. After all, a private right of action can generate anything from only a few lawsuits per year to significant numbers of lawsuits that effectively regulate an entire market. On one end of the spectrum, you can find the South Carolina grave-protecting statute, which leads to almost no lawsuits in any given year. On the other end, take California's Private Attorneys General Act (PAGA), which allows employees in California to sue employers for any violation of California's extensive labor code. Workers can file the lawsuit individually or on behalf of other employees and the State of California. PAGA may be one of the most robust private rights of action in the United States, allowing lawsuits over wages and hours, child labor violations, or smaller infractions like failure to provide itemized wage statements. Since its inception in 2004, PAGA lawsuits have grown by more than ten times, fueling thousands of lawsuits in 2023. A single PAGA private right of action, then, has massive significance for California's economy.

Chapter 3 explores the medieval roots of American private enforcement. Tracing its lineage through English legal history, the chapter reveals how Parliament routinely adopted "penal statutes" that allowed private "common informers" to sue violators of regulatory provisions. By the late 1600s, this system was so entrenched that English political economist Charles Davenant noted how lawmakers deliberately created financial incentives "to stir up the People to put the Laws in Execution."[22] Beyond these general penal statutes, specialized "qui tam" actions allowed citizens to sue on the Crown's behalf while keeping a portion of the penalties, becoming a cornerstone of English regulation by the 1400s. These mechanisms regulated everything from market practices to road maintenance, while a parallel tradition of common law writs empowered private citizens to challenge both private misconduct and government overreach.

Colonial America not only inherited but intensified these private enforcement traditions. The chapter explains how some colonies embedded private enforcement in a large percentage of their laws in the eighteenth century, regulating everything from wandering livestock to gunpowder storage. This pattern repeated across the colonies and subsequent states, with private enforcement overseeing local administration, road maintenance, judicial procedures, elections, and even tax collection. The Founders themselves were intimately familiar with these mechanisms—Thomas Jefferson and James Madison collaborated on Virginia legislation containing numerous informer provisions, while John Adams handled qui tam cases as a colonial lawyer. This historical depth explains why the first Congress used private enforcement to implement nearly all its enumerated powers and why President Washington recognized that he could not override a private citizen's statutory right to enforce federal law. And in the 1800s, Congress adopted dozens of informer claims, building private enforcement into America's early regulatory state. Private enforcement, then, is not a modern tool, but the continuation of a tradition deeply embedded in American governance since its inception.

Chapter 4 then recasts modern US legal history as the construction of a "Republic of Private Enforcement." It shows that, beginning with the Sherman Act's treble damages suit (1890) and continuing through the Clayton Act (1914), the Fair Labor Standards Act (1938), Title VII of the Civil Rights Act (1964), RICO (1970), and the Clean Air and Clean Water Acts' citizen suits (1970–72), every major social movement secured its legacy by placing a private right of action in new federal statutes.

The chapter argues that the true progenitor of the American regulatory system—combining both robust agencies with private rights of action—is the choice Congress made in 1914 to adopt both the Clayton Act and Federal Trade Commission Act. The twin bills established a pattern that would define American regulatory governance for the next century. Rather than choosing between litigation and bureaucracy, Congress regularly paired each new agency (the FTC, the Wage and Hour Division, the EEOC, and the EPA) with a parallel invitation for private plaintiffs and their lawyers to enforce the same statutes. This hybrid, repeatedly justified as "common sense and economical," diffused power beyond resource constrained regulators and resonated with Americans' rejection of bureaucratic monopoly. By the 1970s, the model was supercharged by Ralph Nader's "sue the bastards" consumer crusade, embedding private enforcement so deeply in antitrust, labor, civil rights, environmental, and even racketeering laws that rights to sue became ubiquitous.

Building on this history, part II then develops the causal, theoretical, and procedural foundations of private enforcement.

Chapter 5 explores existing theories of private enforcement's causal origins. Why does the United States end up relying on private enforcement when no one else in the world does to the same extent? First up is the separation of powers theory which "posits that Congress enacts private rights of action when the executive is controlled by another political party."[23]

While this theory has some support at the federal level, it appears to have no support in the states. As I found in a previous article, "[r]egression analyses based on our best estimates of private-enforcement provisions do not yield a statistically meaningful relationship between divided government and private-enforcement adoption."[24] Relatedly, "[w]e even find no correlation between an increased adoption of private enforcement and legislative control by either Democrats or Republicans."[25] Private enforcement in the states, then, may be fundamentally different than at the federal level.

The second prominent theory focuses on structure and culture, positing that American values like individualism, a preference for confrontation, and suspicion of government bureaucracies increase demand for litigation to resolve disputes. But this theory, along with Robert Kagan's adversarial legalism, is somewhat inconsistent with the history and other features of our legal system. Having shown the limitations of these theories, Chapter 5 clears the ground for a fresh explanatory framework developed in Chapter 6.

Chapter 6 rejects other explanations in favor of a layered path dependence account. An inherited toolkit of English penal statutes made delegating enforcement to private parties cheap and familiar; each time Congress or a state legislature copied that language, it further normalized the practice. Separation of powers, federalism, and the lawyers' lobby then reinforced the habit by encouraging lawmakers to hedge against future bureaucratic drift. Whenever legislators built or expanded an agency, they also bolted on a right to sue so that no single institution held an enforcement monopoly. The critical juncture in this story was the 1914 adoption of the Clayton Act and Federal Trade Commission Act. And there was significant contingency in that choice: Political leaders in the early twentieth century repeatedly changed their stance on private enforcement before continuing the tradition. Finally, twentieth-century procedural innovations—sweeping discovery and opt-out class actions—transformed those statutory clauses into a potent litigation engine, lowering the cost of adding them to new bills. The result is a drafting default—rights to sue migrated across the environmental statutes of the 1970s and slipped unnoticed into thousands of state laws. Private enforcement thus became the default, not through ideological design, but through historical inheritance, structural incentives, and uniquely permissive civil procedure rules.

Civil procedure represents perhaps the most critical but underappreciated layer in the architecture of American private enforcement, serving as the essential infrastructure that transforms rights to sue into regulatory devices. A private right of action by itself accomplishes nothing without the procedural mechanisms that enable plaintiffs to actually gather evidence, aggregate claims, and pursue meaningful relief. The chapter explains how French employment discrimination experience demonstrates this vividly: Despite having a formal private right of action, the absence of robust procedural tools renders those rights largely ineffective in practice. American civil procedure, by contrast, provides two uniquely powerful engines that make private enforcement viable: broad discovery rules that emerged from the 1938 Federal Rules of Civil Procedure and modern class actions established through the 1966 overhaul of Rule 23. These new procedures fundamentally distinguish the American system from other legal traditions and explain why private enforcement flourishes in the United States while remaining marginal elsewhere.

Discovery and class actions work in tandem to solve the core challenges that would otherwise cripple private enforcement. Discovery grants private litigants investigative powers comparable to federal agencies, allowing them to compel document production, conduct depositions, and uncover evidence buried within corporations and government agencies. Class actions address the economic barriers that would make most private enforcement impossible by aggregating small-value claims into cases large enough to attract competent counsel and justify the costs of litigation. Together, these procedural tools transform private lawyers into quasi-bureaucrats, capable of policing regulatory violations that public agencies lack the resources to pursue. This procedural foundation explains why the same substantive legal rights generate robust private enforcement in the United States while remaining largely dormant in countries with less permissive procedural rules. Civil procedure is therefore the linchpin that determines whether private enforcement serves as an effective governance mechanism.

While the first two parts of the book focus on history and causal theories, part III shifts gears to explore the theoretical justifications for private enforcement. This shift from explanation to evaluation represents a transition in the analysis. While the previous parts asked "Why did private enforcement develop as it did?" this part asks "Should we want private enforcement to exist at all, and if so, under what conditions?"

Chapter 7 argues that private enforcement is justified when a scheme satisfies a balancing test of three criteria: First, when private enforcement makes up for a *lack of enforcement capacity*. That concept refers to the idea that public enforcement or agencies lack sufficient resources or staffing (capacity) to investigate and police legal violations. By empowering private plaintiffs, governments can achieve higher enforcement of the law—and deterrence—without relying on a costly bureaucracy. Second, and relatedly, private enforcement can diffuse power among hundreds of thousands of plaintiffs and their lawyers. Because of that, private enforcement schemes can avoid the problem of *regulatory dysfunction* due to capture, corruption, and the fear that regulated entities will exercise undue influence on government bureaucrats. Put another way, private plaintiffs can be a failsafe in cases where the bureaucracy is unresponsive. And they can stabilize the enforcement of the law regardless of the political administration in power. Moreover, private enforcement can empower political underdogs or weak constituencies who may otherwise lack the government's attention. Third, private enforcement solves the bureaucratic *problem of informational asymmetries*—it is quite difficult for bureaucrats to discover legal violations and to smoke out relevant information. By giving private parties an incentive to file claims—often via multiple damages and fee-shifting—private enforcement surfaces information that is otherwise hidden.

But of course, even when private enforcement satisfies these criteria, it can impose significant costs. Chief among these is the divergence between private and public interests. As law and economics has long taught us, private plaintiffs will file claims whenever it makes economic sense, but bureaucrats are supposed to take the public interest into account and maintain greater legislative fidelity. This can lead to overenforcement of the law by overzealous plaintiffs' attorneys. On top of that, private claimants lack any democratic accountability and are uncoordinated—this can lead to guerrilla litigation that is wasteful. Yet another effect is that "the piecemeal and unyielding nature of profit-motivated private enforcement will deprive regulatory regimes of needed 'coherence' by, among other things, disrupting the subtle cooperative relationships that arise between regulators and regulatory targets."[26]

Chapter 8 begins with the positive side. There are significant regulatory areas that benefit from private enforcement. Take, for instance, employment law, where the Fair Labor Standards Act of 1938 and all fifty states' wages and hours laws create an almost total reliance on private lawsuits rather than regulation by the Department of Labor (and state equivalents). And in this area, private enforcement draws on all three of its traditional justifications. First, labor regulators at both the state and federal levels are chronically underfunded, leading to a thorough lack of state administrative capacity. For instance, California's Division of Occupational Safety and Health has never been funded adequately, is severely understaffed, and suffers from routine budget cuts. This has forced employees and unions to press for private rights of action, culminating in the adoption of the California Private Attorneys General Act of 2004. This is true, too, at the federal level, where employees are the main enforcers of the Fair Labor Standards Act because the Department of Labor lacks the resources to investigate non-compliance with wages and hours regulations.

Second, and relatedly, large companies and employers invest heavily in courting favor from regulators while simultaneously lobbying for budget cuts to public enforcement budgets. A private right of action responds to this problem by diffusing enforcement power across thousands of employees and their attorneys, reducing the influence of corporate lobbying and ensuring consistent enforcement of the labor code.

On top of regulatory capture and a lack of state capacity, private enforcement also empowers employees who have unique information on whether an employer is violating labor laws. Regulators, by contrast, cannot uncover this information without launching costly investigations. Moreover, without a guaranteed payout, employees have no incentive to flag the problem to regulators because they fear losing their job. Private enforcement steps in and incentivizes employees to identify wage theft, overtime violations, and other infractions with a potential reward of compensatory and punitive damages. This decentralized approach enables private plaintiffs to surface information that would otherwise remain hidden, making private enforcement an indispensable tool for ensuring compliance with labor laws.

All in all, private enforcement is well justified in the employment context and, by most accounts, operates well in this regard.

While the book recognizes the benefits of private enforcement, it also takes it to task where it has failed. Chapter 9 argues that private enforcement is unjustified in the environmental context and has contributed to the undersupply of housing, mass transit, and clean energy in the United States. As discussed above, the United States has some of the highest construction costs in the world. The Transit Costs Project found that "the United States is the sixth most expensive country in the world to build rapid-rail transit infrastructure."[27]

Similarly, a Niskanen Center Report notes: "Over the last few generations, American infrastructure construction costs have exploded . . . even as many peer countries spend a fraction of what the US does on the same bridge or tunnel or high-speed rail line."[28] We face the same problem in housing, where construction of dense multi-story housing is *de facto* illegal in most cities, both due to zoning constraints and misguided environmental regulations.

The book argues that private enforcement became a default method of enforcing environmental law and thereafter played a destructive role in the construction industry. One culprit is the 1970 National Environmental Policy Act, a statute that requires every developer of infrastructure projects (that constitute "major federal action") to prepare an environmental impact statement (EIS).[29] Through the Administrative Procedure Act, any plaintiff can then sue (and stall construction projects) by alleging deficiencies in EISs. Although these are technically administrative claims that do not rely on a private right of action, they effectively turn the National Environmental Policy Act (NEPA) into a private enforcement regime. Many states mirror this federal law with local mini-NEPAs, including California's Environmental Quality Act (CEQA). CEQA applies to almost any construction project in the state, housing or otherwise, and requires cities and developers to prepare extensive environmental impact reports and study any "significant environmental effects of a project."[30] Importantly, any person can file a lawsuit against a city/developer for insufficient compliance with the statute. This turned CEQA into a thermonuclear device that empowers opponents of construction projects. CEQA lawsuits have led to significant problems, recently forcing the state of California to roll back the law in a variety of ways. Yet private enforcement is still core to the statute.

In this context, private enforcement does not draw on any of its traditional theoretical foundations and, worse, is especially vulnerable to rent-seeking. CEQA and the more than 700 private rights of action in state and federal law end up empowering almost anyone to oppose housing or mass transit construction projects. This includes neighbors, local residents, other companies, labor unions, or anyone else who can easily abuse the system through rent-seeking lawsuits that paralyze construction.[31] But none of this is justified. When it comes to policing zoning and environmental laws, there is no lack of state capacity—most of the time, private plaintiffs are filing claims after government regulators have already reviewed and approved construction projects. Nor do private claimants have any particular expertise or access to information that public agents lack. Most of the relevant regulatory regimes operate by asking construction projects to disclose environmental compliance, giving regulators and private parties the same information. Worst of all, there is a clear divergence between the interests of society and neighbors, regular citizens, and labor unions. While all of society benefits from clean energy and housing projects, local populations may see home values drop and neighborhoods change. This leads precisely to the problem of guerrilla litigation that is redundant, wasteful, and burdensome. The constellation of private enforcement therefore increases construction costs in an unjustified manner.

Given these potential problems, Chapter 10 introduces a menu of reforms to sharpen private enforcement. Private enforcement has proven to be a powerful but double-edged regulatory tool, offering unique advantages in complex policy areas while carrying significant risks of overshooting into excessive litigation. Keep in mind that there are two kinds of failed private enforcement schemes. First, statutes like NEPA and CEQA are vulnerable to the problem of litigation capture, even though they provide some benefits like avoidance of regulatory capture and increased state capacity. For this class of statutes, legislatures need new tools to limit lawsuits filed by rent-seeking groups. A second class of statutes, like Texas's SB 8—the statute that bans abortion in Texas and allows anyone to enforce its claims—is simply not justified under any political theory of private enforcement.

To regulate the first class of statutes (NEPA, CEQA, and other environmental laws), this chapter offers a spectrum of possible solutions. On the most intense end, state legislatures and Congress could eliminate private enforcement by prohibiting administrative challenges after an agency has certified compliance with the statute. In the middle of the spectrum, the chapter discusses the incorporation of automatic sunset clauses into private rights of action, requiring legislatures to affirmatively renew enforcement mechanisms after specified periods. On the lighter end, legislatures can make it harder for plaintiffs to file claims. One solution is to increase standing requirements so that only actually harmed parties can file administrative challenges. This would prevent random neighbors, unions, and busybodies from filing environmental claims against construction projects. But it would preserve the legal rights of organizations and citizens who live directly in the path of a new project. At the other end of the spectrum, legislatures could make it procedurally more difficult to file claims by requiring would-be plaintiffs to post large bonds—as an indication of real interest in the lawsuit. This would prevent serial filers from filing dozens of NEPA or CEQA challenges. Finally, legislatures could impose tight timing and aggregation provisions so that judges must consider all legal challenges against projects in one aggregate setting, quickly decide on any challenges, and then close out a short period for legal claims.

---

Below is a high-level outline of the book's parts and chapters.

**PART I: BACKGROUND AND HISTORY**

1. What Is Private Enforcement?
2. The Prevalence of Private Enforcement
3. Historical Roots: Penal Statutes and Qui Tam
4. A Republic of Private Enforcement and the Choice of 1914

**PART II: THEORY AND CAUSAL EXPLANATIONS**

5. Competing Theories of Private Enforcement
6. A Layered Path Dependence

**PART III: A NORMATIVE APPRAISAL**

7. Justifications for Private Enforcement
8. When Private Enforcement *Is* Justified
9. How Private Enforcement Fails: Environmental Law and Housing Construction
10. Sharpening Private Enforcement

---

# PART I

## BACKGROUND AND HISTORY

# ONE

## WHAT IS PRIVATE ENFORCEMENT?

On March 24, 1989, disaster struck the pristine waters of Prince William Sound, Alaska. The *Exxon Valdez,* a massive oil tanker carrying 53 million gallons of crude oil, ran aground on Bligh Reef after veering off its designated shipping lanes.[1] In a series of catastrophic missteps, the ship's captain, Joseph Hazelwood—allegedly impaired by alcohol—left the bridge moments before the tanker needed to correct course, relying instead on his third mate, who failed to maneuver in time. The grounding ruptured the hull, releasing millions of gallons of crude oil into the surrounding waters and triggering one of the worst environmental disasters in US history. Thousands of miles of Alaskan coastline were contaminated, including national parks, wildlife refuges, and forests, devastating fish and wildlife populations and shattering the lives and livelihoods of coastal communities. The spill disrupted commercial fishing, subsistence hunting, and tourism, leading to immediate economic and ecological fallout that reverberated for decades.

The *Exxon Valdez* oil spill is the kind of event that provokes government action—a flurry of legislative, gubernatorial, and presidential efforts to prevent something like that from ever occurring again. When legislators consider how to solve a problem like oil spills, they're typically presented with a choice. They can pass new laws that empower government bureaucracies, be it the Environmental Protection Agency (EPA), Coast Guard, or the National Oceanic and Atmospheric Administration (NOAA), to regulate oil tanker operations more closely. Among other things, legislators could require more extensive licensing or staff training, so that any oil tanker must comply with specific safety guidelines or more thorough vetting of staff. A new law could give officials at the DOJ, EPA, or Coast Guard the power to inspect oil tankers, to require routine safety checks and staff training, and to impose fines or file lawsuits on behalf of the public. This kind of law would be regulatory, because its goal would be to change the behavior of the oil tanker industry, and would rely on government employees and resources, or what we can call, public enforcement.

But empowering government officials is not the only option. In addition to public enforcement, legislators can allow any injured parties to file lawsuits. To do this, legislators would impose new safety guidelines and more thorough vetting, but rather than enforcing it via bureaucratic inspections or licensing, they would also specify in the law that any injured party can sue. In the case of oil spills, this kind of law would give fisheries, coastal communities, and environmental organizations a *private right of action*. Any of these parties could show up in court and demand legal remedies for violations of the new law, a scheme that would rely on private rather than public enforcement. In these cases, private lawsuits turn into "a regulatory tool and the legal system transforms from one where 'one citizen can seek redress from another in an orderly fashion' into one where citizens or groups . . . can enforce the law for systemic regulatory purposes."[2]

In response to the *Exxon Valdez* oil spill, Congress immediately embraced private enforcement via the Oil Pollution Act (1990), a new statute that prohibited the use of single-hulled oil tankers and, among other things, empowered private plaintiffs to file claims against oil polluters.[3] Specifically, the act made "responsible part[ies] for a vessel or a facility from which oil is discharged . . . liable" in private lawsuits.[4] This directly authorized private plaintiffs, not just the Coast Guard or EPA, to execute the new law. By doing so, Congress subjected the oil industry to regulatory oversight from both government and private parties, ensuring more robust enforcement of the law and, hopefully, stronger deterrence.

The choice between public and private enforcement applies to almost every area of society. Take, for instance, minimum wage laws. If a state legislature or Congress wants to raise the minimum wage, it can specify the new wage in a statute. That, by itself, wouldn't do much because employers could continue to pay their employees less. Laws, in other words, are not self-executing. To change actual behavior, the legislature must empower someone to ensure that employers pay the new minimum wage. Legislators can either empower an entity like the Department of Labor (DOL) to conduct inspections and ask employers to produce documents that verify payment of the minimum wage. Or the law can allow any employee to sue an employer for failure to pay minimum wage. The statute would simply say something like, "Any employee may sue an employer for violations of this statute."

The same is true for regulating business monopolies. Governments have long worried about businesses that gain overwhelming control over the supply of a particular product, leading to high prices and weak service for consumers, among other ills. Suppose that Congress or a state legislature is concerned with a large company that dominates a particular area of business and increases prices for a basic good, say the provision of telephone services. A new law can allow lawyers at a public agency, like the Federal Trade Commission, to review potential mergers and acquisitions in the telephone industry and, if they find a violation, impose fines or file a civil enforcement lawsuit. Or the law can allow any business competitor or consumer to sue any telephone company that maintains high prices because of a monopoly. The statute would simply say something like, "Any person or firm injured or damaged by an unlawful trust or monopoly in the telephone industry may, in each instance of such injury or damage, recover the sum of $10,000 and all actual damages from any corporation creating, operating, aiding, or abetting such trust or monopoly."

You get the idea: Legislatures can solve regulatory problems by allowing government officials, injured parties, or both to sue. But this logic can apply in unexpected areas, like the regulation of the legal profession. Suppose a legislature wants to increase the competence and preparation of new lawyers. One intuitive option is to require a more difficult bar exam before someone is licensed to practice law. Many states justify bar exams as a screening device for competence, weeding out lawyers who lack sufficient skill or preparation and ensuring a quality supply of lawyers for the public. But there is another way to do this. A state can adopt a new law that allows clients to easily sue attorneys for malpractice. The statute would simply say something like, "Any client in an attorney-client relationship may sue an attorney for breach of professional standards." Most states do provide malpractice causes of action like this one.

In any of these instances, public and private enforcement can achieve similar outcomes because both forms of enforcement push regulated entities to consider the harms of their conduct. For companies deciding whether to pay the minimum wage or to avoid monopolistic practices, the prospect of a government inspector showing up is not that different from the prospect of a private lawsuit—in either case, the company ultimately fears having to pay a large amount of money. Of course, the form and scale of that payment can differ. Litigating a class action can be more expensive than dealing with a regulatory action, and class action settlements can exceed the fines agencies impose. Nor are these enforcement modes mutually exclusive; a defendant may face both a public investigation and a private suit arising from the same conduct. Still, if public and private enforcement share a credible probability of detecting wrongdoing, the regulated entity should adjust its behavior all the same. Any company subject to the threat of monetary losses should pay the minimum wage to avoid the government fine or the private lawsuit, even if the paths to that sanction differ.

## CONSIDERATIONS ON PRIVATE VS. PUBLIC ENFORCEMENT

The theoretical equivalence between public and private enforcement assumes ideal conditions that rarely exist in practice. While both enforcement mechanisms create incentives for compliance, they differ substantially in their implementation, structures, and practical effects. The choice between empowering government agencies or private litigants involves fundamental tradeoffs that can lead to different outcomes. Understanding these distinctions is important for determining when private enforcement serves as an effective complement or substitute for bureaucracies. Consider the following tradeoffs in choosing public vs. private enforcement:

**Ex Ante vs. Ex Post.** One key feature of private enforcement is that it allows for lawsuits *after* some event has taken place. In the case of the *Exxon Valdez* oil spill, fisheries and coastal communities can sue for compensation but only once the oil damage is clear—*ex post.* By contrast, bureaucratic enforcement allows for regulation to take place before any events happen—*ex ante*. So, for instance, a more robust licensing regime for oil tankers could potentially uncover flaws in a ship's hull and prevent an oil disaster.[5]

One benefit of *ex ante* regulation is that it can, at its best, detect wrongdoing before anyone is harmed. For this reason, many laws create *ex ante* regulatory regimes that seek to prevent irreparable injuries. The Food and Drug Administration (FDA), for instance, requires that new medications go through extensive tests to demonstrate safety and efficacy before they are available for sale. Few Americans would be comfortable relying only on *ex post* private lawsuits against pharmaceutical companies.

But the difference between *ex post* and *ex ante* regimes is often overstated. Some scholars argue that Americans should embrace robust bureaucratic agencies that can implement more *ex ante* regulation of products like cars or medical devices or scrutinize proposed mergers and acquisitions to prevent monopolies.[6] These scholars fear that waiting for actual damage to take place is tragically unjust. No one, for instance, wants shoddy cribs to cause infant injuries or deaths before manufacturers face tort litigation. While superficially appealing, this way of thinking misses the point. The threat of *ex post* litigation should cause regulated entities to consider the harm that they may cause and refrain from imposing it. The crib manufacturer should inspect and ensure that its products are reliable lest it face crippling civil lawsuits if they injure babies. Still, we cannot ignore the danger that sometimes the benefits of selling shoddy cribs may exceed the costs of *ex post* liability, and, therefore, we may need the threat of criminal liability as a complement or, yes, more *ex ante* regulation.

An *ex post* regime of private lawsuits, then, can be robust in two ways: First, criminal laws impose obligations on regulated entities not to intentionally or recklessly cause harm. Those laws still apply, regardless of the legislative choice between public and private enforcement in the civil context. There may well be criminal liability for the intentional or fraudulent sale of shoddy cribs. Second, that leaves only the danger of negligent acts to regulate. But, again, regulated entities study and understand the prospect of heavy lawsuits that can bankrupt them. They take those dangers into account and change their behavior. Because of that, *ex ante* and *ex post* regimes can result in similar levels of safety.

**Salaried Employees vs. Private Lawyers.** Public enforcement empowers salaried employees subject to government control. Government employees have civil service protections and can rely on extensive public resources. They also face different incentives in their jobs. On the one hand, they are supposed to be public-minded, prioritizing the interests of the nation, Congress, and anyone who could be affected by a regulated activity. On the other hand, they may care about ascending their career ladder, gaining prestige, and impressing their superiors, including politicians. They also face statutory constraints imposed by civil service requirements.[7]

By contrast, private enforcement can empower anyone to sue under a particular statute. This can include employees suing for minimum wages; investors filing securities fraud claims; competitors pushing against monopolization of a particular industry; or environmental organizations interested in preventing pollution. Private enforcement mobilizes anyone with a particular interest in enforcing the law, typically because they suffered an injury and want to be compensated. But it may also empower organizations who are interested in pursuing policy goals, like preserving the environment. Incentives here are mixed. Private parties usually care first and foremost about receiving compensation. They are not required, nor should we expect them to, consider the public interest. And often it is the lawyers rather than the named plaintiffs who are shepherding the case. Lawyers are profit-driven because their legal practice is a business. They invest in litigation and need to win cases to stay in business. (This may not apply to public interest organizations that rely on donations rather than profits.) Unlike public enforcers, plaintiffs' attorneys are not always ascending a career ladder; do not have bureaucratic superiors; and are not hemmed in by civil service regulations.

The choice between government officials and private plaintiffs exists regardless of whether a scheme is *ex ante* or *ex post*. So even when legislators choose *ex post* solutions—lawsuits after some incident—they must still choose who initiates the lawsuit. In common law systems, courts cannot initiate cases on their own. There must still be an outsider who prepares a case, gathers relevant facts, assembles witnesses and documents, and presents it to a court. That work can be done by government or private lawyers.

**Costly Bureaucracies vs. Cheap Private Lawsuits.** Another important variable is that public enforcement is fiscally costly while private enforcement is fiscally cheap, at least from a legislature's perspective. Legislators considering public enforcement must appropriate funds to either build new agencies or increase existing agency staff. Designing bureaucracies is complicated—it requires difficult choices about legal structure, distribution of authority, legislative supervision, agency costs, and salaries. But more than anything, it requires scarce public funding that may not exist. But including a private right of action in a statute is almost a fiscal freebie. If there is a capacious judiciary that can handle more lawsuits, then there are few fiscal tradeoffs in allowing more private parties to bring claims.

**Bureaucrats vs. Judges**. Public vs. private enforcement pits decisions made by bureaucrats against decisions made by judges or juries. In deciding whether to empower public bureaucrats, legislators need to consider the kinds of bureaucrats in charge of public enforcement: their ideology, motivations, incentives, salaries, and so on. Some agencies like the Securities and Exchange Commission (SEC) have high-caliber attorneys, can attract career-minded public servants, and enjoy a tradition of competence and high-quality work. Others, however, are underfunded or cannot attract talented employees. The Department of Labor (DOL), for instance, has long faced budgetary and staffing constraints. The DOL's Solicitor's Office has received flat funding since 2013, leading to a 17 percent reduction in personnel. By 2023, staffing had fallen to just 542 attorneys, far below the 770 lawyers employed during the Obama administration.[8] This chronic understaffing means the office often cannot pursue labor law violations even when investigators find evidence of wrongdoing, forcing officials to pick cases to prosecute based on limited resources rather than the merits.

While private enforcement can make up for a lack of bureaucratic resources, it also raises questions about the ideologies and work of courts. Legislators must consider the kinds of judges who will decide whether a private party wins or loses a lawsuit, including those judges' ideologies, incentives, and norms. Both public and private enforcement, then, depend on the background of public officials, bureaucratic or judicial.

**Optimal Deterrence**. When legislators craft new laws to address social issues—pollution, business competition, or minimum wages—they may have a preference on how strict such a regime should be. For instance, in the case of oil tankers, legislators may want to continue to allow the extensive use of certain ships but in as safe a way as possible. Requiring maximum safety would prevent all oil spills, but it may force oil companies to exit the business of oil trade if the costs are too high. Requiring minimum safety would allow too many oil spills and invite more oil shipments, resulting in potentially more disasters. The question for legislators, then, is the level of costs to impose on the regulated activity. This means searching for a *sweet spot* that balances safety and entry into the market.

The choice between public and private enforcement affects deterrence levels. Mobilizing plaintiffs' attorneys to the maximum can result in too many lawsuits, forcing regulated entities to exit the market. While this may be true of regulators too, a legislature can impose a tighter leash on bureaucrats and force them to consider market consequences (through a cost-benefit analysis). A legislative choice of private enforcement can also come with incentives for plaintiffs, including statutory penalties, attorneys' fees, and the possibility of suing as a class of plaintiffs rather than only in an individual lawsuit. Chapter 10 includes a longer discussion of all the different ways legislators can dial private suits up or down.

These tradeoffs between public and private enforcement aren't merely theoretical—they play out dramatically in how different legal systems respond to environmental disasters. As we'll see later in the chapter, a comparison between American and French responses to catastrophic oil spills shows how countries make distinct choices about *ex ante* regulation versus *ex post* liability, about empowering bureaucrats versus private attorneys, and about coordinating enforcement through government agencies versus courts.

## PRIVATE ENFORCEMENT DEFINED

Let's now concretely describe the subject of this book. Broadly defined, private enforcement includes any legal regime that allows private parties to bring lawsuits that deter or regulate misconduct, not just compensate individual harm. This definition encompasses both common law causes of action (like tort claims) and many other private rights of action. But this book focuses specifically on *statutory private enforcement*—the *legislative* choice to empower private parties to file regulatory lawsuits. Notice three key ingredients in this narrower form of private enforcement: legislative choice (discussed in Chapters 3–4), private parties, and enforcement of regulatory statutes. The first two ingredients are self-explanatory. As to the third one, lawsuits are regulatory when they go beyond merely compensating plaintiffs and aim to shape the behavior of private entities, mostly through deterrence. (I explain my focus on statutory rather than common law claims further below.)

Given these ingredients, consider the following types of private enforcement:

1. **Private Rights of Action**: These are statutory provisions that give a private party the right to sue another party (a private right of action, or PRA). PRAs allow employees to sue employers for failure to pay wages, consumers to sue companies for product defects, and anyone to sue a polluter for harming the environment. These provisions can vary in their purpose: Some focus on remediating individual injuries (like wage claims), while others emphasize broader regulatory enforcement (like suits for injunctions against discriminatory policies). Some PRAs even empower parties to "ensure that federal regulations are enforced."[9] Consider, for instance, how the Clean Air Act (CAA) allows "any person [to] commence a civil action . . . against any person . . . who [violates] an emission standard or limitation under this chapter."[10] This was "explicitly justified as a mechanism that would deputize 'private attorneys general' to assist the [EPA] . . . in the enforcement of environmental regulation."[11] Under the CAA, a plaintiff can only sue for injunctive relief and cannot recover damages. Deterrence and the public nature of these lawsuits is obvious.

2. **Informer Claims**: Congress can empower any person (sometimes known as an "informer") to sue and collect a statutory penalty. For instance, a statute might prohibit an act (say, polluting a river) and allow anyone to sue a polluter and collect $10,000. Qui tam is a subset of informer claims that allows the informer to sue *on behalf of the government* and share in any recovery. The most prominent example is the False Claims Act of 1863, which empowers private whistleblowers to sue companies that defraud the federal government. When whistleblowers uncover fraud—like contractors overcharging for military supplies or hospitals submitting false Medicare claims—they can file suit in the government's name. While the DOJ can take over these cases, the whistleblower (sometimes called a "relator") receives a percentage of any damages recovered, creating a powerful incentive to expose fraud against taxpayers.

3. **Suits Against the Government**: Some statutes authorize private parties to challenge government decisions or inaction. This category includes suits against the government for failure to perform a statutory duty (e.g., environmental statutes allow citizens to sue the EPA for missing regulatory deadlines), as well as suits challenging agency approvals of permits or licenses that authorize private conduct. On top of that, some statutes allow private parties to file complaints that trigger agency investigations, participate in rulemaking, or petition for enforcement actions. While these mechanisms target government rather than private entities, they often have significant regulatory effects on private parties' behavior.

Setting aside their differences, the core of statutory private enforcement (referred to as "private enforcement" for the rest of the book) is that a private party can show up in court and challenge the actions of a company, regulated entity, or government agency, either directly via a private claim or indirectly via an administrative challenge. Again, this definition centers on deliberate legislative reliance on private plaintiffs to resolve a regulatory problem.

Note, too, that this definition excludes most lawsuits against the government over constitutional or individual rights. The book is primarily concerned with legislative attempts to regulate private entities, not government officials. Section 1983, for example, empowers plaintiffs to sue state and local officials who violate individual rights under the Constitution or federal law.[12] While that statute contains a private right of action, it is targeted at government behavior. This kind of constitutional litigation implicates fundamentally different questions about individual liberties, democratic accountability, and the relationship between citizens and the government. Those questions deserve separate treatment from the ones addressed below.

Now, to be sure, the book's definition of private enforcement may be overinclusive because sometimes legislators adopt private rights of action that are not regulatory. That is, some statutes authorize private suits that have no effect on the public. Consider, for instance, a new statute that allows a general contractor to file a lawsuit against a subcontractor over the breach of a construction contract. Legislators in that instance may be merely concerned with private injuries to general contractors. Perhaps the statute came in response to lobbying from organizations that represent general contractors. Along the same lines, academics often distinguish "private law" fields like contracts, torts, and property from "public law" fields like constitutional or administrative law. Some areas of constitutional law, international law, and conflicts of law similarly distinguish "regulatory" statutes from merely private regimes. Cases on Article III standing, too, try to distinguish private injuries from public ones. It is important to distinguish statutes that allow claims for private harms from those involving public harm.

But any rigid insistence on clear lines between private and regulatory claims is misguided. In most statutes, it is nearly impossible to disentangle private claims from public regulation. Return to the statute that allows a general contractor to sue subcontractors—did legislators aim to merely remedy private injuries to general contractors? Or did they also mean to decrease prices in the construction industry or deter misfeasance by subcontractors? It is very hard to tell. Or consider a New Jersey statute that allows lawsuits against pet dealers for offering customers pet lease agreements.[13] Again, was that an attempt by the legislature to remedy private injuries to customers? Or was it meant to prevent animal cruelty, regulate the pet industry, and protect cats and dogs?

Indeed, the distinction between truly private rights of action and those that are closer to a public harm may not matter at all. Most public injuries are simply aggregations of private harms—environmental damage affects individual property owners, antitrust violations harm specific consumers, and discrimination impacts particular employees. The regulatory effect of private lawsuits remains the same regardless of whether legislators intended to remedy private injuries or serve broader public goals. What matters is the legislative choice to rely on private suits in the first place. As the French example below shows, even purely private injuries can be addressed through administrative enforcement or criminal prosecution rather than private rights of action. When legislators choose to include a private right of action—whether aimed at individual harms or systemic problems—they are making a conscious choice to mobilize private parties as enforcers of legal norms. This fundamental choice to rely on private enforcement, rather than the muddled distinction between public and private injuries, is what shapes American governance.

## PRIVATE ENFORCEMENT AND THE COMMON LAW

As mentioned above, the book focuses on private enforcement via statutory private rights of action, rather than through common law claims. But these two types of private enforcement are obviously connected in different ways.

Consider first the common law's regulatory role. Just like private enforcement allows anyone to enforce regulatory law, some common law claims are regulatory in nature. Mass torts, for example, are notoriously complex beasts that have significant regulatory consequences for regulated entities. Anyone injured by a product can file a common law claim in any of the fifty states. When aggregated in large numbers, mass claims over asbestos, medical products, tobacco, and the like regulate the marketplace via private lawsuits.

The common law, moreover, serves as background law in almost all regulatory areas, biasing the development of statutory law towards private litigation. Congress and state legislatures do not legislate on a blank slate. Because the United States inherited a full body of common law from England, legislation almost always built upon pre-existing common law rules that already provided remedies through private litigation. This probably created a structural bias toward private enforcement in statutory law. Legislative choices to retain common law remedies—which they could override at any time—reinforced this default. When Congress or state legislatures decided to regulate new areas or modify existing rules, private enforcement was often the default option, creating an inherent entanglement between statutory and common law private enforcement that cannot be ignored.

Yet, despite these connections, private enforcement of statutes "derives legitimacy from Congress's deliberate choice to empower private plaintiffs either to complement or replace administrative agencies . . . . Tort claims, by contrast, rely on a long common law tradition based mostly on state law."[14] When legislatures create private rights of action, they choose between administrative and private enforcement. By contrast, courts develop common law claims and remedies without any choice between public or private enforcement. Courts cannot create new administrative agencies or grant regulatory powers to existing ones; their only tool is to recognize new claims or remedies. This fundamental difference in institutional power and capacity makes legislative private enforcement far more puzzling than judicial development of common law claims. When Congress or state legislatures repeatedly choose private enforcement in addition to administrative solutions, they make a distinctive choice that demands explanation. Common law private enforcement is simply a distinct phenomenon, even if it has similar effects.

More to the point, there is nothing historically or comparatively puzzling about common law claims—they derive from a long English tradition of allowing courts to give remedies for private harms. By contrast, private enforcement via statutory claims appears to be unique to the United States, emerges from hazy origins, and continues to be deeply puzzling because state legislatures and Congress repeatedly make the choice to rely on private rights of action even when most countries refuse to do so.

The key question this book answers, therefore, is specifically about statutory private enforcement: Why do American legislatures employ private lawsuits as a regulatory mechanism when most other democracies do not? While the explanation will inevitably relate to the common law, it is sufficiently distinct to merit an independent study.

## PRIVATE ENFORCEMENT AND ADVERSARIAL LEGALISM

This book's focus on private enforcement is also related to but distinct from what political scientist Robert Kagan called in a seminal book "adversarial legalism." There, Kagan explained that the United States embraces a "unique legal style" that "relies on courts, lawyers, legal threats, and legal contestation in making and implementing public policies, in compensating accident victims, in striving to hold governmental officials accountable, and in regulating economic behavior."[15] In other words, "party-and-lawyer-dominated legal contestation" is a source of "policymaking, policy implementation, and dispute resolution" in the United States. Under Kagan's telling, the American legal system has long suffered from a "weak state" that is fragmented and has limited powers. When citizens demand regulatory action, this fragmented state is unable to respond via bureaucratic enforcement, leading to increased reliance on adversarial legalism. Yet Kagan does not clarify whether adversarial legalism stems from a unique American culture or whether it means anything other than legal contestation over most policy questions.

While private enforcement certainly operates within this broader culture of adversarial legalism, it represents a more concrete and specific institutional mechanism. Again, private enforcement refers to the specific congressional (and state legislative) reliance on private rights of action and the procedural infrastructure that undergirds it. As Sean Farhang has argued, its immediate origins are clear: repeated legislative choices to insert statutory clauses that allow anyone to sue.[16]

Moreover, a country could embrace adversarial legalism with or without private enforcement. For example, the common law system could produce a "legal style" that relies on "lawyer-dominated litigation" as a source of "policymaking," even without any legislative action. That would involve no legislation; it would instead emerge from historical and judicial common law practices. That means a particular state in the US could conceivably rely on adversarial legalism *without* private enforcement. And, *vice versa*, countries that rely on bureaucratic enforcement—like France—sometimes embrace private enforcement in particular areas like antitrust or civil rights. As discussed in Chapter 6, the French parliament adopted a civil rights act that relies on private enforcement. In that particular area, we could observe private enforcement within a system that relies on judicial initiative and energetic management of litigation, not on Kagan's party and lawyer-led process. In that case, we observe private enforcement *without* adversarial legalism. It therefore appears that private enforcement and adversarial legalism are independent concepts.

This book therefore examines not the general cultural embrace of legalistic problem-solving that Kagan described, but rather the specific legislative reliance on private rights of action as a regulatory tool. Understanding why American legislatures repeatedly make this institutional choice requires focus on legislative decision-making rather than legal culture.

## PRIVATE ENFORCEMENT AND OIL SPILLS IN THE UNITED STATES VS. FRANCE

With these concepts in mind, let's return to the example of oil spills. The United States has dealt with at least two major oil disasters in the last forty years: the *Exxon Valdez* oil spill (1989) and the BP oil spill (2010). In both instances, the legal system responded with a mix of public and private claims, criminal and civil suits, and administrative and statutory reforms. Yet, in both instances, regulatory civil lawsuits were at the center of the story. And Congress responded to the *Exxon Valdez* disaster by creating a new private right of action for oil spills—a provision that played a major role after the BP oil disaster of 2010. By contrast, when France faced the 1999 *Erika* Oil Spill, it was the French bureaucracy that took the sole lead, mostly unencumbered by civil litigation. France is a particularly good contrast to the United States because political scientists have long viewed it as the quintessential administrative state in which the bureaucracy enforces the most important statutes. Unlike the United States, private litigation in France is not a pillar of regulatory enforcement but merely a side player in larger bureaucratic schemes.

***1. Exxon Valdez.*** Return to Prince William Sound, Alaska, where 11 million gallons of crude oil were slushing in coastal waters by mid-March 1989.[17] It took only days for lawyers to begin making calls to coastal communities, recruiting clients to take Exxon to court. Within months, plaintiffs' attorneys had filed hundreds of federal and state lawsuits against Exxon Corporation, representing thousands of private individuals and environmental organizations. By September 1989, Exxon faced "over 153 lawsuits, including 58 class actions."[18] Judge Russel Holland noted that "[t]he civil suits came first, but developed slowly because of their number and complexity."[19] Private plaintiffs included over 32,000 fishermen, cannery workers, land and business owners, and others harmed by the spill. They were later divided into three classes: commercial fishermen, Native Alaskans, and landowners. Defendants included several Exxon entities, Mr. Hazelwood, and the third mate, as well as Alyeska Pipeline Service Company for its management role of the Trans-Alaska Pipeline System and the Trans-Alaska Pipeline Liability Fund.

The web of lawsuits was complex, with some suits brought in state court and others in federal court; some filed by the DOJ and others by the State of Alaska. The Department of Justice separately brought criminal charges against Exxon for violations of the Clean Water Act and the Migratory Bird Treaty Act. But private claims had nothing to do with the criminal case; they were instead filed as class actions. Among other groups, Alaska Natives sued over damage and injury "to their subsistence way of life, archaeological sites and artifacts," as well as "to the natural resources and property upon which they depend and/or which are part of their natural habitat and lives."[20] Commercial fishermen claimed damage "to their commercial cultivation, fishing and/or harvesting of the fish, other seafood or marine resources in the Area and in their commercial fishing permits and property rights in the Area."[21] Other fish processing companies complained of sustained harm to "their processing, preparation, marketing, sale or other distribution of fish, seafood or other marine resources cultivated, fished or harvested in the Area."[22] Finally, other businesses claimed injury to property and to their use and enjoyment of the natural resources.

Most plaintiffs based their claims on common law theories of tort and nuisance, while others drew on statutes like the Trans-Alaska Pipeline Authorization Act, which imposed strict liability on owners and operators of gas tankers for all damages resulting from an incident. The Alaska Natives Class claims drew on the Alaska National Interest Lands Conservation Act, a statute that gave "priority" to tribes "over all other takings of fish and wildlife in Alaska."[23] Both of these statutes contained private rights of action.

Litigation went on for more than a decade, developing into a multipronged beast managed by various federal district court judges. Ultimately, the *Exxon Valdez* litigation was mostly a maritime tort case, focused on the harm to commercial fishing and coastal communities, paired with statutory claims under the Trans-Alaska Pipeline Authorization Act and the Alaska National Interest Lands Conservation Act, statutes with private rights of action. As the Circuit Judge noted, "[t]his is not a case about befouling the environment . . . . The reason is that under a stipulation with the United States and Alaska, Exxon had already been punished for environmental harm. The verdict in this case was for damage to economic expectations for commercial fishermen."[24]

On February 25, 1994, the district court granted Exxon's motion to have all claims against it for punitive damages consolidated into one single proceeding. On May 2, 1994, a class action of over 32,000 plaintiffs began its jury trial. "[P]laintiffs asserted that Exxon was liable because Captain Hazelwood was an alcoholic, Exxon knew that he had a drinking problem, and that he had relapsed; and yet, Exxon left him in charge of a supertanker carrying 53 million gallons of crude oil into nature-rich waters."[25] On June 13, 1994, the jury found that Exxon acted recklessly. And on September 16,

1994, the jury returned an award of "$287 million in compensatory damages and $5 billion in punitive damages."[26]

Exxon did not contest the finding of liability for compensatory damages but did contest the punitive damage award. After years bouncing between the circuit and district courts, the Ninth Circuit set the punitive damages award at $2.5 billion.[27] And on June 25, 2008, the Supreme Court agreed that maritime law allowed for punitive damages and awarded the maximum punitive damages: $507.5 million.[28]

The federal government and the State of Alaska brought parallel civil and criminal claims against Exxon. But, back on January 15, 1991, Alaska Governor Walter Hickel proposed a settlement in a personal meeting with Exxon's Chairman Lawrence Rawl: "When Mr. Rawl and I first met in Juneau, we made it clear that negotiations could only be successful if we kept the talks at the highest level."[29] On March 13, 1991, Alaska's governor and Attorney General announced that Exxon agreed to pay "$25 million in a criminal plea agreement, $100 million in criminal restitution," and $900 million in a civil settlement, "resolving all civil claims between [Exxon and the United States and the state of Alaska]."[30] And in October of 1991, the district court approved the plea and settlement agreement.[31] That same year, the parties created the *Exxon Valdez* Oil Spill Trustee Council, composed of government representatives, to use the monies for restoration.[32]

But setting aside the labyrinthine civil and criminal lawsuits, along with quick government action on different fronts, Congress's key response to the disaster was an immediate amendment to the Trans-Alaska Pipeline Authorization Act and the adoption of the Oil Pollution Act of 1990.[33] The main goal of the Oil Pollution Act was to clarify liability for discharges and cleanups of oil spills. The Act specifically provides that any person has the right to sue anyone responsible for an oil spill, for removal costs and for damages to their real or personal property, subsistence use, profits, and earning capacity.[34]

***2. BP Oil Spill.*** It only took a few years before the Oil Pollution Act was at the center of another oil spill. On April 20, 2010, disaster struck deep in the Gulf of Mexico. The *Deepwater Horizon*, a towering semi-submersible offshore drilling rig, was rocked by a blowout, explosion, and raging fire as it drilled into the Macondo Well off Louisiana's coast. In a matter of moments, the rig was transformed into a scene of tragedy, claiming eleven lives, injuring dozens, and unleashing one of the gravest environmental disasters in US history. For nearly three agonizing months, oil poured into the Gulf, devastating marine life, coastal communities, and the livelihoods of thousands. Marine mammals, including dolphins and whales, suffered severe health effects, with many found dead or stranded along the coastline. Coastal communities saw their economies devastated as fishing grounds were poisoned, forcing closures across a vital seafood-producing region. The tourism industry, too, struggled under the weight of oil-blackened beaches and a shattered reputation.

The government's response was quick and multi-pronged. The Department of the Interior (DOI) immediately suspended approval of all drilling permits and later imposed a six-month moratorium on deepwater drilling. President Obama established a National Commission to investigate the causes and recommend reforms. The administration reorganized federal oversight, creating new regulatory bodies and implementing stringent safety measures for offshore drilling operations. But perhaps most significantly, the DOJ launched both criminal and civil proceedings against BP and other responsible parties, securing significant penalties. BP ultimately pleaded guilty to fourteen criminal charges, agreeing to pay over $4.5 billion in fines.

Yet the government's enforcement actions were only part of the story. Within days of the disaster, hundreds of private lawsuits flooded courts across the country. By the time the Judicial Panel on Multidistrict Litigation consolidated these cases in the Eastern District of Louisiana, attorneys had already filed nearly 3,000 cases representing over 100,000 claimants. The plaintiffs included commercial fishermen, seafood processors, recreational business owners, retail businesses, and subsistence fishers—anyone whose livelihood or property had been damaged by the spill.

At the heart of these civil lawsuits was the Oil Pollution Act, born, as we've seen, from the ashes (or sludge) of the *Exxon Valdez* disaster. Plaintiffs' attorneys took full advantage of this powerful private right of action alongside other environmental statutes with citizen-suit provisions, including the Clean Water Act and Endangered Species Act.[35] The scale of private enforcement was staggering—in less than three years after the blowout, BP agreed to pay $13 billion in claims to businesses and individuals, separate from government penalties. Indeed, this amount dwarfed the criminal and civil penalties obtained by the government. The total payout kept growing and by 2016 culminated in one of the largest environmental settlements in history—$20.8 billion.

The contrast between the *Exxon Valdez* and BP oil spills reveals how the Oil Pollution Act transformed private enforcement against oil spills. With *Exxon Valdez*, private claims dragged on for two decades, ultimately resulting in a relatively modest $287 million in compensatory damages and $507.5 million in punitive damages, far below both the government's $1 billion settlement and the initial $5 billion punitive award. The BP litigation tells a different story. Armed with the Oil Pollution Act's clear liability framework, private plaintiffs drove a complex web of settlements that delivered compensation for economic losses with remarkable speed. The BP oil spill settlement provided relief to victims within just a few years, while the government pursued environmental claims separately. This efficient resolution reflected both the Oil Pollution Act's structured approach to liability and improved procedures, including the Judicial Panel on Multidistrict Litigation's consolidation of cases. The BP disaster showcased how American law had evolved to better mobilize both private and public enforcers, each operating in their own sphere but working toward comprehensive accountability.

Yet there is no denying that the BP oil spill prompted a combined force of public and private enforcement, demonstrating how American law mobilizes both government agencies and private plaintiffs to address catastrophic damage. The Obama administration's response to the BP disaster demonstrated the full force of government power. From the earliest days of the crisis, federal authorities orchestrated a whole-of-government response that went far beyond mere litigation. President Obama deployed the Secretary of the Interior and the Secretary of Homeland Security to launch a joint investigation, while Attorney General Eric Holder supervised both civil and criminal complaints. The administration treated the spill as a number one priority, holding multiple weekly meetings for over three months to coordinate the cleanup effort and ensure accountability. Beyond immediate crisis management, the government undertook sweeping regulatory reforms—suspending drilling permits, establishing new oversight bodies, and implementing safety measures for offshore operations. Most importantly, while private plaintiffs focused primarily on economic losses and personal injuries, the government shouldered the broader public interest mandate: stopping the leak, restoring damaged ecosystems, and ensuring BP couldn't cap its liability. This division of labor between private and public enforcement proved remarkably effective (with the Gulf Coast Claims Facility and Ken Feinberg playing a major role in both). Private litigation drove compensation for individual losses, while government action protected broader public interests and reformed the regulatory landscape to prevent future disasters.

The BP disaster is a good case study of America's approach to enforcement—when faced with a massive regulatory failure, the system responds not just through government action but through a parallel and independent wave of private litigation that amplifies the regulatory response.

*3.* ***Erika Oil Spill.*** Unlike the United States, continental European countries, and France in particular, have historically relied mostly on public enforcement of environmental laws. While American legislators routinely empower private parties to enforce regulatory laws, French authorities maintain a tight grip on environmental enforcement through administrative and criminal sanctions. As three scholars highlight, "[i]n continental Europe . . . environmental law is typically enforced using only administrative and criminal sanctions. There is no such thing as a civil penalty. A person suffering harm from pollution may obviously claim damages under tort law, but such civil law claims aim at ensuring compensation for injured parties, not enforcing environmental statutes."[36]

This divergence from the American approach reflects deeper institutional and cultural differences. French citizens have traditionally viewed the state as the proper guardian of public interests, an attitude reinforced by France's development as the quintessential administrative state. The idea that private parties should enforce public law was alien to nineteenth-century French legal thinking, which maintained a strict divide between private interests (defended by citizens) and public interests (defended by the state). The European Union, too, reflects this legal style, traditionally leaving "little room for private participation" in the enforcement of European Union (EU) environmental protection laws (which take the form of "directives").[37] To be sure, this tradition seems to be changing, with many recent EU directives and initiatives embracing a larger role for private claimants.

And so it was that France faced an oil disaster in its own bureaucratic way. On December 12, 1999, another environmental catastrophe unfolded off the French coast when the oil tanker *Erika*, carrying nearly 31,000 tons of heavy fuel oil, broke apart and sank in rough seas. The disaster unleashed an environmental nightmare, contaminating 400 kilometers of coastline and killing between 150,000 and 300,000 birds.[38] Just as with the American oil spills, the economic impact was massive, estimated in the billions of euros. But unlike the American response to *Exxon Valdez* or BP, what followed would showcase a distinctly European approach to enforcement.

To cut to the chase: The French legal response centered on criminal prosecution. The day after the first oiled bird was discovered, the Paris prosecutor's office launched an investigation into the disaster. The prosecution rested on two main charges. First, prosecutors alleged that defendants endangered human life by deliberately violating safety regulations—a charge focused on the immediate risks to human life and safety. Second, they pursued charges of water pollution based on the reckless and negligent operation of a large tanker.[39] These charges drew on France's environmental code and its comprehensive maritime pollution law, which cast a wide net of criminal liability.[40] Specifically, Subsection 4 of Article 8 of Law No. 83–583 of July 5, 1983 criminalizes pollution resulting from a maritime accident caused by a fault that either triggered it or consisted of failing to take measures to prevent it.[41] Unlike American environmental statutes with their citizen-suit provisions, the French law created no private right of action. Instead, it allowed prosecutors to pursue anyone exercising control over the vessel's operation, from the captain and crew to owners, operators, and even corporate officers exercising de facto control. This broad conception of criminal liability allowed prosecutors to target not just the immediate operators but also corporate entities that exercised indirect control over the vessel's operation.

By contrast to America, in France, civil claims are mere appendages to criminal prosecutions. The central criminal prosecution is controlled by public officials: the public prosecutor (procureur de la République) and the judge (juge d'instruction). In parallel, any person who personally suffered damage directly caused by an offense can either file a separate, ordinary civil lawsuit—via the tort system—or victims can choose to seek compensation directly in the criminal proceedings by constituting themselves "civil parties" (parties civiles). In the latter case, the same judge reviews both criminal and civil liability. Rather than a flood of private lawsuits, then, the case proceeded as a single criminal prosecution with an attached civil component—a mechanism that allows victims to join criminal proceedings as civil parties to seek compensation. The defendants included the Italian shipowner Giuseppe Savarese, the society Registro Italiano Navale (RINA), and the oil giant Total SA, along with several other individuals and entities. While 114 civil parties—including regions, municipalities, and environmental organizations—joined the case, they participated within the unified criminal proceeding rather than filing separate civil actions.[42]

The litigation unfolded methodically over thirteen years across three court levels, culminating in a landmark 2012 decision by France's highest court.[43] The trial court convicted several defendants of criminal pollution charges, imposing maximum fines of €375,000 on corporate defendants and €75,000 on individuals. It was only after the culmination of the criminal case that civil claimants could get their full day in court. And so, after a decade of prosecution, the judge granted civil claimants €192 million in damages, with €154 million going to the French Treasury.[44] Most significantly, the court recognized for the first time the concept of ecological damage, allowing environmental groups to claim compensation for harm to natural resources—a pioneering development that French legislators later codified in 2016 (inserting a limited right to sue into the Civil Code). The French high court ultimately upheld these convictions and expanded Total's liability, rejecting arguments that French law couldn't be stricter than international maritime conventions.

Setting aside litigation, one of the most important reactions to the *Erika* Oil Spill was legislative. But, here again, we observe a critical divergence from the United States. The European Union's response to the *Erika* disaster focused on preventing future accidents through enhanced regulatory oversight rather than expanding private enforcement. The Erika I package, adopted in 2000, strengthened port state control, imposed stricter monitoring of classification societies, and accelerated the phase-out of single-hull tankers.[45] Erika II, which followed in 2002, created a new bureaucratic body, the European Maritime Safety Agency, established a new vessel monitoring system, and set up a compensation fund for oil pollution damage.[46] These reforms again displayed Europe's reflexive preference for addressing environmental disasters through expanded administrative oversight.

To be sure, the French system isn't entirely devoid of private influence. Civil parties—including both individual victims and environmental organizations—can shape criminal proceedings in several important ways. They can intervene during investigations to request evidence and additional investigative measures, effectively steering the direction of the probe. More dramatically, when prosecutors decline to pursue a case or drag their feet for more than three months, civil parties can bypass prosecutorial discretion by filing a criminal complaint directly with an investigating judge, triggering a judicial investigation. Environmental organizations enjoy even broader rights under the French Environmental Code. Any certified environmental group can join criminal proceedings as a civil party to defend collective environmental interests, and unlike individual victims, these groups can even claim compensation for indirect environmental damage. This happened in the *Erika* case, where environmental organizations joined the criminal prosecution and ultimately secured compensation for ecological damage. But, again, these mechanisms all operate within a unified criminal proceeding controlled by public authorities—a far cry from the American system where private parties can initiate independent enforcement actions.

———

Three major oil spills—*Exxon Valdez*, BP, and *Erika*—provide a revealing window into how different legal systems enforce the law. In France, the *Erika* disaster triggered a unified criminal prosecution that took thirteen years to resolve. The channeling of all claims through a criminal case reflects a deep-seated belief that public authorities should lead the enforcement of environmental laws. By contrast, both American oil spills unleashed a torrent of private litigation alongside public enforcement, working in parallel but not jointly. The *Exxon Valdez* spawned hundreds of lawsuits and two decades of litigation, leading Congress to immediately adopt the Oil Pollution Act. When disaster struck again with BP's *Deepwater Horizon*, this new statutory framework enabled a more efficient resolution but one still driven by a complex web of private claims beside government enforcement. Critically, private parties operated completely independent from public officials.

Where American courts wrestled to manage parallel public and private enforcement actions, the French system put all claims through a single proceeding. And while American private litigation drove the creation of novel settlement structures and compensation funds, the French system relied primarily on existing mechanisms: criminal fines, civil damages in criminal proceedings, and international oil spill compensation funds. The *Erika* case thus shows how a robust administrative state can address environmental disasters without extensive private enforcement.

Yet these contrasts shouldn't be overstated. The BP disaster invited colossal public power, directly managed by the President of the United States. American enforcement often combines public and private action in sophisticated ways. While private plaintiffs filed thousands of lawsuits, the federal government orchestrated a comprehensive response that included criminal prosecution, regulatory reform, and coordination of cleanup efforts. Similarly, the French system isn't purely bureaucratic—environmental organizations played an important role in the *Erika* case, pushing the investigation forward and ultimately securing recognition of ecological damage as a compensable harm.

The real difference lies not in whether private parties can influence enforcement, but in how their influence is channeled. The American system empowers private parties to initiate independent enforcement actions, while the French system integrates private participation with a proceeding controlled by public authorities. Each approach has its strengths: American private enforcement can respond quickly to violations and detect and surface hidden information, while the French system may better coordinate enforcement and avoid redundant litigation.

## LEGISLATIVE CHOICE

The meaning of private enforcement, and its contrast to public enforcement, should be clearer now. The diverging responses to oil spills in the United States and France bring us back to the scenario posed at the beginning of the chapter. When legislators respond to problems like oil spills, they must choose whether to prioritize regulatory reforms or to also empower private litigants. In the United States, legislators faced this dilemma in 1989 and aggressively chose to do both: stringent regulatory reforms and a brand-new private right of action in the Oil Pollution Act. Yet in Europe, French and EU officials chose differently in 2000, not even considering a new private right of action; adopting instead the Erika I (2000) and Erika II (2002) packages, which strengthened maritime safety regulations along with a brand-new bureaucracy: the European Maritime Safety Agency. (The French parliament did later codify a civil action for ecological harm in 2016, but with significant restrictions on both standing and remedies.) That divergence in behavior is what this book is all about—why, exactly, do American legislators repeatedly choose private rights of action alongside public enforcement?

# TWO

## THE PREVALENCE OF PRIVATE ENFORCEMENT

It turns out that while most countries rely on administrative schemes and robust bureaucracies, Americans like to do things differently across the board, not just in the oil-spill context. On top of bureaucratic governance, the United States relies on a constellation of private rights of action in areas like consumer protection, antitrust, employment, civil rights, and, yes, the environment. Many Americans intuitively know this, but they have no idea how important private lawsuits are in enforcing the law. Journalists routinely note that the United States has "more lawyers per capita than any OECD country,"[1] and that "80 percent of civil legal services [go] to corporate clients,"[2] but they don't seem to understand why that is. Well, one reason is that our regulatory landscape is dominated by private enforcement, enlisting attorneys to either file or defend over 90 percent of antitrust claims, 98 percent of civil rights claims, and most employment, environmental, and securities claims.[3] Of course we're going to end up with a lot of attorneys in a system like that.

If you're camping near Asheville, North Carolina and want to rent a campground, a statute lets you "bring an action" against the campground owner for rescinding your camping agreement.[4] In California, student athletes can "bring a civil action" for $50,000 against a sports agent if the student is "suspended or disqualified from participation in one or more interscholastic or intercollegiate sports events."[5] A New Jersey law creates a private claim against "[a]ny milk dealer or milk company" for violating provisions governing deductions, and the claim can be filed "in the name of the milk producers' association."[6] In Florida, you can sue a hypnotist or "any practitioner of the healing arts" for any damages from their services under a statute that "provide[s] for certain practitioners of the healing arts, such as a trained and qualified dentist, to use hypnosis for hypnoanesthesia or for the allaying of anxiety in relation to dental work."[7]

States create private rights of action to regulate nearly every social area or industry, including campground operations, athletic competitions, the milk industry, or even hypnosis. When legislators confront large social issues they immediately turn to attorneys and plaintiffs to enforce the law.[8] There are more than 350 federal private rights of action and 10,000 across the fifty states. Consider another three areas of cutting-edge regulatory issues that rely on private enforcement:

**Social Media and Children**. The rise of social media and the proliferation of handheld devices have represented a massive governance challenge at both the state and federal levels. There is increasing evidence that social media use can negatively affect the emotional and psychological development of children and teenagers, with studies linking excessive platform use to depression, anxiety, and self-harm behaviors.[9] A burgeoning social movement seeks to regulate these platforms' impact on minors, and, of course, lawmakers have immediately turned to private enforcement. Utah, for instance, has led the states on this front. The Utah legislature initially passed the Minor Protection in Social Media Act, which regulated social media companies by forcing them to implement age verification requirements and higher privacy protections. Notably, this first statute did not create a right to sue.

In 2024, however, Utah tried again with the Harm to Minors by Algorithmically Curated Social Media Service Act, repealing the previous statute (challenged on constitutional grounds) and imposing similar restrictions but now backed up by a powerful private right of action. Under this new framework:

> A Utah minor account holder or [their] parent may bring a cause of action against a social media company in court for an adverse mental health outcome arising, in whole or in part, from the minor's excessive use of the social media company's algorithmically curated social media service.[10]

The statute specifically covers harms including "depression, anxiety, suicidal thoughts or behaviors, and self-harm thoughts or behaviors," effectively transforming what was once a regulatory compliance issue into a litigation-driven enforcement mechanism that allows private plaintiffs to police social media's psychological effects.

**Gun Regulations.** Struggles over the right to bear arms have been a mainstay of political debates for decades. In 2022, California's Governor Newsom noticed that the Supreme Court had both increasingly expanded the Second Amendment's right to bear arms while simultaneously defending states' abilities to regulate contentious regulatory questions through private enforcement. He sponsored Senate Bill 1327, a California bill that would prohibit the sale, manufacture, and distribution of assault weapons in the state. The centerpiece of the law, however, was a right to sue:

> Any person, other than an officer or employee of a state or local governmental entity in this state, may bring a civil action against any person who [manufactures, distributes, transports, sells, purchases, transfers, etc. . . . an assault weapon or other banned firearms . . .]

In other words, "SB 1327 authorizes anyone other than state or local government officials to sue people who violate the state's laws against the manufacture, distribution or sale of assault weapons, ghost guns and other banned firearms."[11] This was an explicit attempt by Newsom to dodge the Second Amendment's protections via an enforcement scheme that did not employ government officials. Newsom challenged the Supreme Court to declare the new law unconstitutional: "The question is whether they are complete and abject hypocrites and frauds if they reject our . . . private right of action."[12]

**Red State vs. Blue City.** Another rising political problem is the clash between state governments and localities. Political polarization has made the problem worse by pitting Republican state officials against Democratic cities and localities. In Texas, there is an increasing divergence between the preferences of Republican politicians who repeatedly clean house in statewide elections vs. Democratic mayors and local officials who dominate politics in the major cities. The divergence extends to "local regulations aimed at a broad range of business activities, including bans on hydraulic fracking, pipeline construction, single-use plastic grocery bags, and the location of wind generation and electric transmission facilities."[13] Rather than pursue direct institutional avenues, in 2023, the State of Texas enacted House Bill 2127, a statute that seeks "to provide statewide consistency by returning sovereign regulatory powers to the state."[14] As you may expect, the state enlisted the help of private enforcers to reappropriate local powers, allowing:

> [a]ny person who has sustained an injury in fact, actual or threatened, from a municipal or county ordinance, order, or rule adopted or enforced by a [municipality or county] in violation [of several provisions] . . . has standing to bring and may bring an action against the municipality or county.[15]

Several cities immediately sued the state government, with San Antonio's mayor declaring "[w]e do not intend to meekly surrender our community's right to self-govern."[16]

---

These are just three examples of recent private enforcement regimes. They show an aggressive willingness to regulate diverse and contentious areas of American life via private rights of action. Let's set aside history, for now, and explore the universe of private enforcement as it exists *today* at both the federal level and in the states.

## PRIVATE ENFORCEMENT AT THE FEDERAL LEVEL: OVER 380 PRAS

Congress has embraced private enforcement in the most important regulatory areas. Drawing on a long history—explored in chapters 3 and 4—of common law claims and penal statutes, Congress placed a private right of action and treble damages in the Sherman Act (1890), making private enforcement a keystone of antitrust regulation. That kicked off a decades-long embrace of private enforcement, including the Clayton Act (1914), Fair Labor Standards Act (1938), Civil Rights Act (1964), and a wealth of environmental statutes in the 1970s. The combination of these areas makes private parties a primary driver of statutory enforcement in most important regulatory areas.

To more fully map out American private enforcement, I assembled a database of private rights of action in federal legislation. I applied dozens of search terms on the US Code, including the phrases "may sue," "file an action," and "shall be liable." This yielded 3,324 subsections for further evaluation. I then used a large language model to determine which of these filtered subsections contained actual private rights of action. And, finally, I reviewed a substantial portion of the results to ensure accuracy. This analysis returned **382** subsections of the US Code associated with a private right of action.[17] Consider the following examples:

Private rights of action predominantly appear in US Code sections related to Commerce and Trade, Public Health and Welfare, Transportation, and Labor. The table below shows the top areas where they appear:

But private rights of actions are just rights to sue, not actual lawsuits. There are many examples of rights to sue that are rarely enforced. Because of that, we also need an idea of how often plaintiffs decide to actually file suit under these statutes. It turns out that they do it *a lot*. In the early 2000s, Farhang found that "private litigants, and not federal agencies charged with enforcement responsibilities, prosecute the overwhelming majority of cases in federal courts. In the [2000s], there was an average of about **165,000 lawsuits** filed per year to enforce federal statutes in United States district courts."[18] That number has increased in the 2010s and 2020s. In fact, most federal lawsuits are private statutory enforcement claims.

Now, to be sure, in these areas, Congress has also created robust administrative agencies like the Securities and Exchange Commission, the Environmental Protection Agency, or the Federal Trade Commission. Private and public enforcement, then, exist in a complex ecosystem of enforcement—with public bureaucrats sometimes initiating cases and private lawyers following on, or *vice versa*. For this reason, it is important to keep in mind that private enforcement is almost never the only method of enforcement; it serves instead as a complement to public regulatory bodies.

With that background in mind, let's examine six important areas of federal law in detail:

***1. Antitrust.*** Private enforcement of antitrust statutes traces its roots to the Sherman Act of 1890, the foundational federal law prohibiting monopolistic practices and anticompetitive agreements. Section 7 of the Sherman Act provides a private right of action, allowing "[a]ny person who shall be injured in his business or property by any other person or corporation by reason of anything forbidden or declared to be unlawful by this act" to "sue therefor" and seek redress.[19] Part of what made that private right of action so powerful is that it allowed plaintiffs to "recover three fold the damages by him sustained, and the costs of suit, including a reasonable attorney's fee."[20] This treble damages provision serves as a powerful deterrent against antitrust

TABLE 1. **Examples of private rights of action provisions in federal statutes.**

| Statute | Private Right of Action |
| --- | --- |
| Servicemembers Civil Relief Act (providing legal and financial protections for members of the armed forces) | Any person aggrieved by a violation of this chapter may in a civil action—(1) obtain any appropriate equitable or declaratory relief with respect to the violation; (2) recover all other appropriate relief, including monetary damages; and (3) be a representative party on behalf of members of a class or be a member of a class, in accordance with the Federal Rules of Civil Procedure, notwithstanding any previous agreement to the contrary.[21] |
| Conrail Privatization (providing for specific expenditures by a railroad corporation) | . . . any person who suffers direct and substantial economic injury as a result of an alleged violation by the Corporation, with respect to the provisions of section 1321(a)(1) and (2) of this title, and section 1322 of this title, may bring an action to require compliance with such provision.[22] |
| Maritime Liability | (a) If a person makes a contract secured by, or on the credit of, a vessel covered by a mortgage filed or recorded under this chapter and sustains a monetary loss . . .<br>(b) A civil action may be brought to recover for losses referred to in subsection (a) of this section. The district courts have original jurisdiction of the action, regardless of the amount in controversy or the citizenship of the parties. If the plaintiff prevails, the court shall award costs and attorney fees to the plaintiff.[23] |
| National Voter Registration (establishing procedures for voting registration) | (b) Private right of action (1) A person who is aggrieved by a violation of this chapter may provide written notice of the violation to the chief election official of the State involved. (2) If the violation is not corrected within 90 days after receipt of a notice under paragraph (1), or within 20 days after receipt of the notice if the violation occurred within 120 days before the date of an election for Federal office, the aggrieved person may bring a civil action in an appropriate district court for declaratory or injunctive relief with respect to the violation . . . .[24] |
| Electronic publishing by Bell operating companies (providing special provisions for the operation of Bell companies) | (e) Private right of action (1) Damages. Any person claiming that any act or practice of any Bell operating company, affiliate, or separated affiliate constitutes a violation of this section may file a complaint with the Commission or bring suit as provided in section 207 of this title, and such Bell operating company, affiliate, or separated affiliate shall be liable as provided in section 206 of this title; except that damages may not be awarded for a violation that is discovered by a compliance review as required by subsection (b)(7) of this section and corrected within 90 days.[25] |

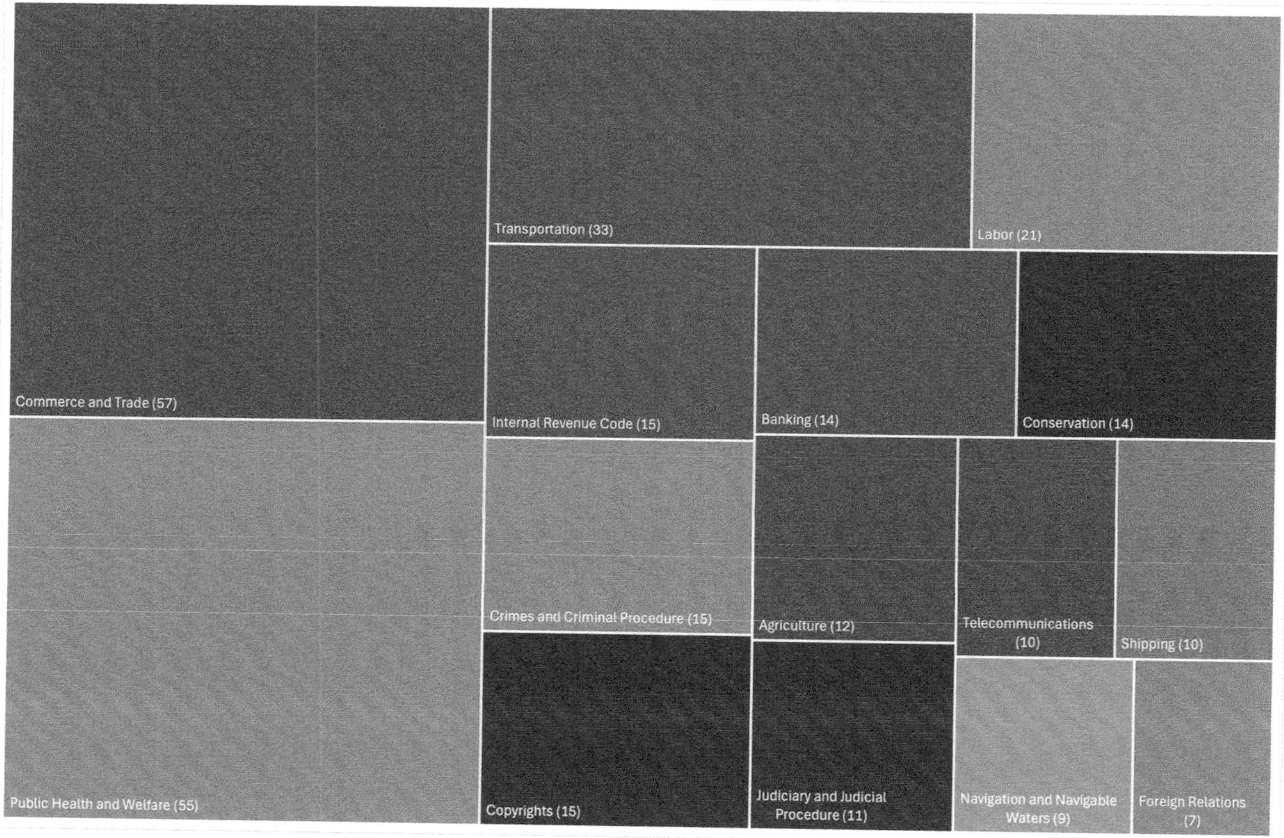


**FIGURE 1.** Areas in which private rights of action are most prominent in federal legislation. Figure based on data previously published in Nitisha Baronia, Jared Lucky & Diego A. Zambrano, *Private Enforcement at the Founding and Article II*, 114 Calif. L. Rev. 131 (2026). Author retained copyright to reproduce.

violations and incentivizes private parties to act as enforcers, supplementing government oversight by the Department of Justice and the Federal Trade Commission. The Clayton Act of 1914 strengthened these provisions, expanding the range of prohibited activities and allowing plaintiffs to seek injunctions.

Private antitrust litigation is a cornerstone of US competition policy, with cases spanning across industries from technology to pharmaceuticals. Private plaintiffs—often consumers, small businesses, or competitors—file most antitrust claims, accounting for over 90 percent of all antitrust enforcement actions in federal courts. These suits challenge practices like price-fixing, market allocation, and monopolistic mergers, driving significant settlements and shaping the behavior of corporations far beyond the direct oversight of regulatory agencies.

Consider a recent case that promises to transform how Americans buy and sell homes. For years, when any seller sold a house, they had to pay not just their own real estate agent, but also the buyer's agent—even though that agent represented the other side of the transaction. This unusual arrangement existed because the National Association of Realtors (NAR), the powerful trade group that controls most home sales in America, required it through what it called the Adversary Commission Rule. The rule forced sellers to offer a non-negotiable commission to buyer's agents if they wanted their house listed on the NAR's essential Multiple Listing Service, the database where most homes are bought and sold.

But private enforcement is now upending this system. In 2019, a class of property listing agents led by Scott and Rhonda Burnett decided to challenge the Adversary Commission Rule. They filed a class action lawsuit in the federal district court for the Western District of Missouri, arguing that the NAR and the nation's four largest real estate brokers were violating antitrust laws by artificially inflating home sale costs. Their core argument was simple: In a normal market, buyers would pay their own agents. Instead, this rule forced sellers to pay both sides' fees with no room for negotiation. The Burnetts weren't alone. Similar lawsuits popped up across the country, including a major case in Illinois. After a trial in Missouri, a jury agreed that this system violated antitrust law and awarded $1.8 billion in damages. Rather than face similar verdicts in other courts, the NAR agreed to settle all the cases for $418 million.[26] More importantly, the NAR agreed to eliminate the controversial rule entirely, changing how real estate agents will be paid across the country.

Now turn to the effect of private enforcement on cutting-edge industries. Consider Epic Games's bold challenge to Apple's control over the iPhone app market. Epic, the company behind the wildly popular video game *Fortnite*, took aim at Apple's iron grip on how iPhone users can download and pay for apps. At the heart of the dispute was Apple's requirement that every app developer play by two rules. First, all iPhone apps must be downloaded through Apple's App Store, where Apple takes a 30 percent cut of each sale. Second, whenever users make purchases within an app (like buying virtual currency in a game), that payment must also go through Apple, which again takes 30 percent of the transaction.

In August 2020, Epic launched a direct challenge to this system, filing a lawsuit that claimed Apple was illegally maintaining a monopoly over iPhone apps. Notably, Epic wasn't interested in money damages—instead, it wanted to fundamentally change how the app market works, asking courts to force Apple to allow alternative ways to download apps and process payments. The complaint sought to promote "fair competition in these two key markets that directly affect hundreds of millions of consumers and tens of thousands . . . [of] third-party app developers."[27] After a lengthy trial, Epic secured a partial victory. While the court rejected most of Epic's claims, it also required Apple to permit app developers to inform users about alternative payment methods beyond the App Store. When Apple appealed, the Ninth Circuit Court of Appeals upheld this ruling in 2022. Although Epic failed to break Apple's control over app distribution, it succeeded in cracking open the door to payment competition, potentially saving app developers and consumers billions in fees.

Sometimes private antitrust enforcement provokes government regulators to pay attention to an industry, leading to government action. In 2005, Advanced Micro Devices (AMD), then a small player in the computer chip industry, decided to challenge Intel's dominance in court. AMD claimed that Intel, which controlled roughly 80 percent of the market for computer processors, was illegally maintaining its monopoly through strong-arm tactics. According to AMD, Intel wasn't winning through better products or lower prices, but by threatening retaliation if computer manufacturers used AMD chips. Intel allegedly offered exclusive deals and special rebates to major computer makers like Dell and HP, but only if they agreed to severely limit their purchases from AMD.[28] The stakes were enormous because computer processors represent the brains of every desktop and laptop computer, a market worth billions of dollars annually. After years of litigation, Intel agreed to a $1.25 billion settlement with AMD to end their legal disputes.[29] But the story didn't end there. AMD's lawsuit attracted the attention of federal regulators, and just a month after the settlement, the Federal Trade Commission filed its own case against Intel.[30] The FTC's follow-on action resulted in another settlement requiring Intel to change its business practices and create a $10 million fund to compensate consumers.

This sequence—private litigation followed by government enforcement—shows how private antitrust suits often surface anticompetitive behavior that later draws regulatory attention. And, of course, the opposite sequence of public litigation followed by private piggybacks is also common.

***2. Civil Rights.*** The Civil Rights Act (CRA) of 1964, a landmark piece of legislation, prohibits employment discrimination on the basis of race, gender, national origin, or religion.[31] Although the statute establishes a dual enforcement model that combines both public and private enforcement mechanisms, it has become predominantly reliant on private lawsuits for its implementation. Yes, the US Equal Employment Opportunity Commission (EEOC) plays a key role in public enforcement, filing 124 federal district court suits in 2021. But that is dwarfed by the private side—private plaintiffs accounted for 98 percent of enforcement actions, initiating thousands of cases every year. This disparity shows the critical role that private litigants play in enforcing civil rights protections, as the sheer volume of private lawsuits far exceeds the limited capacity of the EEOC, making private enforcement the primary vehicle for addressing violations under the CRA.

Similarly, the Americans with Disabilities Act (ADA) of 1990 is another prime example of federal private enforcement in action. The ADA prohibits discrimination against individuals with disabilities in "any place of public accommodation."[32] The motivation behind the statute was that, as one court put it, "there was a 'compelling need' for a 'clear and comprehensive national mandate' to eliminate discrimination against disabled individuals, and to integrate them 'into the economic and social mainstream of American life.'"[33] Beyond delegating authority to the Department of Justice, the statute also empowers "any person who is being subjected to discrimination on the basis of disability in violation of [Title III]" to initiate a civil lawsuit.[34] Notably, private litigants under the ADA are not entitled to damages. Yet, given this ample private right of action, it is no surprise that according to the government, "private suits . . . are an essential complement to the federal government's enforcement."[35] The

Chamber of Commerce claims that ADA lawsuits increased by 349 percent between 2012 and 2021, reaching "12,298 filings" by the 2020s.[36]

Take, for instance, *O'Hanlon v. Uber Technologies, Inc.*, a case that presented a test of how private enforcement mechanisms in the ADA apply to new technology platforms.[37] In 2021, wheelchair users in Pittsburgh sued Uber for failing to provide any wheelchair accessible vehicles (WAVs) in their area, claiming this violated Title III of the ADA's prohibition against discrimination in places of public accommodation. Barred from seeking monetary damages, plaintiffs requested injunctive relief that would force Uber to make WAVs available through its on-demand ridesharing service. When Uber attempted to force the dispute into arbitration, the Third Circuit rejected this strategy, ruling that the plaintiffs, as non-users of Uber's app, had never signed the company's arbitration agreement and thus couldn't be bound by it. The case highlights how private enforcement provisions let groups challenge companies when government regulators are not ready to address emerging regulatory problems. (Although the government eventually sued Uber for related conduct.) As the litigation continues to unfold, it will become a battleground for determining whether digital platforms must comply with the same accessibility requirements as traditional transportation providers.

***3. Wages and Hours Laws.*** The Fair Labor Standards Act (FLSA) of 1938, a landmark New Deal statute, set nationwide standards for minimum wage and overtime pay, reshaping the American labor landscape.[38] Central to its enforcement is a robust private right of action, explicitly providing that "[a]ny employer . . . shall be liable to the employee or employees affected in the amount of their unpaid minimum wages, or their unpaid overtime compensation . . . ."[39] This statutory language empowers individual employees to sue for violations directly, allowing them to recover both their unpaid wages and an equivalent sum in liquidated damages. Beyond that, the statute allows employees to sue collectively, on behalf of other "employees similarly situated."[40] The combination of a private right of action with collective actions turned the FLSA into one of the most litigated labor statutes in the country, with claims frequently involving unpaid minimum wages, overtime violations, and employee misclassification. Wage and hour lawsuits are important in industries like retail, hospitality, and food services, where violations are common.

Sometimes private enforcement under the FLSA helps workers recover wages for tasks their employers refuse to count as "work" and, in doing so, effectively regulates employers. Consider the case of meat-processing workers at Tyson Foods's Storm Lake facility in Iowa. Every day, these workers faced the dangerous job of slaughtering, butchering, and packaging thousands of pigs to distribute cuts of pork across the country.[41] Before they could even start their shifts, workers had to put on extensive safety equipment—hard hats, hairnets, protective gloves, frocks, belly guards, and aprons. This time-consuming process was essential for worker safety and food sanitation, but Tyson wasn't paying workers for the time spent suiting up and removing this equipment.

In 2007, a group of workers filed a collective action lawsuit to recover overtime pay for this unpaid time. The case eventually reached the Supreme Court, but not over whether this "donning and doffing" time should be paid (everyone agreed it should). Instead, Tyson argued that workers couldn't sue as a group because they wore different equipment and thus spent different amounts of time getting ready. Since Tyson hadn't kept records of how long workers spent on these tasks, the workers' attorneys proved their case using a study that showed the average time spent suiting up. The Supreme Court ultimately sided with the workers, allowing them to use this representative evidence to win $2.9 million in unpaid wages. The Court's decision recognized a practical reality: When employers fail to keep proper records, workers need flexibility to prove their claims. Otherwise, the very companies that break wage laws by failing to keep records could use that carelessness to defeat workers' lawsuits. While the Department of Labor could have investigated these wage violations exclusively, private attorneys effectively stepped in as additional regulators, securing both compensation for workers and compliance with federal labor standards.

***4. Securities Markets.*** Congress enacted the Securities Exchange Act of 1934 to regulate and prevent fraud in the securities markets.[42] Like many other statutes, the Act lays out dual enforcement by the Securities and Exchange Commission and, in some instances, private plaintiffs. Private enforcement is primarily anchored in Rule 10b-5, adopted by the SEC to protect investors from deceptive practices in the purchase and sale of securities.[43] Although the rule does not explicitly create a private right of action, federal courts implied a right of action over several cases in the midcentury, culminating with Supreme Court recognition in the early 1970s. This implied right of action allows private plaintiffs to sue for damages resulting from securities fraud. Private securities fraud litigation, especially through class actions, has become a vital component of US financial regulation. While the SEC continues to play a central role in prosecuting securities fraud cases, private plaintiffs are now the primary enforcers of the rule, often driving major changes in corporate behavior and internal compliance practices. Class actions over fraudulent misrepresentations, insider trading, or market manipulation have resulted in some of the largest settlements in history.

The Enron scandal is a famous example of private enforcers stepping in when the SEC had failed to properly regulate fraud *ex ante*. By way of background, Enron was a Texas-based energy conglomerate that, during the 1990s and early 2000s, used sketchy accounting practices and shell corporations to mask its losses and, in the process, defraud its public shareholders. As the fraud was gradually exposed, the stock price tumbled from its all-time high of $90.75 in August 2000 to $0.25 on the eve of its Chapter 11 bankruptcy filing in December 2001. In the ensuing class action against Enron (and the banks and accounting firms that enabled the fraud), investor-plaintiffs won the largest securities fraud settlement to date: $7.2 billion.[44] During this saga, the SEC didn't quite cover itself in glory. A Senate investigation lambasted the SEC for its "systemic and arguably catastrophic failure" in catching the fraud before it wreaked havoc on shareholders.[45] Astoundingly, Enron obtained exceptions and greenlights from the SEC for its practices—including mark-to-market accounting—over the years. In the aftermath, the SEC's enforcement actions targeted only the individual officers responsible for the fraud and generated a mere $440 million for victim compensation. This amount was eclipsed by just the attorneys' fees in the private class action ($688 million plus interest), let alone the staggering loss of shareholder value in the four years preceding the bankruptcy ($74 billion).[46]

***5. Environmental Laws.*** Federal environmental law also relies on private enforcement. These schemes often come in two forms: first, statutes that empower anyone to file a claim against a regulated entity, often polluters; second, schemes that empower private citizens and groups to sue agencies for failure to take environmental concerns into account (these rights "ensure that federal regulations are enforced").[47]

An example of the first kind is the Clean Air Act (CAA).[48] When Congress adopted the CAA in 1970, it included a private right of action in the statute, allowing:

> any person [to] commence a civil action on his own behalf . . . against any person . . . who is alleged to have violated . . . or to be in violation of (A) an emission standard or limitation under this chapter or (B) an order issued by the Administrator or a State with respect to such a standard or limitation.[49]

Through this provision, Congress "deputize[d] 'private attorneys general' to assist the Environmental Protection Agency (EPA) . . . in the enforcement of environmental regulation."[50] Since its adoption, groups like the Natural Resources Defense Council (NRDC) and Sierra Club Legal Defense Fund have become vigorous enforcers of the statute's provisions.[51] Claims often target industrial facilities like power plants and refineries for exceeding emissions limits, as well as regulatory decisions permitting new fossil fuel projects without adequate air quality assessments. Environmental advocates frequently file suits over vehicle emissions standards, the permitting of chemical manufacturing plants, and even agricultural operations that release significant levels of particulate matter and hazardous air pollutants. While plaintiffs cannot sue for damages, they can obtain injunctions against polluters.[52] More recent amendments have expanded the available remedies, permitting plaintiffs under the CAA to seek "civil fines payable to the treasury."[53]

Consider, then, the case of ExxonMobil's Baytown Complex, a massive refinery and petrochemical plant in suburban Houston.[54] The facility operates under thousands of permits that set strict limits on air pollution. But between 2005 and 2013, ExxonMobil repeatedly exceeded these limits, releasing dangerous pollutants into nearby communities thousands of times. Two environmental organizations, the Environment Texas Citizen Lobby and the Sierra Club, filed claims against Exxon under the Clean Air Act's private right of action. Their lawsuit documented a routine pattern of violations: 241 major pollution events, 3,735 smaller incidents, and 901 permit violations. The environmental groups showed how these violations affected nearby residents, who suffered from respiratory problems and were forced to endure foul odors from the facility. While Texas state regulators also fined ExxonMobil about $1.4 million for these violations, a federal court found this penalty inadequate given the scale of noncompliance. In 2017, the court ordered ExxonMobil to pay nearly $20 million in additional penalties—money that would go to the federal treasury rather than the environmental groups. The case demonstrates how private enforcement can supplement state regulation, especially when state penalties prove insufficient to deter violations.

Now let's turn to the second kind of environmental statute, which allows private parties to sue agencies for failure to enforce the law. This category includes the 1970 National Environmental Policy Act (NEPA), a statute that obligates all federal agencies to prepare Environmental Impact Statements

(EIS) on the effects of all "major Federal actions significantly affecting the quality of the human environment."[55] Each EIS must detail any "adverse environmental effects." Note that unlike other private enforcement regimes, NEPA is only procedural because it "does not mandate particular results . . . . Rather, NEPA imposes only procedural requirements on federal agencies . . . to undertake analyses of the environmental impact of their proposals and actions."[56] The EIS serves as the statute's core procedural mechanism. While the Act does not provide an explicit private right of action, private parties can challenge in court an agency's compliance with NEPA. In effect, just like in every other private enforcement regime, anyone can show up in court to contest an agency's action. Each year, dozens of lawsuits are filed by environmental groups and concerned citizens, often resulting in delays or revisions to major infrastructure projects. Typical NEPA challenges come up in large-scale infrastructure projects like highway expansions, oil and gas drilling leases, and the construction of power transmission lines. Environmental groups also frequently contest the approval of logging activities, urban development plans, and even renewable energy projects like wind farms and solar installations, arguing that the required environmental assessments were incomplete or insufficient.

Private enforcers sometimes take advantage of NEPA to stop major infrastructure projects based on allegedly faulty environmental impact statements. Consider the case of Nationwide Permit 12, a streamlined permit that the Army Corps of Engineers used to approve thousands of utility projects, including major oil and gas pipelines, without a detailed environmental study.[57] In 2020, the Northern Plains Resource Council challenged this fast-track approach, arguing that the Corps was rubber-stamping large pipeline projects—including the Keystone XL pipeline—without properly analyzing their environmental impacts. Plaintiffs argued that the Corps failed to analyze the cumulative impacts of their permits on endangered and threatened species in their habitats, violating NEPA's requirement for a thorough environmental review. Moreover, plaintiffs alleged that the Corps failed to consult with the US Fish and Wildlife Service or the National Marine Fisheries Service to ensure environmental compliance. The Corps replied that its streamlined permit only authorized projects with minimal environmental effects. But a federal court in Montana agreed with the environmental groups, ordering the Corps to stop using the streamlined permit for new oil and gas pipelines until it completed proper environmental reviews.

***6. Government Fraud.*** Congress enacted the False Claims Act (FCA) in 1863, during the Civil War, to address rampant fraud by government contractors who supplied defective goods to the Union Army.[58] To combat this misconduct, the Act embraced the ancient legal device of qui tam, allowing private individuals to sue on behalf of the government for fraudulent claims made against federal funds. The statute explicitly "imposes civil liability upon '[a]ny person' who, *inter alia*, 'knowingly presents, or causes to be presented, to an officer or employee of the United States Government . . . a false or fraudulent claim for payment or approval.'"[59] In other words, the FCA targets fraud that directly harms the government's financial interests. Under the Act, a "relator" (a private plaintiff) can bring a qui tam claim "for the person and for the United States Government," effectively acting as a surrogate enforcer of public rights. Because the claim is officially on behalf of the government, the DOJ retains significant control over the litigation, including the authority to intervene and take over the case or to dismiss it altogether. Moreover, qui tam relators are rewarded through a bounty—a portion of the government's recovery—which incentivizes private parties to expose fraud.

One of the largest FCA payouts arose out of the 2008 financial crisis, when several whistleblowers helped uncover Bank of America's role in the crisis. Four separate whistleblowers, including three individuals and one corporation, filed qui tam lawsuits alleging that the bank had defrauded federal housing agencies by selling them defective mortgages with inflated appraisals. The DOJ investigated these claims and incorporated them into a landmark $17 billion settlement with Bank of America, of which $1 billion resolved the whistleblowers' FCA claims.[60] The whistleblowers received approximately $170 million for bringing these violations to light—with one whistleblower's share increasing from $3 million to $48 million after negotiations with the Justice Department.[61] This dramatic increase reflected the government's view that substantial rewards were necessary to incentivize insiders to expose corporate fraud. Qui tam suits sometimes create a partnership between private claimants and government prosecutors: Whistleblowers identify fraud from within institutions, while the DOJ leverages its resources to secure large recoveries. Of course, it doesn't always work like this—in a large percentage of cases, the DOJ lets the private relator prosecute the claim and takes its share of any recovery.

## PRIVATE ENFORCEMENT IN THE STATES: MORE THAN 10,000 PRAS

While federal private enforcement focuses on core regulatory areas, state legislatures have cast a much wider net, implementing private rights of action across virtually every policy domain. Using machine learning to identify private enforcement in state law, I found more than **10,000 private rights of action** across the fifty states.[62] These provisions are all over the statutory map, including banking, labor, taxes, and the environment, among others. By one measure, California and Texas lead other states with about two hundred private rights of action. And most states average somewhere between fifty and one hundred. Under a more expansive measure that captures any statutory provision that gives a private party a right to sue another private party, California has over 1,000 private rights of action, while New Jersey, New York, Illinois, and Texas have around 600 or more.[63]

To get an idea of the kind of language used in these statutes, below are a few provisions from different states:

TABLE 2. **Examples of private rights of action provisions in state statutes.**

| Private Right of Action |
|---|
| Any professional athlete, or any student athlete, or any elementary or secondary school, college, university, or other educational institution, . . . or any other person *may bring a civil action* for recovery of damages from an athlete agent, if [they are] adversely affected by the acts of the athlete agent or of the athlete agent's representative or employee in violation of this chapter.[64] |
| The handler of a search and rescue canine *is liable to* the owner or operator of a commercial lodging establishment or restaurant for any damages to the premises caused by the service canine.[65] |
| *Any person* who shall be damaged or injured by any practitioner of the healing arts, or by any person to whom such a practitioner may refer a patient for treatment, *may bring suit* against the practitioner either severally, or jointly, with the person to whom the referral was made.[66] |
| Failure by any private or public animal shelter to comply with the provisions of this act for euthanizing animals shall constitute a nuisance. *Any person may maintain a civil action* to enjoin the continuance of the nuisance.[67] |

(*continued*)

TABLE 2. **(Continued)**

| **Private Right of Action** |
| --- |
| The driver of a vehicle approaching a person using a service animal shall take all necessary precautions to avoid injury to that person, and any driver who fails to take such precautions *shall be liable in damages* for any injury caused to that person.[68] |
| A [gasoline] dealer *may bring an action* for damages sustained as a result of: (a) Failure to make such disclosures as are required in RSA 339-C:3; or (b) Failure to make an offer in good faith to repurchase as required in RSA 339-C:5; or (c) Wrongful termination of or refusal to renew his agreement as set forth in RSA 339-C:4; . . .[69] |
| No vehicle, unladen or with load, shall exceed a height of 14 feet. Provided, however, that neither the State of North Carolina nor any agency or subdivision thereof, nor any person, firm or corporation, shall be required to raise, alter, construct or reconstruct any underpass, wire, pole, trestle, or other structure to permit the passage of any vehicle having a height, unladen or with load, in excess of 12 feet, six inches. Provided further, that the operator or owner of any vehicle having an overall height, whether unladen or with load, in excess of 12 feet, six inches, *shall be liable for damage* to any structure caused by such vehicle having a height in excess of 12 feet, six inches.[70] |
| A pilot who charges a pilotage rate for pilot services different from the pilotage rates established under this chapter for the port in which the pilot serves *is liable* to each person who was charged the different rate for double the amount of pilotage.[71] |
| Any purchaser injured by any violation of this Article *may bring an action* for rescission and restitution or for recovery of damages and for reasonable attorney's fees.[72] |

While the states all share a broad reliance on private enforcement, there are important state-by-state differences. For instance, as figure 2 below shows, larger states like California and Texas have more private rights of action in absolute terms. But this absolute term count may simply reflect more extensive legal codes. Adjusting for the length of each state's code—that is, measuring private rights of action as a proportion of total statutory provisions—produces a different ranking that better captures each state's relative reliance on private enforcement as a governance strategy (see figure 3 below):

When measured proportionally, states like Wisconsin, Wyoming, and Montana emerge as the most intensive users of private enforcement,

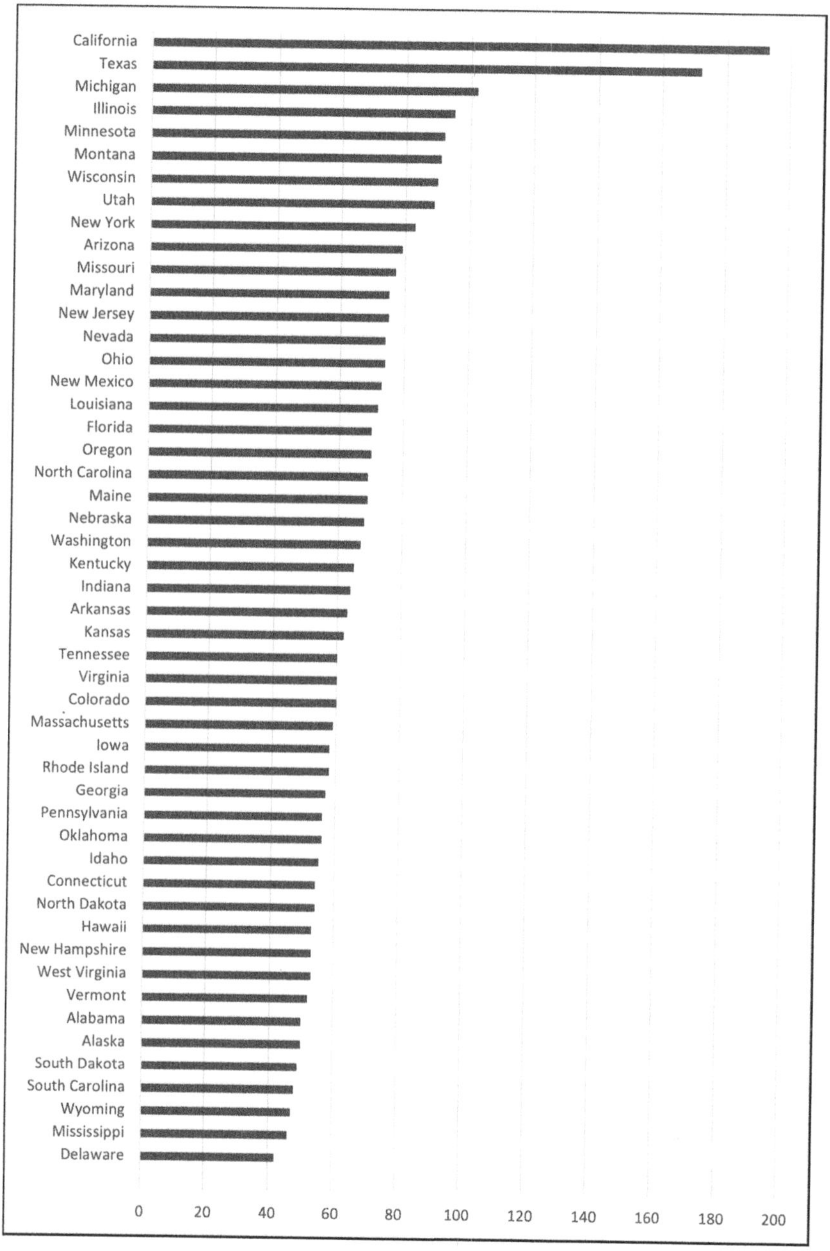


**FIGURE 2.** Number of private rights of action by state, 2021. Figure previously published in Diego A. Zambrano, Neel Guha, Austin Peters & Jeffrey Xia, *Private Enforcement in the States*, 172 U. PA. L. REV. 61 (2023). Author retained copyright to reproduce.

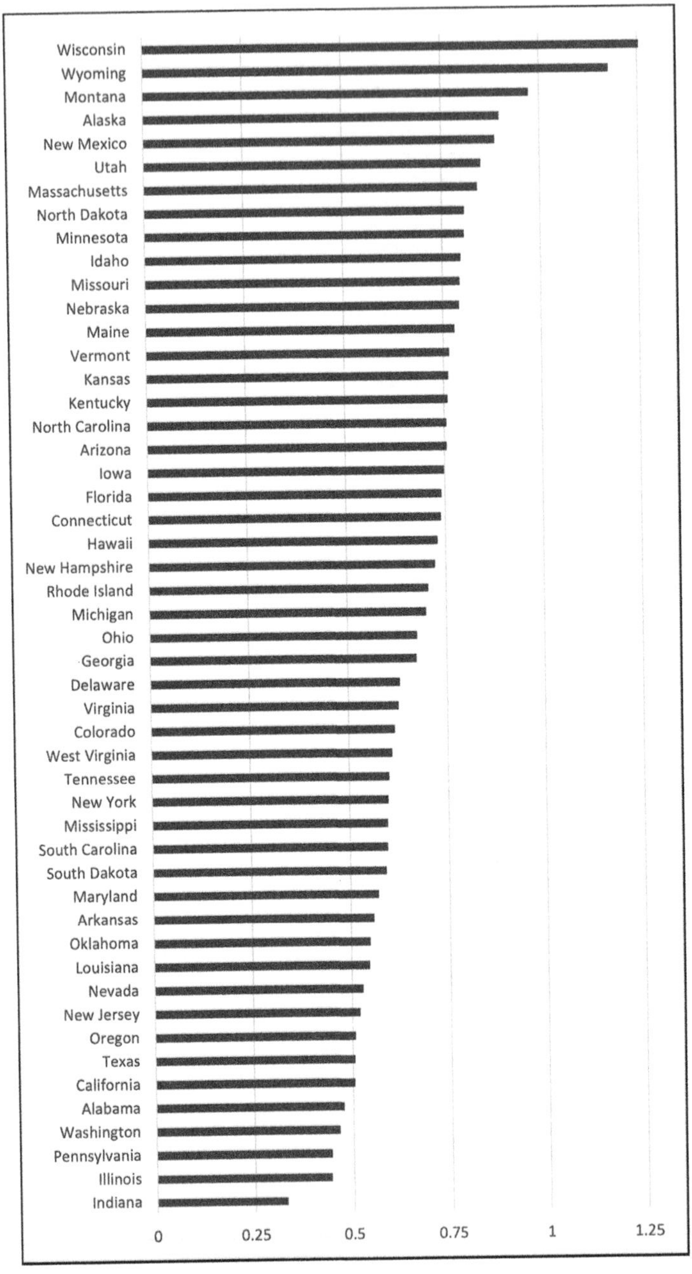


**FIGURE 3.** Number of private rights of action per thousand clauses by state, 2021. Figure previously published in Diego A. Zambrano, Neel Guha, Austin Peters & Jeffrey Xia, *Private Enforcement in the States*, 172 U. PA. L. REV. 61 (2023). Author retained copyright to reproduce.

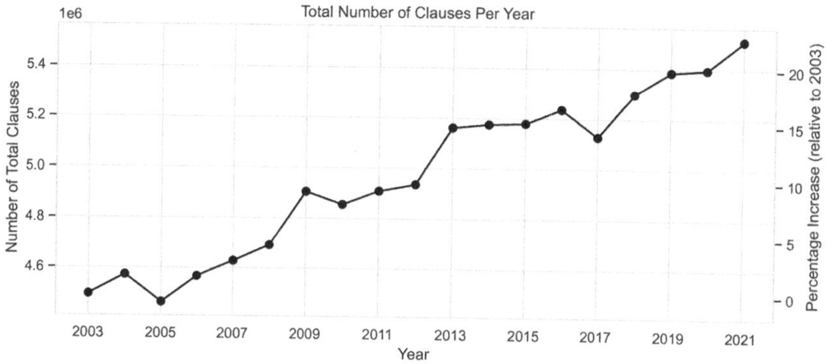


FIGURE 4. Number of private rights of action over time, 2003–2021. Figure previously published in Diego A. Zambrano, Neel Guha, Austin Peters & Jeffrey Xia, *Private Enforcement in the States*, 172 U. PA. L. REV. 61 (2023). Author retained copyright to reproduce.

while large states like California and Texas fall lower in the distribution. Regardless of measurement approach, however, extensive reliance on private enforcement remains a constant across all states, with even the lowest-ranking jurisdictions maintaining dozens of private enforcement mechanisms.

Moreover, over the last twenty years, states have steadily added new private rights of action. (See Figure 4 above.)

Surprisingly, there does not appear to be a correlation between political preferences in a state and reliance on private enforcement. Indeed, private rights of action have been expanding in states across the political spectrum, from conservative Utah and Nebraska to liberal Connecticut and more purple states like New Hampshire and Wisconsin, suggesting bipartisan appeal for this governance mechanism.

Again, private rights to sue do not tell us the actual number of suits—enforcement matters here, too. A 2015 study found that around 17 million civil cases were filed every year in state courts (excluding traffic-related cases).[73] Most state civil cases deal with evictions, debt collection, or family disputes.[74] Only a small minority of these cases deal with regulatory lawsuits, the focus of this book. However, even a small percentage of 17 million cases will result in large numbers of statutory claims. For example, in the calendar year 2018, California employees filed 14,772 complaints with the California Department of Fair Employment and Housing to request an immediate "right to sue" that precedes a court filing—a proxy for a subset of employment lawsuits.[75] And in 2019, plaintiffs filed 190 CEQA claims in California.[76] In 2022–2023, the Florida Office of the State Courts Administrator listed 1,697 employment discrimination claims and 262 "antitrust/trade regulation" suits filed in state courts that year (the antitrust number was unusually large; in other years the number is less than one hundred per year).[77] One study of consumer protection statutes "identified over 17,000 reported . . . decisions in federal district and state appellate courts from 2000 through 2007."[78] (And court decisions are a small subset of filed cases.) These examples are just the tip of the iceberg, but they suggest that there are hundreds of thousands of regulatory claims across the fifty states every year.

Now, to be sure, just like at the federal level, public enforcement plays a significant role alongside private enforcement. A key distinction between state and federal governance lies in the division of executive power at the state level. Unlike the federal government's centralized executive branch, states often split executive authority between the governor and other elected officials, most notably the state attorney general (AG). State statutes empower AGs to initiate lawsuits on behalf of citizens harmed by statutory violations, often bringing these cases as *parens patriae* actions to protect the welfare of residents. However, the strength and independence of AGs vary widely across states—while some have well-funded offices with broad statutory powers, others operate as extensions of the governor's office with limited autonomy and resources.

Additionally, there is a significant administrative bureaucracy in most states. State administrative agencies, much like their federal counterparts, play a critical role in regulating areas such as environmental protection, business practices, and labor standards. However, the landscape of state administrative governance is diverse and varies widely across jurisdictions. While every state has its own administrative apparatus, the size, resources, and sophistication of these agencies differ significantly from state to state. In many cases, state agencies lack the funding and institutional capacity enjoyed by federal agencies. The federal government benefits from broader tax revenue streams and can allocate substantial resources to its agencies, enabling them to hire highly qualified staff and implement complex enforcement programs. By contrast, state budgets are often constrained, with significant portions allocated to essential services like healthcare and education, leaving fewer funds available for public enforcement activities.

Moreover, balanced budget requirements in many states further limit the capacity of state agencies to engage in robust regulatory oversight.

Setting public enforcement aside, let's now explore the world of private enforcement in the states in some discrete areas. The breadth of state-level private enforcement becomes most apparent when examining specific policy domains where states have chosen to supplement traditional government oversight with private litigation. Four areas illustrate this pattern well: antitrust, wages and hours, environmental protection, and consumer protection. In each of these domains, states have not merely adopted federal models but have often gone beyond federal approaches, creating more expansive private enforcement mechanisms that reflect local priorities and political constraints.

***1. Antitrust.*** Every single state has a private right of action to sue for antitrust violations, often mirroring federal statutes but sometimes going even further in scope. These state statutes are typically drafted with similar language, empowering "any person" to "sue" or "recover" damages from monopolistic or anticompetitive practices. Like the federal system, the states embrace a hybrid enforcement model, which allows both private litigants and state attorneys general to pursue claims. For example, the Colorado Antitrust Statute of 1992 targets a range of anticompetitive conduct, giving the attorney general authority to enforce the law either on behalf of the state or the public. The statute provides that "[a]ny person injured . . . in its business or property by reason of any violation of this article" may sue for injunctive relief and recover damages, including attorney's fees and treble damages. Other states, like California, adopt a broader approach.[79] The California Unfair Competition Law (UCL) prohibits "any unlawful, unfair, or fraudulent business act or practice," encompassing a wide range of behavior, including anticompetitive conduct.[80] California's statute, too, employs a hybrid enforcement model that allows for expansive private litigation.

State antitrust laws became even more important after the Supreme Court's *Illinois Brick* decision blocked indirect purchasers from suing under federal law. The case *In re: Lithium Ion Batteries Antitrust Litigation* showcases how states filled this enforcement gap.[81] In *Illinois Brick Co. v. Illinois*, the Supreme Court found that only those who bought directly from defendants could pursue antitrust damages under federal law, barring suits from indirect purchasers who paid higher prices that were passed through a supply chain.[82] In 2012, plaintiffs' attorneys alleged that battery manufacturers were conspiring to fix prices. Lithium ion batteries power most portable consumer electronics, from smartphones to laptops to power tools. By the early 2000s, the market was dominated by Japanese manufacturers (that invented the technology in 1991) and Korean companies like LG and Samsung that entered around 2000. The batteries were highly standardized—all batteries of a particular type had to meet uniform specifications regardless of manufacturer. According to the plaintiffs, this market dynamic drove manufacturers to collude on pricing through secret meetings in Asia, information sharing, and coordinated responses to changes in input costs like cobalt prices. The problem for plaintiffs, however, is that most consumers are only indirect purchasers of lithium batteries. When a company like Apple buys lithium-ion batteries directly from manufacturers to put in iPhones, it's the only direct purchaser. When consumers buy those iPhones containing the batteries, they're indirect purchasers who paid higher prices passed through the supply chain. To dodge this precedent, a class of indirect purchasers relied on seventeen different state antitrust laws that explicitly authorized their claims, ultimately securing $113 million in settlements.[83]

A similar dynamic played out in *In re: Automotive Parts Antitrust Litigation*, where car buyers relied on state statutes to challenge price-fixing and bid-rigging in the auto parts industry.[84] Following a DOJ investigation that produced guilty pleas, piggyback private enforcement under state law secured $1.2 billion in settlements for indirect purchasers.[85] These cases demonstrate how state antitrust laws enable private plaintiffs to both supplement federal enforcement and compensate consumers.

Plaintiffs' attorneys otherwise take advantage of state antitrust laws to target conduct that federal law cannot reach. A 1999 case involving Microsoft is a good example of how state laws enable consumers to challenge anticompetitive practices that inflate prices.[86] California consumers and businesses sued Microsoft under the state's Cartwright Act and Unfair Competition Law, arguing that Microsoft's practice of pre-installing its software and imposing restrictive licensing terms led to overcharges. In short order, the California class secured a landmark $1.1 billion settlement in 2003, with Microsoft providing vouchers to compensate consumers who had indirectly purchased its software licenses.[87]

**2. *Wages and Hours*.** Every state has adopted its own wage and hour laws, creating a vast network of private enforcement across the country. These statutes establish minimum wages, overtime requirements, and mandatory break periods, while empowering employees to sue for violations. The private right of action is essential because state labor departments lack the resources to inspect every workplace or respond to every complaint. Instead, legislators rely on employees and their attorneys to enforce these laws through private lawsuits. In most states, workers can recover unpaid wages, statutory damages, and attorneys' fees, creating sufficient incentives for private enforcement.

But California has gone further than other states. California's Private Attorneys General Act (PAGA) gives employees the right to sue employers for any violation of California's extensive labor code, not just traditional wage and hour claims that most states permit.[88] While other states typically limit private enforcement to recovering unpaid wages, PAGA authorizes lawsuits over the entire spectrum of labor code violations. Employees can file lawsuits individually or on behalf of other employees and the State of California for violations ranging from wages and hours and child labor violations to smaller infractions like failure to provide itemized wage statements and workplace safety violations. PAGA may be one of the most robust private rights of action in the United States. Since its inception in 2004, PAGA lawsuits have grown by more than ten times, fueling thousands of lawsuits in 2023. While a PAGA plaintiff can keep up to 35 percent of the recovered penalty, the rest goes to California's Labor & Workforce Development Agency.[89] In the past few years, that Agency has earned hundreds of millions of dollars in PAGA penalties from employers.

Private enforcement of California labor law takes different forms, as recent high-profile cases illustrate. Through PAGA, Google employees challenged confidentiality agreements that prevented workers from discussing their working conditions, securing a landmark $27 million settlement in 2023.[90] The state received $13.2 million of this amount, while employees who signed these illegal agreements shared the remainder. At McDonald's, hourly workers used PAGA to target the company's overtime calculations and break policies, winning both a $26 million settlement and structural reforms including new training programs and electronic timekeeping systems.[91]

Beyond PAGA's unique public-private framework, California employees also enforce labor rights through traditional class actions. Take, for instance, a case by security guards at G4S Secure Solutions based on the company's failure to provide legally required meal breaks through a class action that resulted in a $130 million settlement, California's largest wage and hour agreement.[92] Similarly, a G.H. Bass store manager led a class action against AM Retail Group over worker misclassification, securing $1.15 million in compensation. Together, these cases demonstrate how employees can act as private attorneys general under PAGA while also pursuing collective remedies through class actions, creating a robust enforcement regime that combines public penalties with private compensation.

*3. **Environmental Laws.*** State environmental law is far more decentralized and dynamic compared to its federal counterpart. Unlike the federal system, which relies on a handful of major statutes like the Clean Air Act and Clean Water Act, state environmental regulation is embedded in a sprawling network of at least 748 distinct statutes with private rights of action. These PRAs are dispersed across a wide variety of laws, often shoehorned into existing legislative frameworks rather than introduced through standalone, comprehensive statutes. To be sure, the states vary in their adoption of environmental rights to sue. As the graph below shows, California and Wisconsin are at the top of the list while South Dakota and Kentucky are at the other end.

Still, every state relies extensively on these rights to sue. This fluid and fragmented approach stands in stark contrast to the federal regime, which has remained largely unchanged since the 1970s, reflecting the states' willingness to experiment with new forms of private enforcement as they respond to local environmental challenges.

The scope of state PRAs in environmental law is vast, covering both broad and highly specific regulatory areas. Some statutes grant sweeping authority, allowing "any person" to sue for the protection of "air, water, land, or other natural resources" from pollution or degradation.[93] Others are narrowly tailored to address particular issues, such as Ohio's private enforcement provisions related to hazardous waste[94] or Texas's statutes regulating surface mining practices.[95] In some cases, PRAs are even more specialized and niche. Nevada, for instance, has a statute allowing lawsuits against those who fail to safeguard poisonous liquids that may harm

FIGURE 5. Environmental private rights of action by state. Figure previously published in Diego A. Zambrano, Neel Guha, Austin Peters & Jeffrey Xia, *Private Enforcement in the States*, 172 U. PA. L. REV. 61 (2023). Author retained copyright to reproduce.

livestock,[96] while New York permits recovery of statutory damages for every tree unlawfully destroyed by fire.[97] California's statutes go as far as authorizing private lawsuits against manufacturers whose tableware releases excessive amounts of lead or cadmium.[98] These examples illustrate the diverse and sometimes idiosyncratic nature of state environmental PRAs, which collectively empower citizens to tackle a wide range of environmental issues that often go unaddressed by federal regulation.

In addition to these niche provisions, some states enacted broader environmental laws that both expand the scope of actionable environmental harm beyond federal standards and eliminate traditional procedural barriers that limit access to courts. New Jersey's Environmental Rights Act (NJERA), passed in 1974, authorizes "any person" to sue for the enforcement of existing environmental statutes, regulations, or ordinances, creating a hybrid enforcement model.[99] NJERA requires prospective plaintiffs to provide thirty days' notice to the state Attorney General and other relevant parties. The legislature intended this statute to give citizens "ready access to the courts to resolve environmental disputes," bypassing the traditional requirement of proving special injury.[100] Similarly, Michigan's Environmental Protection Act (MEPA) empowers "any person," including non-residents, to sue for the protection of natural resources against "pollution, impairment, or destruction."[101] MEPA is widely regarded as a seminal example of state-level citizen suit laws, reflecting its drafters' belief that the public should not only have "a right to a decent environment," but also the ability to enforce that right through private litigation.[102] Together, NJERA and MEPA demonstrate that states can expand private environmental enforcement by removing standing requirements that would bar suits in federal court while simultaneously broadening the definition of actionable environmental harm, creating more comprehensive enforcement mechanisms than their federal counterparts.

*4. **Consumer Protection.*** State consumer protection statutes offer another good example of the expansive use of private enforcement at the state level, often going beyond the scope of federal regulations. Every single state has adopted its own version of a consumer protection statute, known as "unfair and deceptive acts and practices" (UDAP) laws.[103] These statutes are designed to protect consumers from fraudulent business practices, false advertising, and other forms of marketplace deception.[104] Every UDAP statute comes with a private right of action, typically empowering "any person who suffers a loss as a result of an unfair or deceptive act" to bring a lawsuit.[105] Many of these statutes also authorize plaintiffs to recover treble damages and attorney's fees, creating strong incentives for parties to enforce the law.[106]

State UDAP laws vary significantly in their language and breadth. Some, like California's UCL, take a broad approach, prohibiting "any unlawful, unfair, or fraudulent business act or practice."[107] Similarly, the Texas consumer protection law was enacted "to protect consumers against false, misleading, and deceptive business practices, unconscionable actions, and breaches of warranty and to provide efficient and economical procedures to secure such protection."[108] This kind of language allows consumers to bring a wide range of claims, including those not explicitly covered by other statutes, creating a flexible tool for private litigants.

By contrast, states like New York have adopted narrower statutes that focus more explicitly on false advertising and fraudulent sales practices.[109] The structure of all of these laws typically involves a hybrid model, permitting both state attorneys general and private individuals to file suits.[110] Yet state legislatures often adopt these statutes to redress "the demonstrated inability of the [a] state Attorney General to adequately police false advertising and deceptive trade practices."[111] A significant slice of enforcement actions are by private plaintiffs, who flood state courts with consumer claims each year.[112]

The prevalence of private enforcement under these consumer protection statutes has made them a powerful regulatory mechanism, supplementing the limited capacity of public agencies.[113] In many states, private consumer claims outnumber those brought by attorneys general, giving individual litigants a large role in holding businesses accountable. This decentralized enforcement model allows for a dynamic response to marketplace misconduct, as private parties can swiftly bring lawsuits based on emerging issues, from data privacy violations to fraudulent marketing of consumer goods. The resulting litigation landscape is constantly evolving, shaped by a mix of aggressive private lawsuits and selective public enforcement actions that together form a comprehensive consumer protection regime.

Private enforcement of state consumer protection laws targets deceptive marketing across a wide range of industries. In *Bell v. Publix*, consumers used multiple state consumer protection statutes to challenge how major cheese manufacturers labeled their products.[114] The manufacturers had prominently displayed "100% Grated Parmesan Cheese" on the front of packages, while revealing in fine print on the back that the products contained cellulose powder and other preservatives. When the Seventh Circuit allowed the case to proceed in 2020, it established that accurate ingredient lists in fine print don't immunize companies from liability for misleading front-label claims.

State consumer protection laws also enable challenges to broader marketing campaigns. In *Pelman v. McDonald's*, New York consumers sued the fast food chain under the state's consumer protection statute, arguing that McDonald's promotions falsely suggested that daily consumption of its products was part of a healthy lifestyle.[115] While earlier consumer protection cases typically involved specific product claims, the Second Circuit's decision to allow this case to proceed showed how state laws could be used to challenge more general marketing messages. Together, these cases demonstrate the flexibility of state consumer protection laws in addressing both traditional product labeling and more sophisticated forms of potentially deceptive marketing.

## PRIVATE ENFORCEMENT FROM A COMPARATIVE PERSPECTIVE

Countries around the world do not rely on private enforcement of regulatory law as much as the United States. Even nations with similar common law traditions like Canada and the UK show markedly different patterns in how they enforce regulatory statutes, often favoring centralized administrative authority over decentralized private litigation. And even when other nations have borrowed specific elements of American procedure—like adopting private rights of action in the antitrust or civil rights context—they have rejected the core American belief that private suits should play a central role in enforcing public regulations.

Robert Kagan's work on adversarial legalism begins with the premise that "[c]ompared to other economically advanced democracies . . . American economic and political life is more deeply pervaded by litigation (or the threat of it) and by political controversy about the judiciary and legal processes."[116] Indeed, "[t]he United States more often relies on lawyers, legal threats, and legal contestation in implementing public policies."[117] Kagan draws on dozens of studies to support the claim that the United States more often relies on adversarial legalism than other economically advanced democracies.[118] For example, some of these studies:

> compare national systems for compensating injured people; regulating pollution; punishing criminals; equalizing educational opportunity; promoting worker safety; discouraging narcotics use; deterring malpractice by police officers, physicians, and product manufacturers; and so on . . . . [T]he comparative empirical studies . . . are sufficient to show that for one social problem after another, the studies show, the American system for making and implementing public policy and resolving disputes is distinctive.[119]

But setting aside Kagan and older studies, let's get to the point of this book: Other countries do not rely on private litigants—at least to the same extent—to enforce important regulatory statutes. This is true in contexts like environmental pollution, employment wages and hours, securities regulation, discrimination, government fraud, and consumer protection. Indeed, only one nation has more cases and lawyers per capita than the United States—Israel.[120] But even there, two scholars found that "while Israel has many more class actions than the United States on a per capita basis, the cases are much less consequential from a monetary and subject matter perspective."[121]

On securities regulation, for instance, the UK is one of the only countries with a private right of action (but without class actions and other procedural enhancers). The UK Parliament inserted a right to sue in its securities regime in 2006, via the Financial Services and Markets Act.[122] Unlike Rule 10b-5 class actions in the United States, the British mechanism has weaker procedural tools (including opt-in requirements, lack of fraud-on-the-market presumptions, loser-pays fee rules, and tight limits on contingency funding, further discussed in Chapter 6). These missing procedural enhancers sharply reduce the leverage plaintiffs' lawyers wield in US litigation. The loser-pays rule has proven particularly prohibitive, creating a large insurance and reinsurance market that by itself makes individual private claims excessively expensive. Because of those procedural brakes, and the fact that the provision is still relatively young, there is little evidence of widespread enforcement, at least anywhere close to US levels. Plaintiffs have filed fewer than a dozen collective actions, and only a couple have produced large settlements, leaving enforcement intensity low for now.[123]

Consumer protection and government fraud suits look similar to securities. As the Volkswagen case in the introduction shows, while Americans flooded courts with private litigation under RICO and consumer protection statutes, German consumers could not file similar claims.[124] This is a microcosm of a larger phenomenon—most countries around the world allow private suits only over individual personal injury claims. But rarely do countries make it easy to bring a wide range of consumer protection actions like American states do. While some Canadian provinces authorize consumer protection claims, there is no UDAP equivalent in the EU or in Japan.[125] In the related area of government fraud, even the UK rejects the qui tam model of policing government fraud. The UK parliament abandoned that model in the mid-1900s while the United States strengthened it in the 1980s.[126]

American-style private enforcement is an even bigger outlier in environmental law. The United States almost uniquely empowers citizens to sue over pollution and environmental degradation in their individual capacities. Remember that the fifty states have adopted over 700 private rights of action related to the environment. But there is no EU equivalent to American citizen suits. Consider again Chapter 1's contrast of the Oil Pollution Act in the United States (with a private right of action) and the EU/France's agency-focused approach. Some countries like Germany have recognized the right of environmental associations to challenge project approvals. But there is no evidence of widespread adoption or use of these rights to sue. And even in the UK there is no general citizen-suit statute; most of the work is done by the Department for Environment, Food and Rural Affairs. Canada does, however, allow Environmental Protection Actions under the Canadian Environmental Protection Act. But, again, all this pales in comparison to the breadth of American environmental suits.

Antitrust enforcement seems to be one of the only areas where the EU and UK are moving closer to US levels of private enforcement. But even with new damages claims against monopolies, the number of cases still trails the share of private antitrust cases in the United States (90 percent). The EU's Directive 2014/104 instructs member states to ensure that victims of anti-competitive conduct can obtain damages; the UK's Competition Act of 1998 allows private damage claims in front of a specialized tribunal and the Consumer Rights Act 2015 authorizes collective actions.[127] The number of EU damages claims is quickly going up: In 2019, one scholar found 239 antitrust claims under the EU's damages directive and 138 cases filed by public authorities (around 64 percent private).[128] In the UK, a 2023 report found thirty private claims pending in front of the specialized tribunal (filed in multiple years) and thirteen new public investigations in a single year.[129] Both EU and UK regimes are in a nascent stage and may well plateau at current levels. In Canada, while private claims and even class actions are permitted, they are narrower in substantive scope.[130] There is no evidence that these claims are quickly ramping up, and the Competition Act does not provide for treble damages or attorneys' fees, diminishing a major incentive to file private lawsuits.[131] Even when the numbers of claims rises in these countries, these cases are typically heard in specialized tribunals that allow public regulators to manage them, a far cry from the US model.

Employment law is one of the only areas where we see widespread adoption of private enforcement around the world. The EU requires that individuals who suffer discrimination have access to judicial remedies and compensation. The UK, Canada, and even Japan have some form of a right to sue over wages and hours. But, again, the labor and employment bureaucracy in those countries is much larger than in the United States.

Taking all of this in, it still appears that in the United States, "the law and its practitioners have perhaps been the most important single factor making for political and social change and have time and again proved to be the normal instrument for bringing it about."[132]

To be sure, some prominent scholars have pointed out that America may not have unusually high rates of litigation. Marc Galanter, for instance, challenged the conventional wisdom that America is exceptionally litigious. Using empirical data on judges, lawyers, and civil cases per capita, Galanter argued that America's supposed obsession with litigation is largely mythical. His research shows that only a small fraction of grievances ever become lawsuits, with even fewer reaching trial. When comparing international data, he finds that many other advanced democracies show equal or greater rates of formal legal conflict.[133] Yet others who disagree with Galanter have found that US tort litigation far exceeds the comparable volume in the United Kingdom, Australia, and Canada.[134]

The problem with the scholarship on litigiousness is that it is beside the point; private enforcement is *not* fully coextensive with overall litigation rates. That is, litigation rates can be high in a country even with few private enforcement regimes and *vice versa*. Again, the phenomenon addressed in this book is the predilection by American legislators to settle *major regulatory questions* by inserting private rights of action in key statutes. The key empirical question is:

- Do other countries include private rights of action in major regulatory statutes and, if they do, do we observe private litigation as a major driver of regulatory enforcement in those areas?

Sometimes other countries really do adopt private rights of action, especially in areas like antitrust or employment. But even then, we observe that the most important cases are filed by robust public regulators, not private attorneys.[135]

Moreover, a system of private enforcement may or may not result in high litigation rates overall. For example, some of the most important regulatory cases have been part of class actions, which technically count as a single case but represent thousands or even millions of plaintiffs. A simple comparison of litigation rates would miss the importance of class actions to our regulatory apparatus. More on this topic in Chapter 9.

The evidence for American exceptionalism in this context is compelling. As Chapter 6 will discuss, even when other countries adopt rights to sue, a significant procedural infrastructure is absent. Contingency fees, which make American litigation economically attractive for plaintiffs' attorneys, are verboten in many European jurisdictions. Class actions, the key mechanism for aggregating small claims, face restrictions in most countries outside the United States. Even where class action mechanisms exist, as in some Canadian provinces, they operate under more stringent requirements and generate fewer cases. Perhaps most importantly, the combination of broad discovery, punitive damages, and one-way fee-shifting provisions that incentivizes private litigation in America is, again, absent elsewhere.

This brief cross-national comparison teaches us that private enforcement looks very different outside the United States. Even as other nations have selectively borrowed elements of American procedure, including class actions, they have done so without putting private litigation at the center of regulatory enforcement. The persistence of these differences, despite increasing globalization and legal harmonization, shows how deeply private enforcement is embedded in America's distinctive legal and political culture.

## PRIVATE ENFORCEMENT FROM SEA TO SHINING SEA

Take one message from this chapter: Across every regulatory area we care about, statutes empower Americans to enforce the law via private lawsuits. This phenomenon happens in both Washington, DC and your local state legislature. From antitrust to civil rights, environmental protection to consumer welfare, and even hypnosis services in Florida, private rights of action have become a key method for enforcing the law in the United States. Remember, too, that this approach stands in stark contrast to other nations that primarily rely on administrative schemes and bureaucratic governance to achieve regulatory goals.

American governance transforms ordinary citizens into private enforcers of the law and allows bureaucrats to serve as backstops as well. It reflects a practical recognition that government agencies often lack the resources to police violations. This hybrid enforcement model combines public regulatory bodies with private lawsuits and creates a more robust regulatory ecosystem than either approach could achieve alone.

The proliferation of private rights of action at both federal and state levels has deep implications for regulatory compliance. For businesses and individuals, this decentralized enforcement regime means that compliance is not merely about satisfying government agents but avoiding liability from a potentially unlimited pool of private plaintiffs. The resulting litigation landscape is constantly evolving, shaped by a mix of private lawsuits and selective public enforcement actions that together form a comprehensive regulatory framework.

Despite differences in political preferences among states, the reliance on private enforcement appears to be growing rather than diminishing across the country. Over the past two decades, states have steadily expanded private rights of action, suggesting bipartisan appeal. While critics may question the efficiency of this system or worry about overenforcement, the American approach of deputizing private citizens to enforce public law is a deeply ingrained feature of our legal landscape—one that shows no signs of disappearing.

# THREE

## HISTORICAL ROOTS: PENAL STATUTES AND QUI TAM

Molasses was a prized commodity in colonial America, a vital ingredient not just for rum production (one of New England's most profitable industries) but also for everyday cooking and baking. In colonial kitchens, molasses was as essential as salt—its distinctive sweetness flavored everything from brown bread and baked beans to pies and cookies. Housewives stored clay jugs or wooden barrels of the thick, dark syrup in their pantries, carefully rationing out portions for baking. Children would eagerly await fresh-baked molasses cookies or, as a special treat, might be allowed to drizzle the syrup directly onto their morning porridge.[1]

No surprise, then, that importation of molasses into the colonies had been a flashpoint before the Revolution, when British duties on the sweet syrup had sparked colonial resistance. Part of the problem is that throughout the eighteenth century, the British were intent on eliminating sugar and molasses competition from French-controlled islands like Saint-Domingue (modern Haiti) and Dutch territories like Sint Eustatius. The British Parliament tried to force American colonists to buy expensive molasses from British Caribbean islands and imposed steep tariffs on non-British Caribbean molasses, though widespread smuggling meant colonists often ignored it.[2]

When nine state legislatures finally ratified the US Constitution in 1788 and the First Congress assembled over a year later, the new representatives of the United States prioritized serious business: the molasses trade. In 1790, Congress imposed tariffs on sugar imports and prohibited the unloading of molasses at night, presumably to avoid smuggling.[3] Congress also allowed any common informer to enforce the prohibition. But no one expected this statute would lead to the first constitutional controversy over private enforcement.

The problem arose when Samuel Dodge, a customs inspector in New York, allowed a vessel to unload several hogsheads of molasses after dark, in violation of the new law.[4] His actions seemed innocent enough—he probably didn't know about the regulation, which had only gone into effect a few days earlier. But before Dodge could explain himself to his superiors, a private citizen sued him for the violation. It turns out this was quite common; laws of this kind usually allowed any "informer" to sue violators and collect half the fine, in this case $400. When Dodge appealed to President Washington for a pardon, it raised a fundamental question about the American constitutional system: Could the president's power override the rights of private citizens to enforce federal law?

The case landed on President Washington's desk as a plea for mercy. Dodge's explanation seemed reasonable; the regulation had only been in effect for a few days, and he claimed complete ignorance of the new rule. But Washington faced a genuine legal puzzle over presidential power.

The president turned to his trusted Treasury Secretary, Alexander Hamilton, who in turn consulted Richard Harrison, a seasoned lawyer serving as Auditor of the Treasury.[5] Harrison's response revealed the surprisingly limited power of the executive branch: Washington could pardon only the government's share of the fine and lift the ban on Dodge holding future federal office.[6] But the president had no power to stop the private enforcer from collecting his portion of the penalty. The best Harrison could suggest was a conditional pardon that would forgive Dodge only after he paid off the private plaintiff. Washington ultimately followed this advice, discovering that even his constitutional power could not override a private citizen's statutory right to enforce the law.

The Samuel Dodge episode affirmed a striking feature of the new republic: Congress could empower ordinary citizens to enforce federal law, and not even the president could stop them. Yet none of this was new. By 1790, private enforcement was ancient.

## THE ENGLISH TRADITION OF PENAL STATUTES

From the medieval period on, private enforcement by so-called "common informers" was a prominent feature of English law. Parliament routinely adopted a class of laws that were known as "penal statutes"—laws that regulated various industries and conduct, from duties on luxury goods, to restraints on roving horses, to bans on Sunday amusement (due to religious norms), alcohol sales regulations, ship building, and so on. The eminent English commentator Blackstone referred to penal statutes as "acts of parliament whereby a forfeiture is inflicted for transgressing the provisions therein enacted."[7] These acts would empower "any person [to] . . . sue for the [penalty]" as a "common informer."[8] (These "any person" provisions were sometimes known as "popular actions.") In other words, when Parliament wanted to regulate an activity, it would often prohibit the activity (or specify how it should be conducted) and would then allow any "common informer" to file a claim against violators and collect a monetary penalty. Unlike common law claims, discussed below, citizen informers did not seek compensation for an injury; instead, they sought to collect on a statutory penalty.[9] So the key feature of penal statutes was the delegation of enforcement to *anyone* who could file a case.

This precursor to private enforcement was so well established by the late 1600s that Charles Davenant, an English statesman and political economist, could confidently claim that "Law-givers have many times fortify'd their Laws with Penalties, wherein Private Per[s]ons may have a Profit, thereby to [s]tir up the People to put the Laws in Execution."[10]

Penal statutes, and the larger category of popular actions, came in many varieties. Sometimes the penalty went entirely to the King. Or sometimes to the person harmed by the violation. But often it was split between a private enforcer and the government. The system was flexible, and Parliament could choose exactly how to incentivize enforcement based on the problem at hand. If town officials were failing to maintain roads, let any citizen sue them and keep part of the fine.[11] If merchants were evading customs duties, split the penalty between the informer and the Crown.[12] While some of these laws dealt with serious crimes, most regulated ordinary economic and social life—what we would now call administrative regulation. Again, they covered everything from interest rates on loans to the proper training of apprentices. Unlike murder or theft, which were wrong by their very nature, these were wrongs simply because Parliament said so. They were regulatory rules meant to make society run more smoothly. And their enforcement depended on citizens willing to sue.

One standard form of private enforcement was through the legal writ known as "qui tam." The phrase comes from a longer Latin expression meaning "he who brings an action for the king as well as for himself." From at least the 1300s onwards, Parliament used qui tam provisions to allow private citizens to sue violators and keep part of the penalty, typically half. Unlike other penal statutes, which as we've seen were statutes with a penalty that anyone could collect, qui tam claims were a subset of claims where the suit was officially on behalf of the Crown (and the Crown would keep half of the penalty). The concept had deep roots—in ancient Rome, private parties called "delatores" could prosecute and claim a share of forfeited property.[13] But it was in medieval England that qui tam truly flourished. In the 1300s, Parliament used qui tam to regulate everything from the length of market fairs to wages during labor shortages after the plague.[14] One early statute from 1318 used qui tam to prevent local officials from selling goods they were supposed to be regulating.[15] Another in 1350 let citizens sue royal cloth inspectors who failed to properly measure textiles.[16] By the late 1400s, qui tam had become so central to law enforcement that Parliament was passing multiple qui tam statutes each year in almost every area of regulation.[17]

Despite its importance, informers always faced criticism from many angles. Some commentators and elites despised so-called "professional informers." These career enforcers specialized in filing penal statute claims. One historian tracked an English man named George Whelplay who gave up a career in clothing and sewing to file dozens of cases, "employ[ing] something like a small detective agency; it is out of the question that he should have personally rushed about the country in the necessary fashion, on the off chance of getting evidence for a breach of the law."[18] The English jurist Edward Coke called informers like Whelplay "viperous vermin," and tagging someone as a "common informer" became an insult. The problems were obvious—informers could use the threat of lawsuits to extort money from innocent people, or they might collude with wrongdoers to bring weak cases that would prevent more serious enforcement later. During Queen Elizabeth's reign, Parliament adopted new restrictions to tackle these problems (statutes of limitations and limited venues where they could bring suit).[19]

Despite parliamentary constraints, angry mobs sometimes took matters into their own hands. As early as 1566, a riot against informers provoked a proclamation from Queen Elizabeth, stating that "'great routs and companies' had 'assembled themselves together against such as be informers upon penal laws and statutes, commonly called promoters.' The angry citizens 'made great outcries' against the informers and beat them severely."[20] In 1736, Londoners again rioted against informers who brought cases under new gin regulations. Specifically, the Gin Act of 1733 "limited sales of distilled spirits to licensed establishments, and explicitly forbade sales of the same 'about the streets in any wheelbarrow, or upon the water in any ship, boat or vessel.'"[21] What made it a penal statute was that violators were subject to "summary conviction . . . [and] a penalty of £10, half of which went to the informer . . . ."[22] If a violator couldn't pay the penalty, they were "sentenced to one to three months' hard labor at the local house of correction."[23] Similar statutes followed in the late 1730s and early 1740s, expanding the scope of the prohibition. Informers flooded the legal system with accusations of violations, and "prosecutions of middle-class retailers were sufficiently numerous to provoke a backlash against informers."[24] Historians Jessica Warner and Frank Ivis found that informers worked together in large groups, almost like "clearing-house[s]."[25] Dozens of isolated attacks grew into larger disturbances, riots, public beatings, and eventually the dragging of informers through the streets. Some mobs even congregated outside the houses of well-known informers. In one of these mobs, one woman, Sarah Miller, yelled to a well-known informant: "Damn you, you informing Bitch."[26]

Notwithstanding the obvious difficulties with a rudimentary system of private enforcement, the use of common informers was so central to the English legal system that the country didn't even have public prosecutors until 1879.[27] Linguistically, informer statutes referred to informers, not plaintiffs. A modern reader might view informers as merely claiming rewards for providing information or testimony about crimes—in other words, acting as tipsters, not as plaintiffs. But in a world without public prosecutors, there was *no other entity* that could initiate prosecutions or civil enforcement cases. As is widely acknowledged by contemporary sources and present-day historians, references to informers generally meant parties who would act as plaintiffs and bring cases to court.

Moreover, despite all its grandeur, the English Crown had little control over even criminal law enforcement. Instead, as with penal statutes, criminal cases were brought by private citizens, usually victims, who hired their own lawyers to prosecute in the King's name. The King's Attorney General could directly file cases only for a narrow set of political offenses that threatened the government itself.[28] Everything else, from theft to murder, depended on private citizens deciding to take their cases to court.

While the King could interfere in private criminal prosecutions, this same power did not extend to penal statutes. As historian Jared Lucky has explained, in criminal cases, the King could freeze a prosecution by using a tool called the writ of *nolle prosequi* ("unwilling to prosecute").[29] Or, alternatively, the King could use the royal pardon, too. But critically, the King's power to pardon criminals or halt prosecutions did not extend to civil regulatory cases brought under penal statutes. Once a private enforcer filed such a case, not even the King could stop it. The reasoning behind this was that once Parliament gave private citizens the right to sue and collect penalties, that right became a form of property that even the King couldn't take away. This principle remained firmly entrenched in English law for centuries.[30]

The extent of these limits on royal power is illustrated by *Bruse v. Harcourt*, a 1709 case at the Court of the Exchequer.[31] A private informer sued over an illegal shipment of French wine that violated Parliament's trade embargo. But the wine was actually the Queen's, bought "by the Queen's order, with her money." Yet even the Queen herself had to litigate like any other defendant. The case captured the powerful role of penal statutes.

## THE COMMON LAW TRADITION AND THE STATUTE OF MONOPOLIES (1623)

On top of penal statutes and qui tam claims, the final historical precursor of modern private enforcement was the English tradition of common law claims, where private parties could seek redress for injuries. The common law recognized a remarkable variety of writs and private claims—actions of debt permitted recovery of a specific debt, trespass allowed suits for unlawful entry onto property, assault covered threats of violence, trover permitted recovery of stolen goods.[32] Through "actions on the case," courts gradually expanded these writs to cover new situations: nuisance claims for neighbors who created hazards or unpleasant conditions, "assumpsit" for breach of informal promises and agreements, even claims for damage caused by wandering livestock. Public nuisance actions let private citizens sue over obstructed highways, contaminated water supplies, and dangerous structures threatening public safety. The writ of "waste" allowed claims against tenants who damaged property, while "account" required financial agents to justify their handling of others' money. Through these flexible tools, English courts empowered private parties to enforce social norms and protect both individual and community interests, without the need for statutory authorization or government prosecutors.

Two key distinctions between common law claims and penal statutes included the purpose of the claim and the originating institution. The common law courts (led by the King's Bench) developed the common law over time through precedent. Penal statutes, by contrast, were parliamentary creations. Common law claims, moreover, were usually compensatory, allowing an aggrieved party to seek a legal remedy. Penal statutes were instead regulatory penalties determined by Parliament. A common informer could bring a claim under a penal statute even without any injury.[33]

A series of common law writs also empowered citizens to file regulatory claims or police the work of government officials. Members of the public could use the writ of *scire facias* to challenge questionable patents or demand that someone justify their claimed authority. Through mandamus actions, they could force reluctant government officials to perform their duties, often citing harm to the public interest.[34] The writ of *quo warranto* let private plaintiffs challenge the legitimacy of public officials or corporate charters, effectively allowing citizens to police the boundaries of public power. Historians have demonstrated that *quo warranto* allowed private citizens to challenge abuse of public power.[35] Through the writ of prohibition, private plaintiffs could challenge and "prohibit government actors from taking specific actions."[36]

These writs, each with its own specific purpose, gave private citizens powerful tools to enforce public rights centuries before modern statutory schemes emerged.[37] As Jim Pfander has noted, "these 'administrative' writs . . . of certiorari, mandamus, and prohibition—the pillars of common law's system of administrative oversight—enabled public rights suitors to test the legality of action by early administrative bodies."[38] These writs allowed the "King's Bench [the Supreme Court of common law] [to] serve[] as the pre-eminent 'guardian of public rights' in England for well over two centuries."[39]

Focusing on the writ of mandamus gives us an idea of the early role of private enforcement. One of the most important early cases establishing the role of mandamus for judicial review of local government action was *Bagg's Case* in 1615.[40] The case began when the mayor and city council of Plymouth stripped a man, James Bagg, of his rights as a free citizen after repeatedly insulting the mayor in public. After some procedural maneuvering, Bagg asked the King's Bench court to restore his rights. Chief Justice Edward Coke seized the opportunity to establish broad judicial oversight of local officials, ruling that no freeman could lose his rights unless clearly authorized by the town's charter or after a proper legal proceeding. Since Plymouth's leaders had followed none of these paths, Coke ordered them to restore Bagg's status. Although the case concerned a private claim for an individual injury, it established the principle that courts could review the actions of officials who exceeded their authority.[41]

The common law also provided a direct precursor to modern antitrust enforcement—a topic taken up again in the next chapter—a doctrine known as "restraint of trade." This contract claim allowed litigants to invalidate coercive contracts that restricted an individual's ability to act, including "covenants, such as indefinite non-compete clauses, and price-fixing agreements."[42] The doctrine was also commonly employed by defendants as a strategy to prevent the enforcement of void contracts or patents. In addition to the restraint of trade, English common law recognized a tort cause of action for conspiracy where, among other restrictions, plaintiffs could demonstrate personal injury as a result of others' collusion.

Drawing on these doctrines, Sir Edward Coke was among the first to popularize the idea that the common law opposed monopolies. In *Davenant v. Hurdis*, Coke argued that the common law's antagonism toward monopolies extended at least back to the fourteenth century.[43] *Davenant* involved a by-law passed by the Merchant Tailors' guild, which required that guild members who sent "cloth to be finished by outside labor" to reserve at least half of that work for "fellow" guild members. Davenant refused to follow the by-law, and the Guild assessed him a fee of ten shillings. When Davenant refused to pay the fee, the Guild attempted to seize from him goods equal to that value, prompting Davenant to bring a trespass action against the Guild. Interestingly, Hurdis's attorney conceded Coke's argument that monopolies were void under the common law, instead arguing that the by-law did not create a monopoly. Ultimately, the court unanimously found in favor of Davenant, ruling that the by-law was illegal. *Davenant* is the first reported English case on monopolies.

Following *Davenant*, English law evolved to establish even stronger restrictions on the creation of monopolies, targeting the Crown's ability to arbitrarily grant patents and charters. In *Darcy v. Allen*, the court held that a royal patent, granted by the Queen, was void because it tended to create a monopoly and interfered with the rights of others to pursue their trade.

In a monumental move that set the stage for hundreds of years of private enforcement, Parliament adopted in 1623–24 the Statute of Monopolies, declaring unlawful all monopolies as well as associated patents and charters. Coke, again, was heavily involved in the drafting and enactment of the statute. Because part of the statute also laid out important exceptions, it became foundational to the modern law of patents.[44] One provision created what we would today call a private right of action, permitting persons aggrieved by unlawful monopolies to sue and recover three times as much damages as they sustained:[45]

> That if anie person or persons . . . shalbe hindered grieved disturbed or disquieted or his or theire goodes or Chattells . . . and will sue to be relieved in or for anie of the premises . . . the same person and persons shall and maye have his and theire remedy for the same at the Common lawe by any action or actions to be grounded upon this Statute. The same action and actions . . . every such person and persons which shalbe soe hindered grieved disturbed or disquieted, or whose goodes or chattells shalbe soe seized . . . shall Recover three tymes soe much as the damages which hee or they susteyned . . . and double costes . . .[46]

As the language specifies, actions pursuant to the statute were governed by the common law. But, definitionally, this was a statute assessing a regulatory penalty—a penal statute. The law thus blurred the line between the common law and penal statutes. This was not unusual; plaintiffs would often sue to collect on a statutory penalty via the common law "action of debt."[47] No surprise, then, that an English commentator in the late 1800s hesitated on how to categorize the Statute of Monopolies. At first blush, the "whole Act in its general scope is remedial," and is "made in furtherance of the common law [] and for the purpose of giving relief to parties aggrieved [] it gives no penalty to a common informer, but only to an injured party."[48] On the other hand, "although the statute . . . is remedial, [it] does not follow that this particular enactment may not be considered to be penal[], and it falls apparently within the definition that a penal statute is a statute which imposes a penalty[]."[49] The statute, moreover, "creates the offense for which the penalty is given," and actions are "grounded upon this statute," making the claim statutory.[50] "If this view be correct, it is not easy to deny that the action . . . is a penal action."[51] The author then, for other reasons, returns again to the view that this might not have been a penal statute before considering the point moot. Either way, some authorities claim the provision "was never successfully invoked."[52]

After the passage of the Statute of Monopolies, restraint of trade continued to change, evolving into a more direct antecedent for the substantive doctrines that underlie the Sherman Act, as explored in the next chapter.

## COLONIAL ENFORCEMENT

If anything, precursors to private enforcement became even more important in the colonies than they had been in England.[53] Private citizens could sue over violations of shipping rules or illegal imports of luxury goods. They enforced local rules about wandering livestock and hunting seasons. They policed industries like blacksmithing that could create public nuisances. They brought cases about violations of quarantine measures meant to control disease in both humans and animals. And they sued over usury and price gouging.[54]

Colonial courts also embraced the English common law system of writs and expansive claims. American courts adapted these traditional tools to local conditions while maintaining their essential function—allowing private citizens to challenge both individual wrongs and threats to the public interest. Colonial Americans regularly used writs like mandamus and *quo warranto* to challenge official misconduct, while modifying them to fit colonial governance structures. In any regulatory area, colonial governments relied on private enforcers and common law claims to make their laws work.

The colonists lived under multiple layers of laws that allowed some forms of early private enforcement. These combined old English statutes that colonists knew from home, some that were reenacted while others applied despite any official endorsement. Then there were Acts of Parliament that applied only in the colonies. And finally, the colonial assemblies adopted their own statutes. Regardless of their provenance, all three types of laws embraced the tradition of common informers, qui tam, and the common law.

Particularly in Massachusetts, the colonial courts embraced English private enforcement mechanisms, with ordinary citizens regularly using writs to challenge both private wrongs and public misconduct. Historian Jared Lucky found that when Massachusetts received its new royal charter in 1692, it quickly empowered private plaintiffs, informers, and others, via penal statutes.[55] The colonial legislature passed statute after statute allowing private citizens to sue wrongdoers and collect penalties. About 10 percent of all laws passed in Massachusetts between 1690 and 1820 explicitly depended on private enforcement. For example, Lucky describes how the regulation of common lands demonstrates the role of private litigants in practice. In 1693, Massachusetts passed a law to prevent damage to communal fields from wandering livestock. The law limited how many horses each person could keep on the commons and set strict penalties for violations—ten shillings for each unregistered horse, with half going to whoever brought the case. The law even regulated pigs, requiring owners to put yokes on their swine and ring their noses to keep them from squeezing through fences and damaging crops. Owners of unrestrained pigs had to pay sixpence per animal caught on the commons, and twice that plus double damages if the pigs damaged private fields. Again, in both instances, the regulation of horses and pigs could be enforced by anyone.

According to Lucky, Massachusetts used private enforcement across the board, even to handle public safety issues that would have traditionally been governed by the common law. A prime example came in 1809, when the state passed a law about gunpowder storage in Cambridge. In a town full of wooden buildings, large amounts of gunpowder posed an obvious danger to everyone. The law required residents to store gunpowder in metal containers and limited each person to fifty pounds. Anyone who violated these rules would forfeit the full value of their gunpowder, with half going to whoever reported the violation and half to the town.

Massachusetts's approach was representative of a broader national pattern. Every colony—and after independence, every state—passed laws that relied on private enforcement through both damages provisions and qui tam suits. In Virginia, Thomas Jefferson proposed a comprehensive update of state laws in 1776 that included a dozen qui tam provisions and numerous opportunities for private informer claims.

Consider six areas in which historian Randy Beck found extensive reliance on qui tam statutes: oversight of local administration, road maintenance, judicial administration, administrative tasks, elections, and tax collection.[56] Government officials, like sheriffs, were often subjected to qui tam suits for failure to perform their duties. In North Carolina, for example, officials responsible for caring for the poor faced qui tam penalties for neglecting their duties. The law imposed specific fines on sheriffs who failed to advertise elections, overseers who missed meetings, and clerks who didn't maintain proper financial records. Half of these penalties went to the private informers who brought suit. As Randy Beck discusses:

> A Massachusetts town could forfeit £50 in a qui tam action if it failed to appoint a committee to implement a law to prevent overharvesting of certain species of fish. An elected fish warden in New Hampshire could face a qui tam forfeiture for refusing the office. Maryland and South Carolina surveyors could suffer qui tam forfeitures for conducting surveys before taking the oath of office. . . . Other qui tam statutes enforced duties relating to administrative tasks like conducting meetings and keeping records. A Rhode Island town clerk who failed to give notice of a town meeting and a town-sergeant or constable who failed to serve the notice on individual freemen were subject to qui tam forfeitures. A New Hampshire constable who failed to give notice of a town meeting could forfeit £10 "to any inhabitant of the town who will sue for the same," one-half "to the use of the Town and the other half to the use of the prosecutor." A Massachusetts town clerk or county register of deeds could face qui tam prosecution for neglecting record-keeping requirements with respect to lost property or stray animals. A Maryland clerk or register could suffer a qui tam forfeiture for allowing public records to be removed from the office overnight. South Carolina surveyors were required to record surveying instructions in a government office.[57]

In the context of road maintenance, New Jersey's 1774 statute allowed private informers to sue surveyors who neglected road inspection duties or overseers who failed to maintain roads. Connecticut selectmen could face qui tam suits for not maintaining road signs and milestones. Similar laws in North Carolina and New Hampshire used private enforcers to ensure roads and bridges remained passable. As to judicial administration, states used qui tam to ensure officials took required oaths, maintained proper records, and performed their duties faithfully. In Massachusetts, justices of the peace faced qui tam penalties if they failed to transfer official papers to court clerks after leaving office. Informers could sue Virginia court clerks for removing records from the county. Rhode Island allowed qui tam suits against justices who failed to hand over records to town clerks. Some regimes were strikingly niche. So in Rhode Island, Connecticut, and New Jersey, for example, judges could be subject to "qui tam actions for performing clandestine weddings."[58]

The colonies and states also deployed qui tam actions to enforce inspection and regulatory regimes. Maryland used informers to police tobacco shipping regulations, allowing private citizens to call on officials to inspect suspicious barrels. New Hampshire incentivized the oversight of weights and measures by letting informers sue both negligent inspectors and merchants using unapproved measuring devices. Delaware's 1797 port health inspection system included qui tam provisions against doctors who failed to report violations of passenger health standards.

Even the integrity of elections was subjected to qui tam oversight. In Connecticut, anyone could sue anyone involved in vote buying. Pennsylvania allowed qui tam suits against election judges and inspectors who "committed willful fraud."[59] New Hampshire empowered citizens to sue town hall moderators who counted duplicate votes or manipulated vote totals. Virginia and North Carolina authorized suits against sheriffs who failed to conduct polls properly or mishandled election returns. As always, these laws gave private citizens a financial incentive to monitor the electoral process and hold officials accountable.

Finally, qui tam served a role in even the most important of government functions: tax collection and public spending. In New Jersey, anyone could sue tax collectors who failed to make assessment records available for inspection. North Carolina required county clerks to publicly post tax lists and allowed qui tam suits if they failed to do so. County commissioners faced similar liability if they didn't publish accurate records of taxes collected and money spent. Maryland incentivized the oversight of tobacco tax records by letting informers sue clerks who failed to transmit required accounts.

And on and on and on. Nearly every regulatory area one can imagine was subject to penal statutes, either through qui tam claims or informers. And if that weren't enough, there were also common law claims. These precursors to private enforcement were ubiquitous. There were, of course, statutory limits to these claims. The colonies and state governments constantly tinkered with the system, adding new safeguards. In 1786, Madison enacted Jefferson's model legislation in Virginia that prevented collusive private lawsuits from blocking legitimate enforcement actions and required court approval for settlements. Two years later, both Massachusetts and New York passed similar reforms requiring suits to be filed within one year, in the county where the violation occurred. These reforms drew from English precedent but preserved the core system of private enforcement independent of executive control.

By the time of the Constitutional Convention of 1787, private enforcement via penal statutes, qui tam, and expansive common law claims was a deeply ingrained part of the Anglo-American experience. Many framers and other founders had personal experience with this system.[60] Thomas Jefferson and James Madison collaborated on Virginia legislation that included twelve different informers' actions. John Adams, as a colonial lawyer, regularly dealt with qui tam cases, including as a defense lawyer against a suit over local voting procedures. Later on, Justice Story not only helped compile Massachusetts's colonial laws containing dozens of informers' actions but also voted to enact qui tam provisions both as a congressman and state representative.

This practical experience helps explain why the first Federal Congress used informer provisions and qui tam to implement nearly all of its enumerated powers, from military matters to patents to taxation.[61] Far from seeing private enforcement as constitutionally problematic, the Framers viewed it as a standard legislative tool for executing federal law. For instance, the first Federal Congress deployed informer claims in 1794 to enforce laws prohibiting American involvement in the slave trade.[62] The Providence Society for

Abolishing the Slave Trade, a Quaker-led organization, used these private enforcement tools aggressively, bringing suits against prominent slave merchants. The Society hired lawyers, raised funds for litigation, and achieved notable successes in federal court. While enforcement eventually weakened under President Jefferson, these early qui tam cases show how the Founding generation accepted private enforcement and regulatory litigation.

## FROM PENAL STATUTES TO PRIVATE RIGHTS OF ACTION IN THE EARLY NINETEENTH CENTURY

As the 1800s arrived, Congress continued adopting penal statutes across every regulatory domain. From an 1820 statute regulating the work of marshals taking the census,[63] to an 1834 provision regulating the sale of alcohol to native tribes,[64] and an 1841 statute regulating bank operations, penal statutes were at the center of America's early regulatory state.[65]

My systematic review of congressional enactments throughout the nineteenth century—based on text analysis of every statute—finds dozens and dozens of informer provisions adopted between 1800–1891.[66] This new finding challenges existing literature which had previously found only "seven qui tam statutes" in the entire 1800s.[67] In an influential article, Ann Woolhandler and Caleb Nelson claimed that after the 1790s, "subsequent Congresses rarely used the device."[68] Following their lead, Justice Kavanaugh mistakenly asserted in a major case that "until the 20th century, Congress rarely created 'citizen suit'-style causes of action for suits against private parties by private plaintiffs who had not suffered a concrete harm."[69] These scholars and Kavanaugh may have drawn a distinction between qui tam and informer claims (though it is not clear why they would do so). For the purposes of this book, both types of statutory provisions indicated an unbroken and extensive legislative interest in private enforcement.

Informer provisions were routinely litigated throughout the nineteenth century. As I recently documented in a co-authored article, over 1,200 reported cases involving informers were decided between 1800 and 1890 in state and federal courts.[70] This extensive body of litigation addressed fundamental questions about how the informer system operated: Who qualified as an informer? How should penalties be divided when multiple informers came forward? How did informer rights interact with executive pardons and prosecutorial discretion? And could government officers claim informer rewards? Courts were not merely applying these statutes mechanically. Instead, they were building a complex doctrine to manage a system of private enforcement. Fishermen sued neighbors over illegal fishing practices. Revenue collectors claimed their shares of customs forfeitures. Professional informers brought suits against stage line operators, land speculators, and usurers. The sheer volume of this case law reveals that informer provisions were not a historical footnote but a central mechanism through which nineteenth-century Americans enforced regulatory law.

Even more, informer claims did not rely on qui tam—the suit did not have to be in the name of the government—and were therefore "causes of action for suits against private parties by private plaintiffs who had not suffered a concrete harm."[71] As one 1800s treatise noted, "[w]here a penal statute expressly gives the whole or a part of a penalty to a common informer, and enables him generally to sue for the same, debt is sustainable; and he need not declare qui tam."[72] Not only did Congress *often* use the device, but informer claims were also only one kind of private enforcement scheme. Other provisions empowered only injured parties. Counting these related provisions would increase the number into the hundreds.

When Congress employed informers, it mostly used the same colonial language that empowered both informers *and* public prosecutors.[73] Consider a few congressional enactments in this era:

> 1820 – "An Act to provide for taking the fourth census, or enumeration of the inhabitants of the United States, and for other purposes." The statute authorized marshals to take the census in several territories. But, to police the work of marshals, the law also authorized that "every marshal failing to file the [census] returns," was liable for "the sum of one thousand dollars . . . recoverable in the courts . . . by action of debt, information, or indictment; the one half thereof to the use of the United States, and the other half to the informer . . ."[74]
>
> 1834 – "An Act to regulate trade and intercourse with the Indian tribes, and to preserve peace on the frontiers." The statute prohibited trade with "Indians without a license therefor from a superintendent of Indian affairs."[75] The statute also prohibited the sale of liquor or wine to "an Indian," allowing informers to enforce the liquor ban, forcing defendants

to forfeit the value of the wine "one-half to the use of the informer, and the other half to the use of the United States." A more general provision provided that "all penalties which shall accrue under this act, shall be sued for and recovered in an action of debt, in the name of the United States . . . the one half to the use of the informer, and the other half to the use of the United States . . ."[76]

1841 – "An Act to revive and extend the charters of certain banks in the District of Columbia."[77] In addition to reviving the charters of several banks, one provision prohibited banks "from issuing or paying out or offering in payment any bank note or other paper in discharge of their debts or liabilities of any kind . . ."[78] under "pain of forfeiting for every such offence double the sum so paid out or offered in payment of its own debt or debts; one half to the informer, and one half to the use of the town or city in which the offending bank may be situated, to be recovered by action of debt . . ."[79]

State legislatures were just as active as Congress in deploying informer provisions across a sweeping range of regulatory areas. An extensive case law on informers across the states shows them enforcing transportation monopolies,[80] natural resources protections,[81] and even common law subjects like contracts and property.[82] Connecticut granted exclusive stage line privileges and empowered informers to sue competitors for forfeiture of their "stage and horses, or double the value thereof."[83] Connecticut also prohibited destructive fishing practices, splitting penalties between informers and county treasuries to prevent resource depletion.[84] New York's usury statute allowed informers to sue strangers for charging excessive interest, even though the informer was not a party to the contract.[85] New York also used informer provisions to regulate property transfers, empowering informers to sue over defective land conveyances under its statute against maintenance.[86] Across these areas, state legislatures embraced informer provisions as a flexible regulatory tool. There were no substantive limits on what could be regulated through private enforcement—informers policed stage lines and fisheries, and usurious contracts and property deeds, with the same legal mechanism that Congress used to enforce federal revenue laws.

The continued incorporation of informers in an era with American public prosecutors raised new questions that did not come up in the English tradition. Textually, references to "informing" on legal violations can be read to cover parties who served as tipsters in public enforcement cases rather than as plaintiffs. James Pfander's work on early relator claims shows "some blurring of the lines between public and private proceedings," and one judge claimed public enforcers sometimes "represented relators in nominally private enforcement actions."[87] If that were the case, then the continued use of informer provisions does not necessarily refer to private enforcement.

But that reading is contradicted by the historical evidence. Blackstone defined a "common informer" as "any such person as will sue" for a "forfeiture[] created by statute."[88] Courts explicitly called informers "the person prosecuting" the case, noting that "when a statute gives part of a penalty to any one *who will sue for the same*, an action or information of debt is the proper remedy."[89] An extensive case law clarifies that informers usually referred to someone who filed suit, and doctrines routinely addressed the role of informer plaintiffs as distinguished from witnesses or officers. In one case, the court noted that "[t]he provision in the close of the section that one-half of the penalty shall go to the patent fund and the other half to any person or persons who shall sue for the same, leads clearly to the conclusion that the action must be prosecuted by an informer, or, if the name of the United States can be properly used, it must be in connection with a person, to be named as informer."[90]

In the context of customs laws, however, there really was a blurring of the lines. One court clarified that "[i]n its origin the word 'informer' may have meant only one who sues . . ." but "[t]he word also, no doubt, in some of its applications, includes a person who lodges information with a government officer which leads to a suit brought by the government itself. It is so used in the customs revenue laws."[91] This, however, was an outlier area of law.

Moreover, viewing informers as something other than plaintiffs is irrelevant for a few reasons. First, many of the statutes explicitly referenced private lawsuits (i.e., "action of debt," or "shall be sued . . . in the name of the United States"). Congress often specified that moieties went to "persons informing *and prosecuting* for the same,"[92] or "to any person or persons *who shall sue* for the same."[93] Second, and most importantly, Congress knew exactly how to specify the role of tipsters or victims who could receive compensation rather than informer plaintiffs. In the first Collection Act, Congress provided a public enforcement provision with a reward for tipsters:

> [A]ll penalties accruing by any breach of this act, shall be sued for and recovered with costs of suit, in the name of the United States, . . . by the collector of the district where the same accrued, and not otherwise, unless in cases of penalty relating to an officer of the customs; and such collector shall be, and hereby is authorized and directed to sue for and prosecute the same to effect, and to distribute and pay the sum recovered . . . according to law.[94]

This statute empowered only a "collector" to sue. But it also allowed that collector to "distribute" the sum recovered to others, including tipsters. As discussed further below, Congress adopted similar statutes in the 1870s, demonstrating a preference for informer-tipsters rather than informer-plaintiffs in some legislative schemes. Congress, in other words, knew how to differentiate tipsters or victims from plaintiffs and used informer provisions to refer to the latter. It is clear, then, that Congress continued to rely on informers as private enforcers in the 1800s.

Some penal statutes avoided the language of informers and instead referred to "any person . . . who shall sue," along with a reference to the penalty (a "moiety"). This was also common in the English tradition. Consider, for instance, a 1798 statute: "An Act for an amicable settlement of limits with the state of Georgia, and authorizing the establishment of a government in the Mississippi territory."[95] On top of establishing Mississippi, the statute prohibited the importation of slaves therein, imposing a penalty for every slave imported:

> the sum of three hundred dollars; one moiety for the use of the United States, and the other moiety for the use of *any person* or persons who *shall sue for the same.*[96]

Along the same lines, copyright and patent laws used this kind of language, referring to moieties, throughout the nineteenth century:

> 1802 – "An Act supplementary to . . . 'An Act for the encouragement of learning . . .'" The statute protected intellectual property rights over

prints and prohibited printing without authorization of proprietors under penalty of "one dollar for every print which shall be found . . . the one moiety thereof to any person who shall sue for the same, and the other moiety thereof to and for the use of the United States . . . ."[97] The statute had an identical provision for suits against violations of copyrights over maps, increasing the fine to "one hundred dollars" to the "person who shall sue for the same."[98]

1842 – "An Act in addition to an act to promote the progress of the useful arts." The act prohibited, among other things, the use of patent marks by anyone other than the person who obtained the letter patent, making the offender "liable for such offence, to a penalty of not less than one hundred dollars, with costs, to be recovered by action . . . one half of which penalty, as recovered, shall be paid to the patent fund, and the other half to any person or persons who shall sue for the same."[99] A similar provision appeared in another version of the statute enacted in 1870.[100]

When Congress wanted a limited form of private enforcement (with fewer potential plaintiffs), it eliminated any references to statutory penalties at all, moieties, informers, or otherwise. A statute could empower only injured parties or "any person" aggrieved to sue over a regulatory violation. Congress sometimes did this through the common law language of "action on the case" or "action of debt," phrases that were present in federal copyright laws starting in 1790.[101] An 1856 statute regulating copyrights provides holders "the sole right . . . to act, perform, or represent the same, or cause it to be acted, performed, or represented, on any stage or public place during the whole period for which the copyright is obtained." The act then made it unlawful to violate this copyright, noting that violators "shall be liable for damages to be sued for and recovered by action on the case or other equivalent remedy, with costs of suit in any court of the United States, such damages in all cases to be rated and assessed at such sum. . . ."[102]

The story behind intellectual property statutes shows contestation and evolution, but also consistency in informer provisions. Both the 1802 statute ("An Act supplementary to . . . An Act for the encouragement of learning") and the 1856 statute were amendments to the 1790 Copyright Act, which was the United States's first federal copyright law.[103] The British Statute of Anne is a direct precursor to the 1790 legislation.[104] Interestingly, the first version of the 1790 Act "retained" the informer approach "by splitting the penalty sum between 'the author . . . or the proprietor'" and "any person or persons who shall sue for the same."[105] But the final Act "dispensed with this mechanism and split the fine between the [government] and 'the author or proprietor of such map, chart, book or books who shall sue for the same.'"[106] This language, in other words, empowered only directly injured parties.

But by 1802, Congress again went back to a regular informer provision. Senator Bradley introduced the 1802 legislation on March 24, 1802, supplementary to the 1790 "Act for the encouragement of learning."[107] The 1802 legislation explicitly added copyright protection for "historical and other prints,"[108] and in addition to the existing penalties for printing, reprinting, publishing, importing, and selling works, the statute added penalties for engraving, etching, or working on historical and other prints.[109] The penalty was a sum of one dollar for every print "either printed, published or exposed to sale . . . the one moiety thereof to any person who shall sue for the same, and the other moiety thereof to and for the use of the United States, to be recovered in any court having competent jurisdiction thereof."[110] Thus, the 1802 amendment added back in the informer language discarded in the 1790 Act.

Setting aside intellectual property statutes, Congress continued to use qui tam (rather than "informers") in a subset of cases involving government property. The key phrase in this kind of statute was to make the private suit "in the name of the United States." And so an 1845 statute regulating the naval service provided for the enforcement of contracts for naval attire, allowing that "in case of a failure, to supply the articles or to perform the work, by the person entering into such contract, he and his sureties shall be liable for the forfeiture specified in such contract, as liquidated damages, to be sued for in the name of the United States, in any court having jurisdiction thereof."[111] Because the naval service dealt with government property, the statute did not use an informer provision but rather a narrower qui tam claim.

By the mid-1800s, Congress employed private enforcement in all its forms: informer provisions, "any person who shall sue" language, qui tam, and more. On top of the many options at its disposal, Congress occasionally provided for multiple damages, a powerful financial incentive for private enforcement. An 1856 "Act to provide for the Public Instruction of Youth in Primary Schools, throughout the County of Washington" allowed under some circumstances for "the person aggrieved shall have his remedy against such collector by suit or warrant, and if he recover he shall have judgment for double the amount improperly and unjustly extorted from him, and costs."[112] Another provision that same year authorized suits against consular offices who collected fees greater than those authorized by law, making them "liable to pay to the person by whom or in whose behalf the same shall be paid, treble the amount of the unlawful charge so collected."[113]

As discussed above, while we know that colonial governments relied on penal statutes extensively, it is less clear whether state legislatures in the 1800s continued the trend. Historian Jared Lucky found a potential decline of penal statutes in Massachusetts.[114] If that state is representative, there may have been a period after 1820 in which state legislatures (but not Congress!) enacted fewer penal statutes. If so, this trough may be associated with the growth of centralized municipal police departments from the 1830s to the 1880s.[115] Informal watches, local constables, and private and for-profit policing no longer served as effective tools of social control in an age of increasing urbanization and post-Civil War racial and labor conflict.[116] In separate research, we identify multiple potential causes for the late 1800s decline of penal statutes. And, as discussed below, Randy Beck notes that similar developments contributed to the decline of qui tam in England.[117]

## INFORMERS IN THE SECOND HALF OF THE NINETEENTH CENTURY AND SENATOR SHERMAN

Congress ramped up private enforcement when it adopted the powerful False Claims Act with a qui tam provision in 1863. Facing repeated complaints about faulty goods supplied to the army, Congress enacted the FCA, sometimes called the "Informer's Act,"[118] during the Civil War under pressure from President Lincoln.[119] Fraud during the war had become rampant, with the Army often receiving "decrepit horses" or packages of gunpowder filled with sawdust.[120] Congress did not extensively debate the qui tam provision, which allowed "any person, as well for himself as for the United States" to bring suit for violations of the statute.[121] Again, rather than a clean informer claim, Congress used the specific language of qui tam because the suits were over government property. Senator Jacob Howard provided the "only explicit explanation of the qui tam provision":[122]

> The bill offers, in short, a reward to the informer who comes into court and betrays his coconspirator, if he be such; but it is not confined to that class. Even the district attorney, who is required to be vigilant in the prosecution of such cases, may be also the informer, and entitle himself to one half the forfeiture under the *qui tam* clause, and to one half of the double damages which may be recovered against the person committing the act . . . I have based [the qui tam provisions] upon the old-fashion idea of holding out a temptation, and "setting a rogue to catch a rogue," which is the safest and most expeditious way I have ever discovered of bringing rogues to justice.[123]

Less than a decade later, Congress enacted the Civil Rights Act of 1871, allowing private plaintiffs to sue state government officials over "widespread legal abuses and physical violence, often backed by the Ku Klux Klan," targeting Black people and their allies.[124] This statute, however, was aimed at regulating state governments and is therefore not at the core of private enforcement as conceived in this book. Still, the legislative debates are informative.

As the Supreme Court noted in 1961, debates over the Civil Rights Act were "replete with references to the lawless conditions existing in the South in 1871," and speakers drew on a report before Congress that was nearly "600 pages in length, dealing with the activities of the Klan and the inability of the state governments to cope with it."[125] Supporters of the Act argued that even facially neutral statutes were subject to unequal enforcement, with vigorous claims "against Union people" but denial of equal protection to any "man of known Union sentiments."[126] Some members of Congress, including Representative Michael Kerr of Indiana, opposed the private right of action, arguing that it may lead to "numerous vexatious and outrageous prosecutions . . . more reckless and dangerous to society than the alleged offenses out of which the cause of action may have risen."[127] After nearly a week of extensive debate, Congress adopted the bill on April 20, and President Grant signed it later that day.[128]

After the FCA and Civil Rights Act, legislators engaged in significant debates over whether to stick with informers or reject them entirely. John

Sherman—who would come to play a pivotal role via the Sherman Act of 1890 (discussed in the next chapter)—played a major part in these debates, as both Senator and Secretary of the Treasury. In different roles, he showed deep familiarity with informer laws, including as author of an 1877 report on customs-revenue laws and as an active legislator in debates over bills to abrogate informer provisions.

Consider Sherman's role in debates over the proposed 1874 Customs-Revenue Act, "[a]n Act to amend the customs-revenue laws and to repeal moieties." The title of the act referenced its main purpose: to repeal "moieties," that is, rewards for informers who aided in the enforcement of customs regulations.[129] The law eliminated those private bounties, providing that "moieties of any fines, penalties, or forfeitures" would no longer be "paid to informers."[130] Legislative debates show that Sherman supported repealing these informer provisions, arguing that moieties caused "mischief" that needed to be corrected by legislation.[131] As Chair of the Senate Committee on Finance,[132] Sherman was one of the primary legislators in charge of the "amendments reported by the Committee . . . ."[133] Sherman showed deep knowledge of informer laws, referencing moieties in other parts of the tax code that had already been repealed.[134]

Relatedly, on the question of informers as private plaintiffs rather than tipsters, Sherman's discussion again shows that customs-revenues laws were an outlier in blurring the lines between the two. As Sherman noted, amendments to the customs laws replaced moieties with other "remedies," including providing compensation to private citizens who reported violations.[135] For instance, the Secretary of the Treasury could "reward information" provided by tipsters about violations of customs laws.[136] Section 4 of the Act reads:

> whenever any person not an officer of the United States shall furnish to a district attorney, or to any chief officer of the customs, original information concerning any fraud upon the customs-revenue . . . such compensation may . . . be paid to such person so furnishing information as shall be just and reasonable, not exceeding in any case the sum of five thousand dollars; which compensation shall be paid, under the direction of the Secretary of the Treasury, out of any money appropriated for that purpose.[137]

The same section provides that:

> whenever any officer of the customs or other person shall detect and seize goods, wares, or merchandise in the act of being smuggled . . . he shall be entitled to such compensation therefor as the Secretary of the Treasury shall award, not exceeding in amount one-half of the net proceeds, if any, resulting from such seizure . . . .[138]

So even though informers could no longer collect moieties, they could still provide information about violations of the customs-revenue laws in exchange for compensation. Congress knew exactly how to provide tipsters a reward for information that could lead to government prosecution. As Senator Sherman explained, the "object of [Section 4]," the tipsters' information provision, was "to place in the hands of the Secretary of the Treasury a sum of money with which he can reward the actual detection of fraud."[139]

In legislative debates over the customs laws, most senators supported the repeal of informer provisions, and even opponents critiqued the dangers of informers. Echoing the critiques seen throughout English history, Senators implied that informers were "vultures" who extracted settlements. For example, Senator Bayard, who opposed other sections of the act, noted the "division of moieties of spoils among spies and informers" did not lead to convictions for violations, but instead resulted in "[s]ettlement with the informer . . . . Public justice was sold and delivered over to the *private profit* of officials and informers."[140] Similarly, Senator Saulsbury of Delaware called informers "robbers" and "vultures" who "have no right under the guise of protecting this Government to become the robbers of private individuals."[141] He continued, "[t]he men whom [the informers] propose to rob to a certain extent for their own benefit, have some rights as well as these informers, and I propose to protect that class of merchants against these men who have become vultures to prey upon them."[142] Informer provision, according to Saulsbury, gave private informers a "right to prosecute . . . an improper action in order to put money in their own pockets."[143] Senator Carpenter opposed disposing of the private right of action, though he conceded that "these men have become odious."[144]

But much of the debate was over increasing government power to obtain documents. Section 5 of the proposed bill provided that in non-criminal revenue actions, the government could request a court order compelling the defendant to produce documents. If the defendant demurred, "the allegations stated in the said motion shall be taken as confessed," unless the failure or refusal to produce the documents was satisfactorily explained to the court. Sherman defended this provision as "absolutely necessary to the due collection of the revenue" because if there were no informer provisions, then "there will be no means by which the Government can pursue an alleged fraud by a merchant so as to secure the production of his books and papers."[145] In *Boyd v. United States*, the Supreme Court found this disclose-or-confess procedure unconstitutional and an "unreasonable search and seizure," though this opinion was narrowed by later decisions.[146] Congress eventually repealed the moieties and gave the government greater subpoena power.

But three years after Congress's repeal, Sherman changed his tune as Secretary of the Treasury.[147] In a major report on the customs laws, he argued that repealing moieties had severely weakened enforcement of the law: "[The] effect [of repealing moieties] . . . has not been salutary" because "violations of law have not been detected in as great a number" as before the passage of the legislation.[148] He also reported that the New York collector of customs believed that due to the repeal of the moieties/informer provision, there was a "loss of many millions to the Government."[149] However, instead of restoring moieties, Sherman proposed higher incentives for tipsters (parties who can secure knowledge of fraud and alert customs officers) and adopting "specific duties . . . for the purpose of securing simplicity and uniformity in the collection of the revenue from customs."[150] As Secretary of the Treasury from 1877 to 1881, then, Sherman took a pro-informer position in customs-revenue legislation.[151]

---

Sherman's experience with informer claims was a microcosm of private enforcement in the 1800s. Throughout the century, Congress continued to use private enforcement in almost every area of regulation, but legislators were fully aware of existing problems and eagerly explored alternatives. Slowly, the legislative trend was to move away from penal statutes that empowered any informer and, instead, provide a right to sue only for injured parties. The key lesson is that legislators showed dexterity in how they deployed private enforcement, using different forms of language to empower plaintiffs.

## A REPUBLIC OF PRIVATE ENFORCEMENT

Given this historical context, it should be no surprise, then, that when Samuel Dodge's molasses case landed on Washington's desk in 1790, both the President and his Secretary of the Treasury, Hamilton, were accustomed to this type of claim. Both agreed, under the advice of Richard Harrison, that the President of the United States could not dismiss the case or pardon it away. This event effectively launched a new republic dependent on private enforcement. Every ingredient was part of the English and colonial tradition: powerful penal statutes, qui tam claims, and the common law.

# FOUR

## A REPUBLIC OF PRIVATE ENFORCEMENT AND THE CHOICE OF 1914

In a pattern that defies conventional wisdom about American governance, nearly every social movement since the Progressive Era has ultimately secured a private right of action as an enduring legal legacy. Conventional accounts of American political development typically focus on landmark legislation and the creation of new government agencies, while overlooking the private enforcement mechanisms that make these laws effective.[1] Consider the following historical episodes and the resulting rights to sue:

- The Gilded Age and the Progressive Era (1890–1920): When massive industrial trusts emerged in the late 1800s, threatening to dominate entire sectors of the American economy, progressive reformers demanded a government response. Congress first countered with the Sherman Antitrust Act of 1890, including a private right of action empowering "any person who shall be injured" by monopolistic practices to "sue therefor." But early court interpretations limited the Sherman Act's effectiveness, leading Congress to strengthen private enforcement through the Clayton Act of 1914. The Clayton Act expanded the range of prohibited conduct and clarified that private parties could seek injunctive relief to stop anticompetitive practices.[2]

- The Labor Movement and New Deal (1938): As the Great Depression intensified clashes between the labor movement and employers, Congress first enacted the bureaucratic National Labor Relations Act. A few years later it also embraced the Fair Labor Standards Act of 1938 to establish minimum wages and overtime pay. Among other things, the Act provided that "[a]ny employer who violates [these provisions] shall be liable to the employee or employees affected in the amount of their unpaid minimum wages, or their unpaid overtime compensation."[3] This allowed workers themselves to sue for unpaid wages rather than wait for government action.
- The Civil Rights Movement (1964): The civil rights movement brought segregation and racial discrimination into national focus, culminating with Congress's adoption of the Civil Rights Act of 1964. At its core, Title VII of the Act provided that any person claiming to be aggrieved by employment discrimination on the basis of racial or other characteristics could file a civil action in federal court.
- The Law and Order Movement (1970): Even Richard Nixon's conservative crusade against the disorder of the 1960s quickly resulted in a powerful private right of action. As urban violence and organized criminal enterprises dominated headlines in the late 1960s, Nixon campaigned on promises to restore order and crack down on criminal syndicates that had infiltrated legitimate businesses. The result was the Racketeer Influenced and Corrupt Organizations Act (RICO), which not only criminalized racketeering patterns but also empowered private citizens to sue criminal enterprises.
- The Environmental Movement (1970s): Growing awareness of environmental degradation led Congress to pass a wave of statutes in the 1970s, mixing bureaucratic reforms with powerful citizen suit provisions. For example, the Clean Air Act of 1970 allowed "any person [to] commence a civil action on his own behalf . . . against any person . . . who is alleged to have violated . . . or to be in violation of . . . an emission standard or limitation under this chapter."[4]

These statutes give a brief taste of the historical development of private rights of action. To preview the conclusion of this chapter: The American regulatory system embraces a combination of public and private enforcement, but the historical reasoning behind it is not consistent over time. The only clear message from history is that, time and again, legal elites considered it "common sense" to continue the old practice of adopting rights to sue. During most legislative debates after the Sherman Act or the Fair Labor Standards Act, once a congressman proposed a right to sue for any major bill, there was almost no pushback or debate. Moreover, as we'll see, lawyers in Congress almost always led the way: John Sherman, Henry Clayton, Kent Keller, and Edmund Muskie all proposed key private rights of action and all had long legal careers. Zooming out, the persistence of a public-private hybrid across ideological lines and historical periods suggests something deeper than political expediency.

## JOHN SHERMAN'S ACT AND ANTITRUST

In the mid-1800s, the American economy quickly shifted from its agrarian foundations to modern industrial capitalism. New railroads and telegraph lines shrank a continent, while new forms of steel production, oil refining, and manufacturing created economies of scale. As the nation's population nearly doubled between 1860 and 1890, GDP grew at a fast clip, with industrial output exploding in the space of a few years. But this growth brought volatility that devastated industries plagued by "excessive competition."[5] Business leaders, fearing that price wars and overcapacity threatened their survival, sought refuge in combination and consolidation.

When simple price-fixing cartels proved unstable, lawyers invented new legal arrangements to promote concentration. From 1879–1882, Standard Oil's attorneys pioneered the "trust" structure, placing competing companies under unified management while maintaining their separate legal identities. This created a blueprint that was soon emulated by other conglomerates.[6] By the late 1880s, massive combinations controlled entire industries, dictating prices, squeezing suppliers, and crushing competitors. Citizens watched with growing alarm as economic power concentrated in fewer hands, threatening not just market fairness but the foundations of democratic governance.

Newspapers and popular literature propagated the narrative of malicious trusts that affected "everyone, whether as a customer, employee, supplier, or competitor."[7] A report by a New York State Senate committee noted that trusts resulted in:

> [t]he aggregation of capital, the power of controlling the manufacture and output of various necessary commodities; the acquisition or destruction of competitive properties, all leading to the final and conclusive purposes of annihilating competition and enabling the industries represented in the combination to fix the price at which they would purchase the raw material from the producer, and at which they would sell the refined product to the consumer.[8]

There were rudimentary legal tools available in 1889 to tackle corporate monopolies. At the time, some of these tools included state antitrust regimes and the common law restraint of trade doctrine. Some states leveraged corporate law to regulate anticompetitive corporate behavior, such as mergers through trusts. In other states, enforcement authorities could bring *quo warranto* suits to dissolve corporations found in violation of state corporate charters. And authorities used these claims to aggressively police combinations that increased prices or reduced supplies of key products like cotton, sugar, and whiskey.[9] A few states allowed private civil suits against antitrust violations, spurring "private litigants in this period" to bring "many more cases challenging unfair competition than their public counterparts."[10]

But these tools were mostly toothless against trusts. Many states made little effort to enforce their laws, and the limited state suits against trusts were based on outdated common law doctrines or incorporation laws. While the common law made agreements between competitors to fix prices or limit output "void and unenforceable" as contracts in restraint of trade, these agreements weren't criminal offenses or tortious actions that could be challenged by the state or injured third parties.[11] Some states used clever theories to revoke the charters of corporations participating in trusts. But this approach had limited effectiveness, as trusts could reorganize or transfer assets.

Worse yet, many states flat out refused to enforce the law against trusts. One scholar attributes this lack of enforcement at least in part to the lack of independence of prosecuting authorities and the lack of funds to support enforcement efforts.[12] Another scholar found evidence of pervasive regulatory capture and industrial and financial pressures on legislatures.[13] State enforcement authorities may have also been reluctant to prosecute trusts given their contribution to industrial and financial growth. Federal policymakers, both Democratic and Republican, were well aware of weaknesses in the enforcement framework.

From this cauldron of public anxiety (and dissatisfaction with available legal tools) emerged a political movement demanding government action against private economic power. This led both states and the federal government into legislative action around the end of the 1880s. In addition to the common law and corporate law, states adopted constitutional and statutory provisions explicitly outlawing anticompetitive conduct. Right before the passage of the Sherman Act, at least fourteen states had constitutional prohibitions on certain restraints of trade, and at least thirteen states had statutory prohibitions.[14] For the most part, state statutes mirrored the common law and state corporate law: declaring as void contracts made pursuant to an illegal trust or combination, providing a defense for individuals sued under these void contracts, and sometimes authorizing forfeiture of corporate charter. Some states adopted legislation with private rights of action that allowed individuals to recover damages. For example, Kansas's statute provided that persons or corporations injured by an unlawful trust or combination could sue for "the full consideration or sum paid by him . . . or the full amount of money so borrowed."[15] And in lieu of private rights of action, other states like Nebraska permitted private individuals aggrieved by anticompetitive conduct to aid in enforcement proceedings.[16]

In one sense, the federal government took the baton from the English 1623 Statute of Monopolies. In 1888, Sherman, then a Senator from Ohio, introduced an antitrust bill. By this time, Sherman knew both the promise and peril of informer provisions, probably concluding that some form of private enforcement was necessary but with limits to prevent abuse.

After two unsuccessful attempts at passing the bill, he tried once more in 1890, an effort which culminated in the passage of the Sherman Antitrust Act.[17] The Act prohibited "every contract, combination or conspiracy" that restrained interstate commerce,[18] while another section barred firms from "monopoliz[ing]" markets.[19] Sherman declared that the Act was not intended to disrupt pre-existing mechanisms of antitrust enforcement.[20] And the House Committee Report noted that "[n]o attempt is made to invade the legislative authority of the several States or even to occupy doubtful grounds."[21] However, Senator Sherman emphasized that states could not effectively regulate unlawful conduct perpetuated by trusts—like Standard Oil—that extended across state lines. The Sherman Act intended to fill that jurisdictional gap by giving the circuit courts of the United States the power to regulate anticompetitive conduct that extended into interstate commerce.[22]

Senator Sherman modeled the act on state enforcement statutes. On the Senate floor, Sherman declared that the act intended "to enable the courts of the United States to apply the *same remedies* against combinations which injuriously affect the interests of the United States that have been applied in the several States to protect local interests."[23] And he went to great lengths to emphasize the successes of state common law enforcement.

The Sherman Act fixed the common law's weakness by including both criminal penalties and a private right of action that extended directly against trusts (and any other combination in restraint of trade). Moreover, unlike its state equivalents, but like its English ancestor, the statute incentivized lawsuits by giving plaintiffs the possibility of recovering treble damages. The private right of action was worded as follows:

> Any person who shall be injured in his business or property by any other person or corporation by reason of anything forbidden or declared to be unlawful by this act, may sue therefor in any circuit court of the United States in the district in which the defendant resides or is found, without respect to the amount in controversy, and shall recover three fold the damages by him sustained, and the costs of suit, including a reasonable attorney's fee.[24]

Legislators sought to provide an adequate civil remedy to injured plaintiffs. Indeed, the private right of action's reference to *injured* plaintiffs—rather than just any informer—demonstrates Sherman's preference to both employ private enforcement while limiting it to a narrow class of plaintiffs. This, of course, had a direct precedent in the mid-1800s intellectual property laws explored in the previous chapter (employing a right to sue by injured parties). Sherman's original proposal included a right to sue for double damages but was later amended to add treble damages.[25] Sherman defended the inclusion of a private right of action "to give to private parties a remedy for personal injury caused by such a combination" and that "damages should be commensurate with the difficulty of maintaining a private suit against a combination."[26] Moreover, he declared that the "*single object*" of the Act is "to invoke the aid of the courts of the United States to deal with the combinations . . . when they affect injuriously our foreign and interstate commerce and our revenue laws, and in this way to supplement the enforcement" in the states.[27] So in addition to providing individuals with redress, Sherman viewed private lawsuits as an enforcement mechanism to supplement public civil and criminal proceedings, promoting the Act's "single object."

In addition to its evolution of informer claims, there is, of course, a direct connection between the Sherman Act's private enforcement scheme and the 1623 English statute on monopolies. Both created private rights of action and treble damages in suits against monopolies. And, as discussed above, the statute on monopolies was a fusion of the common law and a penal statute. The Sherman Act and the Statute of Monopolies used similar phrasing grounded in both compensation and statutory penalties. Return again to part of the language in the 1623 statute:

> That if anie person or persons . . . shalbe hindered grieved disturbed or disquieted . . . and will sue . . . shall Recover three tymes soe much as the damages which hee or they susteyned . . .[28]

Similarities abound. "Any person" who "shall be" injured (or hindered, grieved, disturbed, etc.) can "sue" and collect "three" times damages "sustained." Indeed, this kind of phrasing ("any person" who "may sue") was common in federal copyright laws throughout the twentieth century. Note, however, that the Statute of Monopolies sought to abolish monopolies that were authorized by the Crown. It was a parliamentary coup against a Crown prerogative. A private right of action was clearly useful in that context precisely because the Crown might not enforce the law against itself (although, as we've seen, the Crown had no independent prosecutorial power). The Sherman Act, by contrast, tackled private monopolies and could rely on both government and private enforcement. Moreover, as discussed previously, the English statute was governed by the common law. The Sherman Act, in a way, fused the historical roots of private enforcement.

The Sherman Act's private right of action provoked an interesting debate in Congress. Skeptical legislators questioned whether ordinary plaintiffs could realistically challenge corporate giants. Senator James Z. George delivered a powerful critique, arguing that average consumers would need to spend substantial resources litigating in distant federal courts, gathering specific evidence of anticompetitive intent, all for relatively modest individual damages. He predicted few private suits would materialize—a prescient forecast, as apparently fewer than two hundred antitrust suits were filed in the fifty years following the Act's passage.[29] Senator John H. Reagan echoed these concerns, calling the private remedy "inadequate" because "the great mass of the people who are the sufferers from these combinations and trusts will not have the means to employ counsel and to take witnesses to the Federal courts, often at a great distance from them, to vindicate and enforce their rights."[30] Reagan warned that "[r]ich corporations and rich men" would be the primary beneficiaries of the provision—a prediction validated decades later when studies revealed that roughly two-thirds of all private antitrust suits between 1973 and 1983 were initiated by competitors and distributors, not consumers.[31]

Senator Sherman himself acknowledged the challenges, noting that even federal attorneys, being underpaid government officers, might struggle against highly compensated corporate lawyers.[32] This concern motivated his support for treble damages to make private suits "commensurate with the difficulty of maintaining a private suit against a combination."[33]

In this original debate over the Sherman Act's private right of action, we observe seeds of what became perennial debates over private enforcement in the twentieth century. Key among these is the belief that private enforcers are necessary when government agencies are underfunded or understaffed. Moreover, even if the Sherman Act's private right of action was well justified, skeptics still worried that private plaintiffs would either lack sufficient incentive or, alternatively, would have the wrong incentives.

The debates also revealed tensions about who should spearhead public enforcement efforts. While Congress did not weigh private enforcement against public enforcement, discussions about government litigation tiptoed around classic concerns. When critics complained that requiring US attorneys to obtain permission from the Attorney General before filing suits would be "too cumbersome," Representative David B. Culberson defended centralized oversight.[34] He argued that the "large and important interests" at stake in antitrust litigation and the risk of "interminable costs" demanded coordination from Washington. Local US attorneys from a "rural district or elsewhere outside of the great commercial centers," he maintained, lacked the necessary expertise to proceed independently.[35] This exchange suggests at least some congressional interest in consolidating enforcement authority within the federal bureaucracy rather than dispersing it widely—an impulse that stands in tension with the Act's ultimate embrace of private enforcement.

Still, substantial evidence suggests that Congress incorporated private enforcement as a primary weapon against anticompetitive conduct. Most telling was Congress's failure to appropriate meaningful funding for public enforcement of the Sherman Act—a glaring omission if government litigation was to be the principal enforcement mechanism.[36]

## WEAKNESSES IN THE SHERMAN ACT AND THE ROAD TO THE CLAYTON ACT

Despite the Sherman Act's embrace of private enforcement, the statute suffered from several shortcomings. First, its provisions were vague and lacked specificity. Section 1 prohibited "every contract, combination or conspiracy" that restrained interstate commerce; Section 2 banned individual firms from "monopol[izing] or attempting to monopolize" markets.[37] Yet this language was read to apply to horizontal cartels—like the oil trusts—but not companies that gobbled up smaller competitors through mergers or acquisitions. In other words, the statute seemed to leave a monopoly-sized loophole.

Second, the Supreme Court further limited the Act's effectiveness through narrow judicial interpretation. In *E.C. Knight* (1895), the Court ruled that the law did not cover the "sugar trust," despite its control of 90 percent of sugar refining. According to the Court, manufacturing was not part of "interstate commerce" and was therefore subject only to state law.[38] Moreover, the Court held that E.C. Knight's existence as a monopoly did not violate the Act without evidence of specific restraint of trade actions.[39]

These limitations created significant gaps that prompted a flurry of changes in the early 1900s and an effort to increase bureaucratic regulation. The first change after *E.C. Knight Co.* was the "great merger movement" of the 1895–1904 period, nearly two thousand firms consolidated into larger units to avoid antitrust scrutiny while achieving the same market control that cartels sought.[40] Following this rush of consolidation came a second change—in *Northern Securities Co. v. United States* (1904), the Supreme Court held that holding corporations could not legally be used to create combinations in restraint of trade. This effectively "revived the Sherman Act"[41] and led to an "Anti-Trust Crusade" against large corporations.[42]

In this period, the pendulum swung back and forth between public and private enforcement. By the late 1890s, some "members of Congress gravitated toward the multi-member 'independent commission' regulatory model that had become popular in England. The idea was that such a commission would be staffed by experts in various fields 'and be shielded from political pressures.'"[43] So in "1898, the President and Congress jointly established the 19-member Industrial Commission to investigate 'the growth of large corporations and trusts' and 'recommend appropriate legislation.'"[44] The problem with public enforcement is that government officials (especially state attorneys general) were "vulnerable to political and economic threats made by corporate actors."[45] This made private enforcement perennially appealing to legislators. So in 1901, a member of Congress proposed strengthening the Sherman Act's private right of action.[46]

Between 1905 and 1908, even President Roosevelt came to embrace a larger role for bureaucratic regulation. Although Roosevelt's administration pursued the *Northern Securities* case,[47] he also argued in his 1905 State of the Union that it is "generally useless to try to prohibit all restraint on competition . . . and where it is not useless it is generally hurtful."[48] And in 1908 he suggested important changes to the Sherman Anti-trust Act, increasing the role of "some popular governmental authority" to review proposed contracts in restraint of trade.[49] As Arthur Johnson notes, "Roosevelt, who had done much to make the Sherman Act a meaningful weapon of public policy, now brought the power of the presidency to bear in support of an effort to weaken it."[50] Judge Gary, chief counsel for the US Steel Corporation Francis Lynde Stetson, and Victor Morawetz prepared a bill incorporating Roosevelt's suggestions for the National Civic Federation, which Representative William P. Hepburn introduced into Congress on March 23, 1908 (the "Hepburn bill").[51] In a March 28, 1908 message to Congress, Roosevelt endorsed the Hepburn bill as a "very good bill,"[52] arguing that industrial combinations were "absolutely necessary."

The Hepburn bill empowered the bureaucracy, allowing non-common-carrier corporations to register with the Commissioner of Corporations "under conditions to be specified by the President."[53] Such corporations could submit proposed contracts or combinations to the Commissioner, who would then determine whether these proposals were unreasonable. If the Commissioner did not make a finding of unreasonableness within thirty days, the applicants were protected from suit by the government for any reasonable restraint of trade.[54] As proposed under the bill, certain contracts that would have been prohibited by the Sherman Act would now be granted a "special immunity," and the "dispensation of this immunity . . . should not be trusted to the courts nor even to that branch of the government concerned in the administration of justice, but rather to a bureau in the Department of Commerce and Labor."[55] In other words, unlike the Sherman Act, which had "left it to the courts to define what combinations were guilty of crime," the sponsors of the proposed Hepburn bill "left it to the Bureau of Corporations or other appropriate executive body."[56]

But the Hepburn bill faced significant opposition in the media, industry groups, and in Congress. Roosevelt withdrew support for the bill before it died in committee.[57] The move towards bureaucratic regulation thus stalled. If there was any ambiguity about the continuing role that Congress intended for lawsuits, the Clayton Act of 1914 eliminated it.

## THE CHOICE OF 1914: THE CLAYTON ACT AND FEDERAL TRADE COMMISSION

If the Sherman Act was an innovative embrace of an old English enforcement tool, 1914 brought an actual novelty: Two bills in Congress directly pitted public regulation against private enforcement in the wake of the 1912 presidential election. Wilson's triumph over Roosevelt validated his commitment to "regulate competition" via legal action against monopolies instead of Roosevelt's proposal to "regulate monopoly" through government oversight.[58] The election turned antitrust policy into a central campaign issue, with each candidate offering different visions for managing America's increasingly concentrated economy. Wilson's campaign rhetoric, heavily influenced by his advisor Louis D. Brandeis, who publicly decried the "curse of bigness," pushed for dismantling monopolies to protect small proprietors and disperse economic power.

Within two years of taking power, then, Wilson was presented with twin bills: one expanding a private right of action against antitrust violations and another proposing to create only the second major federal regulatory agency ever: the Federal Trade Commission. The question, again, was whether to tackle a pressing regulatory problem via lawsuits or bureaucratic state building. Few moments in US history present such a clear legislative choice between private and public enforcement. Which way did Wilson and Congress go? Both ways, it turns out, and so went the rest of the century.

The legislative movement that culminated in the Federal Trade Commission Act began well before President Wilson embraced the proposal. Senator Francis Newlands first introduced trade commission legislation in 1911, reflecting growing concerns that the Sherman Act alone was insufficient to address the trust problem. Despite Wilson's initial resistance to the idea during his 1912 campaign, his position evolved dramatically by 1913. In a significant speech before Congress, Wilson reversed course and endorsed Roosevelt's longstanding proposal for a strong administrative commission. In the speech:

> Wilson requested a more explicit legislative interpretation of the Sherman Act. He stated the country's experience with problems incidental to trusts was now sufficient to make such interpretation possible and the prohibited practices could now be itemized. He added that the country's businessmen desired the guidance of an administrative body or commission which also could be used in the supervision of dissolution proceedings.[59]

Congress responded with twin bills. Representative Clayton introduced his bill on April 14, 1914, expanding the Sherman Act's scope, including its private right of action.[60] Shortly after, on May 22, 1914, Representative Raymond Stevens pushed for an amendment to the trade commission bill that would empower the newly created government agency to "prevent corporations from using unfair methods of competition in commerce."[61] By 1914, Wilson and Brandeis promoted the Clayton Act and the Federal Trade Commission Act as "a coherent legislative package."[62] This dual approach of public and private enforcement revealed legislators' uncertainty about whether administrative expertise or litigation would better address the shortcomings of earlier antitrust efforts.

Bureaucratic state building was a whole different beast, distinct from the Sherman Act's simplicity. The Federal Trade Commission Act granted significant powers to a newly created agency, the FTC, authorized to prevent "unfair methods of competition in or affecting commerce" through a variety of enforcement mechanisms.[63] It could conduct investigations into corporate practices, obtain annual or special reports from corporations, access and copy documentary evidence, and subpoena witnesses.[64] When violations were detected, the Commission could issue cease and desist orders enforceable in federal court.[65] The Act also empowered the Commission to investigate how previous antitrust decrees under the Sherman Act had been implemented.[66] And the Act had to appropriate funds as well as specify how such an agency would be created and composed.[67] After its establishment, the FTC had to defend against dozens of legal challenges brought by industry groups, perhaps evidence of a larger struggle against bureaucratic regulation.

The Clayton Act, meanwhile, was a much simpler bill, meant to expand private and DOJ enforcement by enumerating specific prohibited practices. These included tying contracts, price discrimination,[68] and interlocking directorates.[69] The Act addressed some of the missing gaps in the Sherman Act by prohibiting mergers that "may be substantially to lessen competition, or to tend to create a monopoly."[70] The Act effectively expanded the Sherman Act's private right of action, allowing treble damages for the new antitrust violations:[71]

> Sec. 4. That any person who shall be injured in his business or property by reason of anything forbidden in the antitrust laws may sue therefor in any district court of the United States in the district in which the defendant resides or is found or has an agent, without respect to the amount in controversy, and shall recover threefold the damages by him sustained, and the cost of suit, including a reasonable attorney's fee.[72]

The Act also tilted the playing field toward plaintiffs by introducing a one-way costs rule in their favor[73]—allowing plaintiffs to recover fees if they successfully prosecuted the case—and explicitly authorizing them to seek injunctive relief.[74] On top of that, Section 4 codified treble damages and fees, and Section 16 authorized private injunctive relief. Perhaps most importantly, the Act allowed private plaintiffs to use final judgments from government enforcement actions as prima facie evidence of violations, creating a powerful synergy between public and private enforcement.[75] As the Supreme Court later recognized, these provisions were a shot in the arm to private enforcement, doubling down on Congress's aim for private plaintiffs to serve as essential enforcers of federal antitrust laws.[76]

Together, these acts arguably created the modern American approach to regulation: an embrace of both bureaucratic enforcement and private rights of action. At the apogee of progressivism, with the cult of administrative governance rising, a major progressive president instead reaffirmed the role of private enforcement. The resulting public-private scheme reflected both Wilson's desire for specific prohibitions and the progressive vision of expert administrative oversight, along with the old American tradition of private enforcement. A little bit of the new *and* a little bit of the old. Again, keep in mind that Congress simultaneously created the Federal Trade Commission with broad administrative powers while also strengthening private enforcement through the Clayton Act's more specific prohibitions. The FTC's broad authority to define and address "unfair methods of competition" provided flexibility that the specific prohibitions in the Clayton Act lacked, allowing the Commission to adapt to evolving business practices without requiring additional legislation.

Despite these plaintiff-friendly provisions, private enforcement remained somewhat quiet for decades. The first half-century after the Sherman Act's passage saw only 175 reported private antitrust cases, with plaintiffs prevailing in a mere thirteen instances and collecting just $1.27 million in total damages.[77] Contemporary observers attribute this anemic enforcement to private plaintiffs' inability to match the government's investigative resources.[78] The landscape transformed dramatically in the 1950s and 1960s, when renewed political commitment to antitrust triggered a surge in government prosecutions. Private litigation followed this public enforcement wave, with 396 cases filed in a single decade yielding approximately $500 million in settlements or damages—a direct result of the Clayton Act's provision allowing plaintiffs to leverage government judgments in their own cases.[79]

The evolution of private antitrust enforcement throughout the twentieth and early twenty-first centuries reflects shifting attitudes about its role in American regulatory policy. Initially embraced across party lines, private litigation was championed by both the Eisenhower administration and Democratic lawmakers as a vital complement to government regulation that was "more flexible and less authoritarian."[80] Courts in the 1960s and 1970s enthusiastically endorsed this view, describing private plaintiffs as "private attorneys general"[81] serving "the high purpose of enforcing the antitrust laws"[82] and acting as a "bulwark" against illegal restraints of trade.[83] This period saw rules that facilitated private suits, while Congress and some states expanded standing requirements and remedies available to private plaintiffs.

By the early twenty-first century, however, the Supreme Court's attitude toward private enforcement had dramatically cooled. The Court began expressing preference for expert regulatory agencies over "nonexpert judges and different nonexpert juries" who might "produce inconsistent results" and make "unusually serious mistakes."[84] Concerns about litigation costs and frivolous lawsuits drove significant procedural changes, most notably in *Bell Atlantic v. Twombly*, which revised federal pleading standards to protect against "largely groundless" antitrust claims extracting settlements.[85] Perhaps most significant was the Court's retreat from private enforcement's deterrence rationale. Once celebrated as "an ever-present threat" against anticompetitive behavior,[86] deterrence was later downgraded to "incidental" status.[87] This skepticism reflected a fundamental shift in how the Court balanced competitive markets against business freedom.

The story of America's antitrust battles reveals the enduring tensions that define private enforcement across all regulatory policy. The cyclical embrace and retreat from private litigation—welcoming it when government capacity seems inadequate, then questioning it when concerns about abuse arise—reflects deeper uncertainties about how democratic societies should balance enforcement power between public agencies and private actors. What began as a practical solution to practical gaps evolved into a defining feature of American regulatory strategy, making antitrust both a template and cautionary tale for understanding private enforcement's complex role in modern governance.

## THE LABOR MOVEMENT AND THE FAIR LABOR STANDARDS ACT

Contestation over business monopolies was one of the major concerns of the early twentieth century, but battles over labor rights and wages were not far behind. The early years of the century were consumed by significant labor unrest as workers organized to demand improved working conditions, shorter hours, and higher wages through newly formed labor unions. Between 1900 and 1920, major strikes occurred across industries including mining, textiles, and manufacturing, resulting in gradual reforms to workplace safety standards and limitations on child labor practices. But reformers were biding their time to push for the next big expansion of private enforcement over wages and hours.

Secretary of Labor Frances Perkins quietly prepared for the right moment to unleash her plans. Anticipating constitutional hurdles and aware that there were more immediate concerns during the New Deal and Great Depression, Perkins kept "something up my sleeve . . . two bills . . . locked in the lower left-hand drawer of my desk against an emergency."[88] The bills were centerpiece labor legislation meant to increase wages, protect workers from exploitation, and set maximum hours of work. These bills were the culmination of Perkins's original agreement with FDR to join his administration only on the condition that she could work to establish a "floor under wages" and a "ceiling over hours."[89]

After the Supreme Court softened its stance on the New Deal's aggressive expansion of the administrative state, the Roosevelt administration finally decided to unveil an early version of the Fair Labor Standards Act. Senator Hugo Black and Representative William Connery introduced the legislation in early 1937.[90] The bill proposed a nationwide minimum wage of forty cents/hour, forty-hour workweek, and a minimum age of employment of sixteen.[91] Roosevelt and progressive supporters framed it as essential to lift workers out of poverty.[92] Shortening long hours would spread work to the unemployed, and a wage floor would "underpin the whole wage structure . . . from which collective bargaining could take over."[93]

The road to the FLSA's passage was anything but smooth. Opponents in Congress—an alliance of Republicans and conservative Southern Democrats—decried the bill as a step toward a "tyrannical industrial dictatorship."[94] They warned it would smother businesses under "everlastingly multiplying governmental mandates."[95] Opponents proposed over seventy amendments, all aimed at weakening the bill—by exempting more employers, lowering the wage or overtime standards, or limiting enforcement powers. This resistance made enforcement mechanisms a central point of contention: How intrusive should the new law's oversight be, and who should police compliance?

Just as in 1914, Congress again flirted with both public and private enforcement of the law. The original bill was firmly in the public enforcement camp. It created an independent five-member commission with broad regulatory authority.[96] This proposed Fair Labor Standards Board would have operated with considerable discretion to implement labor protections gradually and selectively across different industries. The Board would have had authority not only to enforce congressional minimums but also to establish higher "fair" wages and "reasonable" hours within statutory limits. This approach reflected New Deal thinking about expert administrative agencies as the preferred vehicle for economic regulation, similar to the structures created for banking, communications, and securities oversight during the same period.

New Dealers were fundamentally committed to administrative solutions and bureaucratic state-building; they were technocrats down to the bone.[97] The New Deal "vision of how public policy should be made" allowed "[t]he democratic process" to "identif[y] social problems at the most general level," and then "experts [would] discern the best way to solve a particular problem and implement the appropriate policy."[98] Accordingly, the Wagner Act of 1935—the landmark labor legislation of the early New Deal—established the National Labor Relations Board (NLRB) as a specialized agency with broad powers to enforce labor organizing rights, deliberately avoiding private lawsuits in favor of centralized administrative enforcement. Similarly, the Social Security Act of 1935 also created a federal administrative apparatus to implement its benefits programs, relying on direct government administration rather than private enforcement mechanisms. Even organized labor—a key constituency of the New Deal coalition—often pushed for administrative enforcement over private litigation options, fearing that robust private rights of action might undermine the collective bargaining system.

Despite its New Deal bona fides, the proposed FLSA board triggered a fight in Congress. Friendly legislators and some union leaders opposed an agency with authority to raise wages for specific industries, fearing excessive government control or interference with collective bargaining.[99] Even supporters of the bill's goals voiced concerns about the proposed five-member board. As Representative Mary Norton (chair of the House Labor

Committee) explained, many of her colleagues "agreed with the principles of the bill but . . . objected to a five-man wage board with broad powers."[100] In late 1937, Norton offered a crucial amendment to scrap the board in favor of a single Administrator housed in the Department of Labor. This change aimed to make enforcement more politically palatable by reining in the "bureaucracy" and concentrating accountability in one official.[101] It was a key concession that revived the bill after an initial defeat on the House floor in December 1937.

Yet, while the question of public enforcement (by either a board or a department of labor official) vexed Congress, almost no one brought up private enforcement. During legislative negotiations, as if by magic, a new provision emerged in Section 16(b) of the Act, giving employees a right to sue their employer for minimum wages or overtime. Multiple provisions specified that:

> Any employer who violates the provisions of section 6 or section 7 of this Act shall be liable to the employee or employees affected in the amount of their unpaid minimum wages, or their unpaid overtime compensation, as the case may be, and in an additional equal amount as liquidated damages.[102]
>
> . . .
>
> Action to recover such liability may be maintained in any court of competent jurisdiction by any one or more employees for and in behalf of himself or themselves and other employees similarly situated . . . The court in such action shall in addition to any judgment awarded to the plaintiff or plaintiffs, allow a reasonable attorney's fee to be paid by the defendant, and costs of the action.[103]

The Committee report noted:

> Section 16 of the conference agreement provides a fine of not more than $10,000, or imprisonment for not more than 6 months, or both, for violations of the act. No person is to be imprisoned upon conviction for a first offense. This section also provides for civil reparations for violations of the wages and hours provisions. If an employee is employed for less than the legal minimum wage, or if he is employed in excess of the specified

hours without receiving the prescribed payment for overtime, he may recover from his employer twice the amount by which the compensation he should have received exceeds that which he actually received.[104]

That such an addition seemed logical and obvious to the conference committee is good evidence of the mindset at the time. The only apparent reference to this private right of action was a statement by Representative Keller, that such a provision would "put[] directly into the hands of the employees . . . the means and ability to assert and enforce their own rights."[105] Workers could sue on "behalf of himself or themselves and other employees similarly situated," and courts were authorized to award not only the owed wages but liquidated damages (an equal additional amount) plus attorney's fees.[106] This, Keller noted, would ensure employees are made whole and "will not suffer the burden of an expensive lawsuit." Just as importantly, he argued, this mechanism "has the further virtue of minimizing the cost of enforcement by the Government," since it avoids giving the government "sole responsibility" for policing every violation.[107]

And here was Keller's *coup de grace*: the right to sue, he told Congress, "is both a common-sense and economical method of regulation."[108]

Congressman Keller's speech serves as an archeological artifact, a perfect little time capsule, capturing how some elites thought about private rights of action in 1938. Those provisions were not new. They were not extraordinary. They weren't particularly sexy. Instead, they were simply common sense. Inserting such a provision in legislation is what any Congressman was supposed to do. How else could the government run? But, of course, as we've seen elsewhere in this book, what was common sense to Keller in 1938 has never been intuitive in most other countries in the world.

Another speaker's testimony, John M. Keating, mirrored Keller's attitude. Speaking on behalf of some unionized workers, Keating argued that employees should of course "be permitted to bring a representative action for the benefit of all employees similarly situated."[109] Echoing themes that would dominate regulatory policy discussions for generations, Keating pressed that employees on the factory floor were "in a better position than the board to institute suit" since they witnessed violations firsthand. He even described private lawsuits as a "psychological weapon" and means to make the act "semi-self-enforcing," revealing an intuitive understanding of private enforcement's deterrent value that modern economic analysis would later formalize.[110]

Again, the ability of an employee to sue for unpaid wages was in line with the old American tradition of private enforcement. The real debate was instead about whether to create a robust new agency that could expand state capacity.[111] Just as in the choice of 1914, American elites seemed to operate on a default of private enforcement and a more skeptical attitude towards public agencies. As others have noted, even at the height of the New Deal there was an "administrative framework of limited capacity and legal uncertainty."[112] Despite the fact that the "bureaucracy had expanded considerably in the 1930s . . . very little of that growth had enhanced the state's capacity to administer industrial production."[113] Indeed, in the mid-1930s, courts were wary of giving agencies the power to subpoena private documents, weakening a necessary tool of public enforcement.[114] Relying on private plaintiffs, then, was sensible. In short, empowering workers to litigate was seen as both "common-sense and economical," a way to leverage private initiative to uphold the new labor standards.[115]

Meanwhile, the final version of the Act provided public enforcement tools as well. The choice of 1914 to stack public and private enforcement as complementary tools was replicated here: The Department of Labor's Wage and Hour Division (led by the Administrator) was authorized to investigate workplaces and refer violations for prosecution. Section 16(a) made willful violations a criminal misdemeanor (with fines or imprisonment), and Section 17 allowed federal courts to issue injunctions (brought by the government) to restrain future violations. But in practice, these public measures were resource-intensive and, at least initially, modestly funded.[116] The public-private compromise reflected the political reality: A more aggressive, purely administrative enforcement scheme was not attainable in 1938, given fears of either insufficiently powerful or, alternatively, overweening government agencies.

Despite the successful incorporation of private enforcement in the FLSA, the labor movement was not always in favor of similar schemes. Consider the case of equal pay laws and private lawsuits in state courts. As legal scholar David Engstrom has documented, in the same year the FLSA was adopted, a group of female factory workers sued General Motors under a Michigan statute that prohibited sex-based wage discrimination. They won a sizable judgment of $55,690—likely the largest employment discrimination payout until the 1970s. Following this victory, women's groups pushed state legislatures across the country to adopt equal pay laws with robust private enforcement mechanisms including class action authority, double damages, and attorneys' fees. But organized labor, despite supporting equal pay in principle, systematically opposed these litigation-enhancing provisions. Labor feared that private lawsuits would function as collateral attacks on the New Deal labor relations system built around collective bargaining. Instead, unions pressed for administrative enforcement that they could more readily control. When twenty-three states enacted equal pay laws before the federal Equal Pay Act of 1963, virtually all channeled enforcement into administratively focused regimes with weak or nonexistent private litigation rights. Even as private enforcement was often seen as "common sense," countervailing incentives sometimes pushed enforcement into more centralized, administrative approaches.[117]

After the FLSA's enactment, the Wage and Hour Division promptly began conducting inspections and overseeing compliance efforts. Many employers adjusted their payroll practices to conform with the new standards, while vulnerable workers, particularly those without union representation, benefited from the ability to sue for back pay. But individual workers rarely, if ever, brought lawsuits. Instead, labor unions served as the "designate[d] . . . representative[s]," to bring cases on workers' behalf.[118] These lawsuits were known as "collective actions" and drew on the FLSA's broad language.

The FLSA's early success provoked a backlash. Immediately after World War II ended, a flood of union lawsuits seeking compensation for "portal-to-portal" time (pre- and post-shift activities) combined with favorable Supreme Court rulings to increase worker lawsuits and compensation. This litigation surge triggered a powerful business response, culminating in the Portal-to-Portal Act of 1947, which significantly amended the FLSA's enforcement provisions. The Act restricted employer liability for past unpaid time and imposed an "opt-in" requirement for FLSA group litigation, preventing workers from being automatically included in group suits.[119] The statute erased any references to lawsuits by "agents" or "representatives," providing that "[n]o employee shall be a party plaintiff to any such action unless he gives his consent in writing to become such a party and such consent is filed in the court in which such action is brought."[120] This amendment was a deliberate recalibration of the public-private enforcement balance in the original FLSA, with Congress acting to constrain what some lawmakers viewed as excessive private litigation.

Despite these adjustments, the FLSA's hybrid enforcement model—combining agency oversight with private litigation rights—would serve as an influential template for subsequent labor and employment legislation. Indeed, by 1944, private enforcement was so well established that the Supreme Court routinely implied private rights of action in federal statutes that did not mention rights to sue at all.[121]

## CIVIL RIGHTS AND TITLE VII

The historical progression from the FLSA to the adoption of the Civil Rights Act is a smooth one. The CRA's private right of action in 1964 was an important step in the development of private enforcement but one that followed previous statutes, all the way back to the Sherman Act.[122] The CRA provided in Title VII that victims of employment discrimination due to race, sex, religion, or other protected categories could bring a private lawsuit against employers and collect backpay or damages. Legal scholar Sean Farhang traced the growth of what he called the "litigation state" to this single provision. While the legislative history of the CRA has been recounted by many scholars, it deserves a quick recapitulation to understand its influence on private enforcement in the twentieth century.

Begin with the pivotal civil rights struggles of the 1950s and early 1960s—from the Montgomery bus boycott to the Birmingham campaign. Growing victories for civil rights created momentum for federal action. After breaking down barriers in education and public facilities, civil rights leaders recognized that true equality required addressing the pervasive discrimination in employment. This shift in focus toward jobs and economic opportunity coincided with a fluid political alignment on racial issues. Republicans sought to appeal to Black voters in northern cities, while Democrats navigated the tension between their northern liberal and southern conservative wings. As public support for civil rights legislation grew, both parties recognized the political stakes—gaining support from an increasingly mobilized Black electorate in key northern states while managing the backlash from white voters. Neither party wanted to be perceived as blocking progress on civil rights heading into the 1964 election, creating a rare window where electoral calculations aligned with moral imperatives.

Debates over a legislative prohibition of employment discrimination proceeded in three key steps that culminated with a powerful private right of action:

First, to craft the enforcement mechanisms for Title VII, legislators began with what had become the standard approach to workplace regulation since the New Deal—public enforcement through a specialized administrative agency. Civil rights advocates had concrete examples to draw upon: More than a dozen states had already established Fair Employment Practices Commissions that investigated discrimination complaints and issued remedial orders.[123] These state-level successes provided a practical template for federal action. At the federal level, proponents looked to the National Labor Relations Board as a model, drawing on the agency's ability to directly address unfair labor practices. Fusing these two precedents, early drafts of the civil rights bill created an Equal Employment Opportunity Commission with parallel powers, including "cease-and-desist" authority that would allow the agency to directly order employers to stop discriminatory practices and provide remedies without court intervention.[124] This public enforcement approach aligned with the preferences of civil rights organizations, which worried that forcing individual victims to navigate federal courts would place an excessive burden on those already beleaguered in the workplace.

Second, just like in the FLSA's original development, the push for a powerful agency ran into strong opposition. Opponents were again wary of an NLRB-like agency (with a monopoly over enforcement) that would crusade against private business. Leading this opposition was Everett Dirksen, the influential Senate Minority Leader, who represented the anti-regulatory preferences of American business. Dirksen's critiques of the administrative state would sound familiar to modern readers. He argued that a large bureaucracy would hound businesses and abuse its power, subjecting employers to the whims of "fishing expeditions by investigators, in their zeal to enforce title VII."[125] In floor speeches and negotiations, Dirksen painted a picture of overzealous liberal bureaucrats wielding unchecked power, creating "layer upon layer of enforcement" that would "draw and quarter" American businesses.[126]

Dirksen's critique was fundamentally about the dangers of overweening government bureaucracies. Dirksen, who stayed in close contact with the National Association of Manufacturers throughout the negotiations, argued that administrators might be biased against businesses and would too easily "infringe[] on business freedom."[127] Southern Democrats, while largely opposed to the bill overall, similarly preferred weaker enforcement if the bill was going to pass.

Third, to quell opposition to a powerful EEOC, Senate Democrats landed on a compromise: bolster the private right of action. Yes, the EEOC could receive complaints, investigate claims, and attempt to conciliate disputes, but legislators watered down all other powers, leaving it without authority to issue binding orders or impose sanctions. Instead, enforcement was placed principally in the hands of private citizens and the courts. If the EEOC could not obtain a voluntary settlement, individual complainants gained an automatic right to file a lawsuit in federal court after a brief waiting period—regardless of the EEOC's own determination. In those circumstances:

> a civil action may be brought against the respondent named in the charge [] by the person claiming to be aggrieved or [] if such charge was filed by a member of the Commission, by any person whom the charge alleges was aggrieved by the alleged unlawful employment practice.[128]

To ensure its effectiveness, Congress built in incentives, including fee-shifting that allowed prevailing plaintiffs to recover attorneys' fees from defendants.

The bill gave some authority to the Department of Justice, which could bring "pattern or practice" lawsuits against systemic discrimination. This compromise reflected Dirksen's view that the DOJ posed "a smaller threat of potential harassment to employers" than a commission would, while the fee-shifting provisions effectively outsourced enforcement to private attorneys. As Sean Farhang observes, "[W]hat Dirksen took away in governmental enforcement power he gave back in private enforcement power."[129] The result was a system in which enforcement would be "totally dominated by private litigation," eventually producing an explosion of civil rights lawsuits in federal courts.[130]

The CRA's compromise of robust private enforcement but weak public power reflected both continuity and departures. On the one hand, the whipsaw was very similar to the FLSA, an initial desire for bureaucratic state building later watered down to some public enforcement paired with robust private enforcement. On the other hand, there was a more vigorous embrace of and even faith in litigation. Some of this was simple political calculus: The federal judiciary was now populated by judges who were, on average, friendlier to civil rights than in other parts of government. That ideological predilection reflected federal judges' elite backgrounds, the influence of the legal profession, and the lack of southern influence on the federal courts. But a lot of the faith was borne out of the NAACP Legal Defense Fund's repeated successes in court. Litigation over civil rights offered individual control over claims when political avenues were closed. Incremental victories shaped the movement's belief that the judicial process would be the best way to secure civil rights. And reliance on courts would also empower existing organizations to continue the struggle, rather than leave the fight to presidential appointees.

The Civil Rights Act's private right of action laid the framework for most private enforcement regimes adopted in the second half of the twentieth century. The Fair Housing Act, the Americans with Disabilities Act, environmental laws, and additional civil rights statutes would all draw and build on the CRA's private enforcement scheme.

But, as discussed in the next chapter, we shouldn't overstate the importance of the CRA because by 1964 there was already a wide legal consensus around private enforcement (even outside of Congress). The Supreme Court was in the habit of implying private rights of action in important federal statutes since the 1940s, and, critically, it recognized an implied right to sue in the securities laws in 1964, the same year the CRA was adopted.[131] The Securities Act's newfound private right of action became a regulatory pillar of the securities markets. The Supreme Court's embrace of rights to sue in tandem with the CRA suggests an elite legal consensus around private enforcement was already in place. The CRA did not create or bolster that consensus—it merely reflected its pre-existence. This elite consensus, however, would need a cultural moment before spreading to the masses.

## THE NADER MOVEMENT AND "SUE THE BASTARDS"

Ralph Nader did not invent modern private enforcement. He did not create cultural change around the role of lawsuits in society. Nor did he partake in particularly innovative litigation. What he did do, however, was raise the salience of private enforcement and the possibility of lawsuits to address the social issues of the day. In other words, he created positive vibes around litigation.

Most stories about Nader begin with his book *Unsafe at Any Speed*—a true classic that exposed the danger of American cars and manufacturers' lax standards.[132] Others focus on the case *Nader v. General Motors Corporation*, resulting in a large settlement for Nader after General Motors's (GM) agents harassed him due to his critiques of auto safety.[133] Most address the significant influence he had on the consumer rights movement and the development of tort law.

Instead of starting with any of those, however, the best way to understand Nader's effect on private enforcement is to begin with John F. Banzhaf III. A longtime public interest lawyer, activist, and later professor of law at George Washington University, Banzhaf popularized the phrase "sue the bastards."[134] After clashing with the tobacco industry in the 1960s, Banzhaf argued that litigation was not merely a means of resolving disputes but "a powerful tool for affecting social change and advancing the public interest."[135] He called some of his approaches "legal leverage," "legal judo," and "guerrilla law," arguing that filing complaints against corporate boogeymen could achieve tangible results. Over a long career, he built on litigation successes against gender-based pricing in haircuts, airlines allowing smoking, and discriminatory drink pricing. In interviews, he acknowledged that litigation was another tool in a continuum that included courting publicity, stating, "Do I actively seek and court publicity? Sure . . . because it gives you tremendous power and clout."[136]

Nader and Banzhaf pioneered a view of litigation as a tool of justice for consumers. But much more than that, they fed a new generation of graduating lawyers a conception of litigation as a redeemer. The reason their movement became, well, a movement is because there was enormous hunger for social change in the budding '60s generation. And that hunger led to expansive new statutes, class actions, a liberal judiciary, and other legal tools that seemed to invite litigation for public interest causes. Historian Paul Sabin notes a "shift from the idea that federal agencies . . . could represent" the public interest to the idea that citizen-led groups must watchdog and even sue the government to enforce the laws.[137]

Both Nader and his young attorneys, "Nader's Raiders," and Banzhaf and his "Bandits" notched win after win in the courts and public opinion. Some of these included:

- In *Nader v. General Motors Corp.* (1970), Nader successfully sued GM for invasion of privacy after the company hired private thugs to follow and harass him following the publication of his book, *Unsafe at Any Speed.*
- Nader's lawsuit against Allegheny Airlines (1976) for being bumped from an overbooked flight reached the Supreme Court, which ruled that fraud claims could proceed without federal regulators weighing in.[138] This litigation directly led to the modern version of compensation requirements for bumped passengers, demonstrating how individual cases could drive industry-wide policy changes.[139]
- Public Citizen Litigation Group, a non-profit law firm founded by Nader, successfully challenged the legal profession's anti-competitive practices. And in *Goldfarb v. Virginia State Bar* (1975), the Supreme Court struck down minimum fee schedules for lawyers as illegal price-fixing, making routine legal services more affordable for ordinary Americans.[140]
- Nader's Public Citizen Health Research Group sued government agencies like the Occupational Safety and Health Administration (OSHA) to force action on workplace hazards.[141] These efforts resulted in court orders or settlements requiring stronger safety standards.
- Groups associated with Nader pioneered using Freedom of Information Act lawsuits to expose government and corporate wrongdoing.[142] For example, Public Citizen litigators fought for thirteen years to release the Nixon White House tapes.[143]

Nader's credo was that if regulators wouldn't protect the public, citizens would, especially via lawsuits and legal petitions to challenge unsafe products, fraudulent business practices, and weak enforcement by government agencies.

To feed this growing movement of lawyers as social protectors, the Ford Foundation played a pivotal role in funding and shaping public interest law.[144] Beginning in 1967 and intensifying through the 1970s, the Foundation channeled millions into new legal organizations. Its funding focused on four new public interest areas: civil rights (NAACP Legal Defense Fund and the Lawyers' Committee for Civil Rights Under Law), sex equality (Women's Law Fund), consumer protection, and the environment (Environmental Defense Fund, Sierra Club Legal Defense Fund, and Natural Resources Defense Council). This substantial financial backing allowed these organizations to increase their litigation activities, hire committed staff attorneys, conduct essential pre-trial discovery, and ultimately expand their involvement in issue areas. This deliberate ecosystem-building approach distinguished Ford from mere charitable giving and turned it into a hub for a growing movement.

Capturing the spirit of the times, future Justice Lewis F. Powell, Jr. lamented the "impotency of business" and the eagerness of "politicians to support almost any legislation related to 'consumerism' or to the 'environment.'" Narrowing on courtroom battles, he noted that "[l]abor unions, civil rights groups and now the public interest law firms are extremely active in the judicial arena."[145] And even more directly, he claimed that "the single most effective antagonist of American business is Ralph Nader, who—thanks largely to the media—has become a legend in his own time and an idol of millions of Americans."[146]

In short, the culture had fully absorbed private enforcement—suing was "in." For consumer activists, the courthouse door was open, and they rushed through it.

## HISTORICAL ECHOES IN THE 1970S: ENVIRONMENTAL LAW, RICO, AND BEYOND

By 1970, the modern synthesis was set: a long history of private rights of action tracing back to the Sherman Act and penal statutes, paired with robust agency-building since the twin bills of 1914 (Clayton Act + Federal Trade Commission) and a burgeoning 1960s culture of young lawyers eager to take advantage of those rights. This combination pushed Congress to adopt even more private rights of action across a range of areas like environmental law and even criminal law. But every single time that Congress did that, individual congressmen drew on the precedents of qui tam and antitrust, drawing a direct connection to the long history of private enforcement.

Here I'll provide a brief review of private enforcement and environmental law—a deeper dive awaits in Chapter 9. The environmental movement emerged alongside Nader's consumer advocacy, with both causes embracing litigation as their primary strategy for change. Following the first Earth Day in 1970 and landmark legislation like the National Environmental Policy Act, organizations such as NRDC and the Sierra Club Legal Defense Fund regularly sued both corporations and government agencies for environmental violations, from dam construction to clean air enforcement failures. The legal strategies and victories of environmental advocates significantly overlapped with consumer protection efforts. So the Clean Water Act's citizen-suit provision (1972), championed by Nader's team, enabled environmentalists to take industrial polluters to court just as consumer advocates could sue manufacturers of dangerous products. These environmental and consumer organizations often shared funding sources, governance philosophies, and even legal talent. Attorneys frequently moved between both types of cases as part of the broader "public interest law" movement that transformed American activism, whether fighting segregated schools, polluted waterways, or dangerous automobiles, into a legal battleground.

On top of support from the new public interest legal movement, backers of private rights of action in environmental law drew on qui tam. Consider the Clean Air Act (CAA), which Congress adopted in 1970.[147] Senator Edmund Muskie and Howard Baker jointly pushed the statute and its "citizen suits," a powerful right to sue, providing:

> any person [can] commence a civil action on his own behalf . . . against any person . . . who is alleged to have violated . . . or to be in violation of (A) an emission standard or limitation under this chapter or (B) an order issued by the Administrator or a State with respect to such a standard or limitation.[148]

This provision empowered private citizens and groups to "ensure that federal regulations are enforced and that environmental problems are corrected."[149] As Professor Barton Thompson describes, the environmental laws gave citizens the role of "prosecutor, monitor, and informant . . . . In authorizing citizen suits in the 1970 Clean Air Act, Congress . . . called on private citizens to play a direct rather than a collateral role in enforcing public laws. Greater deterrence was no longer a collateral benefit but became the primary benefit."[150] To proponents of environmental citizen suits, the most prominent model for private enforcement was the Civil Rights Act. Former Attorney General Ramsey Clark testified in favor of powerful rights to sue, arguing that:

> It will be impossible for government enforcement to control all significant acts of pollution . . . The extension of private right . . . and effective sanctions for the persons directly affected or concerned will be essential if vital interests are to be protected. Our experience in areas of massive unlawful racial discrimination, such as in schooling, employment, and housing tells us that however hard it might try, government will never have the manpower, the techniques, or the awareness necessary to enforce the law for all. Private enforcement of those laws is the only way the individual can be assured that the rights cannot be violated with impunity.
>
> Pollution control is another such area. If we are really serious about controlling the quality of our environment before it destroys the quality of our lives, we must give the individuals affected by, or concerned about pollutions in his life, the power to stop them through legal process . . . it will provide powerful supplementary enforcement . . . and an effective and desirable prod to officials to do their duty.[151]

No doubt, then, that recent private enforcement provisions were in the mind of members of Congress. Yet there is compelling evidence that older precedents like qui tam served as a model, too. Professor Thompson has argued that "[q]ui tam actions provided a highly visible precedent to members of Congress in 1970 when Congress was deciding whether to provide for citizen suits in the Clean Air Act."[152] Part of the reason is that environmental organizations led a series of lawsuits under the 1899 Refuse Act, arguing for an implicit qui tam provision under that statute.[153] Courts eventually rejected that argument, but few had decided by the time Congress voted on the Clean Air Act. Thompson argues, then, that "[g]iven the history of private compensation actions and qui tam provisions, no one involved in the formulation of the 1970 Clean Air Act suggested that citizen enforcement suits were a radical break with the past. As the Nixon administration conceded, citizen suits were built upon the 'trend of existing law.'"[154]

As detailed in Chapter 9, every single major federal environmental statute came with a private right of action, including the Clean Air Act and Clean Water Act. And even statutes that did not have an express private right of action—like the National Environmental Policy Act—were amenable to private enforcement via administrative claims. This represented the full outgrowth of a marriage between environmentalism, legal activism, and the "sue the bastards" ethos of the age. Just like in 1914, these private enforcement schemes were paired with a powerful new agency: the Environmental Protection Agency (EPA). The EPA had authority to issue fines, sanctions, and other measures against violators, as well as establish and enforce air quality standards and police air pollution.

Beyond environmental law, one of the most surprising areas to welcome private enforcement was criminal law. A powerful coalition of congressmen and Nixon's law and order campaign coalesced in the late 1960s to tackle organized crime. Nixon's 1968 campaign for the presidency was riddled with law and order themes, warnings against a "lawless society," and references to "national disorder" and "the decline in respect for public authority and the rule of law in America."[155] Rising crime rates across a range of cities in the US—highlighted by prominent murders and explosive devices detonated on average every few days—led to the creation of national commissions to study the problem.

Many of these commissions emphasized the problem of organized crime's participation in legitimate business. This had been a longstanding concern since the 1940s, particularly prompted by the mafia. The influential Katzenbach Commission, for instance, "conceived of organized crime as a single entity and directed its primary attention toward a single target: the Italian syndicate it believed controlled organized crime throughout the United States."[156] Some of the problems were that even though "24 [La] Cosa Nostra families" had been prosecuted, "not a single one [was] destroyed."[157]

The Racketeer Influenced and Corrupt Organizations Act of 1970 eventually emerged out of this scramble. The statute criminalizes "racketeering activity" by enterprises, which includes the commission of multiple predicate underlying crimes like money laundering, bribery, embezzlement, or wire fraud. RICO contains thermonuclear punishments because it allows prosecutors to impose severe criminal penalties against an enterprise and its high-level officials, not just low-level minions. Strangely, the statute also contains a private right of action allowing civil lawsuits against racketeering.

Return to 1969, as Nixon was about to take power, and several commissions were focused on the problem of crime. A few reform proposals began to take shape, all targeting acts that were criminal in nature: gambling, narcotics trafficking, extortion, and so on. During early debates, several congressmen argued that typical policing and investigatory methods would be insufficient to deal with criminal organizations that were either too powerful or too intertwined in legitimate business to easily smoke them out. The goal of any reform was to root out infiltration of crime into legitimate organizations in order to destroy the financial base of the mafia and other criminal organizations.

The Senate first considered a proposal for what eventually became the Organized Crime Control Act in early 1969. Senator John L. McClellan's original bill authorized a range of new powers to deal with organized crime. But there was no private right of action in sight.[158] Again, the focus was on rooting out expansive organized crime rings that "weaken the stability of the Nation's economic system, harm innocent investors and competing organizations, interfere with free competition, [and] seriously burden interstate and foreign commerce . . . ."[159] But the attention on "competing organizations" quickly led to an idea: What if competitors could sue organizations that are infiltrated by crime? Competitors suffer in those circumstances because of unfair competition.

Pursuing the competitor-lawsuit reasoning, Senator Hruska introduced an early version of RICO, prohibiting money laundering and, for the first time, providing for a right to sue by "businessmen who had been damaged by unfair competition by a 'racketeer businessman.'"[160] Over a year later, Representative Steiger of Arizona proposed an amendment to a different bill that would include a private right of action along with treble damages. Steiger defended a right to sue, drawing on the history of the antitrust statutes and specifically the Sherman and Clayton Acts:

> One possible amendment . . . would add a private civil damage remedy to title IX, similar to the private damage remedy found in the anti-trust laws. Not every businessman, of course, will wish to take advantage of such a remedy, but those who have been wronged by organized crime should at least be given access to a legal remedy. In addition, the availability of such a remedy would enhance the effectiveness of title IX's prohibitions.[161]

In testimony to Congress, the President of the American Bar Association (ABA) came out in support of the right to sue and explicitly mentioned that the "civil remedy of authorizing private damage suits" was "based [on] Section 4 of the Clayton Act."[162] Other supporters included a representative of a business organization.[163] Eventually, Section 1964(c)'s right to sue read as follows:

> Any person injured in his business or property by reason of a violation of section 1962 of this chapter may sue therefor in any appropriate United States district court and shall recover threefold the damages he sustains and the cost of the suit including a reasonable attorney's fee.[164]

The direct analogy to the antitrust laws again shows that congressmen were drawing on historical versions of private enforcement. But there's something farfetched about it here; RICO is primarily a criminal statute. Yet it allows civil plaintiffs to file claims against enterprises that engage in racketeering activity. In a way, this was the apotheosis of private enforcement and a reversal to the common law practice of private prosecution of crimes.

## ECHOES OF 1914

To close the historical loop, the true progenitor of the American regulatory system—combining both robust agencies with private rights of action—is the choice Congress made in 1914 to adopt both the Clayton Act and Federal Trade Commission Act. The twin bills established a pattern that would define American regulatory governance for the next century.

When faced with pressing social problems, American legislators repeatedly chose both bureaucratic expertise and private litigation as complementary solutions. This dual approach reflected an American preference to give private plaintiffs an opportunity to file a lawsuit. In almost every bill debate, once a single congressman proposed a private right of action, other legislators accepted it without much pushback. It isn't clear whether this was entirely due to suspicions of concentration of power (although debates over the Civil Rights Act drew on this theme), skepticism of government bureaucracies (present during debates over the FLSA), or anything similar. While those concerns arose from time to time, they were not the consistent theme in every legislative debate. Rather, the only clear message is that legal elites thought it was "common sense" to continue the old practice of including rights to sue. Or in the words of Senator Steiger, "those who have been wronged . . . should at least be given access to a legal remedy."[165]

This pattern repeated with remarkable consistency across the major social movements of the twentieth century. The FLSA paired a Labor Department Administrator with employee lawsuits to enforce wage standards. The Civil Rights Act created the EEOC while enabling discrimination victims to sue in federal court. Environmental protection relied on both the EPA and citizen-suit provisions across multiple statutes. Even RICO, fundamentally a criminal statute enforced by the DOJ, incorporated private enforcement modeled on antitrust precedents. In each case, legislators could have chosen a purely administrative approach but instead built private rights of action into the regulatory architecture.

The persistence of this public-private hybrid across ideological lines and historical periods suggests something deeply rooted in American governance. Private enforcement disperses regulatory power widely, creating thousands of potential enforcers rather than a single administrative bottleneck. When Representative Keller described the FLSA's private right of action as "common sense and economical," he was articulating an American intuition about how governance should work, one that dates to the earliest penal statutes and qui tam provisions of the colonial era.

As we've seen throughout this chapter, each major social movement built upon earlier precedents while adapting private enforcement to new challenges. The antitrust movement drew on common law restraint of trade and the 1623 Statute of Monopolies. Labor advocates incorporated lessons from antitrust's private enforcement provisions. Civil rights attorneys refined wage and hour collective actions. Environmental lawyers referenced both civil rights and qui tam precedents. This historical continuity reveals private enforcement not as a modern innovation but as an enduring American legal tradition.

# PART II

## THEORY AND CAUSAL EXPLANATIONS

# FIVE

## COMPETING THEORIES OF PRIVATE ENFORCEMENT

We now understand that America's embrace of private enforcement isn't a modern quirk but a four-century legal evolution. We also know that comparative scholars agree that private enforcement is "unusually pervasive" in the United States relative to other developed countries. No other country comes close to America's reliance on the right to sue.[1]

But nothing we have covered so far addresses the causal question: Why does the United States consistently embrace private enforcement when other countries do not? In other words, what about the United States uniquely leads to this phenomenon?

Easy explanations fail when you consider them in a comparative setting. Take, for instance, the common law explanation. Perhaps the United States relies on private enforcement simply because of its common law tradition. At common law, plaintiffs can file all kinds of claims over all kinds of harms. Private enforcement would seem to be a natural outgrowth of this way of law. But this cannot be the case when England, the originator of the common law, does not rely on extensive private enforcement in antitrust, employment, securities, environmental law, government fraud, and other regulatory areas. A few English statutes have moved toward the US model in the past few decades, but the locus of enforcement is still the bureaucracy. Nor were most private enforcement regimes in the United States inspired by the common law. So the common law does not inevitably produce a reliance on private enforcement.

Or consider the easy cultural explanation that Americans are unusually litigious.[2] Set aside that this is empirically contested, this explanation would seem to reverse the causation. To the extent this claim refers to statutory lawsuits (rather than common law claims), wouldn't Americans need rights to sue to engage in their unusual levels of litigation? And why would those rights to sue exist in the first place? There seems to be a chicken-and-egg problem here. Moreover, Americans seem eager to build robust bureaucracies, including the FDA, FTC, SEC, EPA, and NLRB, among many others. In some historical periods, including the New Deal, American elites were keen to embrace administrative solutions. That is somewhat inconsistent with the idea that American culture shows an inherent preference for litigation over bureaucratic regulation.

Likewise, there are political theories that won't be addressed in this chapter because there is not enough evidence to support them. For instance, the "cost-shift" theory posits that legislators turn to private litigation to "shift regulatory costs away from public budgets and onto the private sector," allowing them to claim political victories at little fiscal cost.[3] But two scholars tested the theory in the disabilities context and found little evidence for it.[4]

Given the weakness of these explanations, scholars have produced better and more enduring theories. One is based around America's unique separation of powers and the predictable dynamics between Congress and the President. As explored below, this theory "posits that Congress enacts private rights of action when the executive is controlled by another political party" to avoid an ideologically distant president.[5] While this theory can help explain Congress's actions in the 1960s and 70s, there are several reasons to doubt its explanatory power beyond that time period, including that this dynamic does not appear in the states in the past two decades. Nor does this theory fit neatly with the history of private enforcement.

Another theory suggests that private enforcement emerges from a complex interaction between culture and political structure.[6] By rejecting the monarchy, the Founders created a political culture (and structure) that disaggregates power. This fragmentation produces a reliance on courts to resolve major regulatory questions. This theory better aligns with the evidence. But it, too, suffers from problems, including an inconsistent understanding of the history and prevalence of private enforcement. At the very least, it needs to be refined. Let's dive into both theories before we craft a better one in the next chapter.

## SEPARATION OF POWERS REVISITED

In *The Litigation State*, Sean Farhang argued that private enforcement results from deliberate congressional choices to empower individuals in important regulatory areas.[7] Prior to Farhang's work, scholars often conflated common law and statutory claims, treating them as similar phenomena. Worse, political scientists ignored the role of private rights of action in statutory litigation.[8] By clarifying that we can trace most regulatory lawsuits (and the litigation state) to specific statutes, Farhang put the focus on congressional choices and careful legislative design "to rely upon private litigation in statutory implementation."[9] The key vehicle, then, is the private right of action, along with other important procedural devices like multiple damages provisions and fee-shifting.

After narrowing his focus on private rights of action, Farhang crafted a theory to explain *why* Congress so often adopts these provisions. While he acknowledged multiple contributing factors, he centered on the dynamic between Congress and the President in the 1960s and 70s.[10] Private enforcement, the theory goes, becomes particularly attractive to legislators during periods of divided government with important ideological differences between the legislative and executive branches. In those periods, Congress prefers to shield enforcement away from an ideologically distant president and bureaucracy that it does not trust. This theory makes a clear prediction: The more ideological distance between Congress and the President, the more we should observe the adoption of private rights of action.

Farhang found some support for this theory in the Civil Rights Act of 1964, where Republicans pushed against public enforcement by a Democratic bureaucracy that they distrusted.[11] Similarly, environmental legislation of the 1970s incorporated citizen-suit provisions as congressional Democrats sought independence from Nixon's enforcement priorities.[12] Let's examine the three parts of this theory:

***1. Private Rights of Action.*** As mentioned, one of Farhang's most important contributions is to focus on statutory private rights of action. It is those provisions that create private enforcement of statutory law. In doing so, Farhang correctly leaves to the side tort claims. As discussed in Chapter 1, tort claims are different because they emerge from a long common law process and the evolving judicial recognition of new harms. Moreover, torts are based on state, not federal, law and are mostly litigated in state court. And tort claims are not explicitly regulatory. Farhang's move away from tort claims towards statutory claims also departs from previous political science scholarship and focuses on private rights of action as a driver of adversarial legalism.[13] If we care about major regulatory areas—antitrust, environmental law, wages and hours, discrimination, government fraud, or consumer protection—private enforcement, then, is the study of the legislative choice to adopt a right to sue. So far so good.

***2. 1960–1970s PRAs.*** Farhang's second move is to focus *only* on the development of private enforcement in the 1960s and 1970s. Farhang collected data on statutory lawsuits and found an explosion of those lawsuits in the late 1960s and 1970s. As Farhang explained, "Only at the end of the 1960s did private litigation, which had long been an important part of the federal regulatory enforcement apparatus, begin to outstrip governmental prosecutions by a large margin."[14] Because of this, he concludes that "[t]he overwhelming reliance upon private litigation to enforce federal regulatory policy is not a static feature of the American state, but rather has varied dramatically over time."[15]

This single focus on the statistical growth of private statutory claims lets Farhang set to the side the previous history of private enforcement. He specifically notes that "[w]hile the United States has relied heavily upon private litigation to enforce policies passed into law by Congress since the rise of the federal regulatory state in the late 1880s, the frequency with which it has done so exploded in the late 1960s."[16] On a per capita rate, it does appear to be an "explosion," growing from "a rate of 3 per 100,000 population in 1967 . . . to 13 by 1976, to 21 by 1986, to 29 in 1996, increasing by about 1,000 percent during these three decades."[17]

Much of Farhang's book, then, addresses a few key 1960s and 1970s statutes: the Civil Rights Act, the Fair Housing Act, and several environmental laws, among others.

***3. Congress-Executive Dynamics.*** Despite his limited historical focus, Farhang (a political scientist) is most concerned with persistent congressional-executive dynamics. And these dynamics are not specific to the 1960s. He explains, "[T]he ambition of this book is to illuminate, in general, the institutional foundations of the congressional choice to mobilize private litigants for policy implementation, not specifically to explain the sharp growth in the rate of such litigation beginning in the late 1960s."[18]

Farhang then postulates a clear separation of powers theory of private enforcement: "The legislative choice of private litigation over administrative power emerged from conflict between ideologically antagonistic interests, channeled through America's fragmented political institutions, particularly the dynamic of legislative-executive competition for control of the bureaucracy."[19] The dynamic is as follows: (1) When Congress is controlled by an ideological coalition that (2) is distant from the ideology of the president, (3) Congress shies away from giving more power to the bureaucracy, (4) preferring instead to leave enforcement power in the hands of private plaintiffs. "With respect to why Congress enacts private enforcement regimes . . . the legislative choice is made by purposive, goal-oriented, and strategically minded actors attempting to maximize on policy objectives."[20] Congressional actors choose one form of enforcement that is most likely to carry out their ideological goals. Congress, then, adopts private rights of action to avoid delegating enforcement to ideologically distant presidents.

To be clear, Farhang does not claim that the dynamics of separation of powers are the *only* cause. He points out, for instance, that interest group lobbying is an important variable. But Farhang emphasizes repeatedly that separation of powers is the driving force in the "legislative enactment of private enforcement regimes."[21] He clarifies that this "institutional relationship is by far the most central to the argument of the book, powerful in effect, and pivotal to explaining the steep rise in private enforcement litigation starting in the late 1960s."[22] Or, as he states elsewhere, "legislative-executive conflict over control of the bureaucracy *drives* Congress to rely upon litigants and courts as an alternative to administrative power."[23] And this dynamic has become more important since the 1960s because that is "when divided party control of the legislative and executive branches became the norm and relations between Congress and the president became more antagonistic, a condition that was exacerbated by growing ideological polarization between the parties."[24]

## THE LIMITS OF SEPARATION OF POWERS

But the separation of powers theory does not explain the causal origins of private enforcement. Nor does it fully explain why the United States is so committed to private enforcement relative to other developed countries. While Farhang did *not* purport to make historical or general causal claims—he explicitly cabined his theory to a defined period of time—it is still important to understand why the separation of powers does not account for these important features of private enforcement.

Generally, the theory is limited in the following ways: (1) The adoption of private enforcement at the state level does not always line up with separation of powers dynamics—although there is mixed evidence, it is likely that legislative-executive dynamics do not drive recent state legislative behavior; (2) the long arc of history shows that private enforcement arises in different historical periods regardless of separation of powers dynamics; and (3) it is possible that 1960s data on a litigation "explosion" was not solely due to the growth of private enforcement but to procedural changes in federal litigation. This, again, reduces the relevance of the separation of powers dynamics that drove the adoption of private enforcement in the 1960s and 70s. Below, I explore each of these in turn.

***1. The States Tell a Different Story.*** As mentioned before, there are 10,000 private rights of action in state law, while only around 380 in federal law. If separation of powers is the "driving" force behind legislative adoption of private rights of action, we would expect to see the dynamic replicate across the fifty states. Yet, in the most comprehensive study to date of state-level private enforcement (that I conducted with co-authors), we found no support for the separation of powers theory across the fifty states, at least in our specified study period.[25] Although under some specifications we found very limited support, our preferred way to review the data found no support at all. Whatever it is that "drives" adoption of private enforcement in the United States, a parsimonious account should explain federal and state private enforcement.

Prior to our recent study, there was no available data on the prevalence of private enforcement in the states. Part of the problem is that tracking down these provisions can be tricky because they are worded in a variety of ways. Some provisions allow "employees" to "file suit." Others grant boat captains "damages" under certain conditions. Still others use unique wording found nowhere else. Because of this difficulty, we employed machine learning to develop a model that could identify private rights of action. By conservative estimates, we found over 3,500 private rights of action embedded in the statutory codes of all fifty states, but we believe the best way to count these provisions adds them up to more than 10,000.[26] As discussed in Chapter 2, we found that private enforcement is not confined to traditional regulatory domains like antitrust and employment law but extends to unexpected areas such as gravedigging, pet leasing, and the sale of mislabeled cigarettes. This empirical map of state private rights shows the breadth of private enforcement in American state governance, often in ways overlooked by scholars who focus solely on the federal system.

We then leveraged this dataset to test the separation of powers theory. Specifically, we asked: Do state legislatures adopt private rights of action at higher rates when there is an ideological split between the legislative coalition in control of a state legislature and the governorship? Contrary to federal-level evidence supporting the separation of powers theory, we found no consistent relationship between divided government and state adoption of private rights of action, at least in the past few decades.[27] While under some measures we observed an effect, in general, "[r]egression analyses . . . [did] not yield a statistically meaningful relationship between divided government and private-enforcement adoption . . . . It appears the political economy of private enforcement in the states" is complex.[28]

Nor did we find support for alternative hypotheses centered on lawyer lobbying, fiscal austerity, or partisan control. There isn't even a "correlation between an increased adoption of private enforcement and legislative control by either Democrats or Republicans."[29] This means that state-level private enforcement operates according to distinct institutional dynamics, marked by instability, frequent statutory revision, and some dependence on model laws. Instead of being a surgical tool for a few statutes, state private enforcement appears sprawling, dynamic, and resistant to easy theoretical explanation—posing a challenge to the separation of powers theory and other accounts of how litigation functions as a regulatory tool in the United States. It is less likely that legislative-executive dynamics are the "driving" force behind the adoption of private rights of action when we see virtually no recent evidence of that in the states.

***2. History and Implied PRAs Tell a Different Story.*** As Chapters 3 and 4 explain, private enforcement traces back to the Middle Ages. Penal statutes and qui tam claims were ubiquitous in the colonial era and in the Early Republic.[30] While Farhang's separation of powers theory may explain the federal expansion of private enforcement in the 1960s–70s, it does not account for the phenomenon's much deeper origins or broader prevalence. Governments without modern separation of powers—like colonial governments under the British Crown—adopted these mechanisms at high rates, and contemporary state legislatures embrace private enforcement regardless of a divided government. History, then, suggests that separation of powers dynamics, while relevant to specific episodes of expansion, cannot fully explain why private enforcement emerged and persists as a defining feature of American law.

To be sure, Farhang knew that private enforcement was a key feature of regulatory law before the 1960s. The thrust of his argument refers to a *marginal* increase driven by the separation of powers. He also reasonably believed that private enforcement's history traced back only to the 1880s. As he mentions, "the United States has relied heavily upon private litigation to enforce policies passed into law by Congress since the rise of the federal regulatory state in the late 1880s."[31] Farhang is correct that the Sherman Act of 1890 was an important step towards modern regulatory private enforcement. But we cannot discount the importance of penal statutes in creating America's long dependence on rights to sue. Both informer claims and modern private enforcement played the same regulatory role: to increase detection of legal violations and deterrence via private litigation. For example, Congress adopted the FCA because the Army needed manpower to detect fraudulent contractors. That is the same motivation behind the Sherman Act's private right of action.

There is yet another reason to question the importance of legislative-executive dynamics: The Supreme Court recognized private rights of action in federal statutes after 1944, even without separation of powers drivers. In the 1940s, the Court repeatedly found a private right of action in the Railway Labor Act, holding that "a federal right [was] implied from the statute and the policy which it has adopted."[32] Most importantly, in the same year that Congress adopted the CRA's private right of action (1964)—the key example in Farhang's theory—the Supreme Court independently recognized a private right of action in the securities laws.[33] This right to sue became perhaps the most important private enforcement regime in the country, at least economically. The Court's eagerness to, in effect, create private rights of actions in the 1940s and 1964 suggests that something deeper was driving legal elites, not legislative-executive dynamics.

***3. Procedural Changes are Another Important Variable.*** Farhang's focus on the 1960s and 70s was partially warranted, but his explanation requires refinement. Farhang observed that federal statutory litigation exploded during this period, which would seem to mark a fundamental shift in American governance. However, the timing and pattern of growth in federal filings in the mid-1960s reflect multiple procedural factors rather than simply the creation of new private rights of action.

One important factor was the creation of the modern class action rule in 1966 (and the MDL statute in 1968). A significant uptick in litigation in 1966–68 coincides with these two new procedural mechanisms that increased the attractiveness of federal litigation by allowing plaintiffs to aggregate claims and consolidate related cases.

Jurisdictional changes also likely contributed to the expansion of federal statutory litigation. Stepping back, cases can enter federal court only when there is proper subject matter jurisdiction. Article III of the US Constitution gives federal courts only limited jurisdiction, based only on claims by citizens from different states (diversity jurisdiction) or under federal law (federal question jurisdiction).[34] But Congress controls federal question jurisdiction via statute—it can limit the federal courts' power even further by not authorizing it. And for most of American history, Congress did not authorize federal question jurisdiction. Cases involving federal law were generally litigated in *state court*. The Judiciary Act of 1789 explicitly withheld such jurisdiction from the lower federal courts, entrusting most federal claims to state courts. It was not until the Jurisdiction and Removal Act of 1875 that Congress granted federal courts plenary authority to hear federal statutory claims, marking the beginning of what I have previously described as a second era of judicial federalism.[35] But, importantly, even then, federal question jurisdiction was *limited by an amount-in-controversy requirement*. That meant that plaintiffs with monetary claims under a certain threshold ($10,000 in 1980) could not enter the federal courts.

By the time of the Sherman Act, then, large monetary claims could be litigated in federal court. But many claims under federal law had to be litigated in state court. This situation persisted throughout the twentieth century. This means the Sherman Act, Clayton Act, Fair Labor Standards Act, Civil Rights Act, and any other federal private enforcement claims had to be litigated in state court, unless the claim was sufficiently large.

Congress partially eliminated the amount-in-controversy requirement for claims against the federal government in 1976 and all claims in 1980.[36] The mid-to-late 1970s, then, are an inflection point of federal appropriation of federal statutory claims. Since then, Congress and the federal judiciary have embraced broader interpretations of both diversity and federal question jurisdiction, facilitating the removal or rechanneling of some litigation from state to federal court.

Here's why this story is relevant: Before 1980, there may well have been a significant number of federal private enforcement claims litigated in state court (a kind of submerged federal regulatory state). Even though these claims alleged violations of federal statutes, if the plaintiff alleged a harm that was less than the threshold amount in controversy, these claims would have been litigated in state court. The litigation "explosion" in the 1970s, then, may be partially explained by the expansion of federal jurisdiction over these claims. But not because these claims did not exist before then. Rather, those claims were previously litigated in state courts. Without sufficient data on these claims in state court, we simply do not know whether federal private enforcement was already large before the 1960s and 1970s. Indeed, looking back at the graph of federal statutory claims, one of the largest jumps is between 1980 and 1982 and coincides with the elimination of the federal question jurisdiction monetary threshold. This weakens any attribution of the spike in private enforcement claims to solely Congress's creation of private rights of action. Even the growth of claims before 1976 may be explained by the growth in monetary size of claims that met the federal amount in controversy, not by the appearance of claims that were never filed before then. Increasing inflation, for instance, could equally explain a higher number of claims that can meet the amount in controversy requirement.

Now, to be sure, there are important qualifications. The jurisdictional changes began in the late 1970s and the class action rule was adopted in

1966. But there is no doubt that the institutional and political prominence of private enforcement increased significantly alongside these changes. Congress's choice in this era to rely on PRAs still stands out.

All of this is to say that a systematic understanding of legal changes in the 1960s and 1970s goes beyond merely new private rights of action. There may well have been significant federal private enforcement submerged in state courts.

---

A focus on the separation of powers can tell us why Congress adopted a marginally higher number of private rights of action after the CRA. But it probably does not account for America's long-running commitment to private enforcement.

## THE CULTURAL THEORY

In the face of weak explanations for private enforcement—and cross-country variability—some scholars have long defaulted to culture as the root of unusual American institutions.

A cultural theory of private enforcement would boil down to this—uniquely American values like individualism, a preference for confrontation, and suspicion of government bureaucracies increase demand for litigation to resolve disputes. Congressional adoption of private rights of action simply reflects American cultural preferences for a do-it-yourself version of enforcement as well as a reluctance to empower government bureaucrats.

This cultural preference, the argument goes, traces back to the Founding. The Framers, mistrustful of government power, created a decentralized constitutional structure. This structure renders certain forms of bureaucratic management constitutionally suspect, reinforcing negative perceptions of bureaucracies amongst Americans, and allowing interest groups to channel public demands into the adversarial arena.

Some scholars have made arguments consistent with this theory. Take, for instance, Michael Dominic Meuti's argument that America's adversarial legalism is fundamentally rooted in a cultural commitment to individualism that predates even our constitutional framework.[37] Meuti contends that cultural individualism gave rise to basic structures that increased demand for individualistic legal institutions. An individualistic worldview—independent self-construction, emphasis on personal rights over collective duties, and belief in competition as the optimal path to social good—comes out throughout the legal system. From party-controlled litigation to passive judicial roles and zealous advocacy, each element reflects America's exceptional individualism. Rather than seeing adversarial legalism as merely a product of political structures, Meuti argues we must recognize it as the inevitable expression of America's distinctive cultural DNA—one that prizes individual autonomy and distrust of collective authority as fundamental values.

Similarly, Daniel Polisar and Aaron Wildavsky argue that American adjudication rejects the bureaucracy model, preferring the egalitarian nature of litigation and court-driven dispute resolution.[38] The ultimate root of this is American anti-hierarchical values and reluctance to cede authority to the state. Why are European countries so unwilling to embrace American style tort law? Because European political culture is defined by a hybrid of egalitarianism and hierarchicalism, whereas the United States blends egalitarianism with individualism. Lacking the trust of authority implicit in hierarchicalism, the United States shies away from bureaucratic solutions to personal harm, instead preferring egalitarian (but still individualist) solutions through a robustly pro-plaintiff tort system.

Another theorist, Mirjan Damaška, agrees, arguing that "if ever there was a general political consensus in America, it was—and perhaps still is—an antipathy toward bureaucracy, hierarchical ordering, and the conception of law as a technical discipline, that is, an antipathy towards all the essential aspects of the hierarchical ideal."[39]

A more modern version of the cultural theory focuses on changes in the 1960s. Farhang, for instance, argues that "[t]he cultural transformation explanation comes in two varieties, one pejorative and the other celebratory."[40] The "pejorative cultural transformation" explanation argues that high rates of litigation in the United States "are the result of a process of cultural degeneration from a rights-respecting people to a rights-abusing one . . . . In the 1960s, America's long-standing tradition of individualism morphed into the hyperindividualism of rapid 'rights talk,' rights assertion became far more legalistic, and the American people became much more litigious."[41] A more positive view is that a rise of rights-consciousness during the civil rights movement led to a more assertive form of citizenship, which in turn prompted Americans to vindicate their rights in the courts.[42]

## THE LIMITS OF THE CULTURAL THEORY

These cultural theories are not concrete enough to explain the history of private enforcement and government bureaucracy. As discussed above, Americans adopted some forms of public bureaucracy even before England did, including the powerful office of public prosecutors. So, too, New Dealers were eager to embrace bureaucratic solutions. And the American Food and Drug Administration, the Federal Reserve, FTC, National Labor Relations Board, and other powerful bureaucracies rose in contradiction to an alleged culture of individualism.

That is why the other scholars have pushed back against cultural theories, admitting that culture may be one ingredient but rarely determinative. Farhang, for instance, notes that "explanations rooted in national culture . . . cannot account for the changing level of private enforcement of federal statutory policy . . . such explanations are too global and reductive."[43]

Legal scholar John Langbein agrees that cultural explanations are too reductive, once intimating that differences in American and German civil litigation were probably influenced by culture. But he immediately retreated from a full-throated claim:

> Cultural differences surely do explain something of why institutional and procedural differences arise in different legal systems. The important question for present purposes is what weight to attach to this factor, and my answer is, "Not much." It is all too easy to allow the cry of "cultural differences" to become the universal apologetic that permanently sheathes the status quo against criticism based upon comparative example.[44]

Similarly, Marc Galanter explicitly criticized cultural explanations for a society's litigiousness. In one piece, he noted that Italy has a lower litigation rate than Japan, even though Italians are stereotypically more contentious than the Japanese. Galanter concluded that "we should be wary of assuming that litigation rates are directly reflective of cultural preferences."[45] Instead, he argued that low rates of litigation in Japan, for instance, reflect conscious decisions by political elites to limit the institutional resources given to formal dispute resolution structures.[46]

Relatedly, the argument that Americans prefer private litigation because they distrust bureaucracy faces an internal contradiction: Courts are themselves a kind of bureaucracy. Private enforcement simply substitutes one set of government officials (judges) for another (public administrators). If cultural suspicion of centralized power were truly driving institutional choices, it is unclear why Americans would embrace judicial power while rejecting administrative power. Both involve delegating authority to unelected government officials to interpret and enforce legal rules.

This is not to say that culture plays no role. The history canvassed in Chapter 3 and 4 shows peculiarly American debates about private versus public enforcement taking place among legal elites. Those debates were surely different than similar discussions in England. Cultural frames sometimes shape what is politically possible and how policymakers defend institutional choices. When American legislators throughout history invoke the risks of an expanding bureaucracy or push for "common sense" empowerment of individual plaintiffs, they seem to draw on background cultural principles.

Nonetheless, treating culture as a primary explanation rather than a background condition seems unwarranted. It would explain either too much or too little. And it seems inconsistent with the historical evidence.

## ROBERT KAGAN'S INSTITUTIONAL SYNTHESIS: STRUCTURE & POLITICAL CULTURE

Robert Kagan assembled the best explanation for adversarial legalism, a concept related to but distinct from private enforcement. He argued that reliance on courts as regulatory devices—a "legal style"—emerges because of a mismatch between popular demands for "total justice" and a political system that is decentralized, fragmented, and nonhierarchical.[47] When Americans demand solutions to pressing regulatory problems like pollution or racial discrimination, the system is unable to respond via centralized bureaucratic administration. It therefore defaults into legal contestation led by lawyers and resolved by courts. While this explanation is structural, it leaves some room for America's "political culture."

Kagan argues that there is "a fundamental mismatch between a changing legal culture and an inherited set of political attitudes and structures. Americans have attempted to articulate and implement the socially transformative policies of an activist, regulatory welfare state through the political and legal institutions of a decentralized, nonhierarchical governmental system."[48] When Americans demand solutions that bureaucracies cannot deliver, courts "step into the breach."[49]

The "four basic engines of American adversarial legalism" are: (1) "a politically selected judiciary" with the power to make law via common law adjudication; (2) "litigant-and-lawyer-dominated modes of dispute-resolution and adjudication, structured around the right to trial by jury"; (3) "a large, entrepreneurial, and politically-active legal profession"; and (4) "a legal culture that reflected a view of law, litigation, and courts as important instruments for protecting individual rights, improving governance, and checking . . . political power."[50]

These four structural features lead to a complex interaction of governance and culture, one feeding the other. For instance, Kagan argues that "[Americans] lived in a more pluralistic, more transient society with weaker institutions of social control. Free from traditions of deference to kings and priests and guilds, Americans were not reluctant to mount adversarial legal challenges to authority (and to each other)."[51] By mounting those challenges, Americans fed into the cultural elements discussed in the previous section: individualism, suspicions of government power, and a preference for confrontation.

But Kagan rejects the confrontational-psychology variant of the cultural thesis, pointing out that "institutional alternatives to courts, more than cultural dispositions toward litigiousness, shape the propensity to rely on litigation to resolve disputes."[52] In his clearest statement on culture, Kagan flatly states that "adversarial legalism in the United States does not arise from an inherent American propensity to bring lawsuits."[53] Rather, adversarial legalism is a default when there are no other institutions that "effectively channel contending parties and groups into other ways of resolving disputes, ensuring accountability, regulating business, and compensating victims of injury or economic misfortune."[54]

Kagan's explanation, moreover, makes some small references to history. He argues that the Founders "rebelled and fought against a powerful, distant monarchy. . . . Those attitudes were embedded in the political structures of the young nation. Through written constitutions, both federal and state, government was to be decentralized and divided into cross-checking branches, and limited by law."[55] Despite its eighteenth-century roots, Kagan contends that adversarial legalism intensified in the twentieth century. Specifically, mid-century progressive social movements (e.g., civil rights, feminism, environmentalism) "demand[ed] a major expansion of governmental authority, particularly on the part of the federal government. That demand, however, ran up against . . . structures grounded in distrust of centralized political authority and big government. From that tension sprang increases in adversarial legalism's role in governance."[56] But there was "something new" in the 1960s; an ingredient "had been added to the stew of American law. It became spicier. It was served up more often and in larger portions. It nourished more people—while giving indigestion to others."[57]

Put otherwise, the growth of adversarial legalism was fueled by two strands of US political culture. "One major strand demands comprehensive governmental protections from harm . . . . The other strand, rooted deep in American history, mistrusts governmental power; thus it values the fragmentation of political authority and seeks to keep government (as well as large, powerful businesses) accountable through lawsuits and judicial review."[58] Adversarial legalism provided an answer to this tension: regulatory reformers couched their goals in the form of swelling legal rights, but the legal system then opened legal avenues to individuals. Other contributing factors include lawyers and an activist legal culture.[59]

## THE LIMITS OF KAGAN'S ADVERSARIAL LEGALISM

Revealing as Kagan's theory is, it also paints with a brush so broad that it blurs the very mechanism that makes modern litigation distinctive: Congress's routine decision to add private rights of action into regulatory statutes. That is, while Kagan gives us a structural and politico-cultural style, we know that what fuels the enforcement engine (discussed in the next chapter) is a clause that says, "any person aggrieved may sue" alongside a procedural infrastructure (class actions, fee-shifting, and broad discovery). Because he treats the style as the prime mover, Kagan pays less attention to important features of the system, including its long history.

The discussion below shows why that distinction matters and why Kagan's theory needs refinement.

***1. Focusing on a "Style" Misses Important Drivers.*** By focusing on "adversarial legalism" as a "legal style," Kagan obscured the concrete legislative mechanism that makes private enforcement uniquely American: ubiquitous private rights of action. This oversight is important because it leads Kagan to pay less attention to key drivers of this system.

First, focusing on a "style" does not clarify the source of private enforcement. Despite its relationship, we cannot equate private enforcement with adversarial legalism. While Kagan describes an amorphous culture of legalism, private enforcement refers to the specific congressional (and state legislative) reliance on private rights of action and the procedural infrastructure that undergirds it (leading to a mass litigation engine). As Sean Farhang has argued, its immediate origins are clear: repeated legislative choices to insert statutory clauses that allow anyone to sue. Of course, Kagan was interested in a broader view of American governance through adversarial mechanisms like lawyer and court driven disputes. And those disputes include common law, administrative, or statutory claims.

But distinguishing among these different kinds of claims is important because a country can have adversarial legalism without private enforcement. That is, the United States could have a "legal style" that is "adversarial" but without extensive reliance on private regulatory suits. Indeed, that describes the common law. Common law claims produce a "legal style" that relies on "lawyer-dominated litigation" as a source of "policymaking," even without any legislative action. But by shifting focus away from legislative enactments, adversarial legalism misses the key question: Why do Congress and state legislatures enact these statutes?

Moreover, focusing on a style in a way that encompasses common law claims is inconsistent with the data on private enforcement. The thing that makes the US distinctive from England is not the common law but the regulatory lawsuits discussed in this book. And as Sean Farhang found, common law claims have *not* driven the bulk of federal litigation since at least the 1960s. Instead, it is statutory claims that turn into a regulatory device. That is sufficient reason to move past the "style" and focus on legislative behavior.

More than that, disregarding the relevance of statutes and legislative behavior puts adversarial legalism in conflict with private enforcement.

Kagan's thesis, for instance, weakens when you consider cross-country comparisons. The focus on a style would seem to suggest that a country could embrace adversarial legalism with or without legislative private enforcement. For example, the UK is a common law country with a "legal style" that relies on "lawyer-dominated litigation" for, say, fraud claims that can result in "policymaking." But if the UK has no private right of action for, say, government fraud, then we can clearly observe that it does not employ private enforcement. In that case, we would have adversarial legalism without private enforcement.

And, *vice versa*, countries that rely on bureaucratic enforcement—like France—sometimes embrace private enforcement in particular areas like antitrust or civil rights. As discussed in the next chapter, the French parliament adopted a civil rights act that relies on private enforcement. In that area, we could observe private enforcement within a system that does not rely on Kagan's party-and-lawyer-led process. In that case, we have private enforcement *without* adversarial legalism. It therefore appears that private enforcement and adversarial legalism are independent concepts.

Second, a focus on a style ignores the important role of federal vs. state courts. Whether a right to sue comes from California, Congress, the common law, or a statute matters. It determines whether a case can be litigated in state or federal courts. It also determines the procedure of the lawsuit—a non-trivial component that includes discovery, class actions, punitive damages, right to a jury trial, and so on. But Kagan writes as if these different polities are all the same. This is a significant conflation of very separate things. For example, conflating common law claims with federal statutory claims overlooks key differences. Common law claims come from state courts. A Supreme Court case held in 1938 that federal courts cannot independently interpret the general common law.[60] Is the suggestion that Congress and state legislatures are driven by the same dynamic and style, despite their significant political differences? What is that dynamic? We shouldn't draw conclusions about federal law based on the behavior of state courts.

Third, because of his focus on a style, Kagan also narrows in on elements of the legal system that are probably secondary to private enforcement. Adversarial legalism, Kagan argues, emerges from "a politically selected judiciary" with the power to make law via common law adjudication; and "litigant-and-lawyer-dominated modes of dispute-resolution and adjudication, structured around the right to trial by jury"; and "a large, entrepreneurial, politically active legal profession."[61] As discussed in the next chapter, Kagan is correct to focus on a politically active legal profession. But the other features he highlights are not as critical to private enforcement. Across the fifty states, private enforcement of regulatory law coexists with judiciaries that vary in their composition, from gubernatorial appointments to elected high courts, all the way to judiciaries with civil-law traditions like Louisiana. Political selection, common law adjudication, trial by jury, and other features are neither necessary nor particularly important to private enforcement.

Finally, a focus on a style is so high-level that it cannot help with prescriptive solutions. As Chapter 9 discusses, there is a burgeoning critique of litigation as imposing costs on housing and infrastructure construction. Any references to "adversarial legalism" as the source of these problems miss the point. An eye for private rights of action, by contrast, gives a straightforward solution when there is a problem: abrogate or constrain any PRAs that power lawsuits against construction projects.

On the whole, Kagan was correct about a lot of different features of the American polity. But Farhang was right to argue that litigation's regulatory role arises out of private rights of action. Kagan masterfully provided a larger theory of American politics, but that 30,000-foot view missed the importance of legislation. This book therefore seeks to build on the concept of "adversarial legalism" by looking at other factors that explain private enforcement in the United States.

***2. History and Cross-Country Studies Tell a Different Story.*** Kagan's work does not make direct historical claims but does hinge on key premises about the historical roots of America's political culture. As discussed above, Kagan notes that the Founders "rebelled and fought against a powerful, distant monarchy . . . . Those attitudes were embedded in the political structures of the young nation. Through written constitutions, both federal and state, government was to be decentralized and divided into cross-checking branches, and limited by law."[62] In other words, adversarial legalism's DNA begins with the revolution and founding of the United States and then intensifies in the twentieth century.

But this focus on the Founding misses the important history of penal statutes laid out in Chapter 3. Private enforcement's roots go way back before the

Founding, landing somewhere in the Middle Ages. It is the emergence of qui tam and penal statutes that marks the true beginning of America's reliance on private plaintiffs to enforce regulatory statutes. Nor is the common law tradition the main origin of private enforcement. Again, while the common law does contribute to the phenomenon, the more direct antecedent is the penal statute. Moreover, its origins make private enforcement a shared historical feature with countries like England and Canada, weakening any connections to the American Revolution.

Second, Kagan's argument that Americans embrace a style that relies on litigation also undervalues Congress's repeated embrace of bureaucracies. Remember, Kagan emphasizes a key driver of adversarial legalism: a political system that is decentralized, fragmented, and nonhierarchical. This fragmentation, Kagan argues, produces a default reliance on litigation. But at most key steps of the story, Congress was content to *both* create centralized and hierarchical bureaucracies (the FDA, FTC, DOJ, EEOC, EPA) and on top of that add a private right to sue. There is no unfailing rejection of bureaucracy or a hopeless fragmentation. The story of private enforcement goes hand in hand with robust state building in the United States. As discussed in the next chapter, Americans have not been averse to building bureaucracy and, at times, did it earlier than the UK and Canada.

Third, there are other reasons to suspect that Kagan's decentralization and fragmentation do not drive the adoption of private rights of action. Consider, for instance, that Canada was even more fragmented and decentralized than the United States in the nineteenth century (many of the provinces were independent of any Canadian union until much later). It also shared the same rich common law tradition. Yet Canada did not embrace US-style private enforcement. In 1889, a year before the Sherman Act, Canada adopted an antitrust statute, the first in modern history.[63] Unlike the Sherman Act, however, it had *no private right of action*. The statute—known as the Anti-Combines Act—treated restraints of trade as criminal offenses to be prosecuted by the federal Attorney General, firmly locating enforcement inside the executive rather than in private hands. Throughout the twentieth century, Ottawa repeatedly refined that public-prosecutor model, but it refused to open the courthouse doors to entrepreneurial plaintiffs. A very limited private remedy did not arrive until Parliament's 1976 amendments, and even that cause of action is more limited than its

American analogue.[64] In other words, despite Canada's federal structure and provincial autonomy, the country channeled antitrust policy toward state-led prosecution and away from American-style private litigation. The explanation behind this is that the Canadian federal government did not have the power to adopt a private right of action; only the provinces could do that. In other words, fragmentation pushed *away from* private enforcement at the federal level, not towards it!

## WE NEED A COHERENT ORIGIN STORY

America's reliance on private enforcement is not just a feature of adversarial legalism and inevitable struggles between Congress and the President. Tracing the story from colonial informer actions through the Sherman Act and into the modern statutory landscape shows a continuous legislative pattern: Policymakers repeatedly add private rights of action onto public regulatory schemes. The comparative stories in England, Canada, and the fifty states underscore that common law heritage, federalism, and cultural predispositions cannot, by themselves, explain the pattern. Nor does the separation of powers account drive changes once we see that Congress has often added private suits even when executive and legislative branches were ideologically aligned, the Supreme Court itself implied rights to sue, and that state legislatures adopt thousands of such rights without the separation of powers dynamics.

What emerges instead is a more complex synthesis of structure, politics, and legal culture. A fragmented yet robust state apparatus, entrenched lawyer-driven institutions, and periodic waves of social mobilization interact to make private enforcement an enduring policy tool. Understanding this mix of variables sets up a fuller account, one that treats private enforcement as a choice embedded in America's governing architecture rather than an ideological reflex or a mere by-product of adversarialism. The next chapter develops that account and sketches the conditions under which private and public enforcement have complemented each other across US history.

# SIX

## A LAYERED PATH DEPENDENCE

This chapter lays out a new account of US private enforcement. Before doing that, however, let's understand first how crafting a coherent account of why the United States turns, again and again, to private enforcement is foundational to evaluating the system itself.

First, origin stories matter—identifying the forces that birthed an institution helps us see whether today's arrangements are the result of principled design, political contingency, or historical drift. Second, legitimacy rests on that origin story—if Congress's embrace of private enforcement is merely an accident of legislative drafting, we are free, perhaps obligated, to reconsider it. If it reflects a deep cultural or structural imperative, reform must reconcile with that bedrock. Third, effective change depends on a deep understanding of existing institutions. So, in short, explaining the origins of private enforcement is not a distraction but an important beginning to a broader discussion of its appearance in US law.

Given everything we've covered so far, any good account of this phenomenon should:

1. Be consistent with a long thread of private enforcement from penal statutes and qui tam before the Founding Era, all the way through the Sherman Act, Clayton Act, Civil Rights Act, and the environmental statutes of the 1970s.

2. Explain both federal *and* state private enforcement.

3. Be consistent with Americans' repeated embrace of bureaucratic solutions, especially after the Choice of 1914 to embrace both the Clayton Act and the Federal Trade Commission.

4. And while it can relate to a larger account about the common law, a good account of private enforcement can also be distinct from common law origins because judicial and legislative behavior reflect different dynamics.

So here it is: This chapter lays out an account of *layered path dependence*. In short, an English and colonial tradition of informer suits created an accepted template, weak bureaucratic capacity and wariness of government monopoly over enforcement periodically renewed its appeal, and the powerful lawyers' lobby (unique to the United States) alongside modern civil procedure turned it into a mass-litigation engine. These layers knit together over time, amplifying the role of private enforcement in American governance. While that positive cycle took place in the United States, other countries lacking some combination of that early heritage or legal traditions instead shifted to vast reliance on bureaucratic solutions and public prosecutors.

Note, at the outset, a few important details. In this story, there is a role for culture as one additional layer. As discussed, we may describe Americans' comfort with private enforcement alongside bureaucracies as stemming from America's individualist culture. But relatedly, this account rejects the idea that skepticism of government power (in any amount) is a critical element of the story. No, wariness of government *monopoly* over enforcement (pushing legislators to also add private rights of action) is not the same as skepticism of more government power in general. Private enforcement has been a supplement to bureaucracy, not an anti-statist substitute. American elites have seemed quite comfortable with new bureaucracies. But they have always insisted on giving plaintiffs the opportunity to also file private lawsuits.

In some ways, the most puzzling part of this story is not the United States's reliance on private enforcement, but that other countries, especially Canada and the UK, moved away from it in the late nineteenth and early twentieth centuries, only to embrace it again in the late twentieth century. After all, the United States simply kept doing what it had always done. It was Canada and the UK that decided to *stop* doing that. Why did those countries give up on private enforcement? While I touch briefly on this question, I cannot answer it in this book.

Suffice it to say, for now, that one uniquely American variable is the rise of a powerful and aggressive plaintiffs' bar in the early decades of the twentieth century. The organized power of the "lawyers' lobby" created an entrepreneurial constituency for private enforcement. These lawyers pushed forward not just statutory private rights of action but also the procedural infrastructure and tort doctrines that would make such litigation economically viable. This story, then, cannot be fully separated from the growth of torts and other regulatory common law claims. Private enforcement in the twentieth century developed not in institutional isolation but as part of a broader evolution of American civil litigation, with the organized bar as a major architect and beneficiary.

## LAYER 1: DEEP LEGAL MEMORY AND PATH DEPENDENCE

At its core, a path dependence argument posits that "particular courses of action, once introduced, can be almost impossible to reverse; and consequently, political development is punctuated by critical moments or junctures that shape the basic contours of social life."[1] In other words, institutional choices create self-reinforcing dynamics that make alternative arrangements increasingly difficult to adopt over time. Margaret Levi argues that "[p]ath dependence has to mean, if it is to mean anything, that once a country or region has started down a track, the costs of reversal are very high. There will be other choice points, but the entrenchments of certain institutional arrangements obstruct an easy reversal of the initial choice."[2] Once a particular institutional path is established, it generates powerful feedback effects that lock in that trajectory and foreclose other possibilities. This creates a pattern where early choices have outsized and enduring consequences, as the costs of switching to alternative arrangements grow ever higher.

Leading scholars in history and political science emphasize that a well-founded path-dependence explanation must identify an initial critical juncture (a formative moment) marked by contingency, and then demonstrate the self-reinforcing mechanisms or increasing returns that produce institutional reproduction and stability over time.[3]

***1. Initial Template.*** From the moment the colonists arrived on the East Coast, American lawmakers inherited a template for outsourcing enforcement. We already know that English penal statutes and qui tam had, for centuries, let "common informers" sue in the King's name and pocket part of the penalty.[4] Parliament treated that bounty as the informer's property—so securely, in fact, that not even the Crown's pardon could extinguish it. As Chapter 3 discusses at length, colonists brought the entire template across the Atlantic, embedding private actions in everything from livestock rules to molasses tariffs, and supplementing them with common law writs or causes of action (for example, mandamus, quo warranto, nuisance, restraint of trade) that let citizens police officials and economic abuses alike. Remember that by the eve of independence, roughly a tenth of Massachusetts statutes depended on private plaintiffs willing to enforce public norms.

The common law was the other early ingredient, giving private litigation a major and default role in later statutes. Congress and state legislatures adopted new regulatory frameworks that built on a litigation-focused common law, giving rights to sue a primary role.

Scarce bureaucratic capacity turned this inherited template into a necessity. Colonial assemblies and, later, Congress, repeatedly drafted laws that paired official duties with informer bounties or actions, confident that private incentives would fill the gaps left by thin administrative staffs. The 1790 Samuel Dodge molasses-smuggling incident—where President Washington could pardon only the Treasury's share of a fine, not the informer's—solidified the institution: Once a statute vested enforcement in private hands, even executive clemency could not overwrite it. Far from an exotic workaround, private enforcement was the routine machinery through which early Americans—Jefferson, Madison, Adams, Story—expected regulatory rules, tax laws, and trade embargoes to bite.

***2. Self-Reinforcing Mechanisms.*** That early development set off path dependence, not as a historical relic but a self-reinforcing engine. Because penal statutes were "normal" by the 1790s, each new policy problem found Congress defaulting to the familiar template. Reusing boilerplate rights to sue was easy (there were no new inspectors to fund), politically saleable, and professionally lucrative for legislatures dominated by lawyers chummy with the legal profession. Every further deployment of a private enforcement regime strengthened judicial precedent, procedural infrastructure, and interest-group investment, further lowering the marginal cost of adding the next cause of action. In this way, demands for new statutes presented gaps that private suits could fill, while historical habit supplied the template, making private enforcement a low friction, highest payoff choice time and again.

Adopting private rights of action was cheap for legislators because they could just copy old statutes, avoiding costly negotiations and new regulatory structures. Consider, then, how textual connections between English and American statutes show that legislators were just reusing the English template. As recounted in Chapter 3, informer provisions in the 1800s used the same exact English phrasing: references to "any person" or phrases like "one-half to the use of the informer, and the other half to the use of the United States."[5] Beyond that, two critical examples show the reuse of older language: the Sherman Act and early American intellectual property statutes. First, the Sherman Act's private right of action was a copy-paste job of the 1623 English Statute of Monopolies. Both created private rights of action, treble damages in suits against monopolies, and used the same phrasing. Return again to the Sherman Act's key provision:

> Any person who shall be injured in his business or property by any other person or corporation by reason of anything forbidden or declared to be unlawful by this act, may sue therefor in any circuit court of the United States . . . and shall recover three fold the damages by him sustained, and the costs of suit, including a reasonable attorney's fee.[6]

And then the key language of the 1623 Statute on Monopolies:

> That if anie person or persons . . . shalbe hindered grieved disturbed or disquieted . . . and will sue . . . shall Recover three tymes soe much as the damages which hee or they susteyned . . .[7]

As discussed in Chapter 3, there are copy-pasted words here. "Any person" who "shall be" injured (or hindered, grieved, disturbed, etc.) can "sue" and collect "three" times damages "sustained." American legislators grabbed on to the English template even though the problems were significantly different. As previously mentioned, the Statute of Monopolies targeted Crown monopolies and was therefore a parliamentary victory. A private right of action was necessary. The Sherman Act, by contrast, tackled private monopolies and could therefore rely on public enforcement. Nonetheless, American legislators piled on a private right of action.

By the time of the Sherman Act, Congress could also draw on its own penal statutes and other private rights of action, including in the copyright and patent contexts. Return, then, to the 1790 Copyright Act ("An Act supplementary to . . . An Act for the encouragement of learning"), re-enacted with small updates in 1802 and 1856.[8] Here again we see a copy-paste of a British precedent: the Statute of Anne adopted by Parliament in 1710.[9] Oren Bracha writes that the sheer degree of identity between "the British [Statute of Anne] and the American copyright regime, ushered in by the state statutes of the 1780s and consolidated in the federal 1790 Copyright Act, is striking."[10] For example, the 1790 legislation directly adopted some of the Statute of Anne's text, as both were labeled as an "act for the encouragement of learning," and under both statutes, copyrights were effective for fourteen years. While the Statute of Anne protected only "printed books,"[11] the 1790 Copyright Act more broadly covered "map[s], chart[s], book[s]," and other writings.[12] The Statute of Anne stipulated two remedies: (1) "forfeiture and destruction of infringing copies," and (2) a "punitive sum" of one penny per sheet found to be in violation of the act, with the sum divided between the crown and an informer:[13]

> That every such offender or offenders shall forfeit one penny for every sheet which shall be found in his, her, or their custody, either printed or printing, published, or exposed to sale . . . the one moiety thereof to the Queen's most excellent majesty, her heirs and successors, and the other moiety thereof to any person or persons that shall sue for the same, to be recovered in any of her Majesty's courts of record at Westminister, by action of debt, bill, plaint, or information . . .[14]

Importantly, there was contingency in this initial adoption of informer claims, again supporting a path dependence dynamic. That is, Congress could have chosen a different path but decided to go the cheaper route due to self-reinforcing dynamics. The first version of the 1790 Act still embraced qui tam and split the penalty among:

> "the author . . . or the proprietor" and "any person or persons who shall sue for the same"[15]

But the final draft of the bill rejected this approach, instead dividing the sum between the government and "the author or proprietor of such map, chart, book or books who shall sue for the same."[16] This would've been a weaker form of private enforcement—empowering only a small subset of plaintiffs, rather than the broader "any person" configuration from English practice. But by 1802, Congress again went back to a regular informer provision, providing "one moiety thereof to any person who shall sue for the same, and the other moiety thereof to and for the use of the United States, to be recovered in any court having competent jurisdiction thereof."[17] Thus, the 1802 amendment added back in the informer language that Congress dispensed of in the 1790 Copyright Act.

The lesson here is that from the Founding on, American legislators defaulted to previous statutory arrangements, making private enforcement a cheap statutory design. This generated a continuous deep legal memory and path dependence that shaped every later era. When the Progressive Era and New Deal confronted trusts and wages, Congress simply bolted a right to sue, damages, and fee-shifting onto the familiar framework. Notwithstanding the strong support for statist solutions in the 1930s, the American commitment to private enforcement remained salient. When the civil rights and environmental revolutions feared executive over-or underenforcement, legislators again reached for private suits to supplement public enforcement. Because the United States never dismantled its penal statute heritage, each generation could repurpose it—augmented by new procedures discussed below—into a mass-litigation engine that coexists with, rather than replaces, burgeoning bureaucracies.

Again, this means that part of the puzzle is not only Americans' reliance on private enforcement, but also why peer nations that once shared the same lineage chose, by the early twentieth century, to put their faith mostly in public prosecutors and agencies instead.

***3. Critical Juncture and Contingency in 1914.*** As we've seen, the American tradition evolved to embrace both public and private enforcers, working together in complex legal ecosystems. The congressional decision in 1914 to adopt the twin bills—the Clayton Act and Federal Trade Commission Act—represents a critical juncture that altered the trajectory of American regulatory governance. Critical junctures are key moments that launch or alter path-dependent sequences and can transform the historical trajectories of institutions. In one sense, a critical juncture is a short period of transformation "during which more dramatic change is possible" than normal.[18] Choices made during such junctures have lasting impacts—they "close off alternative options and lead to the establishment of institutions that generate self-reinforcing path-dependent processes."[19]

The 1914 adoption of the twin antitrust bills was just such a critical juncture. President Woodrow Wilson and Congress faced a stark choice between Roosevelt's vision of administrative regulation and the traditional American reliance on private litigation, yet rather than choosing one path, they institutionalized both approaches simultaneously. The American willingness to see private and public enforcers as complementary established a template that would define American regulatory policy for the next century. The Clayton Act strengthened private enforcement through treble damages, fee-shifting, and allowing private plaintiffs to use government judgments as evidence of violations, while the Federal Trade Commission Act created only the second major federal regulatory agency with broad investigative and enforcement powers.

The key American innovation is that legislators did not see a conflict between these two approaches. They decided that American governance could embrace bureaucratic solutions while retaining its historical reliance on private rights of action. This innovation was highly contingent—in the UK, after the emergence of a robust bureaucracy, members of parliament began to see qui tam as unnecessary and counterproductive.[20] The American fusion, by contrast, created the modern American approach to regulation: complex legal ecosystems where private enforcers and public agencies work in tandem rather than as alternatives. This hybrid model became self-reinforcing as subsequent regulatory statutes—from securities law to environmental protection to civil rights—would consistently adopt the 1914 template of pairing robust administrative agencies with private rights of action, making the choice to embrace both enforcement mechanisms a defining characteristic of American governance.

Again, keep in mind that the choice of 1914 was contingent. One hallmark of path-dependent explanations is the concept of contingency—the idea that major historical developments cannot be predicted simply from antecedent conditions, and that seemingly small events can alter the entire course of institutional development. The 1914 antitrust legislation perfectly illustrates this contingency. Wilson initially opposed administrative commissions during his 1912 campaign, favoring instead the dismantling of monopolies through traditional litigation. Roosevelt championed bureaucratic oversight through expert agencies. Either approach could have become the dominant American model—a world of primarily private enforcement resembling today's civil rights law, or primarily administrative enforcement similar to European regulatory systems. Yet a combination of political pressures, Wilson's evolving views, and strategic legislative timing produced an entirely different outcome: the institutionalization of both approaches simultaneously, creating a uniquely American hybrid that neither candidate had originally envisioned.

A remarkable fact is that both Woodrow Wilson's and Teddy Roosevelt's views were evolving in the years before 1914. As discussed in the previous chapter, Wilson initially resisted bureaucratic management of trusts, only to relax his position in a speech to Congress.[21] Between 1905 and 1908, Roosevelt also changed his view of the balance between litigation and *ex ante* review, embracing bureaucratic regulation along the way. After burnishing his trust-busting reputation, Roosevelt shifted his tone in his 1905 State of the Union address, arguing that it is "generally useless to try to prohibit all restraint on competition . . . and where it is not useless it is generally hurtful."[22] And in 1908 he suggested important changes to the Sherman Act:

> The substantive part of the anti-trust law should remain as at present; that is, every contract in restraint of trade or commerce among the several States or with foreign nations should continue to be declared illegal; provided, however, that *some popular governmental authority (such as the Commissioner of Corporations acting under the Secretary of Commerce and Labor) be allowed to pass on any such contracts.*[23]

As Arthur Johnson notes, "Roosevelt, who had done much to make the Sherman Act a meaningful weapon of public policy, now brought the power of the presidency to bear in support of an effort to weaken it."[24] Chairman of the US Steel Board of Directors Judge Elbert H. Gary, US Steel chief counsel Francis Lynde Stetson, and attorney Victor Morawetz prepared a bill incorporating Roosevelt's suggestions for the National Civic Federation, which Representative William P. Hepburn introduced into Congress on March 23, 1908 (the "Hepburn bill").[25] In a March 28, 1908 message to Congress, Roosevelt endorsed the Hepburn bill as a "very good bill,"[26] arguing that industrial combinations were "absolutely necessary." In terms of substance, the Hepburn bill empowered the bureaucracy, allowing non-common-carrier corporations to register with the Commissioner of Corporations "under conditions to be specified by the President."[27] Such corporations could submit proposed contracts or combinations to the Commissioner, who would then determine whether these proposals were unreasonable. If the Commissioner did not make a finding of unreasonableness within thirty days, the applicants were protected from suit by the government for any reasonable restraint of trade.[28] As proposed under the bill, certain contracts that would have been prohibited by the Sherman Act would now be granted a "special immunity," and the "dispensation of this immunity . . . should not be trusted to the courts nor even to that branch of the government concerned in the administration of justice, but rather to a bureau in the Department of Commerce and Labor."[29] In other words, unlike the Sherman Act, which had "left it to the courts to define what combinations were guilty of crime," the sponsors of the proposed Hepburn Bill "left it to the Bureau of Corporations or other appropriate executive body."[30]

But the Hepburn bill faced significant opposition in the media, industry groups, and in Congress. Roosevelt withdrew support for the bill and it then died in committee.[31] The move towards bureaucratic regulation thus stalled.

With matters in flux after 1908, it truly was the adoption of the twin bills in 1914 that finally settled the matter—embracing both private and public enforcement simultaneously.

## COROLLARY: AMERICANS DO NOT FEAR BUREAUCRACY, ONLY MONOPOLY

Some scholars have mistakenly referred to American legal culture as suffused with skepticism of bureaucracies, making private enforcement an anti-statist device. That view misunderstands the development of private enforcement *alongside* public bureaucracies. Taking the deep history into account, it is more accurate to say that legal elites feared giving bureaucracies a *monopoly* over enforcement power, not just additional power by itself. And, moreover, those elites saw no conflict between private and public enforcement.

Begin with an early clue that Americans did not outright reject bureaucrats: The colonies created public prosecutors nearly a century before England. This powerful figure of a public prosecutor, carrying the full might of the state, is according to Professor Jack M. Kress "a distinctive and uniquely American contribution . . . . Whereas Americans typically describe their legal system as based upon English common law, in terms of both its procedural attributes and substantive state penal codes, the public prosecutor is a figure virtually unknown to the English system, which is primarily one of private prosecution to this day."[32] Joan Jacoby traces the history of public prosecutors, noting that the colonies drew on Dutch traditions and "[b]y 1704, one colony, Connecticut, had adopted a system of public prosecution and all others would soon follow."[33]

By the mid-1700s, most colonies, including New York and Pennsylvania, had "officers of the court or representatives of the attorney general" who presented indictments and managed felony trials at public expense.[34] This was the early emergence of bureaucracy, long before Westminster enacted the Prosecution of Offences Act in 1879. England, by contrast, relied entirely on private plaintiffs to hire their own attorneys and prosecute cases on behalf of the King. If anything, early Americans were more comfortable with bureaucrats than the English were at that time. In short, the American colonial instinct was not to exclude bureaucrats, but the opposite.

What American elites have consistently resisted is giving public officials a monopoly on enforcement. That has been a recurrent pattern: Every landmark statute that expanded private lawsuits was partnered with, created, or beefed up a federal enforcement office. Congress followed the False Claims Act (1863) with an enlarged, post-Civil War Department of Justice born in 1870; adopted the twin bills of the Federal Trade Commission (1914) alongside the Clayton Act's treble-damage remedy; created the National Labor Relations Board in 1935 and, three years later, gave workers their own wages and hours lawsuits under the FLSA; created the Civil Rights Division of the Department of Justice in 1957, before embracing both Title VII's right to sue provision and the Equal Employment Opportunity Commission; and, in 1970, launched the Environmental Protection Agency while arming "any person" with citizen suits in the Clean Air and Clean Water Acts. Yes, private rights multiplied, but so did the bureaucracy.[35]

Even more, sometimes Congress specifically refused to give private parties a right to sue, preferring bureaucracy instead. Congress created the FDA in the 1906 Pure Food and Drugs Act and bolstered its power via the Food, Drug, and Cosmetic Act of 1938—but never created an accompanying right to sue for related violations.[36] When it created the FTC, Congress did not fashion a general right to sue over consumer fraud violations either. It did later add a dollop of private enforcement in the Fair Debt Collection Practices Act, allowing consumers to sue for discrete violations.[37] But Congress doubled down on public enforcement later on, adopting in 2010 the Dodd-Frank Act, a statute that built a powerful new agency called the Consumer Financial Protection Bureau (CFPB). Although this agency had wide-ranging power to police the consumer financial industry, Congress refused to provide an accompanying private right to sue. As I previously argued, "[b]y creating the CFPB, and providing that agency with the power to issue broad civil investigative demands, the statute reordered the entire area . . . toward public enforcement. The CFPB . . . occupied the field and displaced the relevance of private claims (both state and federal)."[38]

Why stack these mechanisms? Legal elites trusted bureaucratic expertise for fact-finding and standard-setting yet feared concentrating all coercive power inside a single agency vulnerable to capture, budget cuts, or partisan swings. Delegating a parallel right to sue hedges the project: If the FTC, NLRB, EEOC, or EPA falters, injured parties and entrepreneurial lawyers can still press the law in court. Conversely, agency investigations generate records and liability findings that private plaintiffs can leverage, making litigation cheaper and more accurate. The logic is complementarity, not substitution.

As discussed above, a key feature of American legal culture is to see no conflict between private and public enforcement. Wilson and Brandeis's embrace of the Clayton Act and the FTC Act was premised on the idea of complementarity: Private lawsuits will target different antitrust violations and will dodge any problems with regulatory capture. As we'll see later, in England, once bureaucracies demonstrated high levels of expertise and independence, elites saw private enforcement as redundant or, worse, harmful. This rarely happened in the United States. If there is an American predilection, then, it is to embrace both private and public enforcers and to expect them to play different roles.

Another problem for the claim that suspicions of government bureaucracy fuel demands for litigation is that the judiciary is also a bureaucracy. Private enforcement delegates power to attorneys and judges. Yet there is an American cultural strand of deep skepticism of judges and lawyers, too (think of the insult "ambulance chasers" or defenses of the jury trial as a way to disempower judges). It seems almost self-refuting to say that Americans are so suspicious of government administrators (public enforcement) that they prefer a different set of administrators that go by the name "judge" (private enforcement).

Again, this layered architecture undercuts the claim, common in the "adversarial legalism" literature, that Americans cling to private lawsuits because they distrust bureaucracy.[39] The evidence suggests something else: Congress adds bureaucracy whenever it adds private enforcement, creating a multi-headed system in which public lawyers, administrative experts, juries, and private attorneys all monitor one another. The real fear is exclusive or monopoly power, not administrative power per se. That insight harmonizes with the path-dependence story from the previous section: Inherited penal statutes made private actions cheap and familiar, while a growing, Hamiltonian[40] state supplied the professional officials Americans were perfectly willing to fund, but never to trust alone.

## LAYER 2: STRUCTURAL INCENTIVES, LAWYERS, AND INTEREST GROUPS

If Layer 1 explains why the tool was on the shelf, Layer 2 explains why Congress keeps reaching for it. As discussed above, there are micro-level explanations for why Congress defaults to private rights of action: The reuse of boilerplate provisions is cheap and politically saleable. But at the more structural level, there are two important influences that align with Farhang's and Kagan's work: the American fragmentation of power and lobbying dynamics.

***1. Vertical and Horizontal Fragmentation.*** The separation of powers breaks lawmaking from execution and gives Congress recurring incentives to double up enforcement. When the White House or future appropriations turn hostile, a private right of action (plus multiple damages or fee-shifting) is the one budget line legislators can lock in on day one. Here, Farhang's work shows that divided power at the federal level increases the likelihood of private enforcement clauses, at least in the 1960s and 1970s. In this telling, private suits are thus less a cultural preference than a structural hedge; they ensure the statute against bureaucratic drift or sabotage.

Vertical fragmentation via federalism deepens the logic. Many programs—wage laws, housing, pollution control—depend first on state or local officials whose zeal, resources, and politics vary wildly. A nationwide right to sue bypasses those bottlenecks, letting anyone activate the federal courts. This is where path dependence kicks in: Because the procedural infrastructure is already in place, the marginal cost of adding a right to sue is trivial compared with launching a new bureaucracy. Each successful use of the device (e.g., the Sherman Act, FLSA, Title VII, the Clean Air Act) strengthens that infrastructure, lowering the barrier for the next statute. Structural incentives and accumulated legal machinery reinforce one another in a loop.

Another form of path dependence occurs when a legislative tool becomes a default. After two centuries of private enforcement provisions, legislators treat a private right of action as boilerplate. Faced with electoral pressure to "do something," they can punt the enforcement question to private parties and the courts. A revealing example comes from Mississippi. In 2005 the legislature passed a bill safeguarding the confidentiality of DUI records and, with almost no debate, inserted a sentence authorizing "[a]ny person whose confidential record" had been disclosed to sue.[41] When a litigant later invoked that provision and the state court of appeals upheld standing, lawmakers were startled enough to repeal the cause of action outright at the next session.[42] The episode suggests the clause had slipped in by habit, not design—a rote inclusion until its consequences became visible.

Path dependence, then, is doing two kinds of work. Deep legal memory supplies a familiar template that makes private enforcement cheap and credible. Constitutional structure—the fragmentation of power both horizontally and vertically—makes that template continually attractive. Together they drive Congress almost automatically to add a right to sue even when it is simultaneously building a new bureaucracy.

***2. Interest Groups and the Lawyer's Lobby.*** Interest groups represent another powerful force shaping the legislative adoption of private enforcement. Behind every legislative debate discussed in Chapter 4, interest groups actively mobilized to secure and strengthen private rights of action. The logic here is simple: Pro-litigation interest groups often argue that bureaucracies are unduly influenced by industry and regulated entities (as discussed in the next chapter). Private lawsuits, by contrast, give members of those groups direct power. This dynamic aligns with classic public choice theory, which predicts that concentrated interests can successfully lobby for favorable statutory changes.[43] In most regulatory areas, at least one concentrated interest group has a strong incentive to mobilize for private enforcement: employees in labor law, consumers in antitrust and product safety, shareholders in securities regulation, and environmentalists in pollution control. And, of course, the plaintiffs' bar (and legal profession as a whole) has an incentive to lobby for litigation as a regulatory solution.

From this perspective, private rights of action may represent legislative giveaways to organized constituencies. Rights to sue also cost legislators little in terms of government expenditure while generating political support from key groups. (Though increasing litigation risks alienating business groups, who are likely to be major campaign contributors.) This creates a political economy where private enforcement becomes an attractive compromise that allows legislators to satisfy organized interests without the budgetary commitments of robust public enforcement.

Scholars have long highlighted the influence of interest groups in different historical chapters of private enforcement. Sean Farhang, for instance, demonstrated the influence of interest groups on the 1991 Civil Rights Act, finding that civil rights organizations strategically pushed to expand damages available under Title VII. Those organizations were explicitly responding to what they regarded as "an excessively conservative judiciary that they believed was making it too difficult for plaintiffs to prevail."[44] This tactical use of private enforcement reflected a sophisticated understanding by advocacy groups of the advantages of these statutory rights. Interest groups thus become political entrepreneurs, recognizing that private enforcement can provide durable policy victories that survive changes in political control.

Beyond specific advocacy groups, the legal profession itself represents one of America's most powerful and organized lobbying forces, with attorneys consistently overrepresented in legislatures and maintaining strong professional associations. Lawyers possess obvious financial incentives to support litigation-based solutions to regulatory problems, as private enforcement mechanisms directly expand the market for legal services and create new revenue streams. This dynamic creates a structural bias in favor of private enforcement among the very lawmakers (many of whom are attorneys themselves) responsible for drafting regulatory statutes. The prevalence of private rights of action may partly reflect the legal profession's institutional self-interest rather than purely policy considerations.

America's unique federal structure can amplify the role of interest groups at least over state governments—contrary to Madison's argument in *The Federalist* No. 10—allowing policy entrepreneurs from across the country to lobby particular state legislatures. The development of state consumer protection laws in the 1960s illustrates the combination of federalism and interest group advocacy. Professor Myriam Gilles documented how consumer advocates, energized by figures like Ralph Nader, successfully championed Unfair and Deceptive Acts and Practices (UDAP) statutes across most states.[45] These laws weren't imposed through top-down federal mandates but emerged from coordinated advocacy by consumer organizations working with sympathetic officials, including Federal Trade Commission leadership. These actors actively encouraged states to adopt dual enforcement models combining public enforcement by attorneys general with private rights of action for consumers. Gilles argues that early consumer lawyers "learned the ropes at the newly established National Consumer Law Center" and strategically pushed for robust statutory remedies that would make private enforcement economically viable.[46] This consumer advocacy campaign was systematic and reflected the failures of inadequate federal agencies in policing everyday marketplace abuse. Even something as seemingly scattered as "consumers" resulted in an interest group campaign that successfully mobilized for private enforcement in state legislatures.

But interest group dynamics are more complex than simple advocacy for private rights of action. In every regulatory area, private enforcement creates winners and losers, pitting the interest groups that would benefit from litigation rights against those seeking to avoid them—workers versus employers, shareholders versus companies, consumers versus producers, and so on. Yet this opposition isn't necessarily symmetrical because regulated entities often face a strategic choice between private and public enforcers, and it's unclear which option serves their interests better. Some industries may prefer government enforcement if they believe they can capture or influence regulatory agencies through lobbying, revolving door relationships, or technical complexity that favors industry expertise. But other industries may actually prefer private enforcement to blunt the creation of powerful new regulatory agencies, calculating that dispersed private litigation poses less of a threat than a well-funded, expert bureaucracy.

The classic public choice insight that concentrated interests can outweigh diffused interests adds another layer of complexity here. This dynamic suggests that the more diffuse the potential beneficiary group, the less likely Congress will adopt a private right of action, as diffuse interests struggle to organize effective lobbying campaigns. Consumer protection exemplifies this challenge: While consumer fraud affects virtually everyone, the costs are typically small and widely distributed, making it difficult for consumers to mobilize as effectively as concentrated business interests.

***3. Lobbies and the Civil-Criminal Divide.*** A public choice framework can also help explain the paradoxical contrast between civil and criminal enforcement. While the United States has embraced private enforcement more extensively than other democracies in regulatory areas, it has simultaneously concentrated criminal prosecution authority in the executive branch to a degree that exceeds even England. The Supreme Court explicitly noted in *United States v. Nixon* that "the Executive Branch has exclusive authority and absolute discretion to decide whether to prosecute a case."[47] This is a monopolistic concentration of enforcement power in a public office. The apparent contrast with regulatory statutes seems to be a compelling rejoinder to the path-dependence account laid out above. That is, if path-dependence dynamics (and fear of a public monopoly of enforcement) are so powerful, why do we see a different path in the criminal context? A full answer is outside the scope of this book, but this paradox becomes more comprehensible when viewed through two angles.

First, the distinction is somewhat illusory because the United States continues to rely on private actors to enforce criminal laws. A significant portion of the criminal law literature recognizes that private actors are active players in criminal enforcement, especially when that term is construed to include the front-end investigatory work that is part and parcel of the criminal enforcement machine.[48] Private actors receive enforcement authority both implicitly as a legacy of historical practice and explicitly via statute. For instance, private prosecution of criminal conduct, once the primary force behind criminal legal proceedings, continues today in a variety of modes, both through direct prosecution by private actors as well as outsourcing of public prosecution to private firms.[49] As to the first pathway,

Professor Emma Kaufman finds that at least seven states allow for independent private prosecution of criminal cases.[50] An additional twenty states allow private plaintiffs to prosecute criminal cases alongside, or on behalf of, public prosecutors.[51] Thus, over half of the states allow direct private prosecution in some respect or another. Beyond this, Kaufman notes that many prosecutors outsource the lower rungs of their caseloads to private firms.[52]

Recent literature has identified similar undercurrents of express private prosecution of criminal cases.[53] More than that, some civil suits, particularly under tort law, functionally allow private parties to haul perpetrators into court for conduct that is circumscribed by criminal statute, even if not in criminal proceedings.[54] Or return to the RICO private right of action, which allows civil claims against criminal enterprises. Less formally, many private organizations adjudicate criminal conduct through extrajudicial tribunals—indeed, in the corporate context, human resources and administrative functions play a quiet role in handling conduct which would otherwise be triable in criminal court.[55] More controversially, individual actors may seek to privately negotiate for remedial action from criminal perpetrators, using the long shadow of coercive state power as bargaining leverage.[56] The American criminal justice system, then, gives private actors some enforcement power.

Moreover, as discussed above, criminal reliance on public enforcement emerged during the colonial period. Some of this reliance draws on English traditions, especially the Crown's power over private criminal prosecutions as well as pardons. While the Crown could never control informers, it could employ a writ called "nolle prosequi" to dismiss private criminal indictments. That and the pardon power gave the Crown, and later governors and presidents, a powerful influence over criminal law. And drawing from the Dutch tradition, the colonies departed from English institutions by empowering public prosecutors to enforce criminal penalties, further cementing public enforcement of criminal law.[57] Taking this into account, the paradox nearly disappears—there has been no divergence over time but rather a civil-criminal distinction has existed from the outset.

Second, the interest group angle may explain what remains of the civil-criminal paradox. The fundamental difference lies in the structure of affected interests—regulatory schemes typically create identifiable, concentrated groups of potential "victims" who can effectively lobby for private enforcement. These groups include employees facing workplace violations, environmental groups confronting pollution, shareholders suffering from securities fraud, or consumers dealing with deceptive practices. They are repeat players with ongoing stakes in enforcement outcomes, making political mobilization both feasible and worthwhile. Even more, the plaintiffs' bar is an influential interest group, wielding power through both legislative lobbying and direct participation in elected office. If the relevant interest group is the lawyers' bar, there's even more reason to expect private enforcement on the civil side.

Criminal law, by contrast, affects a diffuse population of potential victims who do not know *ex ante* that they will be harmed and thus cannot organize effective lobbying coalitions before crimes occur. Prosecuting criminal cases is also not a profitable enterprise for plaintiffs' lawyers. This asymmetry in organizational capacity may help explain why private enforcement continued to flourish in regulatory law while somewhat declining in criminal enforcement. If true, this suggests that interest group politics may be as important as constitutional principles in shaping America's distinctive approach to legal enforcement.

## A NOTE OF CAUTION: THE CASE OF FRANCE'S CIVIL RIGHTS ACT

So the legislative adoption of a private right of action leads to private enforcement of the law, right? If that were enough, then a lot of countries would develop private enforcement like the United States. France, for instance, has sometimes adopted private rights of action. And it also has a separation of powers between the legislature and the president. Indeed, in the 1970s, France adopted a private right of action for employment discrimination similar to the Civil Rights Act.[58] Is French private enforcement just like the United States? No, not at all. And the reasons why are telling.

France's post-1972 equality regime at first glance looks strikingly like Title VII. Successive statutes and Labor Code amendments ban hiring, pay, and promotion discrimination on virtually the same list of protected grounds, include burden shifting, and authorize civil lawsuits by victims or representative associations. So far so good.

Yet, as Julie Suk's comparative study reveals, "most employment discrimination cases are litigated through criminal rather than civil proceedings."[59] Far from successfully adopting private enforcement, victim suits are overshadowed by criminal enforcement, the institutional mirror image of the US model. This aligns with the example of oil spills that we covered in Chapter 1, too. Where Americans file civil damages actions in federal court, French complainants proceed through criminal complaints.

The basic reason, Suk argues, is procedural plumbing—or the lack of it—in French civil justice. French labor tribunals offer no pre-trial discovery, depositions, expansive subpoenas, or interrogatories, key ingredients to successful lawsuits in the US. By contrast, a criminal investigating magistrate can subpoena documents, search company premises, and compel witness testimony—the functional equivalents of US civil discovery.[60] Thus, even after Parliament in 2001 eased the civil burden of proof (and even after EU directives mandated effective civil remedies), plaintiffs and advocacy groups kept steering cases to criminal court because that was the only venue where they could obtain evidence.

This institutional inversion means that France's private enforcement scheme exists in name only. Civil judgments remain rare, group actions unusual, and the damages available to individual employees seldom create deterrence.[61] Suk notes that whereas American procedure turns private lawyers into enforcers, French law still relies on public prosecutors.

Finally, Suk argues that France's criminal enforcement results from procedural path dependence. When legislators first responded to employment discrimination in 1972, the country already had a hate speech crime with a ready-made criminal investigative apparatus.[62] Grafting workplace discrimination onto that familiar framework was simpler than building a new civil justice infrastructure. Once the pattern was set, each additional layer—judicial expertise, non-governmental organization (NGO) strategy, doctrinal tweaks—reinforced the criminal preference.

Suk concludes that France's experience demonstrates "how, over time, a regulated behavior comes to be regarded by different legal systems as substantively criminal or civil in nature as a result of the procedural dynamics of enforcement."[63] Lacking discovery, fee-shifting, and aggregation, private civil enforcement has not gained traction. But the US, equipped with those tools, kept expanding them and building on its private enforcement framework.[64]

## LAYER 3: PROCEDURAL ENABLERS IN 1938 AND 1966

French employment discrimination teaches us that undergirding a system of private enforcement is the field of civil procedure. The rules of litigation enable and expand the role of private enforcement in the system. As the French example shows, a private right of action by itself does nothing. It needs to be partnered with procedural plumbing; by deciding who may invoke the courts, what information they can demand, and how costs are allocated, procedural doctrines calibrate the incentives that litigants and judges face. From this perspective, procedure becomes the enabling system for Congress and state legislatures' delegation of enforcement power to private actors: The rules determine whether new statutory rights lie dormant or are energetically vindicated in the real world.

Let's focus on two key procedures that are nearly unique in the United States and necessary to make private enforcement flourish: discovery and class actions.

***1. Discovery After 1938.*** At the center of US civil litigation is the ability of plaintiffs and defendants to find important information that can resolve a case. Our procedural system fills this gap through a robust information exchange process that we call discovery.

At the most basic level, every dispute-resolution system must decide when and how litigants and the adjudicator will learn the relevant facts. Civil law jurisdictions concentrate that task in a judge-directed dossier assembled late in the case, often inside the courtroom itself. The American procedural tradition, by contrast, disperses the fact-finding task into a party-controlled, discovery phase spanning document requests, depositions, and expert reports. Conceptually, trial and discovery perform the same function—each is an information-forcing mechanism designed to narrow uncertainty and permit rational settlement, default, or judgment. But they allocate that function differently: Trial bundles fact-finding into a single public event, whereas discovery stretches it across months of private exchange. Because parties' litigation calculus turns on expected trial value minus costs, the choice between fact gathering at trial and party-led discovery is a critical one for the entire legal system.

Historically, the existence of the lay jury drove the development of procedural rules.[65] In medieval England, the twelve local men sworn on the jury roll were presumed to already know the facts, so the system needed almost no pre-trial information exchange. The primary pre-trial device was a tightly scripted pleading sequence whose sole aim was to crystallize a single issue—law or fact—that could be presented to the panel; everything else waited for trial. Because the jury could be convened only once, parties had no right to depose witnesses or compel records beforehand; if a factual question remained after the pleadings, the case went straight to trial, where examination of witnesses doubled as real-time discovery. That arrangement simplified what an untrained jury would see, but it was costly: Counsel had to assemble twelve lay judges, educate them in open court, and manage the unpredictability of live testimony. Thus, the common law's reliance on trials was not a philosophical choice about adversarialism. Rather, it was a practical solution to the burdens and advantages of using ordinary citizens as the ultimate fact-finders.

But England also had a separate court that eventually came to be known as "equity." In equity, there was no lay jury to shield, so chancery judges felt free to turn the whole pre-hearing phase into a search of the parties' books, letters, and testimony. A complainant filed a bill of discovery that compelled the defendant to answer written interrogatories, could sometimes depose witnesses (especially after the mid-nineteenth century), and could subpoena broad categories of documents. These devices—developed precisely because equity sat away from juries and prized justice over procedural form—made the gathering and testing of facts an elongated, paper-heavy process completed before the Chancellor ever heard argument.

By the twentieth century, that flexible equity toolkit had proven so effective that the 1938 Federal Rules of Civil Procedure (the "Rules") simply transplanted it into a merged civil procedure, turning equitable discovery into the engine of modern American litigation.[66] The Federal Rules, in other words, turned discovery into *the* central process for obtaining information in a civil lawsuit, supplanting the common law trial's role. The Rules (and case law and changes since then) allow litigants to compel one another to turn over virtually every type of information related to the dispute. The Rules supply a full arsenal—initial disclosures, document requests, oral and written depositions, interrogatories, requests for admission, physical or property inspections, and even third-party subpoenas.

Keep in mind, too, that as federal procedure embraced broad discovery for private plaintiffs in 1938, there was intense contestation over the power of administrative agencies to subpoena private documents. Mariano Cuellar writes that the lack of subpoena power weakened the New Deal commitment to administrative enforcement: "Agencies faced constraints from scarce resources, and in many cases were charged with enforcing laws regulating economic, labor, or health-related activity difficult to pinpoint without the ability to subpoena documentary records."[67] The lack of an expansive power to obtain documents was absolutely necessary; without "basic information from regulated parties, it would be difficult for agencies to decide whom to treat as suspicious in the first place."[68] Courts were nonetheless reluctant to allow searching subpoenas, with the Supreme Court noting in 1936 that "leaving the power to subpoena in [some] situations with agencies such as the SEC would place the government at risk of 'becom[ing] an autocracy.'"[69] This skeptical approach faded after 1945, institutionalizing administrative subpoenas *but only after* civil discovery.

Discovery today gives private plaintiffs tools that are very similar to subpoena power. Federal Rules 26 through 37 give litigants a broad discovery power. After the parties exchange their Rule 26(a) initial disclosures, each side may serve interrogatories (written questions answered under oath), requests for the production of any non-privileged documents or tangible things "relevant to any party's claim or defense," and requests for admission.[70] They can issue third-party subpoenas under Rule 45; conduct oral or video depositions of parties, officers, and non-parties anywhere in the world; and, under certain circumstances, compel medical examinations.[71] Because Rule 26(b)(1) defines relevance broadly—"any non-privileged matter that is relevant . . . and proportional to the needs of the case"—these tools reach drafts, internal e-mails, backup tapes, and metadata that would never surface in most civil law systems.[72] Discovery is also iterative: Answers received may themselves create follow-up demands, so the factual record grows until the parties stipulate, settle, or the court decides. All of this creates a fact-finding regime unrivaled in scope.

American discovery is also unrivaled in how much power it gives parties to lead the process away from the court.[73] All of these devices issue without any need for judicial pre-approval. And they operate on a producer-pays norm, so the responding side shoulders the cost of collecting and reviewing its own data. In effect, private parties wield almost every information-forcing tool that federal agencies use.

From a comparative vantage point, the US regime is a true outlier. What Americans treat as an essential component of due process—some scholars even press a constitutional pedigree for liberal discovery—strikes nearly every other legal culture as extravagant or dangerous. Even other common law systems permit only targeted production tied to "specific pleading," impose tight time limits, and read the producing party's obligation narrowly, yielding an exchange of information that is significantly tighter than ours.[74] Civil law jurisdictions go further still: Fact development is micromanaged by the judge, depositions are unknown (and even illegal in many countries), and parties cannot compel the sweeping production of documents. The idea that private attorneys might depose witnesses for seven hours, sift an adversary's e-mail server, or insist on metadata would be unthinkable in France, Germany, or Japan. That is why foreign commentators have long criticized American discovery as costly and abusive.

But with private enforcement in mind, it makes perfect sense for discovery to be so thorough in the United States. After all, some of the most critical regulatory regimes hinge on private lawsuits. Those statutes work only if the plaintiffs who police them can actually uncover the evidence buried inside corporations and government agencies. That is why I have previously argued that modern discovery should be understood as a regulatory device and "the lynchpin of private enforcement," an outsourced analogue to the administrative subpoena power wielded by agencies such as the SEC, FTC, or EPA.[75] Congress deliberately armed private litigants with this investigatory authority because it would not give agencies a monopoly over enforcement. Broad discovery, then, lets plaintiffs act as roving bureaucrats, flushing out wrongdoing, raising the probability of detection, and making lawsuits a credible threat.

We should think of discovery as a critical regulatory device that is fundamental to American governance. Empirical and doctrinal work shows that the prospect of deep, compulsory discovery reshapes behavior far beyond the four corners of any single lawsuit.[76] There are many examples of this in the real world. For instance, in a case by shareholders against Disney Co., plaintiffs discovered thousands of documents of boardroom transcripts, and although Disney ultimately won at trial, the material spurred governance overhauls at Disney and peer companies and informed later SEC compensation rules. Medical malpractice suits have similarly driven systemic safety reforms at hospitals, while employment discrimination discovery has rewritten workplace policies nationwide. Environmental, antitrust, and mass tort cases display the same pattern: Once internal e-mails and other data can be discovered in civil litigation, firms begin to police themselves to avoid future exposure.

In most countries, only the state can compel similar discovery. In the United States, by contrast, the Federal Rules deliberately delegated that subpoena-like authority to plaintiffs. In previous work, I have explained that discovery mirrors agency subpoenas along four dimensions—ex parte issuance, breadth, identical investigative tools, and a producer-pays cost rule—making it the functional twin of the SEC's or EPA's compulsory process.[77] By transforming lawyers into adjunct regulators, this arrangement lets the United States achieve robust deterrence without building a vast public bureaucracy, while still allowing elected legislators to decide where private enforcement should supplement bureaucratic power.

Discovery is why the Civil Rights Act's right to sue is wildly successful while its French equivalent is a failure. It is why the SEC repeatedly argues that plaintiffs' attorneys are necessary to police the securities market. It is also why private antitrust enforcement is robust in the United States (across the fifty states and the federal courts). And it is even why environmental litigation is costly and influential in the country. Private enforcement in these regulatory areas hinges on broad discovery.

***2. Class Actions After 1966.*** In addition to discovery, the Federal Rules of Civil Procedure allow plaintiffs to bring class action claims.[78] A class action is a procedural device that lets one or a handful of named representatives pursue a claim for an entire group whose members suffered the same legal wrong—defective product, discriminatory policy, price-fixing cartel, and so on. Once a court certifies the "class," the representatives and their lawyers control the suit; absent members need not appear, file papers, or even know the case exists, yet a judgment on the merits will bind every person who falls within the certified definition unless they opt out. That capacity to confer preclusive effect on non-participants—turning thousands or millions of dispersed injuries into a single, system-wide adjudication—is what sets Rule 23 class actions apart from other aggregation tools.

Class actions have a long history in England, beginning in 1190 and extending through equity practice and into the modern Rule 23. For centuries, these representative suits allowed plaintiffs to seek injunctions. But the revolutionary moment came when the Advisory Committee (in charge of proposing amendments to the Federal Rules of Civil Procedure) overhauled Rule 23 in 1966.[79] Modern class actions come in two main flavors. One kind—created in the 1960s to tackle school segregation—focuses on winning a single court order that stops the defendant's policy for everyone. For instance, in school desegregation cases, it was important to get one court order against a school district that could force it to desegregate. Because the goal is the same for all class members, no one gets to "opt out"; the ruling automatically protects every student in the group. The second kind, added at the same time but aimed at money claims, lets people band together when each individual loss (a fraudulent fee by a bank or an overpriced product) is too small to sue over alone. Here, group members can step aside if they prefer to go it alone, but most stay because a pooled case is cheaper and stronger. This money-damages model is the workhorse of modern private enforcement: It powers consumer-fraud, wage-and-hour, antitrust, and product-defect cases by rolling thousands of small harms into a single lawsuit big enough to get the company's attention and fund skilled lawyers on a contingency fee.

From a comparative angle, the American opt-out, money-damages class action is still an oddity. Most countries that now allow group proceedings limit them to certified consumer associations or government-approved bodies and require each injured person to opt in before a judgment can bind them. Even the common law cousins who borrowed Rule 23—Australia and Canada copied it only in the 1990s, decades after the United States—and civil law adopters in Europe and Latin America have trimmed its wings with tighter certification tests, no contingency fees, and far narrower discovery.[80] As legal scholar Deborah Hensler notes, more than thirty-five jurisdictions now permit some form of representative suit, yet none match the US model's combination of private lawyers, opt-out membership, and sweeping monetary relief that can reach millions of absent consumers. Those procedural extras make the American class action a uniquely powerful engine of private enforcement—and why, even as other systems experiment with collective litigation, they still stop well short of the Rule 23(b)(3) punch.

Law professor Brian Fitzpatrick argues in *The Conservative Case for Class Actions* that the class action device is a key procedural tool that turns private lawsuits into a private substitute for government regulation. He notes flatly that "[p]rivate enforcement is what makes America different . . . . But, to make private enforcement work here, we need the class action."[81] That is, class actions contribute in three ways:

First, class actions allow plaintiffs to file "negative value" claims—lawsuits where the harm to any one person is too small to justify hiring a lawyer. Fitzpatrick puts it bluntly—without aggregation, "private enforcement of small harms is not possible."[82] A $50 junk fee, a $100 defective electronic device, or a $3 bogus cellphone charge will never be litigated in individual court or arbitration because the filing fee, expert costs, and attorneys' time dwarf the potential recovery. But, as Fitzpatrick notes, tie a thousand identical $100 claims together, and the case suddenly represents $100,000 in damages; a contingency fee lawyer's one-third share is now a meaningful $33,000. The class device converts an unprofitable grievance into a viable lawsuit, giving companies a real incentive to obey the law and consumers a realistic path to compensation.

Fitzpatrick backs the point with a natural experiment from the banking world. During a debit card reordering scandal, thirty banks manipulated transaction sequencing to maximize overdraft fees. Eighteen lacked class action waivers and were sued; they paid roughly $1 billion to 29 million customers. The dozen with arbitration clauses that banned classes faced virtually no exposure—fewer than twenty customers a year pursued individual arbitration nationwide. Same misconduct, two enforcement regimes: one produced near universal redress; the other left victims uncompensated. For Fitzpatrick, the lesson is clear: "to make private enforcement work . . . we need the class action."[83]

A second, closely related virtue of the class action is that it makes claims financially attractive for lawyers. Under the "American rule," each side normally pays its own attorneys' fees, and a contingency percentage of one person's $50 loss will never lure competent counsel. Rule 23 changes the math: By bundling thousands of tiny claims into one lawsuit, it creates a single, sizable recovery pool from which the court can award fees. That "big pot" turns private firms into de facto attorneys general, patrolling consumer fraud, wage theft, and price-fixing that public agencies lack the resources to police. In this way, the class action does more than compensate victims; it deters future wrongdoing by making sure violations are actually prosecuted instead of quietly absorbed as a cost of doing business. Put differently, the device is a market-based substitute for government enforcement—centralizing scattered injuries so that private lawyers have both the incentive and the means to vindicate the law.

Third, class actions help level the playing field when a powerful defendant faces many scattered victims. Fitzpatrick uses an interesting hypothetical to carry the point across. Suppose a company's conduct injures 10,000 people, each by $50,000. If one plaintiff sues alone, her lawyer's recovery is capped at a one-third contingency—about $16,600. She will not pour more than that into experts, document review, or depositions, whereas the defendant may spend *up to the full $500 million* it risks across all parallel suits, and every dollar it invests in the first case can be reused in the next. The imbalance in resources and repeat player incentives can undercut both compensation and deterrence.[84]

A class action changes the economics of the claim. By bundling all 10,000 claims, the case is now worth a collective $500 million; a one-third fee translates into real money and justifies matching the defendant's war chest with top-flight experts and exhaustive discovery. The aggregation also solves an information problem—public notice of the suit alerts victims who never knew they had a claim, swelling the class and increasing leverage. In short, Rule 23 turns plaintiffs' counsel into a counterweight roughly proportional to the defendant's stakes, ensuring that big-ticket wrongdoing faces an equally serious prosecution rather than a series of under-funded skirmishes.

---

There are other important procedures on top of class actions and discovery. US courts, for instance, impose a relatively low standard for claims to survive a motion to dismiss, allowing claims to proceed to discovery (although two major Supreme Court cases, *Twombly* and *Iqbal*, heightened pleading standards). Moreover, contingency-fee financing lets plaintiffs hire counsel without paying by the hour. Together, these two background rules keep meritorious suits from dying at filing and ensure that the cost of investigation is borne from any eventual recovery—advantages largely unknown abroad.

There are two key takeaways here: Broad discovery and class actions are the twin procedural engines that make private enforcement run. Together, they generate the evidence, the economies of scale, and the financial incentives that transform scattered claims into viable cases, allowing private lawyers to perform many of the policing functions a bigger bureaucracy might otherwise assume. Their breadth, party control, and fee potential remain distinctly American.

Both engines emerged in the same mid-twentieth-century window. The 1938 Federal Rules fused equity discovery with common law practice and cemented notice pleading, while the 1966 overhaul of Rule 23—along with the post-war normalization of contingency fees—gave lawyers the aggregation tool they needed. Since then, each new statute that permits private suits has plugged into this procedural machinery, amplifying enforcement without any additional act of Congress.

## COMPARATIVE DIVERGENCE FROM THE UK: QUI TAM

Return to the tricky puzzle I introduced above: If America just kept doing what it had always done, adding a few new layers along the way, why did Canada and the UK diverge? Randy Beck traces how England, once the birthplace of informer suits, killed off the tradition in 1951.[85] In the Common Informer's Act of 1951, Parliament abrogated informer claims, ending a legal institution extending back to the Middle Ages. At the same time, the United States Congress expanded the qui tam claim in a 1986 reform to the False Claims Act. In other words, the two countries diverged around the middle of the century, one moving away from private enforcement; another running even more towards it.

Beck tells us that Parliament's hostility to qui tam dated back a century. As Britain built professional police and public prosecutors, legislators came to see bounty-hunting claims as blackmail. Nineteenth-century critics in parliament grumbled that informers extorted hush money, filed malicious actions over trivial violations—such as Sabbath-breaking or alehouse rules—and pursued penalties that rightly belonged to the Crown. By the early 1900s only a handful of antiquated bounty statutes survived, and no new qui tam law had been enacted since 1875. Indeed, "[o]nly one qui tam statute was adopted in the twentieth century."[86] A member of parliament,

Gerald Hurst, first drafted an abolition bill in the 1930s, calling it "legalised blackmail" and arguing that "a wrong to the State should surely be atoned for by a penalty payable to the State alone."[87] When another abolition bill was introduced in 1951, members of parliament cheered on the proposal, branding informers "parasite[s]" and the procedure a "complete anachronism."[88]

Some members of parliament even wondered why qui tam had not been abolished earlier. Others explained that while qui tam was needed in the past, a more developed bureaucracy had rendered it unnecessary: "[A]t one time the administrative machinery of the state was so incompetent to secure law enforcement that this field of activity had to be left in the hands of private enterprise."[89] Parliament as a whole agreed, abolishing qui tam outright and leaving public enforcement as the exclusive path.

Beck argues that this abolition reflects a structural conflict of interest inherent in bounty suits: The relator's private financial stake can diverge sharply from the public's interest in impartial enforcement. Where the modern administrative state supplies salaried investigators, the rationale for paying citizens to police violations collapses, but the temptation to leverage the statute for extortion persists. England therefore chose to rely on public enforcement alone.

The United States followed a different course, but only near the end of the century. According to Nelson and Woolhandler, the US mirrored the British take in the 1930s: "When a brief wavelet of suits arose between 1930 and 1943, Congress responded with statutory amendments that 'all but eliminated the use of the FCA qui tam.'"[90] But while Congress repealed many informer statutes during the same period, it later retained and strengthened the False Claims Act in the 1980s, which today represents the bulk of American qui tam litigation. Thus, while both countries recognized the abuse potential Beck highlights, only the US decided that the benefits of a carefully tailored bounty law still outweighed its risks; England's experience shows a fork in the road.

Yet again, one potential explanation is that English Members of Parliament (MPs) felt comfortable with a public monopoly on enforcement while Americans hedged and gave themselves an out.

But perhaps one way to understand the story (and to look for points of divergence from the UK) is as follows: The colonies and early American states began with little administrative capacity beyond public criminal prosecutors, making private enforcement the only viable mechanism for regulatory oversight. When the Progressive movement rose to power in the late nineteenth century with its enthusiasm for expert bureaucracies, path dependence and the growing power of the legal profession prevented Progressives from eliminating the existing system of private enforcement. Instead, they could only build new administrative agencies on top of it, creating a hybrid regime. For whatever reason, this same critical juncture did not unfold in the same way in the UK. There are gaps in this story (and some evidence is inconsistent with it), but this is at least a start for future research.

## COMBINING THE LAYERS: AMPLIFIED PENAL STATUTES

The story that runs from colonial penal statutes to today's citizen-suit provisions is not one of a single cause but of path dependence and layers that accumulated and locked into place.

- **Path Dependence (Layer 1).** English penal statutes and qui tam writs gave Americans a template: Outsource enforcement; pay the informer. Because early legislatures routinely copied that language, each new statute made the next insertion cheaper and more familiar. The template survived and evolved, eventually borrowing from the common law, to be grafted onto the Sherman Act (Statute of Monopolies treble damages plus right to sue), elaborated in the Clayton Act and the FLSA, and then replicated in Title VII, RICO, and the environmental citizen suits. The critical juncture was the choice of 1914 to accept both private and public enforcement.
- **Structural Incentives (Layer 2).** Separation of powers, federalism, the lawyers' lobby, and other interest groups give Congress (and state legislatures) a constant reason to double up enforcement. Private rights insulate enforcement of statutes against hostile presidents, budget cuts, or apathetic state officials, and they cost nothing up front. They also satisfy key political constituencies. Over time the clause became almost boilerplate in both Congress and state legislatures.

- **Procedural Enablers (Layer 3).** A private right of action is inert without plumbing that makes lawsuits possible. In the United States, liberal discovery (a privatized subpoena power) and the opt-out class action supply information, scale, and financing; generous notice-pleading and contingency fees keep the courthouse door open. France's experience with discrimination suits, by contrast, demonstrates that when discovery and aggregation are missing, plaintiffs migrate to criminal prosecution and civil private enforcement withers. Discovery and class actions, then, are not peripheral; they are central to the story, turning rights to sue into real-world regulation.

- **Divergent Paths Abroad.** England once shared the same heritage, yet Parliament abolished qui tam in 1951 after condemning informers as "legalised blackmail" and trusting a modern bureaucracy to police public wrongs. As Randy Beck shows, MPs argued that once the state could afford professional prosecutors, "a wrong to the State should surely be atoned for by a penalty payable to the State alone."[91] Something similar may have happened to the broader phenomenon of private enforcement: Canadians and British elites trusted bureaucracies with a monopoly over enforcement. The United States chose the opposite fork, strengthening the False Claims Act in 1986. The contrast shows that path dependence is powerful but not inexorable. And indeed, Canada and the UK later came around to adopt private enforcement regimes at the end of the twentieth century.

## THE ROLE OF CULTURE: A FORTHCOMING SURVEY

Importantly, there is room for culture to play a role between these layers. Even if culture doesn't determine outcomes, it may condition the menu of acceptable options to legislators. In a current project with co-authors, we are deploying a survey of thousands of Americans and Canadians to test preferences for private enforcement and its potential cultural underpinnings. The study offers different areas of social concern—artificial intelligence and environmental pollution—and asks respondents whether they prefer that a hypothetical new statute empower private parties (to file lawsuits) or government bureaucrats. The hypothesis is that if culture is truly behind the roots of private enforcement, then Americans and Canadians will respond differently. But also, Americans from different states will respond differently as well. Do Californians prefer the option of lawsuits as compared to Texans? Do Quebecois prefer bureaucratic regulation as compared with New Yorkers? Is there a correlation between the average preferences of a particular state's citizens and the adoption of private enforcement in that state?

To be sure, cultural preferences may be endogenous to the legal system (i.e., living in a system that relies on private lawsuits may itself generate a preference for more lawsuits). The survey will try to get around this problem by also asking specific questions about respondents' values: the importance of individualism, personal responsibility, perceptions of government corruption, and so on. This means we can connect respondents' preferences between private and public enforcement to respondents' views on the value of individualism, (dis)trust of government, and confrontational litigation.

The survey results will also shine a light on what is called the Free Cantril paradox. In 1967, Hadley Free and Lloyd Cantril conducted a series of wide-ranging public opinion surveys that captured Americans' views on discrete policy issues as well as their ideological beliefs. Their analysis of these surveys yielded a curious paradox: while roughly half of Americans supported "small government," an even larger proportion supported increased government activity across a wide range of social policy areas. Free and Cantril summed up these findings by stating that Americans afflicted with this split political persona were "ideologically conservative" yet "operationally liberal."[92] Further studies have found that the overall proportion of so-called "conflicted conservatives" has grown since at least the 1960s[93] and continues to be a prevalent theme in American politics today.[94]

That future research, then, will provide some answers as to the role of culture in the layers of private enforcement.

# PART III

## A NORMATIVE APPRAISAL

# SEVEN

## JUSTIFICATIONS FOR PRIVATE ENFORCEMENT

The preceding chapters have traced the historical development and causal origins of private enforcement in American law, examining how history, institutional constraints, and strategic calculations shaped the emergence of this governance mechanism. We explored why private enforcement arose when it did, which actors championed its adoption, and how specific political and institutional factors explain its prevalence in the United States and not other democratic systems. This analysis provides context for understanding private enforcement as a phenomenon, but it leaves unanswered a fundamentally different set of normative questions that are equally important for policymakers and legal scholars.

Regardless of its causal origins, perhaps the most important question is whether private enforcement is justified. The fact that private enforcement emerged from political circumstances does not make it a desirable policy, just as understanding why an institution developed historically does not resolve whether it serves the public interest today. Given that most countries do not rely on this form of governance, why should the United States continue to do so? And how should we decide when to include a private right of action in regulatory legislation and when to leave it out? These normative questions require a different analytical approach—one that evaluates private enforcement against theoretical ideals of democratic governance, regulatory effectiveness, and institutional design rather than simply explaining its historical trajectory.

This chapter shifts from explanation to evaluation, marking a transition in the analysis. While the previous chapters asked, "Why did private enforcement develop as it did?," this chapter asks, "Should we want private enforcement to exist at all, and if so, under what conditions?"

---

Here, I argue that private enforcement in the United States is justified when it satisfies a balancing test of three criteria: first, when private enforcement makes up for weak *enforcement capacity*. That is, when public enforcers lack sufficient resources or staffing to investigate and police legal violations. By empowering private plaintiffs, governments can achieve greater enforcement of the law—and deterrence—without relying on a costly bureaucracy. Second, private enforcement may be justified when it avoids the problem of *regulatory dysfunction*—where capture, corruption, and other dynamics render bureaucracies unresponsive. By diffusing power among hundreds of thousands of plaintiffs and their lawyers, private enforcement can be a failsafe in cases where the bureaucracy is unresponsive, and it can stabilize enforcement of the law regardless of the political administration in power. Moreover, private enforcement can empower political underdogs or weak constituencies who may otherwise lack the government's attention. Third, private enforcement may be justified when it solves the bureaucratic problem of *informational asymmetries*. It is quite difficult for bureaucrats to discover legal violations and to smoke out relevant information. By giving private parties an incentive to file claims—often via multiple damages and fee-shifting—private enforcement surfaces information that is otherwise hidden.

But of course, even when private enforcement satisfies these criteria, it can impose significant costs that legislators should consider. Chief among these is the divergence between private and public interests. As law and economics have long taught, private plaintiffs will file claims whenever it makes economic sense, but bureaucrats take the public interest into account and maintain greater legislative fidelity. This can lead to overenforcement of the law by overzealous plaintiffs' attorneys. On top of that, private claimants lack any democratic accountability and are uncoordinated—this can lead to guerrilla litigation that is redundant and wasteful. Yet another effect is that "[t]he piecemeal and unyielding nature of profit-motivated private enforcement will deprive regulatory regimes of needed 'coherence' by, among other things, disrupting the subtle cooperative relationships that arise between regulators and regulatory targets."[1]

This chapter dives into both sides of the debate, including the costs and benefits of private enforcement.

## REGULATORY, NOT COMPENSATORY OR ACCOUNTABILITY STATUTES

Before we get there, however, a quick reminder is appropriate here. The analysis that follows focuses primarily on regulatory statutes—those designed to shape the behavior of private entities through deterrence—rather than statutes with purely compensatory or government accountability purposes. While these categories often overlap in practice, the normative case for private enforcement differs across them. When a statute's only goal is to compensate injured parties for harm suffered, private rights of action are typically straightforward and justified. Similarly, when statutes aim to ensure government accountability by policing official misconduct or protecting constitutional rights, private enforcement makes clear sense as a check on government power from outside actors. The harder normative questions arise with regulatory statutes like the Sherman Act, the Clean Water Act, employment discrimination laws, and so on, where Congress wants to change the behavior of regulated entities and chooses between empowering administrative agencies, private litigants, or both. These kinds of regulatory statutes are what this book is all about.

## PUBLIC ENFORCEMENT IS THE LEGISLATIVE DEFAULT; RIGHTS TO SUE MUST BE JUSTIFIED

Begin with the observation that every major regulatory statute empowers government officials. Congress, in other words, seems to consider public enforcement as a legislative drafting default. This is true for every statutory debate we've discussed so far. At a time with almost no robust bureaucracy, the 1890 Sherman Act was mostly reliant on Department of Justice lawyers, with a right to sue as a secondary option. Antitrust enforcement soon depended on FTC officials after 1914. In 1938, no one disputed that the Department of Labor could investigate FLSA compliance; the question was instead whether to give more or less power to a separate labor board. In 1964, Congress guaranteed the EEOC an important gatekeeping role over civil rights claims. And, yes, the EPA's powerful role over environmental claims was a given from the start. So let's be blunt: There is no major regulatory statute that empowers private parties only. Congress considers public enforcement as the default way to enforce the law.

While Congress always adopts public enforcement, it does not always embrace rights to sue. Return to the example discussed in the previous chapter—when Congress created the FTC, it did not adopt a private right of action for consumer fraud claims. While it partially added one in the Fair Debt Collection Practices Act,[2] Congress doubled down on public enforcement in 2010 by creating the Consumer Financial Protection Bureau. As I previously argued, "[b]y creating the CFPB, and providing that agency with the power to issue broad civil investigative demands, the statute reordered the entire area . . . toward public enforcement. The CFPB . . . occupied the field and displaced the relevance of private claims (both state and federal)."[3]

Congress's preference for public enforcement is constitutionally grounded. Article II provides that the executive shall "take Care that the Laws be faithfully executed." There is a constitutional bias, then, in favor of executive officials and public enforcement. Some of this may go beyond a bias and shade into constitutional obligation territory. While the Supreme Court has not stated this clearly, Article II may in rare instances prevent Congress from disempowering the executive in a regulatory area.[4]

To reinforce this congressional preference, courts, too, have long treated statutes without any specific enforcement provision as "regulatory" statutes that depend on public enforcement only.[5] And while courts sometimes find an "implied" private right of action, even in the face of congressional silence on enforcement, more recently the Supreme Court has rejected that approach. As Justice Scalia clarified in *Alexander v. Sandoval*, Congress must be clear when it creates a private right of action. Otherwise, courts cannot imply it.[6] If Congress adopts a wide-ranging regulatory scheme and does not say anything about enforcement, courts will read that as a public enforcement scheme only.

The combination of ever-present public enforcement, an Article II public bias, and statutory schemes in which Congress rejects private enforcement suggests a preference for public power. It is public enforcement, then, that is the default in the United States.

Now, to be sure, this is not necessarily true in state governments. There are recent prominent examples of private enforcement schemes that explicitly disempower executive officials. For instance, the Texas anti-abortion statute, SB 8, created a powerful right to sue against abortion providers but completely removed any public power over these claims. Congress almost never adopts regulatory statutes enforceable only by private litigants.[7]

Taken together, the evidence points in the opposite direction of the familiar "Americans always prefer litigation" shorthand. In Washington, the baseline rule is still public enforcement, rooted in Article II's command that the Executive "take Care" and reinforced by political habit and administrative capacity. The private right of action, when it appears, is therefore an overlay, not the core. That overlay must carry an affirmative justification—it should solve a problem that bureaucrats or public officials cannot. In other words, the adoption of a private right of action should be justified over and above pre-existing public enforcement.

Framed this way, the policy question flips. The burden is not on critics to explain why a statute shouldn't include a private remedy; the burden is on drafters to show why, given an already-empowered agency, private enforcement adds something the public enforcer is unlikely to deliver.

When we consider the issue this way, we find that private enforcement can make three key contributions to a regime that already relies on public officials. Private enforcement can make up for a lack of enforcement capacity, it can avoid regulatory dysfunction, and it can uncover information that regulators cannot easily access.

## THE FEASIBLE RANGE OF ENFORCEMENT CAPACITY

Scholars across political science, economics, and public administration treat state capacity as a cornerstone of modern governance. But defining the concept is more than tricky. As further discussed below, this chapter focuses narrowly on a specific type of enforcement capacity: a bureaucracy's ability to effectively investigate and police regulatory violations. This is a subset of state capacity broadly, but it is the most relevant angle to the phenomenon we're discussing here—the ability to enforce statutes.

A recent overview of the history of the state capacity literature begins with comparative giants such as Samuel Huntington, Theda Skocpol, and Charles Tilly, who urged academics to "bring[] the state back in," shifting attention from social movements and markets to the machinery of government itself.[8] Luciana Cingolani distilled the emerging definition of capacity as the state's ability to accomplish "official goals against potential resistance, by means of taxation, the bureaucracy, the military, the legislature, and the courts, and throughout its entire domains."[9] In practice, that capacity undergirds everything from enforcing contracts and policing violence to building infrastructure and delivering social insurance. Some of the empirical literature, for instance, finds strong links between high capacity and sustained economic growth.

Most attempts to measure state capacity look to inputs: how much money a government can raise and spend, how many professionals it can attract, and how insulated its agencies are from patronage or political meddling. Francis Fukuyama, for example, points to the Progressive Era replacement of party loyalists with "university-trained agronomists, engineers, and economists" as a leap in US capacity.[10] The same yardstick, Fukuyama points out, explains why central banks across the developing world run far better today than in the 1980s. Bureaucratic autonomy is equally critical: Agencies staffed by experts cannot deliver if elected officials or private interests can constantly veto their decisions.

Yet aggregate scores hide significant variation within governments. Fukuyama notes that Katherine Bersch and co-authors famously found "islands of excellence" inside Brazil—high-functioning federal agencies surrounded by low-capacity neighbors—while China's uneven provincial performance tells the same story.

For that reason, a newer strand of the literature, surveyed by Nicholas Bagley and David Schleicher, asks whether a state can actually provide core public goods such as safe streets, reliable infrastructure, or timely permitting, rather than tallying headcounts and budgets alone.[11] Brink Lindsey pushes the argument further, tying capacity to a government's ability to get stuff done in the face of twenty-first-century complexity.[12]

Thinking about state capacity in a more targeted way is important because, as Bagley and Schleicher emphasize, in the United States most regulation is carried out by state and local officials, not Washington. When scholars map capacity onto variables like "public employment, the security of property and contract rights; crime prevention; the quality and extent of public infrastructure; and the provision of public services,"[13] the pattern that emerges is uneven. Some states can count on professional, well-funded departments; others rely on small staffs and old technology. The result is a mixed system in which national statutes—on, say, environmental protection or wages—hit a capacity ceiling the moment they are delegated to understaffed field offices or inspectors.

For our purposes, the lens is narrowed still further to a subset of state capacity that we can call *enforcement capacity*. This refers to the ability of public officials to detect legal violations and implement the law against violators. Enforcement budgets, expert personnel and legal staff, subpoena power, the ability to bring cases in administrative courts or in the judiciary, and political independence all feed this form of capacity. It is analytically distinct from judicial capacity (federal courts are comparatively well funded and professional) and from the broader state-capacity question of whether a government can deliver welfare benefits or build highways. The simple point is that when agencies lack investigators, laboratories, data analytics, or the political cover to use them, violations go unseen.

Here is where private enforcement comes into the picture. By deputizing plaintiffs' attorneys, who number in the thousands, Congress increases the capacity of the state to hunt for the very violations that understaffed agencies might miss. A right to sue is the starting point, but Congress can build procedures that increase monetary incentives to expand capacity even further: class actions, fee-shifting, contingency fees, and treble or punitive damages. Discovery completes the package. Because Rule 26 lets parties compel documents, depositions, and third-party subpoenas without prior judicial approval, it functions as a delegated subpoena power: The informational fire hose agencies wield through administrative process is, in civil litigation, placed directly in private hands. When those suits surface internal emails, test data, or audit trails, the resulting record can be mined by regulators as well.

One analytical problem with this justification is that enforcement capacity and private rights of action are jointly determined by the legislature.

Both are policy choices rather than independent variables. This raises what economists call an endogeneity problem: Both public and private enforcement are determined by the same body and at the same time. One could argue that pointing to weak enforcement capacity to justify PRAs begs the question: If the superior policy would combine strong public enforcement with no private right of action, then the existence of weak capacity doesn't justify PRAs—it simply reveals that Congress made suboptimal choices on both dimensions simultaneously. Why treat capacity as a given constraint when Congress could have chosen instead to build robust public enforcement without resort to private litigation?

This is an important analytical problem, but it overlooks the realistic constraints that bind legislative capacity-building even when political will exists. The relevant normative question is not whether legislatures could theoretically construct ideal public enforcement, but rather: *what is the feasible range of enforcement capacity* that we are likely to observe in practice? That is, can the legislature, in fact, build a capacious public regulator?

The answer to that question is shaped by several factors beyond legislative control. First, political economy constraints matter: even legislators committed to strong enforcement face entrenched opposition from regulated interests who can block appropriations. That means the legislative choice is heavily constrained by interest groups or political lobbying. Second, the nature and size of the regulatory problem itself impose limits independent of political will. In fast-moving domains like securities markets (discussed in the next chapter), where millions of transactions occur daily, or in areas requiring highly dispersed monitoring like workplace safety across millions of employers, even generous funding cannot overcome the fundamental scale challenges that make public enforcement infeasible. Third, regardless of how much a legislature may want to build enforcement capacity, there can be serious human capital constraints. Building capacity requires specialized expertise that may be scarce regardless of funding, including the availability of, say, scientists, forensic accountants, or technical knowledge. In some developing nations, perfectly drafted regulatory statutes achieve very little because there is no history of a competent administrative state, corruption is endemic, and domestic expertise is nonexistent. Finally, and perhaps most importantly for the United States, constitutional and doctrinal constraints limit what even well-funded agencies can accomplish. So, for instance, the narrowing of Chevron deference and the major questions doctrine limit agencies' legal authority to interpret and implement statutes, creating enforcement gaps that stem from judicial constraints on administrative power rather than from inadequate resources or staffing.

These constraints mean that enforcement capacity, while not entirely exogenous to legislative choice, occupies a narrow feasible range. The normative case for private enforcement therefore rests on whether it improves regulatory outcomes within this realistic capacity range, not on whether ideal capacity could theoretically eliminate the need for private enforcement altogether.

Framed this way, private enforcement is most defensible where public capacity to detect wrongdoing is structurally (and irremediably) weak. And public capacity will vary by government level (federal vs. state) and regulatory area (securities vs. wages and hours). The United States is a mix of systems and laws. At the federal level the Securities and Exchange Commission employs forensic accountants and data scientists, yet labor divisions in many states staff only a handful of inspectors; the Environmental Protection Agency runs sophisticated labs but must rely on state partners with wildly uneven budgets and expertise. It is in these gaps—where public detection fails—that Congress should unleash private rights of action, class actions, and broad discovery.

A focus on enforcement capacity can tell us whether private enforcement is justified, even if it is not a causal account of why Congress adopts private enforcement. But legislative history does support this reading: Congress sometimes adds private enforcement when it fears that public enforcement will be insufficient. In 1914, frustrated by the Department of Justice's anemic use of the Sherman Act, legislators doubled enforcement capacity in two directions at once: They created the Federal Trade Commission and strengthened private treble-damage suits through the Clayton Act. During the 1970 Clean Air Act debates, sponsors pointed to the EPA's inevitable resource limits. It's worth excerpting former Attorney General Ramsey Clark's testimony again:

> It will be impossible for government enforcement to control all significant acts of pollution . . . . The extension of private right . . . and effective sanctions for the persons directly affected or concerned will be essential

> if vital interests are to be protected. Our experience in areas of massive unlawful racial discrimination, such as in schooling, employment, and housing tells us that however hard it might try, government will never have the manpower, the techniques, or the awareness necessary to enforce the law for all. Private enforcement of those laws is the only way the individual can be assured that the rights cannot be violated with impunity.
>
> Pollution control is another such area. If we are really serious about controlling the quality of our environment before it destroys the quality of our lives, we must give the individuals affected by, or concerned about pollutions in his life, the power to stop them through legal process . . . it will provide powerful supplementary enforcement . . . and an effective and desirable prod to officials to do their duty.[14]

The Fair Labor Standards Act's Section 16(b) emerged from similar misgivings about the Labor Department's reach; so did the qui tam revival in the False Claims Act of 1986 after auditors revealed multibillion-dollar frauds the Pentagon had not caught.

By contrast, private enforcement is less justified when Congress has built a well-funded and independent public enforcer. Criminal law is the clearest example: Because prosecutors already command police, grand juries, and compulsory process, our system has discarded private enforcement of criminal law. Consider, too, the context of consumer financial protection. When Congress created the CFPB, it armed the agency with sweeping civil investigative demand power, an independent source of budgetary funding, and high-caliber attorneys. Because the CFPB was granted high enforcement capacity, Congress saw no need to add a private right of action. Congress, then, clearly sees the relationship between capacity and rights to sue.

But even the most robust agencies can use supplemental civil suits. In repeated amicus briefs before the federal courts, the SEC has argued that private securities litigation is a necessary complement to the agency's work, warning that staff and budget constraints leave large swaths of the market unmonitored.

---

There are, however, several reasons why we cannot rely solely on capacity justifications:

First, enforcement capacity is contingent and can change rapidly with shifting political priorities and budget allocations. A new presidency or congressional majority can massively expand a previously anemic agency. Observe the Trump administration's dramatic funding increase for Immigration and Customs Enforcement. Likewise, a new administration can quickly defund or dismantle agencies, as the Trump administration also achieved with USAID's near elimination in a few months. Given this volatility, capacity arguments are most compelling when they address chronic or structural enforcement gaps that cannot be easily remedied through budget adjustments. Or, as Chapter 10 suggests, private enforcement should be designed with built-in responsiveness to state capacity, weakening when government enforcement strengthens. This kind of on-the-go adjustment is reflected in agency gatekeeping provisions that allow regulators to take over cases from private litigants.

Second, and returning again to the endogeneity problem discussed above, adding private rights of action to compensate for inadequate state capacity may inadvertently excuse governmental inaction and create perverse incentives for continued underinvestment in public enforcement. Proponents of robust government regulation can reasonably argue that the proper response to enforcement gaps is increased public capacity, not the further weakening of state authority through privatized enforcement mechanisms. Low enforcement capacity, then, may merely reflect an overreliance on private enforcement, not an independent measure of public capability. That is, rights to sue may undermine the political incentives for building strong regulatory institutions by providing an easy alternative that avoids the challenges of state-building. And if litigation serves as a substitute for adequate government funding, policymakers may systematically underinvest in public institutions.

More fundamentally, enforcement capacity and private enforcement are jointly determined by the legislature, raising the question of whether weak capacity justifies PRAs or simply reflects bad policy choices on both dimensions.

However, these critiques can support the opposite, more pro-private enforcement conclusion. The fact that agency capacity can change dramatically with each election cycle—as we are witnessing with the systematic dismantling of federal regulatory agencies under Trump—may actually strengthen the case for private enforcement as institutional insurance. Private rights of action can serve as more enduring enforcement mechanisms that survive changes in political control, agency capture, or budget cuts that can eliminate public enforcement overnight. This view aligns with Robert Kagan's argument that private enforcement provides inherent benefits in a political system with deep reservations about strong government, offering enforcement continuity that transcends partisan regime changes. This insurance function becomes particularly valuable in policy areas subject to dramatic political swings, such as environmental protection, where agencies like the EPA face periodic efforts at elimination or defunding depending on the party in power.

Moreover, the argument that private enforcement excuses underinvestment in public institutions assumes that private and public enforcement serve identical functions. But in fact, they often (though not always) play complementary roles in regulatory ecosystems. Private enforcement excels at detecting dispersed violations, providing compensation to victims, and maintaining enforcement during periods of government neglect. Public enforcement, by contrast, brings systematic investigation, policy coordination, and democratic accountability that private litigation cannot replicate. Rather than weakening arguments for government investment, private enforcement can enhance the overall effectiveness of regulatory schemes by creating multiple pathways for legal compliance. To be sure, this might imply that legislators should add PRAs even when public capacity is high. But that is only true when public and private enforcement serve as true complements and when other elements of the balancing test (discussed below) are also satisfied.

Some private enforcement regimes also create a positive cycle by generating revenue that funds improved public enforcement capacity. As discussed in the next chapter, California's PAGA demonstrates this dynamic, requiring that a significant chunk of collected civil penalties flow to public agencies. This transforms private litigation into a funding mechanism for the government agencies whose capacity shortfalls originally justified the private enforcement regime. This model demonstrates another dimension of public-private enforcement cooperation, where private lawsuits actively strengthen public enforcement by providing resources that can enhance agency capacity.

The message across a century of statutes is consistent: Public enforcement remains the baseline, but when low state capacity is likely to leave enforcement gaps, Congress uses private lawsuits to supplement them.

## REGULATORY DYSFUNCTION

Relatedly, private enforcement diffuses power among hundreds of thousands of plaintiffs and their lawyers. Because of that, private enforcement schemes can avoid the problem of *regulatory dysfunction* due to capture, corruption, and other bureaucratic pathologies.[15] By dysfunction, I mean that regulators cannot or will not achieve their enforcement goals, creating impunity and suboptimal deterrence.

Start with the most prominent bureaucratic pathology: regulatory capture. This concept refers to the ability of regulated entities—industry, groups, or individuals—to exercise undue influence over regulators, leading regulators to promote the interests of those entities. The classic formulation comes from economist George J. Stigler's "theory of economic regulation," which argued that "as a rule, regulation is acquired by the industry and is designed and operated primarily for its benefit."[16] In this view, regulation can emerge not to protect consumers but to serve producer interests by, for example, erecting barriers to entry or limiting competition. According to public choice theory, concentrated interest groups (e.g., a regulated industry) have strong incentives to lobby and influence regulators, whereas the public (with diffuse, small stakes) faces collective action problems and is less engaged. This asymmetry means organized industries can systematically "capture" the regulatory process, bending rules and enforcement in their favor. To remain legitimate, however, regulators must still deliver some consumer benefits. Capture can be a matter of degree, not a dichotomous variable.[17]

A second wave of scholarship goes further. Daniel Carpenter and David Moss define capture as the redirection of an agency "away from the public interest,"[18] a bar so high that clear examples are rare. Carpenter's work on the FDA shows periods when the agency resisted drug-industry pressure to protect its reputation, concluding there was "abundant evidence against the idea that American pharmaceutical regulation has been built through the attempts of drug companies to limit entry and preserve market power." However, he also noted that "[e]xamining the prospect of capture through other mechanisms . . . suggests . . . [a] degree of cultural capture of the FDA may have occurred."[19] Others have likewise argued that some agencies cultivate professional norms that insulate them from politics and profit. In short, capture is a risk but not inevitable: Expertise, public visibility, and institutional pride can push the needle the other way.[20]

To the extent that empirical studies have tested these dynamics, the evidence continues to be mixed. Closer to our context, according to studies on DOJ prosecutions for government fraud as compared to qui tam lawsuits, the "DOJ is *more* likely to join [False Claims Act] cases brought by former DOJ attorneys" and slower to move against top defense contractors.[21] This suggests that influence can surface through subtle agenda-setting or delay rather than blatant favors.

To be sure, outright corruption can occur from time to time. For instance, in the FDA's late-1980s generic drug scandal, officials took cash bribes and kickbacks to accelerate approvals. This was direct proof that classic corruption, though rarer in US agencies, is still possible.

Yet bureaucratic dysfunction can come from a wide range of sources, including lobbying, career incentives, revolving door dynamics, political pressure on elected officials who lean on agencies, or cognitive capture. Consider the revolving door phenomenon. Scholars have documented the constant movement of personnel between regulatory agencies and regulated industries. FDA officials sometimes move to high-level positions in private drug manufacturers. Similarly, SEC attorneys often leave to work for major Wall Street law firms. The concern here is that regulators will be lax on those industries, perhaps to keep open the possibility of future employment. Alternatively, private industry may hire ex-regulators to exploit their inside knowledge. In this specific context of enforcement, scholars have studied whether the SEC enforcement division is "hobbled by . . . enforcement staff exiting their jobs at the Commission and migrating to lucrative private sector employment."[22] A recent review of those studies finds the evidence "inconclusive as to whether such revolving door practices have weakened the SEC's verve."[23] Still, Cox and Thomas argue that by recruiting top SEC officials from industry, there is a real danger of "cognitive" or "cultural capture," where officials subtly shape the SEC's agenda in industry-friendly ways.

Even without capture, revolving doors, or corruption, bureaucracies can malfunction through red tape and risk aversion. Layer upon layer of procurement, personnel, and procedural rules—each adopted to curb some past abuse—can paralyze agencies that must now spend years justifying a regulation. Francis Fukuyama has recently written about the problem of the never-ending imposition of procedures on bureaucrats, paralyzing them and rendering them ineffective. Nicholas Bagley described the problem as one of a "procedural fetish"—the choice by elites to impose constraining procedures on agencies in pursuit of legitimacy.[24] Relatedly, fear of blame pushes bureaucrats toward safe and slow choices: approve no drug until every doubt is scrubbed away, write 2,000-page cost-benefit analyses lest a court remand the rule. These defensive habits protect careers but can starve enforcement of timeliness and bite.

The broader problem that encompasses these bureaucratic pathologies is one of misaligned incentives. Bureaucrats seek to maximize their own interests, not necessarily the public's.

To round out the problems, a final source of misaligned incentives is the influence of politics. The worst kind of political influence is when politicians force bureaucrats to favor important donors or political allies. In the context of antitrust enforcement, a recent empirical study found that FTC and DOJ antitrust enforcement is relaxed when a company's directors are politically connected to the President:

> Using a sample of domestic mergers under regulatory review [over the period 2000–2016], we find that bidders whose directors overlap with the US President via social club or professional activities experience a lower likelihood of regulatory challenge when they undertake acquisitions. Economically, a bidder with political access to the President is 16.6 percent less likely to face regulatory challenges (consent order or injunction) relative to unconnected bidders.[25]

This appears to be evidence of political influence affecting the likelihood of public enforcement.

Politics, alongside polarization, adds volatility on top of other bureaucratic ills. As partisanship continues to grow, presidents increasingly install ideologically committed agency heads. Between 2017 and 2020, President

Trump selected fossil fuel insiders as directors of the EPA, including a climate change denialist. When leadership is chosen for politics rather than expertise, scientific risk assessments suffer under political influence, enforcement agendas seesaw from one administration to the next, and regulated firms face uncertainty: Today's rule may be tomorrow's rollback, then next year's revival in court. That lack of predictability affects compliance planning and, more critically, can produce multi-year enforcement pauses in which violations go uninvestigated.

Private enforcement cannot make up for all of these bureaucratic ills, but it can help at the margins. Begin with capture—regulated entities cannot "capture" hundreds of thousands of entrepreneurial lawyers dispersed across fifty states; they cannot promise every attorney an attractive new job; and they cannot affect procedural rules that give private plaintiffs access to key information. Because plaintiffs' counsel finance cases with contingency fees and expect payment only if they win, their incentives point relentlessly in one direction—prove the violation and recover as much as possible. That profit motive sidesteps the revolving door temptations, efforts to maximize budgets, and avoidance of blame that can blunt agency enforcement. Nor does private litigation grind to a halt under layers of procurement rules or protracted bureaucratic reviews: Once a complaint is filed, counsel can serve subpoenas the next morning without bureaucratic clearance, political sign-off, or notice-and-comment. In short, the competitive market for plaintiffs' lawyers is resistant to the classic capture channels of lobbying, campaign donations, and inside access that afflict centralized bureaucracies.

Professor Brian Fitzpatrick argues in *The Conservative Case for Class Actions* that profit-driven private enforcers avoid regulatory capture.[26] Drawing on the conservative commitment to privatization, he contends that contingency-fee lawyers function like market entrepreneurs: They spend only private capital, pursue cases only when expected recoveries exceed costs, and are rewarded in direct proportion to the money they win for victims. That profit-seeking structure, he notes, supplies sharper incentives, deeper resources, and more innovative strategies than chronically under-funded, politically constrained government offices can muster. Because thousands of competing firms—not a single bureaucracy—decide which violations to chase, enforcement is decentralized, less susceptible to regulatory capture, and carried out at no taxpayer expense, all while preserving a smaller state.

For conservatives, Fitzpatrick concludes, private lawyers are therefore not a necessary evil but the most efficient and freedom-preserving way to police the marketplace.

Private suits can also cushion the enforcement system against political whiplash and bureaucratic risk aversion. In periods of ideological flux, the availability of private suits and independent courts supplies a stabilizing influence—keeping statutory mandates from turning on the outcome of a single election cycle and ensuring that, even when an agency's leadership changes hands, legal enforcement continues unabated. Put another way, plaintiffs can be a failsafe in cases where the bureaucracy is unresponsive. And lawyers can stabilize the enforcement of the law regardless of political changes.

To be sure, private plaintiffs bring their own pathologies (opportunistic filings, nuisance settlements, and the possibility of over-deterrence). Those concerns warrant careful gate-keeping and calibrated procedural checks, which later chapters will tackle.

## INFORMATIONAL ASYMMETRIES

Every regulatory system begins with a simple logistical hurdle: Officials must discover whether regulated entities are actually following the rules on the books.[27] Yet the day-to-day conduct—and the relevant paper trail—resides inside the regulated entity, not in a public database or a regulator's file cabinets. Insiders to the regulated entity usually know whether it is or is not in compliance with relevant regulations. Everyone else is an outsider with very little visibility into compliance. This insider-outsider asymmetry is a central obstacle to effective oversight because it grants regulated entities a decisive informational advantage, relegating public authorities to a largely reactive posture.

Scholars across economics, political science, and administrative law have long dissected this detection dilemma. Gary Becker's work on the economics of "crime and punishment" frames compliance with criminal law as a gamble in which actors weigh the illicit gain against the expected sanction, discounted by the probability of getting caught.[28] George Stigler and public choice scholars have argued that information itself is endogenous: Agencies, chronically understaffed, must often rely on data curated by the very firms they regulate, giving industry room to filter or withhold facts and thereby tilt oversight to its advantage.[29] Legal scholars have long argued that "[i]nformation is the lifeblood of regulatory policy,"[30] and that "[t]he central problem of the standard-setting process and the most pressing task facing many agencies is gathering the information needed to write a sensible standard."[31] Administrative law scholars added a procedural layer on top of this, noting that notice and comment, mandatory disclosures, judicial review, and whistleblower channels are all attempts to narrow the information gap—yet each can be gamed or ignored when regulated entities act strategically. Across these literatures, the message is similar: Scarce public resources and private incentives combine to weaken the probability of detection.

One fundamental cause of enforcement information gaps is limited monitoring capacity. Agencies often lack the personnel and funding to proactively audit or inspect more than a small fraction of the activities under their jurisdiction. For example, the US Department of Labor's Wage and Hour Division (WHD)—responsible for enforcing federal wage laws—has only roughly 1,100 inspectors to oversee over 135 million workers nationwide.[32] Similarly, federal workplace safety enforcement is stretched thin: As of 2023, federal OSHA had so few inspectors that each workplace could expect an inspection only once every 186 years on average.[33] Environmental enforcement faces the same crunch; the EPA and state environmental agencies oversee hundreds of thousands of facilities (power plants, factories, waste sites, etc.) but conduct only tens of thousands of inspections per year. In recent years, the EPA's inspection activity actually declined—the agency averaged about 10,000 civil inspections per year in 2018–2021, roughly 46 percent fewer than the annual inspections in the prior decade.[34]

And this limited monitoring capacity is not fully endogenous to the legislative choice because of the external constraints discussed above *and*, importantly, the inherent structure of regulatory problems. Regardless of the number of public agents, there will inevitably be an insider-outsider asymmetry in access to information. Private parties have access to information that agencies can never efficiently obtain through external monitoring, regardless of staffing levels. And the severity of this asymmetry will change depending on the regulatory domain. In some areas, modest capacity increases can substantially improve detection—monitoring a discrete set of facilities for specific pollutants, for instance, is achievable with sufficient inspectors and technology. But in fast-moving, high-volume domains like securities markets, with their millions of transactions per day, the informational challenge is orders of magnitude greater. The information asymmetry problem is inherent to regulation even if its severity varies considerably across domains.

Still, keep in mind that agencies have significant power to flush out information. Agencies can inspect facilities, issue subpoenas and civil investigative demands, mandate filings, and host whistleblower hotlines. As I've argued before,

> The absolute "backbone of an administrative agency's effectiveness is the ability to investigate rapidly the activities of entities within the agency's jurisdiction." Although regulated entities usually provide information voluntarily, agencies' main investigatory tool is the administrative subpoena, an agency request compelling the production of documents or testimony without preapproval from courts or grand juries. That is why almost all agencies have subpoena power.[35]

Subpoena power plus procedural requirements like notice and comment create a powerful combination. While this toolkit is powerful in theory, it cannot be deployed everywhere, especially against sophisticated actors. The combination of these instruments, moreover, reaches only a sliver of potential wrongdoing.

Compounding the problem of scarce oversight is the strategic behavior of firms intent on concealing violations. Regulated actors often exploit the information asymmetry actively, by hiding evidence of wrongdoing, misrepresenting compliance, or structuring their activities to evade detection. A recurring theme in the literature is that firms have strong incentives to keep regulators in the dark.

The securities regulation arena provides clear evidence of strategic concealment. Corporate fraud—such as accounting fraud, earnings manipulation, or insider trading—is by nature hidden, often involving falsified records or collusion among insiders to mislead investors and regulators. Agencies like the SEC face an uphill battle in uncovering such fraud without inside information. An influential empirical study by Alexander Dyck, Adair Morse, and Luigi Zingales examined how large US corporate frauds are detected and found that regulatory enforcers themselves (such as the SEC) played a surprisingly small direct role in discovering these incidents.[36]

In antitrust enforcement, informational asymmetries are also significant. Price-fixing cartels, for obvious reasons, run their schemes in secret. Cartel members have strong mutual incentives to keep their unlawful agreements hidden from customers and authorities—meetings are covert, records are minimal or coded, and communication is often conspiratorial. The DOJ Antitrust Division and FTC thus struggle to detect cartel behavior through normal market observation alone, and direct evidence is hard to obtain without an insider. The DOJ's leniency program, introduced in the 1990s, was essentially a solution to an information problem: It created a race for conspirators to confess because traditional detection was so difficult. The academic literature has since documented the effectiveness of leniency in increasing detection (by encouraging self-reporting)—but also the limits of agency-led discovery without such tools. An influential empirical piece by Peter G. Bryant and E. Woodrow Eckard estimated that without informants, the annual probability of a given cartel being detected (between 1961 and 1988) was on the order of 13–17 percent.[37]

Environmental law enforcement also shows firms' strategic evasion of detection. In regulatory regimes like the Clean Air Act and Clean Water Act, regulators impose reporting requirements on companies (e.g., annual emissions reports, spill notifications) and conduct inspections, but companies have found ways to game these systems. A notorious example was the Volkswagen emissions scandal: VW programmers installed "defeat device" software in diesel cars that made emissions appear compliant under testing conditions, while in real-world driving the cars polluted far above legal limits. This deception fooled US and European environmental regulators for years. The truth emerged only when independent researchers performed road tests outside the standard protocol.

In sum, the literature converges on the understanding that enforcement agencies struggle to uncover violations largely because the informational deck is stacked against them. Regulated entities typically know far more about their own operations and any wrongdoing; regulators have limited means to independently obtain that knowledge. This core asymmetry is exacerbated by resource limits, deliberate concealment, and institutional incentives on both sides. It is a problem that spans administrative law, political economy, and regulatory design.

Private enforcement ameliorates some of the informational asymmetries. By giving private parties an incentive to file claims—often via multiple damages and fee-shifting—private enforcement surfaces information that is otherwise hidden. A right to sue empowers insiders, people who sit closest to misconduct—disgruntled employees, short-changed consumers, neighbors breathing contaminated air—into a dispersed detection network. Because of the financial incentives of litigation, those insiders suddenly have a personal stake in exposing information the government would struggle to obtain (or could not legally compel) on its own. Antitrust suits often begin when a purchaser notices anomalous, uniform price increases; wage claims surface fraud known only to front-line workers; environmental citizen suits turn downstream landowners into groundwater monitors. By opening the courthouse door, Congress reverses the usual information asymmetry: Firms can still try to hide records, but any individual who sees a violation now has a clear, monetizable path to bring it to light.

Private plaintiffs often use their insider information to bring meritorious cases that public agencies cannot pursue. According to one study by Stephen Choi and Adam Pritchard—comparing SEC actions with class action claims—class action plaintiffs in the securities context pursue cases that are as strong, or stronger, than the government's. This study suggests that private enforcers are filing good claims, not meritless lawsuits to extract costs.[38]

The American discovery system intensifies that dynamic. As I argue in *Discovery as Regulation*, discovery confers on private litigants "the functional equivalent of administrative subpoena power," allowing them to flush out information without prior judicial approval.[39] This pre-trial exchange of documents and testimony turns into a regulatory mechanism that compels firms to disgorge internal data. In regimes that hinge on private enforcement, this compelled disclosure deters wrongdoing and produces industry information for everyone to consume, including competitors and regulators. Discovery is thus more than a truth-finding aid for an individual case; it is an institutional mechanism.

Information surfaced through private litigation, moreover, does not remain isolated in civil dockets. Regulators piggyback on private filings—issuing parallel subpoenas, launching enforcement actions, or leveraging settlement agreements that copy the factual admissions already extracted from defendants. The SEC's ability to investigate corporate fraud after a securities class action, OSHA's reliance on whistleblower complaints, and the EPA's practice of shepherding citizen suits all illustrate a feedback loop in which privately generated evidence lowers the public cost of detection and proof. Even when agencies decline to intervene, the litigation record itself reshapes regulatory priorities by spotlighting problems (e.g., opioid diversion, diesel emissions cheating) that had escaped earlier notice. In this way, private enforcement smokes out information, channeling knowledge into the public domain and enabling more coherent regulatory oversight.

The informational case for private enforcement may evolve as detection technologies advance. Emerging AI-powered monitoring systems could dramatically enhance agencies' capacity to detect violations systematically. These technological developments suggest that informational asymmetries favoring private enforcement are not permanent features but contingent on monitoring capabilities. As these technologies mature, the relative informational advantage of private enforcement may diminish in some domains.

## THE RULE OF LAW AND POLITICAL POLARIZATION

Private enforcement offers a distinctive benefit for the rule of law: consistent enforcement across political administrations. As discussed above, private plaintiffs can serve as a failsafe when bureaucratic enforcement becomes unresponsive, politically compromised, or subject to large swings with each change in administration. This failsafe addresses a specific pathology that goes beyond mere enforcement capacity—the problem of inconsistent enforcement that strongly correlates with political affiliations rather than legal violations. While dysfunctional enforcement reflects regulatory capture or institutional weakness, inconsistent enforcement represents a clear threat to legal predictability and equal treatment under the law. In certain policy areas that depend on steady, predictable enforcement to maintain compliance cultures and prevent regulatory gaming, the promise of consistent private enforcement can provide an additional justification beyond typical dysfunction arguments.

This benefit is particularly salient in an era of high political polarization, when each new presidency brings considerable shifts in regulatory philosophy and enforcement priorities. Agencies like the EPA and Consumer Financial Protection Bureau have experienced significant reversals between the Obama, Trump, and Biden administrations, with enforcement priorities changing every four years. Such volatility can undermine the deterrent effect of regulation as regulated entities learn to simply wait out unfavorable administrations rather than investing in genuine compliance. Private enforcement, by contrast, provides a more stable enforcement baseline that persists regardless of which party controls the White House or regulatory agencies.

Consider the Trump Administration's flat-out refusal to enforce the TikTok ban.[40] Large congressional majorities adopted the Protecting Americans from Foreign Adversary Controlled Applications Act with significant bipartisan support, requiring ByteDance to divest from TikTok or face a ban.[41] The Supreme Court unanimously upheld the law shortly before its deadline. Yet as the ban took effect on January 19, 2025, the Trump administration immediately announced executive orders to prevent enforcement, first delaying the ban by seventy-five days, then extending it twice more for additional ninety-day periods through September 2025. These orders explicitly instructed the Department of Justice to "take no action to enforce" the statute and to issue letters to companies "stating that there has been no violation of the statute and that there is no liability"[42]—effectively dispensing waivers of enforcement reminiscent of the royal prerogatives that English kings exercised before 1688. There is no question that this non-enforcement was unlawful. Under the Take Care Clause, the president lacks discretion to refuse enforcement of congressional commands, and the Trump administration has offered no justification beyond the president's personal preference. This is a clear case of what legislators have feared for over a hundred years: a president who simply refuses to enforce a congressional command and excuses non-compliance with the law.

A private right of action against companies that continue to host TikTok would have prevented this problem and provided predictability for regulated entities. That predictability is especially important in regulatory areas where intermittent enforcement can trigger harmful equilibria or allow damaging practices to become entrenched. In such contexts, private enforcement serves not merely as a complement to government action but as an essential stabilizing force that prevents the regulatory equivalent of boom and bust cycles from undermining policy objectives.

But private enforcement introduces its own form of inconsistency: Private parties exercise enforcement discretion without democratic accountability, creating enforcement patterns that reflect private priorities rather than public policy goals. This dynamic varies significantly depending on the type of private enforcer involved. Profit-driven plaintiffs' attorneys have relatively consistent incentives to pursue cases with strong financial prospects, creating predictable if not necessarily optimal enforcement patterns. However, ideologically motivated legal organizations that rely on donations face different pressures that can produce their own forms of enforcement volatility. When policy areas like environmental protection or civil liberties attract surges of philanthropic support, enforcement activity may spike dramatically, driven by the priorities and resources of a small number of wealthy donors rather than the systematic assessment of legal violations or public need. This can create enforcement patterns that are just as politically contingent as government action, albeit responsive to different constituencies and funding cycles.

Despite this limitation, private enforcement generates an important additional benefit—it builds and sustains robust legal organizations that serve as institutional counterweights to government power. Organizations like the American Civil Liberties Union (ACLU) have used private enforcement mechanisms to develop sophisticated legal expertise, build institutional capacity, and maintain persistent advocacy that transcends electoral cycles. These organizations provide a form of institutional memory and legal infrastructure that can challenge government overreach and maintain pressure for legal compliance even during periods when government enforcement agencies are compromised. In this sense, private enforcement serves not just as an alternative enforcement mechanism but as a rule-of-law-strengthening institution that creates independent centers of legal expertise capable of holding both government and private actors accountable.

## PRIVATE ENFORCEMENT AND DEMOCRACY

Some scholars have argued that private enforcement does much more than play back-up to administrative agencies—it is a vehicle for democratic participation. Drawing on the Civil Rights Movement, scholars have long highlighted that private suits can empower political underdogs or weak constituencies who may otherwise lack the government's attention. That is, after all, what Title VII of the CRA was about.

Recently, legal scholar Luke Norris built a larger democratic justification for private enforcement as a mechanism that folds ordinary people into the regular work of governance.[43] Drawing on Progressive Era debates over expertise and popular sovereignty, Norris argued that private enforcement accomplishes three objectives beyond the reach of public acting alone: It counterbalances concentrated power, injects practical knowledge into fluid regulatory settings, and facilitates public deliberation.[44] Traditional regimes like environmental citizen suits, antidiscrimination actions, or False Claims Act qui tam suits score high on all three dimensions.

First, private enforcement can serve as countervailing power by enabling the little guy, thus inverting information and resource asymmetries that favor large firms or recalcitrant officials. Giving everyone the right to sue avoids the dangers of concentrated power and its effect on regulators and democracy.[45] Fee-shifting, treble damages, and collective actions turn workers, cheated consumers, and owners of polluted land into watchdogs who can haul powerful defendants into court without waiting for a reluctant agency.[46]

Second, private plaintiffs bring a wealth of expertise that informs fluid regulatory regimes. Agencies possess technical expertise, yet they often lack visibility into evolving workplace practices, cartel tactics, or emissions cheats. Insider plaintiffs supply that missing data. In Norris's terms, they bring "the expertise of experience" to dynamic regulatory environments, translating experienced harms into legal claims and obliging courts (and, often, regulators who piggyback on the record) to confront problems they might otherwise miss.[47] The discovery process arguably amplifies this contribution by forcing defendants to disgorge internal documents that ripple far beyond a single case.

Third, private lawsuits engage in a kind of democratic deliberation that shapes the law and regulation. Lawsuits are public events—citizens file complaints, evidence enters open dockets, opinions circulate, and legislators revise statutes in response. This iterative dialogue among citizens, courts, agencies, and Congress gives regulatory norms a connection to the experience of regular people and keeps them contestable. Successful or not, private suits thus widen the channels through which people debate the rules that govern them.[48]

While Norris's argument praises the potential of private enforcement done well, there are significant problems that point against its democratic bona fides. It is true that, on the one hand, private litigation can democratize legal enforcement by empowering individual plaintiffs to achieve policy outcomes that might be impossible through electoral processes. But this democratizing potential comes at the cost of democratic accountability. After all, private lawsuits often operate in a counter-majoritarian fashion, allowing judges to override public policy decisions that better reflect the majority will. While judicial insulation from politics enables the protection of minority rights, it also raises legitimacy concerns about the separation of powers, particularly when judges assume legislative-like roles. On top of this, private enforcement is typically driven by plaintiffs' attorneys with financial incentives to pursue profitable cases rather than socially optimal ones, or by well-resourced plaintiffs who can afford to employ these attorneys. These financial incentives create a system where enforcement patterns reflect economic rather than democratic priorities. In contrast, the administrative state maintains accountability to elected officials. In other words, the democratic angle is complicated.

## COSTS AND CRITIQUES OF PRIVATE ENFORCEMENT

Yet despite private enforcement's many benefits, it also comes with significant costs. Chief among these is that private enforcement can produce an excessive number of claims, inefficiently increasing enforcement and over-deterring conduct beyond socially optimal levels. These concerns fall into three analytically distinct, though overlapping, categories: incentive misalignment, democratic deficit, and regulatory incoherence.

A powerful critique of private enforcement is that it generates too many claims, imposing costs that diminish public welfare. In practice, this can mean duplicative suits against the same defendant or conduct, heavy judicial and agency burdens, and excessive overall sanctions. Private plaintiffs, driven by potential damages awards, may pursue marginal or repetitive cases because they incur little cost of enforcement relative to the defendant and society, leading to a "waste of judicial resources."[49] In short, private enforcement over-deters legal violations and produces redundancy: When every misstep risks damages suits plus fee awards, firms may forgo good ventures or innovative practices that society would otherwise welcome. Private suits can "lead to overzealous and inefficient enforcement of federal statutes" since private litigants do not internalize many social costs.[50]

Law and economics scholars long ago highlighted that private enforcement can both increase deterrence and over-deter. Scholars like William M. Landes and Richard A. Posner originally argued that private enforcement is a cost-effective substitute for government enforcement because it deploys bounty hunters who expand the probability of detection without burdening the public fisc.[51] But they also argued that competition between enforcers could lead to overenforcement of the law because profit-maximizing private parties would overinvest in cases. Subsequent work—most prominently Steven Shavell and Mitch Polinsky's—expanded the model.[52] Shavell demonstrated why private plaintiffs would be likely to over-enforce the law. The main reason is divergence between private and public interests—private litigants capture the full reward of a judgment yet bear only their own costs.[53] That means they sue whenever the expected payoff is positive, not when expected social gains are positive. Private enforcers, then, ignore key costs, including expenditures, court congestion, and the chilling effect of outsized penalties on beneficial conduct. Bureaucrats, by contrast, must weigh those system-wide considerations and remain (at least formally) answerable to elected overseers. The upshot, Shavell warned, is a risk of overenforcement: a proliferation of marginal or duplicative claims that drives total sanctions above the efficient level and channels scarce judicial resources toward private rent-seeking rather than public welfare.

Economic critics highlight how financial incentives can drive overzealous litigation. Contingent-fee lawyers and entrepreneurial plaintiffs may pursue cases primarily for profit or notoriety, not because they serve the public interest. Working on contingency, lawyers enjoy the upside of a large percentage if they win or settle, but only sunk time if they lose.

That asymmetric payoff pushes attorneys to identify any colorable violation, bundling borderline cases into mass filings, and using the prospect of treble damages or discovery costs to extract settlements. In that calculus, the public value of the lawsuit is secondary; what matters is the expected private return in a litigation portfolio. Still, as discussed above, a major supporter of private enforcement, Professor Brian Fitzpatrick, argues that the profit motive is a benefit, not a cost, of private enforcement.

A second line of critique focuses less on incentives than on legitimacy: Private enforcers answer to no electorate and coordinate with no cabinet agency, so their litigation agenda can diverge sharply from democratically chosen priorities. Elected prosecutors and agency heads can be hauled before voters or congressional overseers if they squander resources or derail policy; plaintiffs' lawyers and their clients face no comparable discipline. Plaintiffs are simply not insulated by any democratic checks.[54] The result is, again, what critics call guerrilla litigation: multiple, uncoordinated lawsuits that flood dockets, collide with negotiated compliance programs, and force agencies to clean up the wreckage after the fact. Because those suits land in the chambers of generalist judges—rather than within expert bodies that care about an entire regulatory field—case outcomes can fragment policy and undermine carefully tailored regulatory strategies that modern governance is supposed to deliver.[55]

A final objection targets programmatic coherence. Modern agencies often pursue careful regulation, combining guidance, negotiated compliance, and strategic sanctioning to steer whole industries toward better behavior. Financially driven private suits can weaken that arrangement. Without any systemic interest in mind, individual cases are resolved on terms attractive to individual claimants and may impose remedies that clash with agency consent decrees, trigger cross-cutting precedents in different jurisdictions, or frighten firms away from voluntary disclosures that regulators actively encourage. As Engstrom warns, the "piecemeal and unyielding nature of profit-motivated private enforcement will deprive regulatory regimes of needed 'coherence,'"[56] undoing the bargains that make oversight possible. The upshot is a landscape in which no single actor—least of all the expert agency—can plan with confidence, because each new lawsuit threatens to redraw the compliance map overnight.

Critics often support their arguments with reference to specific sectors. In antitrust, skeptics warn that private treble-damage actions can over-deter procompetitive conduct or duplicate government antitrust efforts. Early law and economics scholars noted tensions: Firms have strong incentives to sue rivals (even for competitive behavior), while duplication of DOJ cases could impose "extortionate" damages on companies.[57] In securities law, private class actions are accused of spawning speculative lawsuits and imposing high litigation costs on capital markets. Critics claim these suits often add little beyond the SEC's work and can encourage frivolous claims or "piggybacking" on weak public enforcement. The same critiques bear out in the environmental context, as we'll see in Chapter 9.

One final concern to highlight here is the problem of ideological litigation. Private enforcement can impose significant costs when plaintiffs are driven not by the profit motive—as Brian Fitzpatrick praises—but by political or ideological goals.[58] This commitment short-circuits one of the benefits of private enforcement—that lawyers will file meritorious cases because they're interested in a financial payout. Ideological litigants instead will file claims for many reasons, regardless of the merits. Private enforcement can thus impose large social costs when plaintiffs sue to advance a political agenda: Because their payoff is intangible—perhaps victory in the culture war—they are willing to press marginal, even money-losing, claims simply to burden their opponents. Abortion "bounty" suits under Texas SB 8 illustrate the dynamic: Ideological funders absorb the filing fees, volunteers supply free labor, and defendants face ruinous discovery and reputational harm even if the cases collapse on the merits.[59] Unlike profit-minded lawyers, these plaintiffs are immune to the disciplining effect of economics. The result is a weaponization of procedure that can chill lawful behavior, clog dockets with weak cases, and destabilize carefully balanced regulatory schemes; precisely the "guerrilla warfare" that critics of private enforcement despise.

## A TEST FOR LEGISLATORS

Developing a good justification for private enforcement is important for legislators. It allows them to answer the question: If we're interested in regulating some behavior, should we do it through public or private enforcement? The default, of course, is public enforcement. Article II's Take Care Clause, Congress's comprehensive reliance on agencies, and the Supreme Court's modern hostility to implied causes of action all signal that government lawyers remain the default executors of federal statutes. So the question is whether to add that private overlay on a public enforcement baseline.

This chapter argues that the justification is strongest when three conditions converge: (1) Public enforcers lack the capacity to police violations at scale, (2) the risk of capture, corruption, or partisan changes threatens to weaken agency enforcement, and (3) deep informational asymmetries insulate wrongdoing from official detection. Where those gaps loom large, Congress and state legislators should empower private plaintiffs to supply workforce capacity, disperse power, and surface hidden evidence.

Yet legislators must balance out these benefits with an array of potential costs. The same market incentives that nudge lawyers to chase hidden misconduct can overshoot, producing redundant suits, punishing efficient conduct, and taxing courts and regulators with ever-expanding dockets. Democratic accountability is weaker as well: Plaintiffs' lawyers and funders are not answerable to voters, so their litigation agenda can drift away from democratically chosen priorities and weaken regulatory strategies. Worse still, when lawsuits are driven by ideology rather than the profit motive, normal economic discipline evaporates; litigation becomes a form of political combat that can chill lawful behavior and destabilize entire regulatory domains.

So legislators need to take a calibrated approach. They should view private enforcement neither as an automatic default nor as a necessary evil, but as a targeted instrument suited to specific governance deficits. Where agency capacity is robust, capture risks low, and information readily verifiable, the public enforcer should lead. Where those conditions falter, a carefully designed private remedy—tempered by fee-shifting rules, class certification standards, or agency veto gates—can supplement state power while containing the dangers of over-deterrence and regulatory incoherence.

A legislative checklist might ask the following key questions:

- Capacity Gap: Would violations likely go undetected or unremedied if we rely on public enforcement alone? Ask whether projected staffing, expertise, and appropriations give the public enforcer a realistic chance of monitoring regulated entities.

- Dysfunction Risk: Is the agency unusually vulnerable to capture, partisan swings, or procedural paralysis? Indicators include heavy industry lobbying, a revolving-door workforce, highly polarized oversight committees, or statutory mandates that routinely stall.

- Information Asymmetry: Do potential plaintiffs possess superior, insider knowledge that the agency cannot easily obtain? Whistleblower access to internal ledgers, emissions data, or payroll records signals that a private right of action will unlock evidence otherwise hidden behind corporate walls.
- Social Costs and Legitimacy: Is there a potential divergence between private benefits and social welfare that goes beyond the normal divergence inherent to private litigation? Is public legitimacy an important goal in this area of law?

Only when private enforcement satisfies this balancing test should Congress add a private right of action—and even then only after a second-round screen that weighs the classic critiques of social costs and lack of legitimacy. Legislators should estimate the marginal deterrence gained against the likely social costs of duplicative filings, fragmented policy, and democratic deficit. If expected recoveries (net of litigation expenses) substantially exceed those costs, the legislature should adopt the right to sue; if not, Congress should bolster public capacity instead or cabin private suits with agency-approval requirements, damages caps, or other safeguards. Applied rigorously, this test ensures that private enforcement is deployed where it is most needed.

This chapter's analysis of normative justifications leaves unaddressed several developments that complicate private enforcement in practice. Most significantly, the past two decades have witnessed a systematic procedural retrenchment aimed at constraining private litigation. The Supreme Court has repeatedly blessed the use of mandatory arbitration in consumer and employment contracts, weakening private enforcement. On top of that, the Court has also heightened pleading standards, made class actions more difficult to certify, limited the breadth of discovery, and narrowed standing doctrine. These constraints raise questions about whether private enforcement retains the capacity to serve the supplementation and information-forcing functions identified here.

The chapters that follow pick up from this balanced assessment. They examine, in turn, the procedural levers that can sharpen the benefits and blunt the costs of private suits, evaluate evidence from antitrust, securities, and environmental law, and propose reforms that align private incentives with the public good. The overarching lesson is simple: Private enforcement is most effective when used carefully, strategically, and in concert with a vigilant, adequately funded public sector.

# EIGHT

## WHEN PRIVATE ENFORCEMENT *IS* JUSTIFIED

There are major regulatory areas that benefit from private enforcement. As expected, in these areas we see a powerful convergence of weak enforcement capacity, chronic regulatory capture, and informational asymmetries that shield wrongdoing from official detection. Chief among these is employment law, where the Fair Labor Standards Act of 1938 and all fifty states' wages and hours laws create an almost total reliance on private lawsuits rather than regulation by the Department of Labor (and state equivalents). And, as discussed below, in this area, private enforcement draws on all three of its traditional justifications.

But not every regulatory area neatly satisfies the capacity, dysfunction, and informational asymmetries trifecta. Areas like securities law or antitrust are supervised by robust and independent agencies like the SEC and FTC. In those areas, we don't see regulatory dysfunction but nonetheless still find informational and capacity problems that call for a right to sue. That is why the capacity, dysfunction, informational asymmetries test is a *balancing* test that weighs multiple factors, alongside a consideration of the social costs of litigation.

To better understand when and why private enforcement is justified, this chapter begins with the neat story of employment law before complicating the picture with securities litigation. It applies to both of these regulatory domains the framework laid out above: (1) Capacity Gap: Would violations likely go undetected or unremedied if we rely on public enforcement alone?; (2) Dysfunction Risk: Is the agency unusually vulnerable to capture, partisan swings, or procedural paralysis?; (3) Information Asymmetry: Do potential plaintiffs possess superior, insider knowledge that the agency cannot easily obtain?; and (4) Social Costs and Legitimacy: Is there a potential divergence between private benefits and social welfare that goes beyond the normal divergence inherent to private litigation? Up first, then, is California's powerful right to sue for labor violations.

## CALIFORNIA'S PRIVATE ATTORNEYS GENERAL ACT

California's Private Attorneys General Act (PAGA) of 2004 creates a unique state-level mechanism for enforcing labor and employment protections.[1] The statute grants California's workers a private right of action against current or former employers for labor code violations that would otherwise be enforced by the Labor Workforce Development Agency (LWDA).[2] Since its enactment, PAGA lawsuits have increased significantly, drawing sharp critiques from California's business community.[3] To understand why PAGA emerged as a key mechanism for labor law enforcement in California, we must dive into its history.

***1. Legislative History.*** Prior to the introduction of PAGA, the California Assembly commissioned several studies on the efficacy of the LWDA's enforcement efforts, with an eye towards understanding the wage and hour legal landscape. One of the first big conclusions to emerge from these studies was that public enforcers were chronically underfunded and understaffed, reducing their enforcement capacity. The Senate Rules Committee, for instance, concluded that the LWDA had grossly underenforced labor protections due to severe budgetary shortfalls and structural limitations on public agency enforcement. The LWDA and other enforcement agencies within the California Department of Industrial Relations (DIR) had for decades failed to hire new staff to keep pace with the overall growth of California's labor force.[4] Even in "targeted" industries such as the food service sector, studies found it would take a century for government agencies to inspect California's businesses under their pre-PAGA enforcement rate.[5] Enforcement efforts were particularly poor in California's growing "underground economy."[6] Moreover, some labor violations were subject only to criminal enforcement. Prosecutors devoted insufficient resources to investigating and prosecuting these low-level criminal violations, allowing employers to avoid punishments for code violations.[7]

In response to these studies and to a recession in the early 2000s, Senator Joe Dunn proposed the Private Attorneys General Act as SB 796 in February 2003. Dunn, a Democrat representative of Santa Ana from 1998–2006, was primarily known at the time as "the Man Who Cracked Enron" for his work as Chair of the Senate Judiciary Committee during the 2001 California energy crisis.[8] Dunn had a relatively brief career in elected office, never holding another government position after he hit his term limit in the California Senate. Dunn's work on the Senate Judiciary Committee and his work prior to office likely informed his support for PAGA's private enforcement regime; he was a prominent personal injury and consumer attorney prior to his 1998 election,[9] and he returned to private practice after stepping down.[10] Key to his proposal was a private right of action that empowered any employee to sue for any labor code violations.

Support for SB 796 splintered along partisan lines as the bill made its way through the Senate Labor and Industrial Relations and Rules Committees.[11] Neither sponsors nor interest groups supporting PAGA had a strong ideological preference for a private right of action. Senate President Pro Tempore John Burton, a progressive Democrat, and his allies in organized labor recognized that the business community was pushing to gut public enforcement agencies. Their arguments seemed to recognize both an enforcement capacity problem but also a question of regulatory dysfunction. They urged Senator Dunn to introduce PAGA as a compromise measure that he would pull from consideration if pro-business groups ceased lobbying for weakened public enforcement. The business community, however, did not back down, and Burton and his allies in the Assembly used their political capital to get the bill through both chambers.[12]

In an ordinary legislative session, Governor Gray Davis would have almost certainly vetoed PAGA. He was well known for allying with industry groups and was opposed to Burton for personal and ideological reasons. However, Davis faced a close recall election the same year PAGA was introduced in the legislature. With the bill sitting on his desk, Sen. Burton and organized labor groups were able to exert enormous political leverage over

Davis; if he failed to sign the bill, union organizers would withhold their campaign contributions and mobilization efforts to defeat the recall challenge. SB 796 narrowly passed in both chambers before lame-duck Davis signed the bill on October 12, 2003.[13]

***2. Political Support.*** SB 796's co-sponsors,[14] the California Labor Federation, the California AFL-CIO, and the California Rural Legal Assistance Foundation, argued that California's inability to enforce labor laws effectively required a "creative solution" to address structural gaps in staffing and the predicted growth of the underground economy.[15] Another proponent of the bill, Protection & Advocacy, Inc., a disability rights advocacy group, argued that it would specifically support people with disabilities by providing them "some mechanism by which to get an employer to comply with the Labor Code."[16]

Most statewide business and employer associations opposed the bill on two grounds. First, as articulated by the California Chamber of Commerce, the original version of PAGA did not include any exhaustion requirements for administrative or procedural remedies.[17] Second, employers were seriously concerned that PAGA would allow private attorneys to weaponize the law to profit from frivolous litigation on behalf of employees. As the California Motor Car Dealers Association wrote in opposition to the bill, "a private enforcement statute in the hands of unscrupulous lawyers is a recipe for disaster."[18]

Contemporary media and scholarly analysis of PAGA focused on employer organizations' primary concern about the potential costs of a surge of private litigation. Los Angeles law firm Ervin Cohen & Jessup described PAGA as the "Sue Your Boss Bill" and the "Bounty Hunter Law" in its legislative analysis,[19] and scholars warned that the law "effectively deputizes California's more than 17 million workers to enforce the Labor Code themselves."[20] Business groups have maintained consistent arguments against PAGA for the last two decades, advocating for expanded funding to the Division of Labor Standards Enforcement (DLSE) as an alternative to lawsuit-driven enforcement mechanisms. These business groups found support in a report by former regulators, which found that agency adjudication led to greater employee awards and faster resolution times than PAGA cases.[21]

***3. The Passage of PAGA.***[22] The California Legislature finally enacted PAGA in 2003 to empower workers as "private attorneys general" for labor enforcement. PAGA creates a representative cause of action for "aggrieved employees" (those who worked for an employer and were subject to at least one Labor Code violation). Unlike a class action, each plaintiff sues individually but "in the name of" the State and on behalf of all similarly aggrieved workers. To initiate a PAGA claim, an employee must first send a written notice to both the employer and the LWDA, identifying the alleged Labor Code violations and giving the agency sixty-five days to investigate or intervene. If the LWDA does not take the case, the employee may then file a civil lawsuit in court on behalf of the State and other affected employees.

The remedy in a PAGA action is strictly statutory penalties, not unpaid wages or back pay. In fact, PAGA suits cannot recover wages, interest, or injunctive relief—only the Labor Code's civil penalties. As set by statute, the penalty proceeds are split three ways: 50 percent goes into the State's general fund, 25 percent to a special labor law enforcement fund, and 25 percent to the aggrieved employee(s). In practice, plaintiffs' attorneys typically petition the court for these penalties on behalf of everyone named in the notice.

PAGA has generated thousands of lawsuits. In the first decade after enactment, filings grew roughly fourfold.[23] For example, one report noted 759 PAGA notices in 2005 versus 3,137 in 2013.[24] The growth has accelerated in recent years: Tracking data show PAGA notices skyrocketed in the early 2020s. One analysis found over "2,000 more PAGA notices were filed in 2023" than in 2022, reaching an all-time high of roughly 760 notices in October 2023 for just that month.[25] Many commentators view this as evidence of an exponential rise in representative wage and hour litigation in California.

PAGA cases overwhelmingly involve wage-theft claims. One recent report notes that roughly 91 percent of PAGA suits allege wage and hour violations; most commonly, unpaid overtime (in 79 percent of cases) or unpaid regular wages (76 percent).[26] The monetary impact of these suits is large. California's 2019 fiscal year saw $88 million collected in PAGA penalties.[27] By contrast, average payouts per worker from PAGA cases have often been modest—a CalChamber analysis found average individual recovery of ~$1,264 in PAGA court cases—but those figures reflect high attorney fees and litigation costs.[28]

***4. New Reforms.*** PAGA remains controversial. Supporters (mostly labor and worker advocacy groups) praise it as essential to catching wage theft that agencies miss. A UCLA labor report concludes there is "no evidence of a negative effect on the economy or a flood of frivolous litigation" from PAGA; rather, "PAGA has demonstrably enhanced Labor Code compliance among employers [and] built enforcement capacity."[29] Proponents argue PAGA creates a powerful compliance incentive because it threatens substantial penalties and lawyers' scrutiny, whereas before, such violations might have gone unpunished.

Critics—chiefly business associations and some Republican legislators—paint PAGA as a "sue your boss" shakedown. They note that (1) PAGA lawsuits have increased roughly 1,000 percent since 2004;[30] (2) statutory penalties can dwarf actual harm (an infraction only discovered years later may trigger hundreds of dollars per day in penalties per employee);[31] and (3) most of the payout often goes to attorneys.[32] Employers complain that even minor or technical violations become leveraged, forcing settlements "regardless of the validity" of the claim.[33] California's LWDA itself has observed that many private PAGA settlements "fell short of protecting the interests of the state workers," implying that the negotiations often prioritize lawyers' fees over workers' recovery.[34]

As a result of these debates, there have been numerous reform proposals. The Fix PAGA coalition, backed by the California Chamber of Commerce and many of the State's business and trade associations, supported an initiative to put the question of repealing and replacing PAGA before voters on the 2024 California general ballot.[35] After qualifying for the ballot in 2022, the initiative's proponents reached a compromise with PAGA supporters, resulting in Governor Newsom's June 2024 PAGA reform measures.[36]

In July 2024, Governor Gavin Newsom signed two bills that significantly overhauled PAGA.[37] AB 2288 and SB 92 modify the right of action and other PAGA provisions codified in Labor Code §§ 2699–2699.5. The reformed law includes a number of new pro-employer provisions. First, to have standing to bring a PAGA claim, an employee must have personally suffered the same Labor Code violation as the employee(s) they claim are aggrieved. Previously, aggrieved employees were able to file PAGA suits against any Labor Code violation. Second, there is now a one-year statute of limitations to initiate a claim.[38] Third, the new law caps penalties for employers' non-negligent Labor Code violations. If an employer can show that they took "all reasonable steps to be in compliance" before a PAGA notice is received, their liability will be capped at 15 percent of the normal statutory penalty.[39] The existence of a Labor Code violation is not sufficient to establish that the employer's conduct was not reasonable. Fourth, plaintiffs are required to comply with a sixty-day notice and cure period.[40] If an employer remedies a Labor Code violation during this period, their liability will be capped at 30 percent of the normal statutory penalty unless their violation was found to be malicious or fraudulent.[41] Fifth, the legislation expanded the list of Labor Code violations that may be cured to avoid civil liability under PAGA.

***5. Other State Labor Enforcement Laws.*** California's adoption of PAGA ignited debates about similar laws across the country. Every state has a wage and hour statute that depends on private enforcement. But not all states embrace California's general private right of action to enforce any violation of the labor code. The Maine legislature came close to passing a law similar to PAGA in 2021, but the governor vetoed the bill after it passed both houses of the state legislature.[42] Maine's proposed law would have authorized not only aggrieved employees but also advocacy groups and other workers to bring enforcement suits on behalf of workers.[43] Connecticut's legislature contemplated two narrow private rights of action for labor violations. The first would have allowed private suits for labor standard breaches at certain "warehouse distribution centers" as an additional enforcement mechanism to public administrative proceedings.[44] The second would have enabled private suits for violations of the State's expanded paid sick leave standards.[45] Both bills died in committee.

While New Jersey lacks a private right of action for permanent workers, it recently created a private right of action for temporary laborers. The Temporary Workers Bill of Rights finds that temporary workers require greater legal protections, as they are typically underpaid and far less likely to receive employer-sponsored benefits compared to full-time workers.[46] Aggrieved temporary workers may bring civil actions against their employers and the temporary help services that placed them, with no administrative exhaustion requirement and a six-year statute of limitations.[47]

New York City recently adopted a private right of action to supplement its public enforcement regime for employee leave protections, though there is no statewide right of action in New York. When the New York City Earned Safe and Sick Time Act (ESSTA) was passed in 2014, employees seeking redress for statutory violations were limited to filing administrative complaints with the NYC Department of Consumer and Worker Protection (DCWP). In January 2024, the City Council unanimously amended the law to create a new private right of action.[48] There is no notice or administrative exhaustion requirement, and plaintiffs may commence administrative complaints and private suits concurrently as long as they notify the DCWP if their civil action has commenced. However, the DCWP has not clarified whether it will stay administrative investigations if there is an ongoing lawsuit.[49]

## WHY PRIVATE ENFORCEMENT IS JUSTIFIED IN EMPLOYMENT LAW

Setting aside debates over policy, for our purposes the key question is: Assuming California will continue to prohibit a wide array of labor code violations, is a private right of action *justified* in addition to the LWDA's investigatory powers? Applying the framework developed in Chapter 7—focusing on enforcement capacity, regulatory dysfunction, and informational asymmetries alongside social costs—suggests that, yes, it is.[50]

***1. Capacity.*** First, we ask whether labor law violations would likely go undetected or unremedied if California relies on public enforcement alone. The evidence suggests that California's labor agencies, like labor regulators at both the state and federal level, are chronically underfunded, leading to a thorough lack of enforcement capacity. Every analysis of CalOSHA or the LWDA funding structure and history has found that these agencies have never been adequately funded, are severely understaffed, and suffer from routine budget cuts. In 2023, the state had roughly one field investigator for every 113,000 workers—a ratio that leaves entire industries functionally unmonitored.[51] Administrative wage-theft complaints now sit in a queue that tops 47,000 backlogged cases, with workers waiting more than six times the statutory deadline for a hearing.[52]

Some of the chronic underfunding is due to business cycle reasons, but there are also important structural problems. On the temporary side, some resource and staffing shortages are due to budgetary shortfalls around recessions. For example, in the late 1990s the State faced a short-term recession and budgetary shortfall that led to cuts at several agencies. But here is where the structural problems come in: Any time California deals with funding shortages like that one, industry groups target the LWDA for defunding, knowing they are easier for legislators to trim than, say, schools or firefighting. In a difficult business climate, the LWDA is an easy target and becomes among the first agencies to lose funds. In the early 2000s, industry groups seized on the opportunity to advocate for slashing the enforcement budgets of the State's labor regulatory agencies, which were already understaffed and under-resourced. Because the political rewards for cutting expenditures are immediate while the costs are dispersed among low-wage workers, the LWDA's staffing levels have never recovered. The result is a structural deficit in enforcement capacity—even in boom years, appropriations do little more than back-fill prior cuts, and during recessions, regulators again find themselves on the chopping block.

California's chronic underfunding illustrates how enforcement capacity can be effectively exogenous despite being formally under legislative control. In addition to the structural issues raised above, California operates under constitutional constraints on fiscal capacity. Several propositions and ballot initiatives make it extremely difficult to legislate tax increases. These constraints mean that even legislators committed to robust enforcement face practically immovable fiscal ceilings. Combined with the political economy dynamics where industry groups systematically target labor agencies during budget crises, enforcement capacity becomes locked at chronically low levels regardless of legislative preferences.

The combination of constitutional constraints, concentrated industry opposition to labor regulators, and political incentives that reward cost-cutting means that we can expect a structural lack of enforcement capacity. Projected staffing and appropriations give no credible prospect that the government alone can police the state's workplaces.

PAGA's private enforcement scheme is a direct way to increase enforcement capacity. By deputizing employees, it effectively multiplies enforcement agents. UCLA researchers observed that PAGA has "built enforcement capacity" because it brings thousands of additional cases into the system. In practice, workers in high-violation industries have used PAGA to pursue claims at a rate far above what the Labor Department can investigate. Those suits yielded more than $88 million in civil penalties in 2019 alone, money split between the state and the affected employees.[53] Because of PAGA, millions of dollars that might have gone undetected now flow into state coffers and worker recovery. On the first prong of our framework, then, PAGA squarely passes: It replaces missing public capacity with privately financed detection and prosecution.

***2. Dysfunction.*** Second, and relatedly, we scrutinize whether labor agencies are unusually vulnerable to capture, partisan swings, or procedural paralysis. Some key indicators include heavy industry lobbying, a revolving door workforce, highly polarized oversight committees, or statutory mandates that routinely stall.

California's wage and hour history answers in the affirmative. Employer pressure routinely stalls agency rule-making and blunts enforcement priorities; political appointees must weigh campaign donors' interests against workers' claims. In this area, regulatory dysfunction is clear because companies and employers invest heavily in courting favor from regulators while simultaneously lobbying for budget cuts to public enforcement budgets.

A private right of action responds to this problem by diffusing enforcement power across thousands of employees and their attorneys, reducing the influence of corporate lobbying and ensuring consistent enforcement of the labor code. By enabling private citizens to enforce labor laws, PAGA diversifies enforcement beyond a single bureaucracy that might be influenced by industry. In theory, this makes it harder for powerful business interests to quietly soften penalties or bias inspections. California's experience suggests that PAGA serves as a public check on lax enforcement. For example, the state's own agencies sometimes choose not to act on PAGA notices, but the lawsuits still proceed in court. This partly bypasses the normal budget and political pressures on regulators. In its legislative findings, California emphasized that PAGA actions would be subject to the same primacy rule as state actions, but otherwise left enforcement to "aggrieved employees" when needed. In short, PAGA reduces sole reliance on state regulators, helping prevent a situation where the agency is "captured" or suffers from corruption and other problems.

***3. Information.*** On top of regulatory capture and a lack of state capacity, labor enforcement faces a classic information asymmetry between employers and regulators. Labor violations of all kinds—failure to provide breaks, unpaid overtime work, falsified wage statements, or the failure to reimburse uniforms—all take place behind closed doors. Unless an investigator happens to be at that workplace, or an insider speaks up, those violations remain invisible. Contrast employment from other areas of law where legal violations are public—securities violations can be determined by analyses of public market trades; environmental pollution is visible in surrounding communities; antitrust violations affect consumer prices. But when an employer fails to pay an employee, the information is solely between them. The answer to our third question, then, is yes, potential plaintiffs possess superior, insider knowledge that public enforcers cannot easily obtain.

Employees are quintessential insiders: They work within regulated entities and have access to confidential information. They see whether timekeepers round down, whether supervisors shave tips, or whether meal periods are skipped to meet production quotas. The only way for outside agencies to discover this information is to send inspectors on-site. But, for structural reasons discussed above, regulators have insufficient staff to do so. Moreover, even when inspectors are available, employers can game the system by shielding information from them. Employers have much more information than regulators about day-to-day practices (break timing, off-the-clock work, wage statements, etc.). And they have access to different techniques on how to game that information.

Regulators could try to give incentives to employees; many whistleblower regimes operate this way. But without a guaranteed payout, employees have no incentive to flag the problem to regulators because they fear losing their jobs.

Private enforcement cures these informational and incentive problems. A statute like PAGA leverages employees' insider knowledge: Empowered with a right to sue, workers bring cases forward (and evidence) that an agency cannot see. Empirical data support this: From 2018 to 2021, workers filed over 4,200 PAGA claims in certain industries, nearly triple the number of official inspections in those sectors.[54] This suggests that employees are surfacing widespread violations that labor law enforcers would likely never detect on their own. In effect, PAGA converts private information into enforcement. California's legislative findings spoke to this need to police the "underground" economy of hidden violations—exactly what informational asymmetry describes.

Private enforcement also incentivizes employees to identify wage theft, overtime violations, and other infractions with a potential reward of compensatory and punitive damages. Without a statutory bounty, most employees would stay silent—reporting wage theft risks retaliation, black-listing, and legal costs. PAGA's penalty sharing flips that calculus. The prospect of a monetary award compensates for the risk of losing a job, while shifting the legal costs lets plaintiffs' counsel front the litigation costs. In short, the statute harnesses private gain to overcome information asymmetries that make public policing so difficult.

This decentralized approach also enables private plaintiffs to surface information that can both help their cases and help regulators. PAGA turns insider vantage points into a public asset: A worker who spots non-compliance can step into the shoes of the LWDA, file a notice, and compel discovery that would otherwise require a costly, formal investigation. PAGA notices are therefore not duplicative; they fill blind spots. Between 2018 and 2021, workers lodged more than 4,200 PAGA claims in industries such as warehousing, food service, and janitorial services.[55] Each notice unlocks discovery, giving employees subpoena power to obtain payroll records, scheduling software logs, or manager emails (documents that agencies rarely see absent a raid). Regulators can (and routinely do) piggyback on that evidence, using the private record to launch parallel investigations or to calibrate industry-wide guidance. And PAGA also provides a procedural advantage by allowing employees to bring representative claims on behalf of other workers even when bound by individual arbitration agreements.

*4. **Social Costs.*** Of course, a powerful private right of action like PAGA's brings up classic concerns with guerrilla litigation to extract settlements, duplicative filings, fragmented policy for employers, and a lack of democratic checks on unions and employees. Yes, PAGA filings have grown—from around 1,000 notices in 2013 to more than 7,000 notices in 2023—but most notices never ripen into lawsuits, and the data do not show a runaway flood of cases.[56] A 2021 empirical review for the Legislative Analyst's Office found "no evidence of a negative effect on the economy or a flood of frivolous litigation."[57] Another common critique is that "PAGA has resulted in a proliferation of litigation that has mostly benefited plaintiffs' attorneys with large fee awards and resulted in minimal payments to employees."[58]

Despite these problems, any concerns with PAGA's ability to produce frivolous litigation can be checked via procedural calibration, precisely the approach California has pursued. Take first the litigation-flood argument.

One way to address this problem has been the 2024 reform package negotiated by Governor Newsom, a statutory cap on penalties for employers that promptly cure violations, and an expansion of the list of curable infractions.[59] Second, any critiques that plaintiffs' attorneys bring cases that public regulators would not bring—because they're socially costly—are weakened by the fact that every PAGA case begins with a notice to public regulators and settlements cannot take effect without both LWDA review and judicial approval (though the regulator does not have an actual veto).[60] Moreover, private plaintiffs keep only 25 percent of any civil penalties while the public keeps the rest, giving the statute a democratic element. Third, new reforms also require that employee-plaintiffs have personally experienced violations. This weakens any potential ideological misuse of the statute, ensuring that only injured parties participate in each case.

PAGA certainly imposes costs, but its procedural checks—agency notice, judicial review, penalty discretion—and legislative amendments meaningfully blunt the classic objections of over-deterrence, democratic deficit, and regulatory incoherence. What remains is a statute that still mobilizes insider information and plaintiffs' attorneys to make up for enforcement gaps, while now offering outs for employers and guardrails against abuse.

## SECURITIES CLASS ACTIONS AND THE SEC

Unlike employment claims, most areas of law do not have such a clean justification for private enforcement. Consider securities litigation, a major regulatory area with significant consequences for the US economy. As discussed in Chapter 2, securities litigation is heavily dependent on private enforcement. The Supreme Court held in a series of 1960s and 70s cases that the Securities Exchange Act of 1934 contained an implied right of action, leading to the creation of a powerful securities plaintiffs' bar.[61] Securities class actions allow a large group of investors to collectively sue a company (and its officers, directors, or other parties) for securities fraud, typically when a material misrepresentation or omission causes a stock price drop. In these class actions, courts can presume that investors relied on the integrity of the market price. This mechanism makes it feasible to aggregate many small claims into one lawsuit, which can yield substantial potential damages.

Most of the action in securities litigation is taken up by large securities fraud class actions. Plaintiffs' attorneys file roughly two to three hundred new federal securities class actions per year. For example, a report found "229 new federal securities class action suits" in 2024, matching the 2023 total.[62] Technology and healthcare firms consistently account for roughly half of new suits.[63] Newer trends include a rise in AI-related claims (thirteen suits in 2024) and a decline in crypto and other suits.[64] Approximately ninety to one hundred class actions settle each year. One report found aggregate settlements of about $3.8 billion.[65]

Given the vast regulatory implications for the US economy, is private enforcement of the securities laws justified? Decades of literature have addressed this question, rife with heated arguments on both sides, empirical findings, and significant disagreement. Applying the capacity, dysfunction, and information trifecta, however, helps clarify these debates. The answer is a qualified yes: Private enforcement in the securities context is justified but only when partnered with significant guardrails.

***1. Capacity.*** Few observers doubt that the Securities and Exchange Commission is the highest-capacity regulatory agency in the federal bureaucracy. In 2024, the SEC's overall budget stood at about $2.15 billion,[66] and the Division of Enforcement alone employs roughly 1,400 lawyers and investigators[67]—numbers that dwarf those of most domestic regulators. In the last year, the agency filed 583 enforcement actions and secured a record $8.2 billion in monetary remedies.[68] On paper, capacity hardly looks like the problem.

Yet the scale of the US securities market overwhelms even the most capacious regulator. Thousands of domestic companies are listed on US exchanges, and average daily equity trading routinely tops $500 billion.[69] Add tens of thousands of registered advisers, brokers, funds, and crypto assets, and the math becomes stark: One SEC enforcement lawyer would need to police hundreds of entities and billions of dollars of trading every single day.

Unsurprisingly, the agency's own leadership has long conceded that it lacks the resources to patrol the entire market. The Commission has for decades argued that private suits are indispensable, and in amicus briefs it has reiterated its "longstanding commitment to private enforcement of the securities laws." A recent brief by former SEC officials argued that "[e] nforcement resources . . . are stretched thin, and the SEC alone cannot ensure a level playing field for honest market participants."[70] The Supreme Court has echoed that view, calling private Rule 10b-5 actions a "necessary supplement" to agency enforcement.[71] The message from the SEC and courts is that private enforcement is necessary.

Scholars have also argued that private plaintiffs fill a gap that the SEC cannot: direct investor compensation. While private class actions provide a direct remedy for defrauded shareholders, SEC penalties usually flow to the US Treasury. For instance, class settlements returned $3.8 billion to shareholders in 2023 alone. The compensatory function is not mere rhetoric: Scholars argue it bolsters deterrence by ensuring that wrongdoers, not taxpayers, bear the cost of fraud. Empirical work supports the claim that private plaintiffs are filling in a different niche. Choi and Pritchard find that top officers resign more often in class-action-only cases than in SEC-only investigations, suggesting that shareholder suits target serious frauds at least as precisely as public actions. Parallel studies show that class actions hit roughly the same disclosure violations the SEC pursues but also arise in hundreds of matters where the agency never files a case.[72]

Bolstering the capacity argument, in a recent paper, legal scholar Fernán Restrepo found that when the UK introduced an opt-in private right of action for some securities disclosures, the change made trading in affected stocks noticeably smoother and a bit more valuable.[73] Put simply, shares of companies newly exposed to these lawsuits traded at tighter spreads—meaning investors could buy and sell them more cheaply—and the share prices ticked up by about 1–2 percent compared with similar firms that were already subject to US litigation. The takeaway is straightforward: Even a minimal lawsuit option gives markets extra confidence that bad information will be surfaced, and that extra confidence shows up almost immediately in better liquidity and higher valuations.

How do we reconcile the SEC's sizable enforcement capacity with its professed need for private enforcement? It may be that the enormous scale of the securities markets makes any kind of public enforcer insufficient. The size of the markets creates a policing surface so vast that even a gold-standard agency can cover only its edges. Private class actions fill the inevitable gaps: They mobilize insider information, provide direct restitution the Treasury cannot deliver, and multiply deterrence by raising the marginal cost of fraud far beyond what any single agency budget could sustain. Far from being an admission of weakness, the SEC's repeated endorsement of private litigation reflects a pragmatic recognition that, in securities regulation, capacity is always relative to complexity—and true market oversight requires both public and private reach working together.

***2. Dysfunction.*** Moving on to regulatory dysfunction, begin again with the recognition that the SEC is a top-performing agency with high competence and nonexistent corruption scandals. From almost any comparative angle, the SEC looks particularly *functional*—it is independent from political influence, lawyers are highly capable, and there appears to be zero corruption.

Yet a body of research highlights a subtler pathology: revolving door capture. Former SEC Chair Mary Schapiro warned during a congressional hearing that the SEC must work harder to "avoid conflicts" of interests when employees "walk[] out the door and go[] to a firm and leav[e] everybody to wonder whether they showed some favor to that firm during their time at the SEC."[74] A report by the Project for Government Oversight found that former officials were routinely representing clients in front of the SEC, even immediately after leaving the agency.[75] Of course, much of this is natural and should not raise any alarms. Similarly, researchers James Cox and Randall Thomas found that since the late 1990s, most SEC Enforcement Directors now cycle directly from and back to the defense bar.[76] Obviously, industry groups are interested in hiring lawyers with experience at the SEC. But some researchers have found slight evidence of revolving door dynamics. Michael Shen and Samuel Tan, for instance, found that issuers who retain former SEC lawyers during negotiations with the SEC obtain softer disclosure outcomes, perhaps gaining a strategic advantage due to their former SEC insiders. (Or this could just be a case of former SEC attorneys bringing unique experience.) Still, while the studies reveal no systemic bribery or major problems, they sometimes document pockets of preferential treatment for Commission alumni.[77]

In sum, the SEC's institutional integrity remains high, but career incentives and professional networks create identifiable blind spots. Neither budget increases nor additional headcount can fully eliminate these effects because they are inherent to labor markets rather than resource shortages. In this area, private securities litigation could provide an important counterweight: Shareholder suits follow different incentives, draw on independent investigative resources, and can press claims that slip through the agency's agenda or negotiation culture. Thus, under the dysfunction prong of the trifecta, private enforcement serves as a slight safeguard against selective leniency and agenda capture.

***3. Information.*** An array of regulations and statutes obligates regulated entities to produce vast amounts of information to the SEC. Public companies must produce data to the Commission through periodic forms, current reports of material events, annual proxy statements, specialized disclosures, and—when an inquiry begins—parties "voluntarily" produce a whole slew of documents, even before any subpoena is issued. On top of that, the SEC receives thousands of whistleblower tips each year, a massive compendium of data.[78] The SEC is, in a sense, the greatest gatherer of information about financial markets in the world.

On the other hand, just like with the capacity prong, the SEC insists that it does not possess enough information to police the markets. In a comprehensive sample of large corporate frauds from 1996–2004, a group of scholars found the SEC itself unearthed only 6 percent of cases; the vast majority were exposed by employees, journalists, or industry watchdogs, with regulators often reacting only after the story was public.[79] Closer to this book's context, Professors Choi and Pritchard examined market reactions to SEC enforcement actions and class action lawsuits.[80] They found that the stock market reacted more negatively to a possible violation in cases that led to a class action alone, compared to cases that triggered only an SEC investigation. In other words, standalone class action cases involved larger stock drops on the news of wrongdoing, suggesting these private suits target more serious or surprising fraud revelations. This implies that private litigation is often focused on significant misconduct events—possibly the kind the SEC might overlook or at least had not yet acted upon.

Critics, however, question whether private class actions provide additional deterrence and truly reveal new information or merely piggyback on facts the SEC (or the market) already knows. Many securities fraud suits are filed only after a company's malfeasance has become evident following a major earnings restatement, whistleblower disclosure, or stock price crash.[81] This dynamic means that private suits typically react to public revelations rather than proactively unearthing secret misconduct. In this view, private litigation may add little informational value because the key facts were coming to light regardless.

Indeed, some research suggests that private securities litigation often overlaps with SEC enforcement based on the same underlying facts, raising concerns about duplication.[82] Legal scholars William Bratton and Michael Wachter, for example, have argued that diversified shareholders might be just as well protected by public enforcement, proposing to limit class actions and rely more on the SEC in many cases.[83] From this skeptical perspective, class actions rarely generate new revelations of corporate fraud; rather, they impose additional penalties based on information regulators and investors already had.

Still, other researchers highlight that only a minority of securities class actions run parallel to SEC investigations (although that may be intentional on the SEC's part). Others argue that the SEC tends to focus on "weaker targets," allowing class actions to target the big fish.[84]

A useful test is whether plaintiffs in securities cases occupy the same "insider" position that aggrieved employees do in employment suits. Workers know the timecards, the pay stubs, the internal directives—facts regulators almost never see without their help. By contrast, the lead plaintiff in a securities class action is usually an institutional investor drafted by a plaintiffs' firm, not a CFO or auditor with knowledge of the books. The shareholder's toolkit is public: quarterly filings, earnings calls, price anomalies, perhaps an investor's report. That places the plaintiff midway between insider and stranger—better informed than the average bystander but still relying on information already available (in theory) to the SEC. In most cases, therefore, securities plaintiffs do not enter the courthouse bearing novel, non-public facts. Rather, they hope to use discovery to find those facts during litigation.

***4. Social Costs.*** Finally, scholars and class action critics have long complained about the social costs of securities cases. Critics argue that these lawsuits frequently produce "blackmail" settlements and "strike suits," imposing heavy costs on companies and shareholders with little social value. A recent law review comment summarized the critique: "The primary criticism of private securities litigation is that rent-seeking attorneys abuse the system by bringing frivolous litigation aimed at achieving a settlement and a fee."[85] In this view, plaintiffs' lawyers file weak claims (often hinging on stock drops not tied to fraud) and pressure defendants into nuisance settlements. The result can be enormous defense costs for companies and managers, even if cases lack real evidence of fraud.

The reason these claims impose "social" costs is that class actions often shift the cost of fraud onto shareholders themselves, with little effect on culpable insiders. John Coffee argues that in practice, officers rarely pay anything toward settlements. Instead, corporations and insurers foot the bill. Thus "the cost of such actions . . . falls on largely diversified shareholders," akin to "punishing the victims of [fraud] for their negligence."[86]

Others similarly argue that public and private dual enforcement can be counterproductive. With both SEC and class action penalties imposed on the same event, total fines may exceed what is socially optimal and chill legitimate business. The Supreme Court has warned of the danger of "vexatious" securities suits.[87]

---

Taking the private enforcement trifecta along with social costs produces a mixed result. It is not at all clear that private enforcement of securities laws is justified. It is difficult to dismiss the critics' argument that plaintiffs' attorneys do not surface unique information and can engage in blackmail settlements. Still, there is no doubting the SEC's lack of capacity; it is impossible for a single agency (no matter its size and prestige) to police the entire financial market. Nor can the SEC avoid, on the margin, some revolving-door problems.

All of this suggests *qualified* support for *limited* private enforcement. However, the system has already landed at a good equilibrium: one that welcomes private enforcement but with severe procedural restrictions. This is especially true after the 1995 Private Securities Litigation Reform Act (PSLRA) imposed sweeping changes on securities class actions. Congress's stated purpose was to deter "meritless" or "professional" lawsuits that had burdened companies.[88] Legislators and supporters worried that plaintiffs could file flimsy claims (with bare allegations) and then use costly discovery to extort settlements. The PSLRA sought to raise the bar by requiring plaintiffs to front-load evidence of fraud before a case could proceed. Congress expected that the PSLRA would make it harder to file securities claims.

Some key PSLRA reforms included: (1) Automatic discovery stay while a motion to dismiss is pending. This prevents plaintiffs from fishing for evidence before surviving dismissal. (2) Heightened pleading standards: Complaints must plead each alleged misstatement "with particularity." In practice, this forced plaintiffs to be much more detailed in their complaints. (3) Lead plaintiff selection: Courts must appoint the "most adequate plaintiff"—typically the investor with the largest losses—to serve as lead plaintiff. This was intended to discourage so-called bounty hunters and empower institutional investors, whose interests are presumed to align with the class. (4) Other reforms including damage limitations and sanctions reviews.

The PSLRA's package of reforms, then, already imposes a *qualified* and *limited* version of private enforcement, one that is entirely appropriate in this context.

---

As a final note, notice how the relative weight of the individual prongs in the balancing test (capacity, dysfunction, information, and social costs) varies across regulatory domains. In employment law, informational asymmetries and capacity gaps dominate; in securities regulation, capacity concerns must be balanced against overdeterrence and coherence risks. While the framework's criteria remain constant, how we weigh them inevitably depends on the specific enforcement context.

# NINE

## HOW PRIVATE ENFORCEMENT FAILS: ENVIRONMENTAL LAW AND HOUSING CONSTRUCTION

Despite its many benefits, private enforcement is not justified in many areas of law. This chapter addresses one area that is simultaneously most reliant on private enforcement and yet has the least justification for its use: environmental regulation. In the 1960s and '70s, Congress embraced a wave of environmental statutes that almost universally employed "citizen suit" provisions, a new name for private rights of action. More than traditional private enforcement regimes, these statutes empowered plaintiffs to police public harms like water and air pollution, endangered species, and environmental compliance by both the government and private parties.

But, as this chapter discusses, these lawsuits have played a negative role in the current undersupply of housing, mass transit, and clean energy in the United States. Over the past forty years, it has become extraordinarily expensive to build things in the United States. This includes infrastructure (mass transit, energy, etc.) and housing. The Transit Costs Project found that "[t]he United States is the sixth most expensive country in the world to build rapid-rail transit infrastructure."[1] Similarly, a Niskanen Center Report notes: "Over the last few generations, American infrastructure construction costs have exploded, even as many peer countries spend a fraction of what the US does on the same bridge or tunnel or high-speed rail line."[2] We face the same problem in housing, where construction of dense multistory housing is illegal in most cities, both due to zoning constraints and misguided environmental regulations, among other problems.

What drives these costs? No doubt there are many different causes, including zoning restrictions, burdensome administrative procedures, and so on. But this chapter focuses on the problem of legal process and what I call rent-seeking litigation. Some of the most important environmental statutes increase costs by empowering anyone to bring lawsuits that challenge construction projects. These statutes include the National Environmental Policy Act (NEPA), the Clean Water Act, the Clean Air Act, and related state laws. The question, then, is whether the ability of private plaintiffs to file lawsuits under these laws is justified. Keep in mind that from a comparative angle, the United States is an outlier—most peer countries do not empower private citizens to the same extent in environmental law.

Below, I argue that private enforcement is not justified in this area because it does not make up for a lack of state capacity, creates more capture problems than it solves, and fails to produce unique information.

## PROBLEMS IN ENVIRONMENTAL PRIVATE ENFORCEMENT

As discussed in Chapters 2–4, private enforcement spread like wildfire in the new environmental statutes of the 1960s and 1970s. Drawing on state laws and the general pro-plaintiff attitude of the 1960s, Congress included a private right of action ("citizen suit" provision) in the Clean Air Amendments of 1970.[3] Proponents in Congress argued that environmental degradation was such a generational challenge that no public body, even those "well staffed or well intention[ed]," could address the problem.[4] Echoing the same arguments, President Nixon's 1970 address to Congress noted: "The task of cleaning up our environment calls for a total mobilization by all of us. It involves governments at every level; it requires the help of every citizen."[5] Citizen-plaintiffs could provide both manpower and important information about environmental pollution that was difficult to detect, and they could overcome the problem of regulatory capture of existing public bodies. This powerful combination carried the day and led to the inclusion of citizen-suit provisions in almost every single major environmental law, including the Clean Air Act and Clean Water Act.

Even laws that did not have explicit private rights of action, like NEPA, came to rely on private enforcement. In 1969, Congress adopted NEPA as a procedural statute that would force public agencies to consider the environmental impact of major regulatory decisions.[6] The motivating concern was that agencies were routinely engaged in massive infrastructure projects without any consideration of environmental impacts. Examples included the construction of interstate highways that bulldozed through neighborhoods and ecosystems, large-scale dam projects that flooded vast areas, and federal agencies approving nuclear power plants, oil drilling, and mining operations with minimal consideration of their ecological consequences.

The statute seemed to address this problem head-on with a simple procedural requirement, instructing agencies to examine the environmental effects of their choices. Agencies can do this by preparing extensive "environmental impact statements" (EIS) for major federal projects. But NEPA did not include an explicit private right of action. Over time, however, it became clear that plaintiffs could sue agencies under the Administrative Procedure Act for failure to comply with NEPA. Via this administrative channel, NEPA gained, in effect, something equivalent to a private right of action.[7]

In short order, NEPA and the Endangered Species Act became "the most litigated natural resource statutes, accounting for approximately 85% of the natural resource cases filed annually."[8] This is because judicial interpretations of NEPA extended the statute beyond major federal projects and expanded EISs from procedural box-checking into enormously costly research studies. As researchers Brink Lindsey and Samuel Hammond explained:

> Projects that do not meet [the NEPA "major projects"] threshold must still be accompanied by an "environmental assessment" that establishes that an EIS is not needed . . . . In the early days, NEPA's procedural requirements were modest: An EIS could be as short as 10 pages, and the legislation didn't provide for a private right of action. Courts soon declared a private right of action, though, and under the pressure of litigation the law's demands grew ever more onerous: Today the average EIS runs more

> than 600 pages, plus appendices that typically exceed 1,000 pages. The average EIS now takes 4.5 years to complete; between 2010 and 2017, four such statements were completed after delays of 17 years or more. And remember, no ground can be broken on a project until the EIS has made it through the legal gauntlet—and this includes both federal projects and private projects that require a federal permit.[9]

To make matters worse, more than a dozen states adopted their own NEPA-style statutes, including California's all-powerful CEQA statute. CEQA applies to almost any construction project in the state, private or public and housing or otherwise, and requires cities and developers to prepare extensive environmental impact reports and study any "significant environmental effects of a project."[10] Just like NEPA, any person can file an administrative lawsuit against public bodies for certifying projects that arguably did not comply with CEQA's requirements. As I wrote in a previous article:

> CEQA specifically applies to projects that "require discretionary approval from a California public agency and . . . have the potential to result in direct or reasonably foreseeable indirect impacts on the physical environment." But in the 1970s, the California Supreme Court read the statute to apply to nearly every project, public or private. Like many other states' laws, CEQA is both substantive and procedural—it requires cities and developers to prepare extensive environmental impact reports (EIR) and also imposes a substantive requirement that projects adopt all feasible mitigation measures. Each EIR is supposed to explore in detail any "significant environmental effects of a project" and ways to "mitigate or avoid the effects." In practice, EIRs have evolved to explore any potential impact, including on shadows, traffic, insects, and, really, anything you can possibly imagine.[11]

NEPA and CEQA lawsuits impose costs on both regulatory agencies and regulated entities, usually developers. Legal scholars Zach Liscow and Leah Brooks found that "citizen voice" played an important role in increasing costs after the 1960s and '70s because, among other things, it "empowered" people to police environmental review.[12] A growing body of scholarship has assessed the effect of NEPA and CEQA lawsuits, finding conflicting results. A comprehensive analysis by David E. Adelman and Jory Reilly-Diakun found that environmental citizen suits are filed in surprisingly small numbers given the breadth of laws allowing them.[13] And some environmental scholars claim that NEPA litigation is "not unreasonably burdensome."[14] But this argument misses the point. The costs of NEPA cannot be boiled down to the actual cost of litigating a handful of actually filed cases. Rather, NEPA imposes significant indirect costs via two main channels:

First, NEPA and CEQA impose significant indirect financial costs by forcing all developers to prepare projects *in expectation of potential litigation.* Litigation creates both direct and indirect costs that significantly inflate infrastructure development expenses. While direct costs include legal fees for specific cases, the more substantial problem is that litigation forces developers, consultants, and cities to permanently alter their practices to avoid lawsuits. This "litigation-proofing" behavior leads to cumulative changes over time—such as mandatory unionized labor, exhaustive environmental analyses, and "bulletproofed" construction plans—that become standard practice and inflate costs.[15] The result is a system where the threat of litigation drives up costs across the entire industry, with some projects costing significantly more than comparable international equivalents. As Zach Liscow has shown, many infrastructure projects in the United States are designed in costly ways that are unseen in other countries.[16] Expectations of litigation shape project design at the outset.

This means we cannot assess the statutes' impact by solely observing existing lawsuits. Worse, other than missing inflated costs due to *expectations of litigation*, we can also never observe the large-scale projects that do not get started because of NEPA legal threats. As one report noted, "even the specter of litigation can tie up projects for years, preemptively discouraging developers."[17] In other words, 100 percent of projects are planned and budgeted under the threat of a NEPA lawsuit, inflating costs for everyone. Counting legal costs in actually-filed cases completely misses this problem.

Second, NEPA and CEQA lawsuits (and the expectations of a lawsuit) impose costly *delays* rather than simply additional design or legal costs. As I've previously discussed, under CEQA, "[i]f a court 'rules that an agency has not completed the required level of analysis,' the 'most likely remedy . . . is for a judge to vacate the agency's project approval, and require more

CEQA study.' That process is likely to take '2–4 years (or more)' to 'repeat the agency CEQA process.' And a plaintiff can challenge CEQA compliance anonymously and by simply filing a short petition."[18] Regardless of the outcome, then, delays associated with legal process can effectively kill infrastructure projects. For these reasons, NEPA and CEQA are powerful litigation devices.

---

Just a year after adopting NEPA, Congress also passed the Clean Air Act of 1970 (CAA), a foundational environmental statute that launched the modern environmental legal movement. Prompted by severe smog episodes and growing scientific evidence of air pollution's health effects, Congress passed the 1970 CAA (signed by President Nixon) to create national standards and a federal-state partnership for the cleanup of the nation's air. The statute had both public and private enforcement components. As a recent paper summarizes:

> The CAA is perhaps most aptly conceptualized as a multilayered combination of interrelated pollution control regimes. The heart of the statute is the National Ambient Air Quality Standards (NAAQS), which establish minimum standards for the concentration of a select set of air pollutants widely emitted throughout the country. These standards are complemented by three types of technology-based regulations: two sets of standards for "new" sources—New Source Performance Standards (NSPS) and New Source Review (NSR)—and one for sources emitting toxic air pollutants—National Emissions Standards for Hazardous Air Pollutants (NESHAPs). Motor vehicle emissions are regulated separately by the Environmental Protection Agency (EPA) at the national level. Each regime presents numerous opportunities for rulemaking challenges to be filed. Importantly, the CAA also has two judicial review provisions that define where challenges are filed: a citizen suit provision and a direct appeal provision for certain types of rulemaking decisions.[19]

One provision authorizes the EPA to regulate air quality standards and common pollutants. The citizen-suit provision empowers:

> any person [to] commence a civil action on his own behalf . . . against any person . . . who is alleged to have violated . . . or to be in violation of (A) an emission standard or limitation under this chapter or (B) an order issued by the Administrator or a State with respect to such a standard or limitation.[20]

This private right of action is unusually powerful for two reasons. First, the statute enlists private plaintiffs as co-regulators who explicitly pursue public (not private) aims. Congress's "primary goal . . . was to protect the public interest," and the provision was justified as "a mechanism that would deputize 'private attorneys general' to assist the Environmental Protection Agency (EPA) . . . in the enforcement of environmental regulation."[21] Private plaintiffs can't even collect damages—suits are for injunctions (to stop pollution emitters) and for "civil fines payable to the treasury."[22] This kind of explicitly public-minded private enforcement goes beyond previous statutory regimes. Second, private plaintiffs can also sue to force action by the EPA. As others have explained, "citizen enforcement may compel the Administrator [of the EPA] to perform a nondiscretionary duty."[23] On top of that, many amendments in the 1970s–90s expanded the Act's scope over more sources of pollution. All of this makes the CAA a powerful statute.

Congress built on this model in the 1972 Clean Water Act (CWA), a statute that sought to combat water pollution across the country. The statute imposes permitting requirements for any discharge of pollutants into navigable waters and sets certain water quality standards. Just like the CAA, the CWA empowered both the EPA and citizen plaintiffs.

As we've come to expect, both EPA and citizen suits combine for widespread enforcement of the CAA and CWA. Since 2010, there has been a general decline in the number of EPA-led CAA enforcement cases, punctuated by a few very high-impact cases. The EPA's annual enforcement statistics show that the number of civil enforcement cases (judicial and administrative) initiated and concluded each year has dropped. For example, in 2009 the EPA concluded over 3,500 civil enforcement cases across its programs, but by 2019 that number was around 1,600.[24] The EPA couples this with more than 10,000 inspections or evaluations of pollution sites per year.[25] In the air context, enforcement often involves large, complex cases against major emission sources (power plants, refineries, vehicle manufacturers), and these have sometimes resulted in significant penalties or injunctive relief. A prime example is the Volkswagen Dieselgate case: In 2017, the EPA and DOJ secured injunctive relief "requiring over $15.9 billion" in compliance costs by Volkswagen for installing illegal defeat devices to cheat emissions tests.[26] On the private enforcement side, an overwhelming number of suits (90 percent) involve challenges to EPA rulemakings or policies, with only a small minority involving direct suits against polluters.[27]

But when it comes to the CWA, citizen suits have become more frequent than government enforcement. Already by 1990, "twice as many CWA suits [were] filed by citizens than by state governments and the national government combined."[28] Cases include claims against industrial dischargers for permit violations, often brought by environmental groups seeking injunctive relief and penalties. While citizen suits are numerous, they are still limited by procedural requirements (e.g., short timelines to give notice to regulators and violators, and no overlap with ongoing government enforcement). Many citizen suits end in settlements that require the polluter to take corrective action and sometimes pay penalties (which, again, go to the US Treasury) or fund supplemental environmental projects. A recent example is the Formosa Plastics case in Texas (in 2019), where a volunteer group sued over plastic pellet pollution and won a significant settlement and cleanup commitments.[29]

---

Given the widespread private enforcement of NEPA-style and CAA/CWA environmental laws and the added costs that these statutes impose on construction and housing, the key question is whether private enforcement is justified in this context. To summarize: No, it isn't justified. Below, I tackle this question in separate sections for the different styles of laws.

## PRIVATE ENFORCEMENT OF NEPA-STYLE LAWS IS NOT JUSTIFIED

Private enforcement of NEPA-style laws does not draw on any of its traditional foundations and, worse, is especially vulnerable to a public choice failure. NEPA, CEQA, and similar laws empower almost anyone to oppose housing or mass transit construction projects. This includes neighbors, local residents, other companies, labor unions, or anyone else. As environmental scholar Anna Mance recently argued, the system has been captured by self-interested groups that are completely opposed to the construction of housing and infrastructure projects.[30] Just as agencies face problems with regulatory capture, private enforcement regimes can invite litigation capture and rent-seeking. Private plaintiffs of different stripes—labor unions, homeowners averse to construction, and wayward environmental organizations—abuse this system through lawsuits that paralyze construction.

If the system were otherwise justified, we might accept these costs. But NEPA-style laws do not draw on traditional capacity, dysfunction, and information justifications.

Note, too, that NEPA is not a traditional government accountability statute. Some private enforcement schemes are justified because they allow citizens to vindicate rights against government illegality or misfeasance, particularly statutes protecting constitutional rights. But NEPA does not fit this category. While NEPA suits formally target government agencies for inadequate environmental review, the statute creates no substantive individual protections and imposes compliance costs primarily on private developers. The government acts as a regulatory intermediary, but private entities bear the burden of compliance. This places NEPA squarely in the regulatory private enforcement category central to this book: statutes empowering private litigants to enforce regulatory standards against private entities.

***1. Capacity.*** Proponents of key environmental statutes have long argued that private plaintiffs complement the scarce resources of public regulators. This was an important premise in the 1970s for both theoretical and practical reasons. Like any other area of law, one theoretical underpinning of citizen enforcement is the deterrence model of regulation. Increasing the probability of detection and punishment raises the expected cost of non-compliance, thereby motivating polluters to obey the law. Citizen suits heighten enforcement risk because they multiply the enforcers—not only must violators fear inspections and prosecutions by government agencies; they must also anticipate lawsuits from private watchdogs.

More practically, NEPA preceded the EPA and served as the first statute to obligate administrative agencies to consider environmental pollution. Enforcement manpower in 1969 was necessary. Legislators worried that a mere declaration of policy, asking agencies to consider environmental impacts, would be insufficient without a mechanism to ensure agency compliance. Senator Jackson stated that "what is needed in restructuring the governmental side of this problem is to legislatively create those situations that will bring about an action-forcing procedure the departments must comply with. Otherwise, these lofty declarations are nothing more than that."[31] APA lawsuits enforcing NEPA's provisions could be seen as a necessary vehicle to force the hand of reluctant regulators.

But, under closer scrutiny, rationalizations that made sense in 1969 have grown extremely weak over time. Consider how the process of NEPA compliance actually works for federal infrastructure projects.

1. A federal agency (or a private applicant seeking federal permits, funding, or approvals) proposes a "major federal action" and performs an initial screen to see whether the project is categorically excluded from review, requires a brief Environmental Assessment (EA), or demands a full Environmental Impact Statement (EIS).

2. If an EA shows no significant impacts, the agency issues a Finding of No Significant Impact (FONSI), and the process ends. Otherwise, the agency, often with help from the applicant and outside consultants, embarks on the multi-year task of preparing a comprehensive EIS that analyzes every potential environmental effect and possible mitigation.

3. Early in that EIS process the agency publishes a scoping notice in the Federal Register, inviting other agencies, tribes, and the public to raise issues that the EIS must cover.

4. When the Draft EIS is finished, it is noticed in the Federal Register and released for public comment. Anyone may submit written objections or point out analytical gaps.

5. The agency must evaluate every substantive comment and then issue a Final EIS that addresses those comments, updates the analysis, and identifies mitigation or monitoring commitments.

6. At least thirty days after the Final EIS is noticed, the agency produces a Record of Decision (ROD) formally approving, modifying, or rejecting the proposed action and its mitigation plan.

7. Only after the ROD, any person or group with standing can file suit under the Administrative Procedure Act claiming the agency's NEPA review was inadequate. Although the defendant is the federal agency, the practical target is usually the project proponent, whose project may be enjoined, delayed, or forced back to an earlier NEPA step.

The actual capacity question is whether litigation by private parties is adding critical enforcement manpower to this process. It simply does not for three reasons:

First, by definition, private plaintiffs can file NEPA challenges only after a government regulator has reviewed and approved a construction project. The NEPA process involves public regulatory oversight from the get-go, with an initial assessment by a federal agency, and then multiple steps of regulatory review. That means the regulator is fully on board and has devoted significant manpower to reviewing and approving construction projects. Private enforcement, in this context, is entirely redundant.

Contrast this with areas like employment law where employees file wage and hour suits because the Department of Labor has not assigned inspectors to police compliance with the FLSA. Or consider securities litigation, where a class action plaintiffs' attorney files a claim against a company that the SEC overlooked. Now, to be sure, sometimes plaintiffs file piggyback claims after a regulator has already investigated wrongdoing. But in those cases, the employee or shareholder plaintiff files a claim *to receive compensation.* By contrast, the NEPA plaintiff cannot receive compensation. The only purpose of the lawsuit is to contest the regulator's decision, made after an extensive and thorough process. Again, private enforcement, uniquely here, cannot compensate and is therefore entirely redundant.

Second, there is no evidence that regulators are devoting insufficient manpower to reviewing NEPA compliance. In fact, agencies have developed robust internal teams to review and ensure compliance with NEPA and environmental laws. The Council on Environmental Quality obtains information on NEPA by working "closely with its federal agency NEPA contact group, composed of key officials responsible for implementing NEPA in each agency."[32] The Federal Highway Administration's liaison guidebook explains that many resource-agency NEPA liaisons are full-time or part-time federal employees funded under 23 U.S.C. 139(j) to accelerate environmental reviews.[33] Surely, some of this occurs precisely because of the expectation of private litigation. But the problem is that private plaintiffs can file cases regardless of whether regulators devoted significant resources to a particular case. There is no consideration of capacity in this process at all.

And worse, to file an *ex post* suit, plaintiffs can only bring claims that were already fully aired out during the notice and comment process. Administrative exhaustion requirements mean that a plaintiff cannot bring up an argument for the first time during an APA challenge. This triples the level of redundancy because by the time of an *ex post* lawsuit, regulators have already considered and dismissed all specific complaints multiple times.

Of course, the availability of private enforcement keeps agencies on their toes. Some research suggests that the presence of active citizen enforcement spurs agencies to be more vigilant. For instance, one economic analysis found that citizen suits in the Clean Water Act context "crowd in" public monitoring activity, leading agencies to conduct more inspections when they know private watchdogs can file a claim.[34] But, notably, the study focused on the Clean Water Act, a statute that does not require an extensive NEPA-style *ex ante* process. We have no reason to believe that in the context of NEPA, where procedures are both extensive and already include notice and comment, we would observe similar effects.

Third, to make up for a lack of enforcement capacity, we would expect to observe more private enforcement in areas with weak regulatory enforcement or funding. Yet we observe the opposite. Consider first one finding from my previous work: Out of the 700+ private rights of action in the country, it is some of the larger states with more robust regulatory agencies that, at the same time, have *more* private rights of action.[35] California, for instance, leads the way both on environmental regulatory capacity and private rights of action. It seems that public capacity and private enforcement go together, rather than making up for shortcomings.

Along the same lines, the distribution of citizen suits appears skewed toward certain jurisdictions with robust public enforcement. A striking result from Adelman and Reilly-Diakun is that most cases were filed in states or circuits with strong pro-environment constituencies, notably California and Washington, DC. The authors noted: "The regressions we conducted show that third-party suits under the pollution statutes are not associated with the rigor of enforcement programs. In other words, the effectiveness of government enforcement is not a statistically significant factor in determining where citizen suits are filed."[36] There is no other way to put it: Private enforcement is *not* making up for a lack of enforcement capacity; instead, it is doubling down in areas with the most capacity.

Consider the odd fact that relatively few citizen suits are filed in the industrial Midwest or Southeast, even though those areas have many polluting facilities and often weaker state enforcement. Citizen enforcement has simply not penetrated uniformly across the country; it tends to reinforce areas with robust public enforcement, occurring in places where there are active environmental organizations and support for environmental regulation. This weakens the argument that citizen suits fulfill their role of preventing "races to the bottom." If few are filed in states with lax enforcement, then those states may still under enforce.

Fourth, and perhaps most concerning of all, private enforcement can distort regulatory regimes by distracting regulators and weakening regulatory capacity. Private enforcement allows any plaintiff to set the agenda for regulators. By tying any regulator in a thicket of NEPA lawsuits, often over ideological disagreements, private enforcement forces agencies to devote significant legal staffing and time to address NEPA litigation. Expanding on this, a common critique targets the dynamic where citizen groups sue agencies and then enter settlements that effectively dictate regulatory priorities.[37] The dynamic is simple: Through repeated litigation, NGOs can effectively force regulators' hand in prioritizing certain areas or industries.

Again, again, again, and again the problems of NEPA are clear—instead of overcoming capacity problems, NEPA produces overenforcement, over-deterrence, and may actually weaken regulatory capacity. It cannot, by definition, offset for a lack of capacity when lawsuits are entirely redundant to regulatory oversight.

**2. *Dysfunction and Rent-Seeking Litigation.*** The strongest defense of private enforcement of environmental laws leans on the problem of regulatory capture. Powerful lobbies like Big Oil have a strong interest in shaping environmental regulators. By opening agency decisions to judicial review at the behest of citizens, private enforcement creates a check on executive discretion. For example, if the EPA fails to act against an industrial polluter, a citizen suit can force the issue into the courts and onto the public record.

This mechanism has prompted agencies to issue overdue regulations (such as setting new air quality standards) or to enforce the law against politically powerful violators.

Private enforcement, in essence, can counteract the problem of regulatory capture by vested interests, because citizens independent of industry can demand enforcement action in court. The classic works in environmental law, such as Joseph Sax's *Defending the Environment*, and subsequent scholarship, support this argument. They cast private enforcement as a necessary innovation that leverages citizen energy to ensure the ambitious environmental statutes of the 1970s achieve real results.

While this argument rings true in this context, the problem has been the development of what I call rent-seeking litigation (and Anna Mance calls "litigation capture")—the phenomenon of self-interested groups suing under the environmental laws but for non-environmental ends. Rather than alleviating the problem of regulatory dysfunction, private enforcers have introduced an analogous problem by filing lawsuits that are completely against the goals of the environmental laws. Mance even claimed that private enforcement is "exacerbating climate change."[38] This happens when citizen suits target green infrastructure like solar or wind farms or mass transit and dense housing.

The reason we should refer to this as rent-seeking (distinct from merely profit-seeking) is that NEPA/CEQA plaintiffs are motivated by goals that are not aligned with environmental laws. Consider first profit-seeking litigation. A plaintiffs' firm is a business that invests in a litigation portfolio with the aim of making a profit. Because of this, plaintiffs' attorneys usually have an incentive to take cases that are meritorious and are therefore more likely to produce a damages award. When a state legislature or Congress employs private enforcement, legislators deliberately enlist plaintiffs' attorneys who can file meritorious cases. A plaintiff attorney seeking profits, then, can actually promote statutory goals. There is a nice match here between legislative goals and attorneys' incentives.

Granted, some plaintiffs have an incentive to file meritless claims to force monetary settlements. But the system addresses this problem via sanctions for frivolous suits as well as counterclaims for abuse of process. But it bears emphasis that, rationally, plaintiffs' attorneys should choose cases that have some merit because they are more likely to produce larger settlements or judgments. Financial and procedural incentives in the system provide a check on frivolous litigation.

By contrast, as discussed below, NEPA-style laws cannot result in damages awards; a "good" outcome is only more process, never a victory on the merits. Because of that, NEPA/CEQA cases rely on plaintiffs interested in extracting a different set of benefits (that we can call "rents"): higher property prices for neighbors, settlements that provide labor benefits to unions, preservation of the status quo for high-income incumbents, and on top of that, attorneys' fees.[39] Crucially, none of those rents come from filing meritorious cases. The reward of a NEPA case, again, is *more process*, not a win on the merits. But meritless cases *also* result in more process. Plaintiffs derive rents simply by stalling construction projects or forcing settlements. And the key to these rents is that NEPA permits injunctions against the approval of major federal action. The environmental legal ecosystem is therefore dominated by rent-seeking NGOs and plaintiffs not interested in monetary payouts. One analysis of NEPA litigation from 2001–2013 noted that "litigation [is] being driven by political activism."[40] Government officials have observed plaintiff groups who use legal cases to fundraise.[41]

All of this means that, unlike the profit-seeking plaintiffs' attorney, it is quite easy for the NEPA plaintiff's preferences to diverge from the legislature's goals. A plaintiffs' attorney usually makes money by filing meritorious cases. But a NEPA plaintiff derives rents by stalling construction projects, not by filing a meritorious case. The plaintiff attorney is an expected part of the legislative design of private enforcement, while the NEPA plaintiff is often an unforeseen rent-seeker.

With that in mind, let's review the significant evidence that specific groups of plaintiffs file NEPA and CEQA lawsuits to pursue non-environmental goals:

*NGOs Against Growth.* The quintessential NEPA filer is an environmental NGO or community group that claims an interest in environmental degradation. The problem, however, is that ideology points the wrong way here. As scholars have found, the environmental movement of the 1970s developed a degrowth model that opposes development in principle. The 1970s degrowth wing of the environmental movement framed almost any new construction as an ecological harm rather than a public good. That degrowth legacy is still visible in modern NEPA fights. Empirical data shows how that mindset plays out in court today: A 2023 study of 355 large energy and transport projects found that 28 percent of proposals requiring an EIS were sued before ground-breaking. But most telling, a high percentage of utility-scale solar projects faced litigation—and 89 percent of those suits alleged NEPA violations.[42] That environmental NGOs oppose solar farm construction is the clearest evidence that they are not interested in longer term environmental goals.

Degrowth plaintiffs file NEPA claims knowing that their likelihood of success on the merits is low, but that imposing costs and delays on large projects can effectively kill them. One researcher flatly notes that NEPA lawsuits can be used as a "weapon by activist groups to try to stop projects they don't like."[43] NEPA cases land on top of an already protracted administrative timeline, where the average EIS takes roughly 4.5 years to complete even before a judge reviews it. The result is that activist plaintiffs can wield NEPA as a procedural veto, delaying or killing projects—including renewable-energy and housing developments—despite the statute's original, more balanced promise of informed decision-making rather than blanket opposition to growth.

*NIMBYs and Neighbors.* Similarly, CEQA filers are often motivated by preserving existing neighborhood character (a significant financial rent) rather than legitimate environmental concerns. While NEPA applies only to major federal actions, CEQA applies to every housing project in California, allowing neighbors to pursue ideological and financial aims. Neighbors have a financial interest and a cultural preference in maintaining the status quo of a community. Researchers have repeatedly found that incumbent households tend to prefer neighborhoods in their current form, viewing new development as a threat to property values, local amenities, and the familiar social fabric of their area. For instance, in a study of CEQA claims, Jennifer Hernandez found that in Los Angeles, "CEQA housing lawsuits disproportionately target new housing in . . . wealthier . . . communities."[44] That is, wealthy NIMBYs oppose construction around their neighborhoods and can afford to file cases with no prospect of direct compensation.

Because of these non-environmental goals, CEQA claims often result in absurd cases that are contrary to the purpose of the statute. CEQA lawsuits, for instance, have stalled affordable housing for students and low-income residents, transit-oriented developments, bike lanes, and solar farms, all projects that benefit the environment or community.[45] A striking example involved a lawsuit by a local lawyer against a Habitat for Humanity housing project in Redwood City, CA. Habitat for Humanity is an NGO that builds low-income housing using volunteer labor. This project was located in an already dense downtown area. The plaintiff, however, was a neighboring law firm that was apparently against sharing the same block with a Habitat for Humanity apartment building. The lawsuit successfully delayed the project even though everyone acknowledged it was a frivolous attempt by project neighbors who felt the building was too large for their neighborhood. This is a microcosm of a larger problem: NIMBYs and neighbors use CEQA as a weapon to prevent any construction. As the Habitat for Humanity CEO noted, CEQA has "become a loophole for anti-development interests to preserve a world they remember from the 1960s."[46]

Another piece of evidence indicates that claims by NIMBY groups are not outliers but serious problems. Geographically, the distribution of citizen suits appears skewed toward certain jurisdictions. Again, a key result from Adelman and Reilly-Diakun is that most environmental cases are filed in states or circuits with strong pro-environment constituencies (California and Washington, DC). Relatively few citizen suits are filed in the Midwest or Southeast, even though those areas have many polluting facilities and often weaker state enforcement.[47] To be sure, some of this geographic skew is explained by the amount of public land in western states, where major forestry, mining, and fossil fuel projects take place.

*Unions.* Rent-seeking lawsuits by labor unions have also become a significant problem under CEQA (but not NEPA). Labor unions have transformed CEQA from an environmental protection statute into a sophisticated tool for extracting economic concessions from developers.[48] Labor unions file CEQA lawsuits to coerce developers into paying higher wages and/or committing to hiring union workers.[49] According to some researchers, unions may file up to 10 percent of all CEQA cases.[50] The practice has become so routine that specialized law firms now handle these cases. Two firms, Lozeau Drury and Adams Broadwell Joseph & Cardozo, are engaged in many of these lawsuits. Between 2016 and 2017, "these two firms [filed] more than 100 CEQA complaints against a variety of California development projects."[51] A newspaper report notes that "the threat of CEQA litigation has been the longstanding strategy of an association of four building trade unions—that demand high-priced, no-bid contracts from developers in exchange for an agreement to stand down on meritless CEQA claims."[52] This approach reveals that unions are not responding to genuine environmental concerns on a case-by-case basis, but rather implementing a coordinated strategy to leverage environmental law for labor market control.

When unions abuse environmental enforcement, they increase the cost of housing and infrastructure. One researcher found that "[w]hen developers are forced to use union labor, costs can be '10–20% higher than those that would go out to bid.'"[53] Researcher Alon Levy found a case in Los Angeles where "a union sued a rolling stock vendor . . . for environmental remediation." But instead of pursuing the CEQA claim, the union settled the claim as soon as the stock vendor committed to employ unionized labor. Levy found that this commitment to employ unionized workers increased train construction costs, "which may play a role in why the trains cost around 50% more than equivalent European products."[54]

Perhaps nowhere is union abuse of CEQA more apparent than in renewable energy projects, where unions often sue to block the very solar and wind developments meant to advance environmental goals. Unions notoriously do this across the board, from teamsters suing to block truck facilities, to nurses opposing new hospitals, to grocery workers targeting retail competition.[55] But there are also numerous instances of CEQA lawsuits against green infrastructure,[56] filed to force developers to sign "project labor agreements" that favor unions. Of course this increases the costs of renewable energy projects.[57]

---

Return to a key justification of private enforcement: It can be a failsafe tool that allows plaintiffs to avoid regulatory dysfunction. But the proliferation of rent-seeking NEPA and CEQA claims instead introduces dysfunction into the system. And this dysfunction is not at all the typical claim that plaintiffs' attorneys bring frivolous litigation (a recurring claim by the Chamber of Commerce in securities, antitrust, and tort claims). Rather, this dysfunction is structural and inherent to NEPA/CEQA. As discussed above, the statute is not compensatory, so every plaintiff is already motivated by either rent-seeking or narrow goals, rather than the likelihood of success on the merits. And the mere act of filing a NEPA/CEQA case imposes significant delays on construction projects, immediately increasing costs. Rather than dodging captured regulators, NEPA and CEQA lead to an analogous problem of rent-seeking and "captured" litigants and courts.

To be sure, rent-seeking lawsuits do not necessarily constitute the majority of NEPA and CEQA litigation. It is possible that most environmental challenges are filed by genuine environmental groups or neighbors concerned about local impacts.

But even if rent-seeking lawsuits constitute a minority of claims—and it is not clear that they do—that does not diminish the significance of the litigation capture problem they create. Just as regulatory capture theory does not require that all regulators be captured or that all regulatory decisions serve private interests, the systematic abuse of environmental law by rent-seeking plaintiffs need only be substantial enough to distort the legal framework's operation and impose widespread costs. One study of CEQA lawsuits in a three-year period, conducted by a law firm, found that "recognized state and national environmental advocacy groups . . . comprise only 13% of the CEQA petitioners."[58] This is suggestive evidence that claims are filed by small groups without a recognized interest in environmental goals. It may well be that CEQA cases are mostly filed by plaintiffs for non-environmental reasons.

Either way, the threat of NIMBY or union litigation has become so predictable and costly that developers modify their practices to avoid these challenges, creating industry-wide effects that extend beyond the individual cases where ideological plaintiffs actually file suit. In this way, even a minority of cases can generate systemic regulatory dysfunction when the potential costs of non-compliance (delays, project abandonment, or mandatory union agreements) are severe enough to alter behavior across the entire sector.

In simple terms, these statutes are not justified under the regulatory dysfunction prong and, instead, seem to make the problem worse.

*3. **Information.*** Some of the original proponents of citizen suits highlighted that "environmental violations are difficult or prohibitively expensive for the government to detect."[59] This rationale made sense for traditional pollution cases where local residents might observe midnight dumping of toxic waste into streams, notice unusual odors from chemical plants that suggest illegal emissions, witness trucks disposing of hazardous materials in abandoned lots, or detect changes in groundwater quality from their wells that indicate contamination from nearby facilities. These classic nuisance claims involve observable harms where neighbors possess unique, location-specific knowledge about ongoing violations that distant regulators would struggle to monitor.

Unlike typical environmental claims, NEPA-style laws *cannot* produce unique information for three reasons discussed here: (1) NEPA plaintiffs rely on information already produced to regulators before litigation; (2) because of NEPA's broad standing requirements, NEPA plaintiffs are *outsiders* to the process with no particular inside information; and (3) any information NEPA plaintiffs may provide can be harnessed through notice and comment, rendering litigation wholly redundant.

An important problem with private enforcement of NEPA-style laws is that plaintiffs cannot contribute any unique information that regulators cannot already access. Unlike most private enforcement regimes, NEPA and CEQA challenges target the adequacy of government agencies' own environmental impact analyses for proposed projects, not ongoing violations that require local detection. In these procedural challenges, private plaintiffs add no informational value that agencies lack; instead, they simply second-guess the thoroughness of studies that agencies are already required to conduct and make publicly available.

Uniquely among private enforcement regimes, NEPA and CEQA operate on top of a set of procedures that already disclose significant information prior to any litigation. Administrative agencies must prepare detailed environmental impact statements that analyze potential harms, consider alternatives, and propose mitigation measures, all of which become part of the public record. Administrative exhaustion requirements further force project challengers to reveal their complaints during the notice and comment period, creating an additional information-flushing process that brings potential issues to light before any lawsuit is filed. This comprehensive disclosure framework leads to thorough documentation of environmental compliance considerations, giving regulators and private parties access to the same information set.

Unlike securities fraud cases where whistleblowers reveal hidden misconduct, or employment disputes where workers expose concealed violations, NEPA and CEQA challengers typically work from the same publicly available environmental analyses that agencies have already compiled and reviewed. The result is a private enforcement system that operates without the informational asymmetries that justify citizen suit provisions in other areas of law, creating opportunities for strategic litigation based on procedural technicalities rather than substantive environmental protection.

Worse, NEPA plaintiffs are *outsiders* to the process, without any access to special inside information. Return to the discussion in the previous chapter: Private enforcement works best when *insiders* produce information that is difficult to access. In securities law, whistleblowers possess inside knowledge of corporate misconduct or financial irregularities that outside regulators cannot easily detect. In antitrust cases, competitors and consumers observe price-fixing conspiracies, exclusive dealing arrangements, or predatory practices that occur behind closed doors. In employment law, workers witness workplace safety violations, discrimination, or wage theft that happens away from regulatory oversight. In each case, we see the shareholder, consumer, or employee with inside information that adds genuine value to enforcement efforts.

Contrast that with NEPA plaintiffs who are outsiders to the very process they challenge—they typically lack any special knowledge about project impacts, scientific methodologies, or regulatory compliance that isn't already contained in the public environmental impact statements prepared by agencies. Part of the problem is that NEPA and CEQA have what proceduralists call broad standing requirements. Typically, in federal courts, plaintiffs must demonstrate an injury that is concrete, particularized, and traceable to the defendant's conduct, requirements that limit litigation to parties with genuine stakes in the outcome.[60] But NEPA and CEQA allow plaintiffs to skirt these requirements by asserting generalized environmental or procedural interests that courts routinely accept as sufficient for standing. CEQA gives an entity standing to sue if "beneficially interested," and parties can just claim "public interest in environmental quality."[61] Any motivated party, then, can challenge agency decisions regardless of whether they suffer distinct harms from the proposed project.

NEPA and CEQA plaintiffs are not insiders reporting hidden violations, but rather external critics second-guessing publicly available analyses using the same information accessible to everyone else. This fundamental difference explains why private enforcement works well in securities and employment contexts but creates perverse incentives in environmental procedural review, where plaintiffs contribute no unique informational advantage while imposing substantial litigation costs.

Nor do private claimants have any particular expertise that agencies cannot access through conventional regulatory processes. To be sure, some environmental organizations can develop specialized expertise in certain areas—wetlands ecology, air quality modeling, or endangered species habitat requirements—but all of that expertise can already be harnessed through the notice and comment period, where agencies routinely receive detailed technical submissions from scientists, environmental consultants, and advocacy groups. Agencies can also commission their own expert studies, consult with other government scientists, and require applicants to fund independent environmental assessments. The rulemaking process is specifically designed to aggregate technical knowledge from diverse sources before decisions are made. Litigation is simply not needed to bring this expertise to bear on environmental review. When environmental groups later challenge agency decisions in court, they rely on the same scientific studies and expert opinions that were submitted during the administrative process. The litigation system thus creates a redundant and more expensive mechanism for presenting information that agencies could access more efficiently through their existing procedural requirements.

*4. **Social Benefits and Costs.*** So far, private enforcement of NEPA-style laws looks unjustified. But the analysis worsens when we consider the clear divergence between the interests of society and some of the typical NEPA or CEQA plaintiffs: neighbors, regular citizens, and labor unions. Environmental pollution can surely harm society in significant ways. But let's be more precise: NEPA and CEQA police major projects that were already reviewed and approved by regulators. In that subset of projects, society usually benefits from the construction of housing and infrastructure. But neighbors and local populations may see home values drop and neighborhoods changed. As discussed above, this can lead to the problem of rent-seeking litigation that is redundant and wasteful. That is why private enforcement of NEPA-style laws increases construction costs in an unjustified manner.

Return again to the basic problem: Rent-seeking plaintiffs take advantage of NEPA-style laws to promote non-environmental goals. That is, the union seeks labor agreements, the neighbor wants to preserve property values and neighborhood character, and NIMBYs oppose any change to the status quo regardless of environmental merit. More narrowly, NIMBYs take advantage of every tool in the legal shed to prevent construction—not just environmental laws but also zoning appeals, historic preservation claims, traffic studies, and procedural challenges of all kinds. The problem is that NEPA-style laws give a uniquely powerful weapon to these plaintiffs because environmental review requirements are so comprehensive and procedurally complex that virtually any project can be challenged on technical grounds. Unlike zoning disputes that focus on specific land use compatibility issues, or historic preservation claims that require demonstrable cultural significance, NEPA and CEQA create broad mandates to study "all significant environmental impacts," a standard so expansive that determined opponents can almost always find some aspect of the analysis to attack. This gives rent-seeking plaintiffs a reliable litigation tool that sounds publicly defensible while serving their true non-environmental objectives, whether those involve labor organizing, property value protection, or simple resistance to change.

Again, that is not to say that there are no benefits to these lawsuits; some undoubtedly catch genuine regulatory failures, force agencies to consider overlooked environmental impacts, or compel more rigorous analysis of complex projects. Environmental litigation occasionally exposes inadequate studies of air quality impacts, prevents development in sensitive habitats, or requires better mitigation measures for significant ecological harms. The citizen suit mechanism can serve as a valuable backstop when agencies lack resources, face political pressure to approve projects quickly, or simply make analytical errors in their environmental review. Moreover, the mere threat of litigation may encourage agencies to conduct more thorough initial assessments, knowing that their work will face potential judicial scrutiny.

However, these legitimate benefits must be weighed against the systematic costs imposed by rent-seeking litigation that exploits procedural requirements for non-environmental purposes. The question is not whether private enforcement of NEPA-style laws ever serves environmental goals, but whether the current framework creates perverse incentives that allow too many meritless challenges to proceed while imposing excessive costs on beneficial development projects. Again, at least under some measures, only a small minority of CEQA claims are filed by recognized environmental organizations (but this is probably not the case with NEPA claims).[62]

There is, in general, a clear divergence between plaintiffs' and society's interests that is inherent to environmental law. Unlike many other areas of law, environmental law deals with large-scale impacts that are geographically dispersed, temporally extended, and affect diffuse populations who may not be represented in litigation. Environmental harms often cross jurisdictional boundaries: air pollution from one county affects neighboring regions, watershed contamination impacts downstream communities, and climate change represents a global problem. The benefits of environmental protection, similarly, accrue to broad populations including future generations who cannot participate in current legal proceedings. This creates a fundamental mismatch between the narrow, localized interests of typical NEPA/CEQA plaintiffs—who may be concerned primarily with their immediate neighborhood, property values, or organizational objectives—and the broader societal interest in rational environmental policy that balances protection against economic development, housing needs, and infrastructure requirements. A local resident opposing a transit project may care little about regional air quality improvements or affordable housing goals, while a union challenging a solar farm is indifferent to statewide renewable energy targets. This divergence means that environmental litigation often reflects parochial concerns rather than genuine environmental optimization, leading to outcomes that may actually harm broader environmental and social welfare.

When it comes to construction, most beneficiaries are low-income residents or people who do not currently live in the area but want to move there for better job opportunities, affordable housing, or access to services. And their interests are systematically underrepresented in environmental litigation. The people who would benefit most from new apartment buildings, transit projects, or commercial developments typically lack the resources to intervene in CEQA lawsuits, while the costs of participating in lengthy administrative and judicial proceedings are prohibitive for working families. Meanwhile, the established residents who worried about neighborhood change have both the financial means and organizational capacity to sustain extended legal challenges. This creates a problem where those who most need new housing and infrastructure have no voice in the legal proceedings that determine whether these projects get built, while those who already enjoy economic security and homeownership can weaponize environmental law to block developments that would serve broader social needs. We thus have a litigation system that favors the status quo and existing interests over the interests of future residents and regional housing or environmental goals.

In complex regulatory situations like this (with diffuse interests and a mismatch between parochial plaintiffs and regional goals), we give power to an entity that can balance all of this: the public regulatory agency. Administrative agencies are specifically designed to consider broad public interests, weigh competing policy objectives, and account for stakeholders who may not be directly represented in adversarial proceedings. Unlike private litigants who pursue narrow self-interest, agencies have mandates to serve the general welfare and are equipped with technical expertise and institutional capacity to evaluate complex tradeoffs between environmental protection, economic development, and housing needs. Agencies can consider regional impacts and long-term consequences that transcend the immediate concerns of local opponents. They operate through transparent processes that invite public participation while maintaining professional staff capable of analyzing scientific evidence and balancing competing values.

When private enforcement allows parochial interests to override agency expertise and democratic accountability, it undermines this carefully designed institutional framework. The result is that narrow interest groups can impose their preferences on broader communities through procedural challenges that courts are ill-equipped to resolve on the merits, rather than through the democratic and technocratic processes that agencies represent.

---

Any claims that NEPA is justified because it ensures that regulators pay attention to information provided during notice and comment fail to distinguish between information generation and judicial review of agency reasoning. The information asymmetry justification requires that private parties surface information that agencies cannot efficiently obtain themselves (again, whistleblowers disclosing securities fraud, or employees reporting wage theft, and so on). NEPA does not fit this pattern. Environmental impacts are precisely the type of information agencies commission through their own experts or obtain through notice and comment. When environmental groups submit technical studies during the administrative process, agencies already have access to this information. NEPA litigation challenges whether agencies adequately considered submitted information, but this is judicial review of agency decision-making, not private enforcement surfacing hidden violations.

Moreover, any reliance on a government accountability defense of NEPA proves too much. If it were enough that agencies might ignore notice and comment, we should impose NEPA-like review on every regulatory decision—FDA approvals, national security determinations, monetary policy. Yet we do not, because democratic governance requires vesting authority in politically accountable officials. NEPA creates an intensive procedural review that allows project opponents to delay approved activities based on analytical thoroughness rather than substantive violations. And critically, NEPA does not fit the accountability model because compliance costs fall on private developers, not the government. True accountability statutes impose liability on the government for its own misconduct. NEPA makes the government a regulatory intermediary while private parties bear the costs.

## WHAT ABOUT THE CLEAN AIR AND CLEAN WATER ACTS?

Other environmental statutes do not suffer from the exact same problems as NEPA-style laws but may still be unjustified. First, only NEPA-style laws create comprehensive procedural review requirements that apply to virtually every major development project, making them uniquely vulnerable to strategic litigation by parties with non-environmental motives. The Clean Air Act and Clean Water Act, by contrast, target specific pollution sources and ongoing violations rather than the adequacy of government planning documents. Second, the CAA and CWA typically involve concrete, observable environmental harms—illegal discharges into waterways, excessive emissions from smokestacks, or contamination of drinking water supplies—where local residents can genuinely possess unique information about violations that regulators might miss. These statutes address the traditional enforcement gap that citizen suits were designed to fill, allowing neighbors to report midnight dumping or unusual plant emissions that government inspectors cannot monitor continuously. Third, CAA and CWA enforcement focuses on established pollution standards with clear legal requirements, rather than the open-ended mandate to study "all significant environmental impacts" that makes NEPA and CEQA challenges virtually impossible to defend against.

It seems like the CAA and CWA are at least partially justified under the capacity, dysfunction, and information analysis. These statutes address the traditional enforcement challenges that citizen suits were designed to solve: Government agencies cannot monitor every pollution source continuously, regulated industries have strong incentives to capture their regulators, and local residents often possess unique observational knowledge about ongoing violations that distant bureaucrats would struggle to detect.

Unlike NEPA-style procedural challenges, CAA and CWA enforcement typically involves situations where private plaintiffs can genuinely supplement regulatory capacity by reporting violations that might otherwise go undetected. CAA and CWA claims do not double up on an extensive *ex ante* regulatory process. Cases often arise when regulators are unable to police some environmental discharge. This makes CAA and CWA suits different.

However, even these statutes may warrant reform to prevent abuse by competitors using environmental law to harass business rivals, or to ensure that citizen suits genuinely complement rather than duplicate existing regulatory oversight. The key distinction is that traditional pollution statutes address ongoing violations with observable harms, while NEPA-style laws create opportunities for endless procedural challenges to government decision-making processes. As discussed in the next chapter, however, these statutes need procedural fixes, not complete elimination.

## SANITY CHECK: OTHER COUNTRIES DO NOT RELY ON PRIVATE ENFORCEMENT OF NEPA-STYLE LAWS

A final way to assess whether private enforcement of NEPA-style laws, or of environmental laws in general, makes sense is to examine it from a comparative angle. As discussed in Chapter 2, other countries have selectively adopted American-style private enforcement mechanisms in various regulatory areas, particularly antitrust, securities, and employment law. The European Union's Directive 2014/104 instructs member states to ensure that victims of anti-competitive conduct can obtain damages, the UK's

Competition Act allows private damage claims, and the EU requires that individuals who suffer discrimination have access to judicial remedies. Even in securities regulation, the UK recently adopted a private right of action through its Financial Services and Markets Act. While these foreign adaptations typically lack the procedural enhancers that make American private enforcement so powerful, they nonetheless represent a conscious decision by other democracies to harness private litigation for regulatory enforcement in these specific areas.

Environmental law, however, is an entirely different story. Despite decades of global environmental cooperation and the widespread adoption of American regulatory innovations in other fields, foreign countries have largely rejected the American model of citizen suits for environmental enforcement. There is no EU equivalent of American citizen suits under the Clean Air Act or Clean Water Act. While some countries like Germany have recognized limited rights for environmental associations to challenge project approvals, there is no evidence of widespread adoption or use of these mechanisms. Even the UK, which has borrowed heavily from American legal innovations in other contexts, provides no general citizen suit statute for environmental enforcement, leaving most regulatory work to public agencies. Canada does allow "environmental protection actions" under its Environmental Protection Act of 1999,[63] but this pales in comparison to the nearly 800 private rights of action related to the environment that American states have adopted. Moreover, Canada's statute is more analogous to the Clean Air and Water Acts than to anything like NEPA.

This selective rejection of American environmental enforcement mechanisms by other developed democracies is particularly telling given their willingness to experiment with private enforcement elsewhere. It suggests that sophisticated legal systems with robust environmental protection records have concluded that citizen suits are either unnecessary or counterproductive for environmental regulation. Instead, these countries rely on well-funded environmental agencies and direct government enforcement, precisely the institutional capacity that American environmental statutes were designed to supplement but that other nations have chosen to strengthen rather than circumvent through private litigation.

## DELETE NEPA-STYLE PRIVATE ENFORCEMENT

Based on the analysis above, private enforcement of NEPA-style laws fails under every traditional justification. On capacity, these statutes create redundant enforcement on top of already extensive regulatory processes, with private litigation occurring only after agencies have devoted substantial resources to multi-year environmental reviews. On dysfunction, rather than correcting regulatory capture, private enforcement has created its own form of "litigation capture" where unions, NIMBYs, and ideological groups exploit environmental procedures for non-environmental ends. On information, NEPA and CEQA plaintiffs contribute no unique knowledge that agencies cannot access through existing notice and comment processes, instead merely second-guessing publicly available analyses using the same information available to regulators. The result is a system that generates systematic costs (delayed housing, inflated infrastructure expenses, and blocked renewable energy projects) without any corresponding benefits that justify those impositions.

The evidence against private enforcement in this context is not marginal or debatable; it is clear and convincing. Unlike other areas of law where private claims serve legitimate enforcement functions, NEPA and CEQA private enforcement operate as regulatory dysfunction, allowing narrow interests to impose high social costs through procedural gamesmanship. When unions can block solar farms until developers agree to labor contracts, when affluent neighbors can halt affordable housing through environmental pretexts, and when the very statute designed to protect the environment is used to prevent environmentally beneficial projects, the system has become divorced from its original purpose. The traditional justifications for private enforcement not only fail to apply here but are actively undermined by a regime that enables strategic litigation unrelated to environmental merit.

Return to the legislative checklist from Chapter 6:

- Capacity Gap: Would violations likely go undetected or unremedied if we rely on public enforcement alone? **No.**
- Dysfunction Risk: Is the agency unusually vulnerable to capture, partisan swings, or procedural paralysis? **No, and we have reason**

**to worry about rent-seeking litigation and a different form of capture.**

- Information Asymmetry: Do potential plaintiffs possess superior, insider knowledge that the agency cannot easily obtain? **Usually no.**
- Social Costs and Legitimacy: Is there a potential divergence between private benefits and social welfare? **Yes, and to an unusual extent**.

In short, private enforcement of NEPA-style laws represents a textbook case of private enforcement failure, where procedural protections have been weaponized by interest groups to serve goals antithetical to both environmental protection and broader social welfare. Wholesale reform is not just advisable. Rather, it is essential to restore these environmental statutes to their intended function of promoting rational decision-making rather than enabling procedural obstruction by parochial interests.

# TEN

## SHARPENING PRIVATE ENFORCEMENT

One lesson from the preceding chapters is that private enforcement is a powerful regulatory tool that *can* effectively supplement traditional government oversight. The contemporary legal landscape demonstrates both the promise (e.g., employment and securities law) and perils (e.g., abortion and environmental law) of private enforcement experimentation. The legislative innovations we started with in Chapter 2—from social media regulations protecting children to novel gun control measures to the growing tensions between red state policies and blue city ordinances—show how private enforcement can serve as a policy instrument that may grow more sophisticated and effective over time. This ongoing experimentation deserves continued support because private enforcement offers unique advantages in addressing complex regulatory challenges where traditional government enforcement may prove inadequate or politically constrained.

The main problem with continued experimentation is that private enforcement can easily overshoot. To be sure, private enforcement regimes can undershoot by creating enforcement mechanisms that prove too weak and give insufficient incentives to attorneys or plaintiffs. But Congress has demonstrated the ability to readily strengthen private enforcement regimes through amendments adding fee-shifting provisions or treble damages (as demonstrated with civil rights legislation that grew more powerful with time). By contrast, overshooting creates far more intractable problems. As Sean Farhang has observed, private enforcement regimes exhibit remarkable stickiness once established, as affected constituencies mobilize to defend their litigation rights, making subsequent legislative weakening extraordinarily difficult.[1] Historical evidence supports this concern: Congress has rarely scaled back private enforcement mechanisms once they've taken root.

So here's where we land: a continued need for experimental uses of private enforcement along with asymmetric risks between under- and overshooting and a stickiness problem. The goal is for state legislatures and Congress to create private enforcement regimes where they are justified and can avoid overshooting or stickiness.

This chapter provides a list of potential solutions, ranging from the wholesale elimination of private enforcement, automatic sunset clauses in private rights of action (provisions that would lapse private enforcement authority after a specified period), all the way to softer procedural tinkering. Consider this a list of options, or perhaps a menu, for legislators who may worry about the health of a private enforcement regime. The menu is deliberately comprehensive because different statutes face different problems and operate in different political contexts—what works for reforming CEQA in California may not be feasible for amending federal environmental laws, and what seems politically impossible today may become viable as the costs of dysfunction become more apparent. Some reforms target the incentive structures that enable abuse, while others focus on procedural barriers to frivolous litigation. Still others attempt to preserve the legitimate functions of citizen suits while eliminating their pathological applications.

The key insight is that private enforcement regimes are not binary choices between perfect citizen oversight and complete regulatory autonomy—they exist on a spectrum of design choices that can be calibrated to maximize benefits while minimizing costs. Legislators facing pressure to reform dysfunctional private enforcement systems can choose among these options based on their assessment of political feasibility, administrative capacity, and the severity of the problems they seek to address.

## INTENSE: ABROGATE PRIVATE ENFORCEMENT

On the most intense end, state legislatures and Congress could eliminate private enforcement. While it seems radical at first blush, state legislatures routinely do it. Take, for instance, an example discussed in earlier chapters: Mississippi's elimination of a private claim for DUI records. In 2005, lawmakers passed legislation protecting the privacy of drunk driving records and allowed "[a]ny person whose confidential record" was improperly disclosed to sue. The provision appeared unremarkable until a plaintiff actually used it and won in the state court of appeals, prompting legislators to eliminate the private right of action entirely in the following session.[2]

Or consider the example of a qui tam provision in a patent statute. The false marking statute prohibited deceiving the public by falsely labeling products as "patented" and included a qui tam provision since 1842 that allowed private parties to sue on behalf of the United States, but this provision remained largely unused for over 150 years due to modest $100–500 penalties. In December 2009, a Federal Circuit decision in *Forest Group v. Bon Tool* increased enforcement incentives by ruling that penalties applied per falsely marked item, causing cases to grow from roughly eighteen in 2009 to 661 in 2010. Legal scholar Zach Clopton recounted how Congress quickly responded to this litigation "gold rush" by eliminating the qui tam provision entirely through the America Invents Act of 2011.[3]

Another example comes from abroad. As discussed in Chapter 6, faced with growing critiques against the excesses of qui tam, the United Kingdom simply abrogated every single informer statute.[4] Complaints about qui tam resemble some complaints against some private enforcement regimes today—bounty-hunter plaintiffs taking advantage of expansive informer statutes to extort settlements. Malicious plaintiffs pursued claims over the most trivial violations. And they were increasingly perceived as usurping the role of the Crown. When a bill to cleanly abolish all informer claims was introduced in 1951, MPs embraced it, calling informers "parasite[s]" and qui tam a "complete anachronism."[5] Randy Beck noted that abolition came in response to the divergence between relators' financial incentives and the public interest which, as we have seen, can diverge sharply.

To be sure, Sean Farhang has argued that private enforcement provisions are particularly sticky.[6] Once enacted, these provisions create powerful constituencies, including specialized attorneys and enforcement entities, who have strong financial incentives to resist any legislative attempts to weaken or eliminate their enforcement rights. This dynamic makes private enforcement mechanisms harder to repeal than other types of legislation, as the beneficiaries actively mobilize to protect their lucrative litigation opportunities.

But, regardless of the political feasibility of eliminating private enforcement provisions, the point here is to say that some private enforcement regimes cannot be reformed; instead, they must be abrogated. This solution applies to Texas's SB 8 statute. By way of reminder, in 2021, Texas adopted SB 8, a bill that empowered anyone to sue abortion providers for aiding an abortion of a fetus with a heartbeat (after around six weeks of gestation). But the statute was a bizarre combination of three features. First, it allowed extremely broad standing, empowering anyone to enforce its claims. Second, it explicitly prohibited public officials from enforcing the statute. The crafters made this odd choice to avoid federal actions to enjoin the statute (because those statutes require a state official defendant to request equitable enjoinment of enforcement). Third, the statute was partnered with several procedures that advantaged plaintiffs in a lopsided manner. There seemed to be no concern with capacity, dysfunction, or information benefits at all. The statute did not provide enhanced capacity because it was deliberately designed to *neuter* public capacity. Nor was it aimed at fixing any dysfunction problem. Rather, it was a transparent political attempt to avoid federal courts. Finally, it did not purport to provide information benefits because it does not make up for a lack of state capacity and is not even related to the problem of regulatory capture. It appears that the statute was purely a tactical way to get around federal constitutional challenges. Given that SB 8 could proffer no reason to rely on private enforcement, it should be abrogated without question.

As discussed in the previous chapter, abrogation is probably the best way to tackle the failures of NEPA-style laws. Now, to be sure, some technical work is necessary here because there is no explicit private right of action in NEPA. Everything hinges on the ability of plaintiffs to bring APA challenges against agencies that allegedly don't comply with NEPA's procedural gauntlet.

Fortunately, Congress has repeatedly limited APA review in different areas of law. Keep in mind, first, that courts begin with a presumption that every agency action is subject to judicial review under the APA "except to the extent that . . . statutes preclude judicial review."[7] Some of this is rooted in the text of the APA, but much of it is based on judicial precedent.[8] To overcome this presumption, Congress must clearly prohibit judicial review. Sometimes Congress provides that "no court shall have jurisdiction to review" certain agency actions, as in the Immigration and Nationality Act.[9] In other statutes, Congress instead provides that a particular agency action "shall not be subject to judicial review."[10] To be sure, sometimes courts try to get around even these explicit jurisdiction-stripping provisions.[11] But if Congress is explicit and clear enough, it can avoid judicial review under the APA.

## MEDIUM TOUCH: SUNSETTING PRIVATE ENFORCEMENT

For most areas of law, state legislatures and Congress will continue to create private enforcement regimes where they are justified. The main difficulty is avoiding the asymmetric risks between under- and overshooting and the stickiness problem.

One way to thread this needle is to incorporate automatic sunset clauses into some private rights of action—provisions that would lapse private enforcement authority after a specified period unless the legislature affirmatively chooses to renew it. While sunset provisions are common features in many regulatory schemes, they remain conspicuously absent from private enforcement regimes. This oversight represents a significant gap in legislative design, as sunset clauses would preserve the benefits of private enforcement experimentation while creating regular opportunities for legislative reassessment and course correction, preventing the entrenchment of overly aggressive or misdirected enforcement mechanisms.

*1. **Need for Experimentation**.* Contemporary regulatory challenges will continue to demand the innovative enforcement mechanisms that private rights of action can provide. The lessons from existing private enforcement regimes demonstrate their ability to supplement traditional government oversight where it proves inadequate or politically constrained. Employment law regimes like PAGA have proven not merely well-justified but operationally effective. The SEC consistently emphasizes that private securities class actions perform essential work in market regulation, while private antitrust litigation has achieved breakthrough victories in opening Apple's app store ecosystem and dismantling the real estate industry's anticompetitive practices. These successes highlight private enforcement's unique capacity to address complex regulatory problems that traditional government enforcement struggles to tackle.

The states will continue to lead the way, with legislators across the political spectrum looking to private enforcement as a solution to previously intractable policy issues. Look around, and you'll find continued experimentation—attempts by Utah and other states to regulate social media's effect on children through private enforcement, and a more recent wave of state privacy laws incorporating private enforcement provisions.

Perhaps a more pressing and notable example comes at the federal level: The Department of Government Efficiency (DOGE) under Elon Musk has conducted unprecedented attacks on the federal workforce, dismissing thousands of federal workers and causing mayhem across the regulatory state. DOGE's chaotic approach included firing entire agencies like USAID, dismissing probationary employees, and eliminating critical positions.[12] Yet affected federal employees discovered a stark reality: Traditional government oversight mechanisms provide virtually no immediate recourse against these mass dismissals. The Privacy Act has emerged as the primary and only remedy available to federal workers, granting individuals a private right of action to sue federal agencies that fail to comply with the Act's provisions on handling personal records. When a court determines that an agency acted intentionally or willfully, the United States becomes liable to the individual for actual damages (with a minimum of $1,000) plus costs and reasonable attorney fees.[13] However, the Act's remedial scope is limited—federal courts have interpreted it as not providing the injunctive relief necessary to stop ongoing violations. Representatives Eugene Vindman, Sam Liccardo, and Dave Min are developing legislation to strengthen private enforcement mechanisms against federal agencies, including private rights of action under the Impoundment Control Act with substantial penalties of $1,000 per day per violation, again putting private enforcement at the center of responding to the latest regulatory problems.[14]

This ongoing experimentation deserves continued support, as private enforcement offers unique advantages in addressing complex regulatory challenges where traditional government enforcement may prove inadequate or politically constrained.

***2. Public Enforcement Failures Are Contingent.*** We know from Chapter 7 that private enforcement is justified when there is regulatory dysfunction, inadequate agency capacity, and informational asymmetries that prevent effective government oversight. However, these underlying conditions are not permanent fixtures—they represent contingent institutional failures that can evolve over time, requiring legislatures to remain highly responsive to changing enforcement needs. Agency capacity and competence fluctuate based on political priorities, resource allocation, leadership quality, and institutional learning, creating a dynamic landscape where today's enforcement gaps may become tomorrow's regulatory strengths. The key, then, is for private enforcement to remain flexible and responsive to changes in public enforcement.

The historical trajectory of civil rights enforcement shows how changing political representation can alter the necessity of private enforcement mechanisms. During the 1960s and early 1970s, private rights of action in civil rights legislation were necessary because Black citizens lacked meaningful political representation and faced indifferent government enforcement. Private litigation became the primary vehicle for challenging discriminatory practices when federal agencies either refused to act or actively supported segregation. However, as Black Americans gained substantial political influence through voting rights protections and increased representation in elected offices and federal agencies, the relative importance of private enforcement has diminished. Government agencies have become more responsive to civil rights concerns, reducing (but not eliminating) the critical need for private enforcement as the primary accountability mechanism.

Environmental law presents a parallel evolution, where the initial necessity for robust private enforcement has gradually receded as agencies developed greater expertise and commitment. CEQA and NEPA emerged in the 1960s and 1970s during a period when federal and state agencies routinely ignored environmental consequences and lacked both the technical capacity and political incentive to conduct meaningful environmental review. Citizen suits became essential to force reluctant agencies to consider environmental impacts they would otherwise dismiss. Over subsequent decades, however, environmental agencies have developed sophisticated technical expertise, environmental review has become institutionally embedded across government, and political pressure for environmental protection has increased substantially. While private enforcement remains valuable for addressing specific violations and maintaining accountability, the systematic dysfunction that originally necessitated extensive private enforcement has largely been remediated through improved agency capacity and changed political priorities.

*3. **The Under- and Overshooting Asymmetry***. There is a fundamental asymmetry between the danger of under- and overshooting with private enforcement regimes. Start with the observation that Congress has consistently shown a willingness to expand and strengthen private enforcement mechanisms over time. The Civil Rights Act of 1964 serves as a prime example of this pattern—the original legislation created relatively modest private enforcement provisions, but Congress subsequently enhanced these mechanisms throughout the 1970s by adding fee-shifting provisions and other incentives designed to encourage plaintiff participation. This evolutionary strengthening reflects Congress's general comfort with bolstering private enforcement when initial mechanisms prove insufficient to achieve policy goals. The pattern extends well beyond civil rights law, appearing across numerous regulatory domains where legislators have repeatedly amended statutes to increase damages, expand standing, or provide additional procedural advantages to private enforcers.

However, the reverse dynamic—Congress weakening or scaling back private enforcement regimes—proves remarkably rare. Despite extensive discussion in earlier chapters about instances where private enforcement has clearly overshot its intended targets, Congress has almost never deleted private rights of action or reduced multiple damages provisions once they become established. The patent qui tam provisions eliminated around 2009 represent one of the few documented examples of legislative rollback, making it an exception that proves the rule. This reluctance to weaken established rights to sue reflects more than mere legislative inertia; it represents a political economy dynamic where affected constituencies develop vested interests in maintaining their litigation rights.

The underlying cause of the asymmetry between under- and overshooting lies in the dynamics of interest group mobilization that Sean Farhang has documented.[15] This is another classic tale of public choice theory: a concentrated constituency (usually plaintiffs' attorneys) successfully defending its interests. Once private enforcement regimes become established, they create concentrated constituencies—including plaintiffs' attorneys, advocacy organizations, and affected interest groups—who have strong economic and political incentives to defend their litigation rights. These groups can mobilize effectively to resist any legislative efforts to weaken their enforcement mechanisms, creating what amounts to a classic public choice scenario where a small, concentrated group successfully defends its interests against broader but more diffuse opposition. This political reality transforms private enforcement into essentially a one-way ratchet—these regimes can grow stronger through legislative amendment, but they almost never become weaker through subsequent legislative action, regardless of their actual performance or unintended consequences.

Of course, political opponents of private enforcement have found other ways to limit private enforcement beyond direct legislative rollback. At the state level, the tort reform movement has proven both powerful and successful in constraining private litigation through caps on damages, restrictions on punitive awards, and other procedural limitations. Similarly, the sustained political campaign against class actions culminated in the Class Action Fairness Act (CAFA) of 2005, a significant procedural reform designed to weaken private enforcement by making it harder to bring large-scale litigation in state courts.[16] This anti-class action movement achieved additional victories by convincing presidents to appoint federal judges with more conservative views on class certification, personal jurisdiction, and other procedural doctrines.[17] Over time, these judicial appointments resulted in a systematic procedural retrenchment that significantly constrained private enforcement, demonstrating that opponents of aggressive private litigation can achieve meaningful victories through indirect routes when direct legislative assault proves politically impossible.[18]

Yet none of these examples involve Congress directly amending the substantive statutory provisions that create private enforcement regimes, particularly at the federal level where most significant private enforcement mechanisms operate. This book focuses specifically on the legislative design of private enforcement regimes—the statutory language that creates private rights of action, establishes damages formulas, and defines enforcement parameters. Indeed, the fact that successful attacks on private enforcement have consistently operated through indirect channels—tort reform at the state level, procedural changes like CAFA, and judicial appointments that gradually shift doctrinal interpretations—actually confirms the central point about legislative stickiness. These indirect strategies exist precisely because direct congressional modification of substantive private enforcement provisions proves so politically difficult that opponents must resort to weakening the procedural foundation rather than attacking the statutory superstructure directly.

*4. **Sunset Solutions***. Sunset clauses in private rights of action offer a surgical solution that addresses multiple structural problems with private enforcement regimes simultaneously. By requiring periodic legislative reauthorization, sunset clauses create natural checkpoints for evaluating whether private enforcement mechanisms remain necessary and appropriately calibrated, transforming what would otherwise be permanent institutional fixtures into adaptive policy tools subject to regular democratic review.

First, sunsets directly solve the stickiness problem that makes private enforcement regimes so difficult to modify once established. As discussed above, without sunset provisions, constituencies that benefit from private enforcement mobilize powerful political opposition against any legislative attempts to weaken litigation rights. These entrenched interests create a political ratchet effect where private enforcement can only expand, never contract, regardless of changing circumstances. Sunset clauses flip this dynamic by requiring proactive legislative action to continue private enforcement rather than to eliminate it. This shifts the political burden from those seeking to constrain private enforcement to those seeking to extend it, creating regular opportunities for legislative reassessment without the extraordinary political effort typically required to roll back established regimes.

Second, sunset provisions align perfectly with the underlying justifications for private enforcement by recognizing that regulatory dysfunction, agency capacity constraints, and information asymmetries are *contingent* conditions that can change over time. As discussed above, the need for private enforcement often emerges from specific institutional failures that may be remediated through subsequent reforms, personnel changes, or evolving political priorities. A responsive legislature requires mechanisms to adjust enforcement strategies as these underlying conditions change. Sunset clauses provide this essential flexibility by creating regular opportunities to evaluate whether the original justifications for private enforcement remain valid or whether improved agency capacity has reduced the need for private supplementation.

Third, sunset provisions could help the federal government achieve the adaptive capacity that states have demonstrated in managing private enforcement regimes. State legislatures routinely create, modify, and eliminate private rights of action based on changing needs and accumulated experience, showing a responsiveness that the federal government lacks. States have proven willing to substantially modify private enforcement mechanisms when they prove problematic or when government capacity improves, while Congress has shown remarkable reluctance to scale back federal private enforcement regimes regardless of changing circumstances. Federal sunset provisions would import this state-level flexibility to the national level, enabling Congress to experiment with private enforcement while maintaining the ability to course-correct based on evidence and experience.

Sunset mechanisms are well-established in federal law and have proven effective in other contexts requiring periodic legislative review. Different surveillance authorities, defense programs, and emergency powers operate under sunset provisions that force periodic reconsideration. These precedents demonstrate both the political feasibility and practical utility of sunset mechanisms for consequential federal programs.

Indeed, the implementation of sunset clauses would likely accelerate the adoption of private enforcement mechanisms by reducing legislative risk aversion and encouraging policy experimentation. Currently, legislators face a binary choice: Either enact permanent private enforcement regimes that may prove difficult to modify if they overshoot, or forgo private enforcement entirely due to concerns about creating politically entrenched constituencies and litigation abuse. This dynamic strongly favors the status quo, as the potential downside risks of permanent private enforcement can outweigh the perceived benefits for risk-averse legislators. Sunset provisions fundamentally alter this calculus by transforming private enforcement from a permanent institutional commitment into a time-limited policy experiment with built-in exit ramps. Legislators should feel significantly more comfortable authorizing innovative private enforcement mechanisms knowing they retain the ability to let them expire naturally if problems emerge. This reduced political risk would particularly benefit experimental approaches to emerging regulatory challenges, like AI governance, where legislators currently hesitate to create new private enforcement tools due to uncertainty about their long-term effects. The experimental mindset that sunset clauses enable would likely produce more creative and targeted private enforcement mechanisms, as legislators could test novel approaches with the confidence that unsuccessful experiments would terminate automatically.

The primary risk of sunset provisions is that a particular administration interested in underenforcing existing law may choose not to support reauthorization of effective private enforcement mechanisms, potentially creating enforcement gaps during periods of government indifference. However, this risk is counterbalanced by significant benefits that sunset provisions provide to public enforcement agencies. Sunset clauses allow public enforcers to observe and learn from private enforcement litigation, gaining valuable information about violations, enforcement strategies, and legal theories before taking over primary enforcement responsibility. They also provide a structured timeline for public agencies to develop the capacity and expertise necessary to assume greater enforcement responsibility as private enforcement mechanisms wind down. Rather than creating an enforcement vacuum, well-designed sunset provisions can facilitate a planned transition from private supplementation to enhanced public enforcement based on institutional learning and capacity development.

## LIGHT TOUCH: MAKE IT HARDER FOR PLAINTIFFS

In the light end of the spectrum, legislatures can make it harder for plaintiffs to file claims in a variety of ways. As discussed below, legislatures can narrow the number of people who can file a case through the rules of standing, and they can make it procedurally more difficult to file claims by requiring would-be plaintiffs to post large bonds—as an indication of real interest in the lawsuit. This would prevent serial filers from filing dozens of NEPA or CEQA challenges. And legislatures can impose tight timing and aggregation provisions so that judges must consider all legal challenges against projects in one aggregate setting, quickly decide on any challenges, and then close out a short period for legal claims.

To maintain a consistent example for all of the solutions discussed below, I'll focus on California's CEQA statute. Again, this is an extraordinarily powerful NEPA-style law that allows anyone to sue. For political reasons, it has been nearly impossible for the California legislature to engage in wholesale reform of the statute. How, then, could reformers weaken private enforcement of this law? Here are several options.

*1. **Standing.*** The rules of standing determine whether a party has an adequate injury to bring a lawsuit in court. At the federal level, Article III of the Constitution requires "a case or controversy" that the judiciary can properly address. Courts have developed this language to mean that "a plaintiff must have suffered an 'injury in fact'—an invasion of a legally protected interest which . . . is concrete and particularized."[19] At the state level, however, the rules vary widely. Some states mirror the federal approach while others provide much broader standing requirements that allow parties without concrete injuries to file claims.[20]

Standing rules can serve as a powerful calibrator of private enforcement regimes.[21] As discussed throughout this book, there is a frequent divergence between the interests of private plaintiffs and the goals of a statute (or even social welfare). Plaintiffs' attorneys motivated by profit sometimes have an incentive to file claims that are legally questionable but can force the defendant to settle for a small monetary amount. Other plaintiffs are engaged in rent-seeking and represent narrow interests rather than a statute's broader purpose. Limiting standing to plaintiffs with direct, concrete injuries narrows the pool of potential lawsuits to those with genuine stakes in the outcome, filtering out opportunistic litigation while preserving legitimate enforcement mechanisms.

This calibration effect can be enormously important for managing strategic litigation. When standing requirements are tight, only a limited number of genuinely affected parties can sue, making it easier for defendants to identify and potentially negotiate with real stakeholders rather than face waves of ideological challengers. Restrictive standing also prevents the kind of serial litigation that can be frivolous, where the same groups file dozens of challenges against some particular act. For instance, in the context of endangered species, the US Supreme Court held that plaintiffs do not have standing to bring a lawsuit against a project that allegedly harmed a protected species. That is, harm to a species did not produce a cognizable injury for plaintiffs who had merely "visited" the areas or who "observe[] or work[] with an endangered species," elsewhere in the world.[22] Standing, then, can serve as a calibrator—the legislature can expand standing rules if there is insufficient private enforcement or narrow them if there's too much.

Let's see how this would work in the context of CEQA. A common problem is CEQA lawsuits by NIMBYs, unions, and ideological groups who exploit CEQA's broad statutory standing provisions. CEQA allows anyone with a "beneficial interest" to file a claim, including those with merely financial interests. There is also an exorbitant "public interest" exception that allows plaintiffs to file claims ostensibly in the public interest. While courts have noted that "public interest standing is not 'freely available to business interests lacking a direct beneficial interest in the litigation,'" this standard remains far too permissive.[23]

Standing requirements can limit this abuse. The most direct solution is to increase standing requirements so that only parties suffering concrete and particularized harm can file administrative challenges against CEQA projects. This would prevent random plaintiffs, unions, serial litigants, and many (though not all) NIMBYs from filing environmental claims against construction projects, while preserving legal rights for organizations and citizens who live directly in the path of harmful developments. Some reformers, including Arthur Coon, have proposed this solution, arguing that California should adopt a statutory fix to "more firmly establish the 'beneficial interest' standing requirement as the rule, and 'public interest' standing as a strictly circumscribed exception."[24] However, Coon would still allow standing for non-profits "presumptively," which doesn't go far enough. I would argue that only those with direct, concrete stakes in a construction project should be able to sue—actual neighbors who will suffer tangible harm, not advocacy organizations often created specifically to manufacture environmental opposition. To be sure, tightening standing requirements cannot eliminate all NIMBY litigation by proximate neighbors with parochial concerns, but it would at least prevent lawsuits by plaintiffs with no direct stake.

***2. Posting Bonds.*** A time-honored solution to the problem of vexatious litigation is the requirement that a plaintiff post a bond. The gist of it is that forcing the plaintiff to put up a nontrivial amount of money at the outset is a signal of genuine intention to file a legitimate claim. The goal is both to deter frivolous filing but also to prevent serial litigants who file dozens of similar cases. In a major 2013 Supreme Court case, Justice Stevens noted that bond requirements have long been "bound up" with substantive policy goals, like shielding certain industries from frivolous lawsuits.[25] At the same time, policymakers must avoid turning bonds into barriers for good faith and meritorious plaintiffs.

Courts have upheld the use of bonds by both the states and the federal government, although bond-posting statutes are more common in the states. Take, for instance, a mid-century New Jersey statute that sought to tackle the problem of overlitigation by shareholders in securities claims. One provision provided that "'In any [shareholder] action, . . . the corporation in whose right such action is brought shall be entitled, at any stage of the proceeding before final judgment, to require the complainant or complainants to give security for the reasonable expenses, including counsel fees, which may be incurred by it in connection with such action."[26] The law targeted plaintiffs with a small ownership interest, presuming that major shareholders are less likely to sue frivolously. In one case that ended up in front of the Supreme Court, the defendant asked for a bond of $125,000 pursuant to the statute, and the plaintiff challenged the law as unconstitutional. The Supreme Court upheld the constitutionality of the statute because "[a] state may set the terms on which it will permit litigations in its courts," and "it cannot seriously be said that a state makes such unreasonable use of its power as to violate the Constitution when it provides liability and security for payment of reasonable expenses if a litigation of this character is adjudged to be unsustainable . . . . [I]t is within the power of a state to close its courts to this type of litigation if the condition of reasonable security is not met."[27] In other words, so long as the bond amount is not punitive and is tied to expected costs, it's within a state's power to require it.

After the Supreme Court upheld the use of bonds, states either expanded or retained similar provisions. Some historical reports defended the use of these provisions as a key safeguard and perhaps the best way to fight against strike suits in the securities context.[28] A current New York law, for example, provides that in any shareholder derivative action, if the "plaintiff owns" less than a certain threshold, the corporation "shall be entitled . . . to require the plaintiff to give security for the reasonable expenses, including attorney's fees, which may be incurred by [the corporation]" in the defense.[29] Similarly, Section 1030 of California's Code of Civil Procedure permits a defendant to require an out-of-state or foreign-corporate plaintiff to post a bond if the defendant shows a "reasonable possibility" of defeating the claim. Upon motion, the court orders the plaintiff to give security in an amount sufficient to cover anticipated costs and attorney's fees; failure to post the bond within the time set leads to dismissal of the case.[30] But while states continue to use them, some scholars have worried that particular kinds of security requirements can become "an absolute barrier to entry for even the most well-intentioned plaintiffs acting in good faith with a legitimate concern, who simply lack the funds to post the required bond."[31]

Sometimes the states use bond-posting provisions to target vexatious litigants directly. A California statute lets a court order a designated vexatious plaintiff to post a bond if they file a new lawsuit and the judge finds there is no reasonable likelihood of success.[32]

Requiring plaintiffs to post a bond can be a powerful mechanism to control the filing and prosecution of civil cases. But while bond-posting requirements can be a useful tool to regulate private enforcement, they must be carefully calibrated not to overdeter meritorious claims. I won't address here many implementation questions (including the conditions under which bonds are returned versus forfeited, appropriate bond amounts, recipients of forfeited funds, etc.). These design choices matter but are beyond this discussion's scope. This section serves only as an introduction to bond posting as a potential calibration tool for private enforcement regimes, not as a full implementation guide.

***3. Statutes of Limitation.*** Time limits on statutory claims have always been there. From the earliest penal statutes in England, reformers who disliked informers sought to restrain them via time limits on their claims. The gist of it is that legislatures use time limits on claims to protect defendants from stale claims or unreliable evidence. Sometimes, too, legislatures use time limits to simply regulate the number of claims against a particular industry. Scholars and judges have long struggled to balance the need for "extinguishment of untimely claims" and the desire to decide "all claims . . . on their merits."[33] Critics worry that an unwarranted time limit is a denial of justice; Oliver Wendell Holmes once quipped, "What is the justification for depriving a man of his rights, a pure evil as far as it goes, in consequence of the lapse of time?"[34]

Still, the states and Congress continue to use time-limit provisions to limit private enforcement. California, for instance, has "thousands" of these provisions, including several across CEQA. To challenge a project approval under CEQA, petitioners must act swiftly. When a Notice of Determination is filed, a thirty-day clock starts to file suit. (If no notice is filed, a 180-day limit applies.) Courts strictly enforce this thirty-day deadline, even requiring that the notice remain posted for the full period.[35] But the fact that CEQA litigation continues to present problems despite these time limits is a warning that statutes of limitations can be toothless in some contexts.

Beyond CEQA's environmental context, California employs abbreviated limitation periods across numerous regulatory domains as tools of enforcement control. Section 65009 of the state's Government Code imposes a strict ninety-day limit for challenging local land-use approvals, with courts emphasizing that this provision "contains no exceptions" and reflects "plain intent . . . to limit the time to seek review" of agency decisions.[36] Similarly, California's Tort Claims Act compresses the ordinary two-year personal injury period into what practitioners call "the Rule of Six"—six months to present a claim to the public entity, then six months to file suit after rejection.[37] Insurance disputes face their own truncated timeline under Section 2071 of the Insurance Code, which mandates a one-year deadline from the date of loss, with the clock starting upon the insurer's effective denial of a claim.[38]

New York follows a parallel approach, using compressed deadlines to channel and constrain private enforcement actions. The state's Article 78 procedure for challenging government actions must be commenced within four months of the final agency determination—a window far shorter than ordinary civil statutes of limitations.[39] Even for complex environmental harms, Section 214-c of New York's Civil Practice Law and Rules requires suit within three years of discovery. Federal law similarly employs strategic time limits, from Title VII's 180-day EEOC filing requirement to the Federal Tort Claims Act's compressed two-year administrative claim period followed by six months to sue.

Courts have consistently upheld these abbreviated periods as valid expressions of legislative policy rather than mere procedural technicalities. In *Schmidt v. Southern California Rapid Transit District*, California's

Court of Appeals characterized the Government Claims Act as "a thoughtfully devised statutory plan that is designed to control the basis under which public entities may be liable," rejecting any suggestion that claimants could invoke both the Act's six-month deadline and longer general limitations periods.[40] As legal scholars have observed, these compressed deadlines function as policy tools to filter out marginal or delayed suits while concentrating litigation within narrower time windows, ultimately serving legislative goals of reducing case volume and providing defendants with earlier repose.

***4. Other Tools: Aggregation, Attorneys' Fees, and Narrow Remedies.***

***Aggregation.*** Aggregation mechanisms in US litigation serve the dual purpose of streamlining dispute resolution while controlling the proliferation of repetitive lawsuits. These tools—including interpleader, class actions, and multidistrict litigation—can be a useful way to calibrate private enforcement because they force multiple lawsuits to be litigated in one forum at one time. The fundamental policy behind aggregation is judicial economy: avoiding duplicative litigation that wastes resources.

The legal system employs several aggregation tools to consolidate related disputes. Interpleader allows stakeholders facing competing claims to a single pot of money to force all claimants into one proceeding. Class actions under Federal Rule of Civil Procedure 23 let representative plaintiffs sue on behalf of similarly situated individuals, binding all class members to a single judgment and avoiding hundreds of individual suits. Multidistrict litigation under 28 U.S.C. § 1407 centralizes related cases from different districts before one judge for coordinated pretrial proceedings.

While aggregation clearly promotes efficiency and consistency in litigation, it creates complex trade-offs. The benefits include reduced litigation costs, protection against inconsistent judgments, prevention of tactical abuse through multiple small suits, and conservation of judicial resources. Defendants gain protection from being dragged to court by conflicting obligations across different courts. However, aggregation can also incentivize more litigation by making collective actions economically viable—class actions and MDLs often attract additional claimants who might never have sued individually. The challenge for policymakers remains striking the proper balance: using aggregation to prevent wasteful repetitive litigation while maintaining adequate deterrence of wrongdoing.

***Attorneys' Fees.*** Attorney fee-shifting is a familiar lever for shaping private enforcement. By giving a plaintiff or defendant the ability to collect attorneys' fees, fee-shifting statutes change incentives for lawyers. Congress has long employed this tool, especially in the Civil Rights Attorney's Fees Awards Act of 1976 (42 U.S.C. § 1988), which guarantees prevailing plaintiffs their "reasonable" fees. Dozens of other federal and state regimes adopt the same model. On the other side, legislatures sometimes invert the incentive by saddling an unsuccessful plaintiff with the defendant's fees, thereby discouraging suits—an approach now common in securities, patent, and certain state consumer-protection statutes.

Some recent work shows that fee-shifting provisions do far more than reimburse lawyers: They determine whether cases are filed, how much discovery is pursued, and whether settlement values track social harm.[41] The way that lower courts calculate attorneys' fees (by looking at hourly rates or market-wide averages) can determine the value of a claim to an attorney, shaping levels of enforcement, while the defense-side fee awards in "frivolous" litigation can eliminate meritorious claims when set too aggressively. In short, fee rules function as dials that can be tuned up or down to calibrate the volume of private enforcement.

Many reformers have pushed for fee-shifting as a tool to regulate California's CEQA. A *Los Angeles Times* op-ed urges a categorical loser-pays rule, insisting that parties who sue under CEQA and lose "shouldn't be allowed to skip out . . . without having to pick up the tab of the prevailing party."[42] State Senator Andreas Borgeas pursued the same logic in a proposed bill to authorize courts to award fees against petitioners whose CEQA claims were "frivolous."[43] These proposals illustrate how fee-shifting, long used to spur public interest suits, can also be redeployed to discipline opportunistic litigation and recalibrate the overall mix of private enforcement.

***Narrow Remedies.*** Narrowing the remedies available to private litigants is another classic tool to limit private enforcement. Some of the most potent private enforcement regimes have a built-in limit by providing only narrow remedies. For instance, Congress wrote the federal Clean Air Act citizen-suit provision so that a successful plaintiff may obtain only injunctive relief plus civil penalties that are paid into the US Treasury, not to the plaintiff. Along the same lines, the Americans with Disabilities Act similarly denies private damages, confining victories to injunctions and attorneys' fees awards. By eliminating the prospect of monetary windfalls, these statutes still permit suits that compel compliance while muting the profit motive that can over-incentivize filings.

Just like with other remedies, critics of CEQA have proposed limiting its remedial structure. As many have highlighted, CEQA remedies are robust—filing a petition for a writ of mandate effectively freezes financing for construction projects because lenders fear that a court may later vacate the project approval in its entirety.[44] Courts must issue a peremptory writ if they find "prejudicial abuse of discretion," and critics say judges often set aside a whole approval for relatively minor defects in an environmental impact report—turning what should be a small fix into a de facto injunction that can kill a construction project outright. This is clearly an extremely powerful remedy.

Reformers therefore propose narrowing CEQA remedies to recalibrate enforcement without gutting environmental review. Two scholars, Michelle Ouellette and Ali Tehrani, recommend remanding EIRs to agencies as the presumptive remedy—ordering agencies to fix only the deficient portions of an EIR—rather than nullifying the entire approval.[45] A report by law firm Holland & Knight urges alignment with ordinary equitable principles so that injunctive relief issues only when irreparable environmental harm is likely, and a remand without vacatur when agencies commit technical errors.[46] These proposals would preserve the statute's disclosure goals while dialing back the collateral leverage that broad vacatur currently gives CEQA plaintiffs.

# CONCLUSION

This book began with an apparently simple yet puzzling question: Why does the United States consistently rely on private enforcement when virtually no other developed democracy does so to the same extent? The answer, as we have seen, is neither simple nor reducible to familiar explanations about American culture, separation of powers, or accident. Instead, private enforcement represents the cumulative product of layered path dependence—an inherited tradition of English penal statutes, and structural incentives created by separation of powers, lobbying, and federalism. Supporting this are a uniquely powerful lawyers' lobby and civil procedure rules that transformed scattered statutory clauses into a mass-litigation engine capable of regulating entire industries.

The story we have traced spans centuries, from medieval English informer suits through colonial penal statutes to today's sprawling network of more than 10,000 private rights of action across federal and state law. What emerges is not the tale of a single legislative choice or cultural preference, but rather the evolution of a distinctly American approach to governance, one that systematically mobilizes private attorneys and everyday citizens as roving regulators who can enforce the law.

## THE ARCHITECTURE OF AMERICAN PRIVATE ENFORCEMENT AND THE CHOICE OF 1914

The empirical landscape we have mapped reveals private enforcement operating across every area of regulatory concern. From California's Private Attorneys General Act, which has generated hundreds of millions of dollars in penalties for labor violations, to the Clean Air Act's citizen suit provisions that empower environmental organizations to police industrial emissions, to securities class actions that have secured tens of billions of dollars in settlements from corporate fraud, private enforcement has become the dominant mechanism for implementing regulatory policy. We started Chapter 2 with numbers that are worth repeating here: Private parties file over 90 percent of antitrust claims, 98 percent of civil rights cases, and a significant chunk of employment, environmental, and other enforcement actions. In many regulatory domains, private lawsuits are not merely supplemental to government enforcement; they are the primary vehicle through which law is enforced.

This vast system operates through a sophisticated procedural infrastructure that has no parallel elsewhere in the world. The combination of broad discovery rules that function as privatized subpoena power, opt-out class actions that aggregate scattered injuries into economically viable lawsuits, low pleading standards that keep courthouse doors open, and contingency fee arrangements that align lawyer incentives with client recovery has created what amounts to a parallel regulatory state (what Sean Farhang appropriately called the "Litigation State"). When Congress or a state legislature includes a private right of action in a statute—often with treble damages, fee-shifting provisions, and other plaintiff-friendly enhancements—they are not merely creating a cause of action. They are plugging that statute into a pre-existing enforcement infrastructure capable of generating thousands of cases, compelling discovery of internal corporate documents, and imposing sanctions that can exceed what government agencies can achieve on their own.

The historical roots of this system run deeper than most scholars have recognized. Rather than emerging from 1960s social movements or New Deal administrative struggles, private enforcement traces its lineage to medieval English penal statutes and qui tam actions that empowered "informers" to police regulatory violations in exchange for a share of the penalty. Colonial America not only inherited but intensified these traditions, with roughly 10 percent of Massachusetts laws in the eighteenth century explicitly depending on private enforcement. By the time of the Constitutional Convention, private enforcement was so familiar that the first Congress used qui tam and informer actions to implement nearly all of its enumerated powers. President Washington, too, discovered he could not even pardon away a private citizen's statutory right to collect a penalty.

This deep legal memory created path dependence that persists today. Each new statute that included a private right of action made the next insertion cheaper and more familiar, turning private enforcement into legislative boilerplate. The 1890 Sherman Act's treble damages provision accelerated the trend by drawing directly on the 1623 English Statute of Monopolies. And then came the key moment: the 1914 congressional adoption of both the Clayton Act and the Federal Trade Commission Act, demonstrating that private enforcement could continue to operate alongside a new bureaucracy. This is what fused the tradition of rights to sue with an emerging bureaucratic state, forcing them to operate side-by-side for the rest of the century.

Developments later in the century just copied the choice of 1914. And so the 1964 Civil Rights Act's enforcement mechanisms built on 1914's twin bills as well as the Fair Labor Standards Act precedents. Environmental citizen suits of the 1970s explicitly referenced both civil rights and qui tam models. New schemes like Utah's social media regulation and California's gun control measures continue this pattern, demonstrating how private enforcement has become the default legislative response to regulatory challenges.

## WHEN PRIVATE ENFORCEMENT WORKS AND WHEN IT FAILS

The normative framework developed in this book provides clear criteria for evaluating when private enforcement serves the public interest. Private enforcement is most justified when three conditions converge: (1) Public enforcers lack the capacity to police violations at scale, (2) regulatory capture or partisan dysfunction threatens to blunt agency enforcement, and (3) informational asymmetries prevent government officials from detecting violations that private parties can readily observe.

Employment law exemplifies private enforcement at its best. California's PAGA demonstrates how employee lawsuits can effectively supplement chronically underfunded labor agencies that have only one field investigator for every 115,000 workers. With a backlog of 47,000 wage theft complaints and waiting times exceeding six times the statutory deadline, private enforcement through worker lawsuits provides essential capacity that government agencies simply cannot match. Moreover, the informational asymmetries are stark—only employees witness whether employers round down time records, skip meal breaks, or misclassify workers to avoid overtime obligations. The deterrent effect is substantial: PAGA generated $88 million in civil penalties in 2019 alone, money that flowed both to affected workers and state enforcement agencies.

By contrast, environmental law reveals private enforcement at its most dysfunctional. NEPA and CEQA lawsuits fail every traditional justification for private enforcement while imposing significant social costs. These procedural challenges occur only after government agencies have conducted multi-year environmental reviews, making private litigation entirely redundant rather than capacity-enhancing. Private plaintiffs contribute no unique information that agencies cannot access through notice and comment proceedings, yet they can delay or kill beneficial projects—affordable housing, renewable energy, mass transit—through strategic litigation that exploits procedural complexity for non-environmental ends. Labor unions file CEQA lawsuits to extract project labor agreements, wealthy neighbors oppose developments that might affect property values, and even environmental organizations challenge solar farms that would advance climate goals. The system has become captured by interests antithetical to its stated environmental purpose.

The comparative evidence reinforces these distinctions. While other developed countries have selectively adopted American-style private enforcement in areas like antitrust and employment discrimination, they have consistently rejected environmental citizen suits. This selective borrowing by sophisticated legal systems suggests that environmental private enforcement represents a uniquely American pathology rather than a regulatory invention worth emulating.

## SEARCHING FOR MORE EFFECTIVE PRIVATE ENFORCEMENT

This book's analysis may leave readers uncertain about whether America has too much or too little private enforcement overall. That uncertainty is deliberate. Private enforcement operates so differently across regulatory domains that it would be unwise to make an aggregate judgment. Maybe PAGA-like regimes that genuinely supplement underfunded agencies outnumber NEPA-like problems, but the latter impose disproportionate costs in critical areas like housing and infrastructure. The question is not whether we have the right amount of private enforcement in the abstract, but whether specific regimes continue to serve public welfare under evolving conditions.

The reform agenda emerging from this book is therefore complex because different private enforcement regimes face different problems and operate in different political contexts. For new statutes, legislators should consider incorporating sunset clauses into private rights of action. This approach would preserve the benefits of regulatory experimentation while preventing the entrenchment of overly aggressive or misdirected enforcement mechanisms that prove politically impossible to modify once established.

For existing regimes that have overshot their targets, the book provides a menu of calibrated responses. At the most intensive end, wholesale abrogation may be appropriate for statutes like Texas's abortion enforcement law that were designed to circumvent constitutional protections rather than serve legitimate purposes. NEPA and CEQA's private enforcement schemes similarly warrant elimination because they impose massive costs without corresponding benefits and enable rent-seeking litigation unrelated to the environment.

For statutes that serve legitimate purposes but need recalibration, more targeted reforms can sharpen private enforcement's benefits while blunting its costs. Tightening standing requirements would limit lawsuits to parties with concrete stakes rather than allowing anyone to file challenges. Bond posting requirements could deter serial litigants while preserving access for good-faith challengers. Aggregation mechanisms could prevent duplicative lawsuits while maintaining adequate deterrence. Fee-shifting provisions could discourage frivolous litigation while maintaining incentives for meritorious claims. The goal is not to weaken private enforcement but to ensure it serves public rather than narrow interests.

## LESSONS FOR GOVERNANCE AND DEMOCRACY

The story of private enforcement touches on broader themes about American governance that extend beyond litigation and regulatory policy. At its core, private enforcement reflects an American solution to the eternal problem of controlling government power while ensuring effective governance. Rather than choosing between bureaucratic expertise and democratic accountability, the American system systematically creates dual enforcement mechanisms that check each other while serving complementary functions.

This approach has generated significant innovation in regulatory enforcement. Private securities litigation has developed sophisticated techniques for detecting corporate fraud that government agencies have missed. Employment law class actions have created compliance standards that have spread throughout entire industries. Environmental citizen suits have forced government agencies to meet statutory deadlines and consider previously ignored ecological impacts. Private enforcement has proven capable of adapting quickly to new forms of misconduct, deploying entrepreneurial energy and financial incentives to police behavior that bureaucratic agencies might miss or choose to ignore.

Yet private enforcement also reveals the limitations of American governance. The system's emphasis on diffusing power creates coordination problems that centralized approaches avoid. Private lawsuits can work at cross-purposes with agency enforcement strategies, fragment policy implementation across multiple jurisdictions, and subject defendants to inconsistent legal obligations. The entrepreneurial energy that makes private enforcement effective can also produce rent-seeking litigation when financial incentives diverge from social welfare. And the system's historical stickiness means that private enforcement regimes often persist long after the conditions that justified their creation have changed.

Perhaps most fundamentally, private enforcement demonstrates how procedural choices become substantive policy. The rules governing discovery, class certification, fee-shifting, and standing do not merely determine how lawsuits proceed—they calibrate the level of regulatory enforcement. When Congress creates a private right of action, it is not simply adding another enforcement mechanism; it is connecting that statute to a procedural infrastructure that can amplify or constrain its regulatory impact. This has profound implications for how we think about the relationship between courts and agencies, procedure and substance, and private and public power in American governance.

## AN AMERICAN INNOVATION: WHY NOT BOTH?

Private enforcement represents one of America's most distinctive contributions to the global menu of governance techniques. Like federalism or judicial review, private enforcement has been exported selectively to other legal systems while remaining most fully developed in its country of origin. Understanding why requires appreciating both the historical contingency, structural logic, and procedural infrastructure of American legal development.

The historical contingency lies in the particular sequence through which American law evolved. The early inheritance of English penal statutes, combined with weak colonial bureaucratic capacity, made private enforcement a necessity that became normalized through repetition. The structural logic lies in how the separation of powers and federalism create ongoing incentives for legislators to hedge against future administrative drift by empowering private enforcers alongside public agencies. And the procedural enablers that emerged in 1938 and 1966 transformed this inherited preference into a mass-litigation engine capable of regulating modern economic activity.

Other countries that developed stronger administrative traditions during the nineteenth and early twentieth centuries never experienced the same need to rely extensively on private enforcement. And they often decided that private and public enforcement were alternatives rather than complementary. When they faced similar regulatory challenges, foreign elites typically responded by building more capable bureaucracies rather than mobilizing private litigants. And when pushed to keep private enforcement, legal elites in countries like England wondered: Why would we do that? We have expert public agents to take charge now. Time to let go of that old enforcement tool.

Americans, by contrast, welcomed the new bureaucracies and decided that the ancient tool of private enforcement could work alongside it. Why not both? The different paths taken during formative periods may help explain why American and European approaches to regulation continue to diverge.

Yet private enforcement's American origins do not diminish its broader significance for governance theory and practice. As regulatory challenges become more complex, the limitations of purely bureaucratic approaches become more apparent. Private enforcement offers a way to harness distributed knowledge, align private incentives with public goals, and maintain regulatory pressure even when government agencies face resource constraints or political interference. The Trump Administration's attacks on the bureaucracy, refusal to enforce the TikTok ban, and artificial intelligence governance all present challenges that may benefit from the kind of adaptive, decentralized enforcement that private litigation can provide.

## FUTURE DIRECTIONS

The analysis in this book points toward several important areas for future research and policy development. First, the most important question left largely unaddressed in this book is how to optimally combine private and public enforcement rather than simply evaluating each in isolation. The framework developed in Chapter 7 treats private enforcement primarily as a supplement to public enforcement, but this framing understates how private and public enforcement can serve genuinely complementary functions. The California PAGA revenue-sharing model hints at more sophisticated integration possibilities, where private litigation funds public agency capacity while public agencies provide guidance and oversight. Similarly, agency gatekeeping provisions that allow regulators to supervise or even take over private cases are another mechanism for channeling private enforcement.[1]

Second, the interaction between private enforcement and emerging technologies demands careful attention. Popular demands to regulate artificial intelligence, biotechnology, and digital platforms will present legislators with familiar questions about whether to rely on government agencies, private lawsuits, or some combination. The framework developed here suggests that private enforcement will be most valuable where government agencies lack technical expertise, industry influence threatens regulatory capture, and private parties possess superior information about violations or harms. Moreover, as briefly suggested in Chapter 7, AI may empower public regulators with new ways of gathering information, weakening the information asymmetries that partly justify private enforcement.

Third, the international dimension of private enforcement requires more systematic study. As American-style private litigation spreads to other jurisdictions, we need a better understanding of how different procedural contexts affect the performance of private enforcement regimes. For example, the German development of collective redress mechanisms—some of it prompted by the Volkswagen scandal discussed in the opening paragraphs of the book—represents a fascinating experiment in adapting American tools to civil law systems with different litigation cultures and procedural traditions.

Fourth, the relationship between private enforcement and democratic legitimacy deserves continued theoretical and empirical investigation. This book has argued that private enforcement can serve the rule of law and democratic values by empowering political underdogs, generating information for public deliberation, and providing checks on concentrated power. But private enforcement can also enable special interests to weaponize legal process for anti-democratic ends, as environmental litigation abuse demonstrates. Understanding when private enforcement enhances versus undermines democratic governance requires more nuanced analysis of how litigation intersects with political representation, interest group mobilization, and bureaucratic accountability.

## A CONTINUING AMERICAN EXPERIMENT

Private enforcement will continue to evolve as American governance confronts new challenges and adapts to changing political and economic conditions. Recent schemes in state privacy law, social media regulation, and gun control demonstrate that legislators across the political spectrum reflexively view private enforcement as a valuable tool for addressing difficult policy problems. Government employees' response to DOGE's attacks on the civil service has highlighted how private enforcement can serve as a check on executive overreach when other accountability mechanisms prove inadequate.

Yet this book's analysis also suggests reasons for caution about the continued expansion of private enforcement. The stickiness problem identified here means that today's experimental private enforcement regimes may become tomorrow's entrenched pathologies, resistant to modification even when their costs clearly exceed their benefits. Texas's SB 8 anti-abortion statute or the environmental law experience provides a sobering reminder that private enforcement can be captured and weaponized by political or rent-seeking interests.

The path forward requires rejecting both wholesale embrace and categorical rejection of private enforcement in favor of more discriminating analysis of when and how private enforcement serves the public interest. The framework developed in this book provides tools for making such discriminating judgments. But applying this framework effectively requires sustained attention to how private enforcement regimes perform in practice, not just how they appear on paper.

Private enforcement is neither a panacea for regulatory dysfunction nor a pathological departure from proper governance. It is a distinctively American institution that can serve democratic values when properly designed and constrained but can also undermine those values when captured by narrow interests or poorly adapted to changing circumstances. Our task is not to embrace or reject private enforcement entirely, but to understand how this powerful governance tool can be wielded more effectively in the service of public welfare.

The American experiment with private enforcement continues. Whether it serves as a model for good governance or a cautionary tale about institutional dysfunction will depend on whether we can learn from both its successes and its failures. This book has attempted to provide the analytical tools necessary for that learning.

# ACKNOWLEDGMENTS

I first want to thank the people who matter most to me: my wife Silvia and my two beautiful children, Oliver and Hannah, whose patience and support made this book possible.

I'm deeply grateful to mentors and colleagues who shaped my thinking on procedural issues. My colleagues at Stanford provided invaluable feedback and guidance, including Amalia Kessler, Mark Lemley, David Sklansky, and Lisa Larrimore Ouellette. I'm also grateful to colleagues who taught me much about civil procedure, including David Freeman Engstrom, Nora Freeman Engstrom, Shirin Sinnar, and Norm Spaulding. Steve Burbank and Sean Farhang first helped me think about procedure from an institutional angle. I'm of course grateful to my own law school professors: Glenn Cohen for teaching me that civil procedure was interesting, and Mark Wu for being a mentor and pushing me into academia. My Bigelow Fellowship mentors deserve special thanks: Saul Levmore for always pushing me to think harder about legal puzzles and for his mentorship along the way, and William Hubbard for nudging me to think about civil procedure empirically.

This book draws on several of my previous works on private enforcement, particularly: Diego A. Zambrano, Neel Guha, Austin Peters & Jeffrey Xia, *Private Enforcement in the States*, 172 U. Pa. L. Rev. 61 (2023); Nitisha

Baronia, Jared Lucky & Diego A. Zambrano, *Private Enforcement at the Founding and Article II*, 114 Calif. L. Rev. (2026); and Diego A. Zambrano, *Discovery as Regulation*, 119 Mich. L. Rev. 71 (2020).

For generously reading the manuscript and providing thoughtful comments, I thank Rachel Bayefsky, Brian Fitzpatrick, Myriam Gilles, William Hubbard, Jared Lucky, Rick Marcus, and James Pfander.

For outstanding research assistance, I thank Dayle Dahae Chung, whose indefatigable help was invaluable throughout this project. I also thank Ian Kenneth Woods, Estefania Bolivar, and Liana Van Nostrand. For research assistance in the earlier stages of drafting, I thank Anna Kuritzkes, Haaris Zaid Siddiqi, Avi Dugginapeddi, Justin Iannacone, Carlos Lapuerta, and Parker Elizabeth Grove. For help with proofing and finishing touches, I thank Esther Lawrence, Faith Fisher, Lucy Ricca, and Katerina Kaganovich.

I am thankful to the team at Stanford University Press, including the several anonymous reviewers who provided invaluable feedback as well as my editor Marcela editorial, design, and production editor David Zielonka; production editor Tiffany Mok; and Charlie Clark at Newgen.

# NOTES

## Introduction

1. Notice of Violation of the Clean Air Act from US EPA to Volkswagen AG, Audi AG & Volkswagen Group of America, Inc. (Sept. 18, 2015), https://www.epa.gov/sites/default/files/2015-10/documents/vw-nov-caa-09-18-15.pdf.

2. In re Volkswagen "Clean Diesel" Mktg., Sales Pracs., & Prods. Liab. Litig., MDL No. 2672, 2016 WL 4204369 (N.D. Cal. Apr. 12, 2016).

3. Andrea Thomas, *Germany Set to Allow Collective Lawsuits Following VW Scandal*, Wall St. J. (May 9, 2018).

4. Diego A. Zambrano, Neel Guha, Austin Peters & Jeffrey Xia, *Private Enforcement in the States*, 172 U. Pa. L. Rev. 61, 77 (2023).

5. Diego A. Zambrano, *Discovery as Regulation*, 119 Mich. L. Rev. 71, 75 (2020).

6. Zambrano et al., *Private Enforcement in the States*, *supra* note 4, at 63.

7. *Id.*

8. *Id.*

9. *Id.*

10. Zachary Liscow, *Getting Infrastructure Built: The Law and Economics of Permitting*, 39 J. Econ. Persps. 151, 164 (2025); World Bank Group, *Worldwide Bureaucracy Indicators Dashboard* (May 31, 2023), https://www.worldbank.org/en/data/interactive/2019/05/21/worldwide-bureaucracy-indicators-dashboard.

11. World Bank Group, *Worldwide Bureaucracy Indicators Dashboard* (May 31, 2023), https://www.worldbank.org/en/data/interactive/2019/05/21/worldwide-bureaucracy-indicators-dashboard.

12. Robert A. Kagan, Adversarial Legalism: The American Way of Law 3 (2d ed. 2019).

13. *Id.*

14. *Id.*

15. Sean Farhang, The Litigation State: Public Regulation and Private Lawsuits in the U.S. (2010).

16. Anna A. Mance, *How Private Enforcement Exacerbates Climate Change*, 44 Cardozo L. Rev. 1493, 1495–96 (2023).

17. Jim Carlton, *Solar Power's Land Grab Hits a Snag: Environmentalists*, Wall St. J. (June 4, 2021), https://www.wsj.com/us-news/climate-environment/solar-powers-land-grab-hits-a-snag-environmentalists-11622816381.

18. Jeremy B. White, *California Invites Court Fight with Gun Law that Mimics Texas on Abortion*, Politico (July 22, 2022), https://www.politico.com/news/2022/07/22/california-gun-law-newsom-00043539.

19. Miller v. Bonta, No. 22-cv-1446-BEN, slip op. at 5 (S.D. Cal. Dec. 19, 2022).

20. Zambrano et al., *Private Enforcement in the States*, *supra* note 4, at 66.

21. *Id.* at 125.

22. Nitisha Baronia, Jared Lucky & Diego A. Zambrano, *Private Enforcement at the Founding and Article II*, 114 Calif. L. Rev. 131 (2026) (manuscript at 4-5).

23. Zambrano et al., *Private Enforcement in the States*, *supra* note 4, at 62.

24. *Id.*

25. *Id.*

26. David Freeman Engstrom, *Agencies as Litigation Gatekeepers*, 123 Yale L.J. 616, 634 (2013).

27. *What the Data Is Telling Us*, Transit Costs Project, https://transitcosts.com/what-does-the-data-say/ (last visited Aug, 7, 2023); Eric Goldwyn, Alon Levy, Elif Ensari & Marco Chitti, Transit Costs Project: Understanding Transit Infrastructure Costs in American Cities (2023), https://transitcosts.com/wp-content/uploads/TCP_Final_Report.pdf.

28. Alon Levy, Niskanen Ctr., So You Want to Do an Infrastructure Project 1 (2021), https://www.niskanencenter.org/report-so-you-want-to-do-an-infrastructure-project.

29. National Environmental Policy Act of 1969, 42 U.S.C. §§ 4321–4347.

30. California Environmental Quality Act, Cal. Pub. Res. Code §§ 21000–21189 (West).

31. *See* Mance, *supra* note 16.

**Chapter 1**

1. *See* Alaska Oil Spill Commission, Spill: The Wreck of the *Exxon Valdez* (1990).

2. Zambrano, *supra* note 5, at 75.

3. 33 U.S.C.A. § 2701 *et seq.* (West).

4. *Id.*

5. See also Brian Fitzpatrick, The Conservative Case for Class Actions 59, 25–27 (U. Chi. Press 2019) for a related discussion.

6. *See, e.g.*, Brian Galle, *In Praise of Ex Ante Regulation*, 68 Vand. L. Rev. 1715 (2015); Peter Huber, *Safety and the Second Best: The Hazards of Public Risk Management in the Courts*, 85 Colum. L. Rev. 277 (1985).

7. *See also* Fitzpatrick, *supra* note 36, at 31–34.

8. Robert Iafolla, *NLRB Facing 'Lost Year' on New Precedents Despite Path to Quorum*, Bloomberg Law (July 21, 2025), https://www.bloomberglaw.com/daily-labor-report/nlrb-facing-lost-year-on-new-precedents-despite-path-to-quorum.

9. Jonathan H. Adler, *Stand or Deliver: Citizen Suits, Standing, and Environmental Protection*, 12 Duke Env't L. & Pol'y F. 39, 48 (2001); *see also* Barton H. Thompson, Jr., *The Continuing Innovation of Citizen Enforcement*, 2000 U. Ill. L. Rev. 185, 192 (2000).

10. 42 U.S.C.A. § 7604 (West).

11. Mance, *supra* note 16, at 1497–98.

12. 42 U.S.C. § 1983.

13. N.J. Stat. Ann. § 56:8-211 (West 2025).

14. Zambrano, *supra* note 5, at 79.

15. Kagan, *supra* note 12, at 7.

16. Sean Farhang, *Public Regulation and Private Lawsuits in the American Separation of Powers System*, 52 Am. J. Pol. Sci. 821 (2008).

17. *Exxon Valdez Spill Profile*, US EPA (Nov. 19, 2024), https://www.epa.gov/emergency-response/exxon-valdez-spill-profile.

18. Christopher V. Panoff, *In Re The Exxon Valdez Alaska Native Class v. Exxon Corp.: Cultural Resources, Subsistence Living, and the Special Injury Rule*, 28 Env't L. 701, 703 (1998).

19. In re *Exxon Valdez*, 236 F. Supp. 2d 1043, 1047 (D. Alaska 2002).

20. Amended and Consolidated Class Action Complaint and Demand for Jury Trial, In re *Exxon Valdez*, No. 2:89-cv-00095, 1989 WL 1690640 (July 17, 1989 D. Alaska).

21. *Id.*

22. *Id.*

23. *Id.*; *see also* 16 U.S.C. § 3114.

24. In re: the *Exxon Valdez*, 270 F.3d 1215, 1221 (9th Cir. 2001) (emphasis added).

25. Wendy Rose Parcells, *A Monumental Decision or Just an Environmental Catastrophe? An In-Depth Look at the Ramifications and Shortcoming of the US Supreme Court Decision in* Exxon Shipping Co. v. Baker, 16 U. Balt. J. Env't L. 1, 6 (2008).

26. *Id.* at 7; *See also* Lieff, Cabraser, Heimann & Bernstein, *Exxon Valdez Oil Spill Class Action*, https://www.lieffcabraser.com/environment/exxon-valdez/ (last visited July 22, 2025).

27. In re *Exxon Valdez*, 472 F.3d 600, 602 (9th Cir. 2006).

28. Exxon Shipping Co. v. Baker, 128 S. Ct. 2605 (2008).

29. EPA, *Exxon to Pay Record One Billion Dollars in Criminal Fines and Civil Damages in Connection with Alaskan Oil Spill* (Mar. 13, 1991), https://www.epa.gov/archive/epa/aboutepa/exxon-pay-record-one-billion-dollars-criminal-fines-and-civil-damages-connection-alaskan.html.

30. Press Release, US Dep't of Just., United States and the State of Alaska Opt Not to Recover Additional Damages from Exxon Mobil Under Reopener Provision of 1991 *Exxon Valdez* Oil Spill Settlement (Oct. 15, 2015), https://www.justice.gov/opa/pr/united-states-and-state-alaska-opt-not-recover-additional-damages-exxon-mobil-under-reopener. *See also* Nat'l Oceanic & Atmospheric Admin., *Exxon Valdez* (Aug. 17, 2020), https://darrp.noaa.gov/oil-spills/exxon-valdez; EPA, *Exxon to Pay Record One Billion Dollars in Criminal Fines and Civil Damages in Connection with Alaskan Oil Spill* (Mar. 13, 1991), https://www.epa.gov/archive/epa/aboutepa/exxon-pay-record-one-billion-dollars-criminal-fines-and-civil-damages-connection-alaskan.html.

31. Eyak Native Village v. Exxon Corp., 25 F.3d 773, 775 (9th Cir. 1994).

32. *See* Press Release, US Dep't of Just., *supra* note 30.

33. Oil Pollution Act of 1990, Pub. L. No. 101–380, 104 Stat. 484 (1990).

34. To be sure, the Oil Pollution Act (i) does not grant every person the right to sue for damages to natural resources, (ii) does not contain an explicit provision on injunction or attorney fees, and (iii) caps liability.

35. Endangered Species Act of 1973, 16 U.S.C. §§ 1531–1544.

36. Rod Hunter, Frederic Hendrickx & Koen Muylle, *Environmental Enforcement in Europe*, 7 Eur. Envtl. L. Rev. 47 (1998), 49 (emphasis added).

37. Josephine van Zeben, *The Untapped Potential of Horizontal Private Enforcement within EC Environmental Law*, 22 Geo. Int'l Envtl. L. Rev. 241 (2010), 242.

38. *ERIKA, West of France, 1999*, Int'l Tanker Owners Pollution Fed'n (Dec. 12, 1999), https://www.itopf.org/in-action/case-studies/erika-west-of-france-1999/.

39. *Le Procès Erika*, Ministere de la Justice (July 10, 2024), https://www.justice.gouv.fr/actualites/actualite/proces-erika.

40. Code de l'environnement [C. env.] art. L. 218-19 (Fr.).

41. Loi n° 83-583 du 5 juillet 1983 réprimant la pollution par les navires, art. 8(4) (Fr.).

42. International Oil Pollution Compensation Funds, Incidents Involving the 1992 Fund — Erika 1–2 (40th Exec. Comm., Feb. 19, 2008).

43. Cass. crim. Erika, No. 10-82.938 (Cour de cassation Sept. 25, 2012) (Crim.).

44. *1999 – L'Erika*, LPO (Nov. 10, 2021), https://www.lpo.fr/la-lpo-en-actions/agir-pour-la-faune-en-detresse/reponse-aux-catastrophes/historique-de-nos-interventions/1999-l-erika.

45. Eur. Parl. & Council, *Erika I Package: Maritime Safety Legislation*, EUR-Lex (Sept. 5, 2007), https://eur-lex.europa.eu/legal-content/EN/TXT/?uri=legissum:l24230.

46. Eur. Parl. & Council, *Erika II Package: Maritime Safety Legislation*, EUR-Lex (Jan. 25, 2007), https://eur-lex.europa.eu/legal-content/EN/TXT/?uri=legissum:l24242.

**Chapter 2**

1. Derek Thompson (@DKThomp), X (May 10, 2024, at 3:23 PM), https://x.com/DKThomp/status/1789013301805961531.

2. Rowan Moore Gerety, *Lawyer Up? Increasingly, Americans Won't, Or Can't.*, N.Y. Times Magazine (Apr. 17, 2025), https://www.nytimes.com/2025/04/17/magazine/lawyers-civil-court.html.

3. Zambrano et al., *Private Enforcement in the States, supra* note 4, at 77.

4. N.C. Gen. Stat. § 66-247 (2019).

5. Cal. Bus. & Prof. Code §§ 18897.8–18897.97.

6. N.J. Rev. Stat. § 4:12–44 (2024).

7. Fla. Stat. §§ 485.002, 485.005.

8. On top of private rights of action, statutes and rules provide a web of plaintiff-friendly procedures: low pleading standards, broad discovery, class actions, multidistrict litigation, punitive damages, fee-shifting, and so on.

9. Jonathan Haidt, The Anxious Generation (2024).

10. Utah Code Ann. § 78B-3-1103 (West 2025); David Stauss & Shelby Dolen, *Utah Legislature Repeals and Replaces Utah Social Media Regulation Act*, Husch Blackwell (Mar. 11, 2024), https://www.bytebacklaw.com/2024/03/utah-legislature-repeals-and-replaces-utah-social-media-regulation-act/.

11. John Healey, *Californians Have a Green Light to Sue the Gun Industry. How Will That Work?*, L.A. Times (Jan. 1, 2023), https://www.latimes.com/california/story/2023-01-01/californians-will-soon-have-their-chance-to-sue-the-gun-industry.

12. Jeremy B. White, *Judge Strikes Down California Gun Law Modeled On Texas Abortion Measure*, POLITICO (Dec. 19, 2022), https://www.politico.com/news/2022/12/19/california-gun-law-texas-abortion-00074689.

13. *Legislature and Attorney General Limit Local Regulation of Businesses*, Baker Botts (Mar. 5, 2024), https://www.bakerbotts.com/thought-leadership/publications/2024/march/legislature-and-attorney-general-limit-local-regulation-of-businesses.

14. *Id.*

15. H.B. 2127, 88th Leg., Reg. Sess. (Tex. 2023).

16. Craig Huber, *San Antonio Sues Texas Over So-Called 'Death Star' Bill*, Spectrum News 1 (July 24, 2023), https://spectrumlocalnews.com/tx/south-texas-el-paso/news/2023/07/24/san-antonio-sues-texas-over-so-called--death-star--bill-.

17. For a longer discussion on the methodological details, see Nitisha Baronia, Jared Lucky & Diego A. Zambrano, *Private Enforcement at the Founding and Article II, supra* note 22.

18. Farhang, *supra* note 16, at 10.

19. 15 U.S.C. § 7.

20. United States v. Cooper Corp., 312 US 600, 605 (1941).

21. Burnett v. NAR, Final Settlement Approval Order, No. 4:19-cv-00332 (W.D. Mo. Nov. 27, 2024).

22. Complaint at 2, Epic Games, Inc. v. Apple Inc., 559 F. Supp. 3d 898 (N.D. Cal. 2021), *aff'd in part, rev'd in part and remanded,* 67 F.4th 946 (9th Cir. 2023).

23. Advanced Micro Devices, Inc. v. Intel Corp., No. 1:05-cv-00441 (D. Del. June 2005) (consolidated into In re Intel Corp. Microprocessor Antitrust Litig., No. 1:05-md-01717).

24. In re Intel Corp. Microprocessor Antitrust Litig., Case No. 1:05-md-01717, Settlement Agreement (D. Del. Nov. 12, 2009).

25. In the Matter of Intel Corp., FTC Matter No. 951 0028, No. 9288, Decision and Order (Aug. 6, 1999) (consenting to cease unfair methods of competition in CPU/technical information markets).

26. Civil Rights Act of 1964, 42 U.S.C. §§ 2000a–2000h-6.

27. Americans with Disabilities Act of 1990, 42 U.S.C. §§ 12101–12213.

28. PGA Tour, Inc. v. Martin, 532 US 661, 674 (2001).

29. ADA Title III Technical Assistance Manual, § III-8.2000 (US Dep't of Just.).

30. Brief of the United States as Amicus Curiae Supporting Neither Party, Acheson Hotels, LLC v. Laufer, 601 US 1 (2023) (No. 22-429), 2023 WL 4028533, at *9.

31. Brief of the Chamber of Commerce of the United States of America et al. as Amici Curiae in Support of Petitioner, Acheson Hotels, LLC v. Laufer, 601 US 1 (2023) (No. 22-429), 2023 WL 3040228, at *7.

32. O'Hanlon v. Uber Techs., Inc., No. 2:19-cv-00675, 2019 WL 5895420 (W.D. Pa. Nov. 12, 2019).

33. Fair Labor Standards Act of 1938, 29 U.S.C. §§ 201–219.

34. *Id.* § 216.

35. *Id.*

36. Bouaphakeo v. Tyson Foods, Inc., 564 F. Supp. 2d 870, 878 (N.D. Iowa 2008).

37. Securities Exchange Act of 1934, 15 U.S.C. § 78a.

38. 17 C.F.R. § 240.10b-5.

39. John C. Coffee Jr., *What Caused Enron? A Capsule Social and Economic History of the 1990s*, Columbia Law Sch. Pub. Law & Legal Theory Working Paper Series, Paper No. 193 (2003).

40. US Senate Comm. on Gov't Affs., Financial Oversight of Enron: The SEC and Private-Sector Watchdogs 2 (2002).

41. *Enron Fast Facts*, CNN (July 2, 2013), https://www.cnn.com/2013/07/02/us/enron-fast-facts.

42. Adler, *supra* note 9, at 48.

43. Clean Air Act, 42 U.S.C. §§ 7401–7671q.

44. 42 U.S.C. § 7604.

45. Mance, *supra* note 16, at 1497–98.

46. Adler, *supra* note 9, at 47, 50; Thompson, Jr., *supra* note 9, at 192.

47. *See* Adler, *supra* note 9, at 47.

48. *Id.*

49. Environment Texas Citizen Lobby, Inc. v. ExxonMobil Corp., No. 4:10-cv-4969, 2017 WL 2331679 (S.D. Tex. Apr. 26, 2017).

50. 42 U.S.C. § 4332(2)(C).

51. Dep't of Transp. v. Pub. Citizen, 541 US. 752, 756–57 (2004) (quoting Robertson v. Methow Valley Citizens Council, 490 US 332, 350 (1989)).

52. Northern Plains Res. Council v. US Army Corps of Eng'rs, 454 F. Supp. 3d 985 (D. Mont. 2020).

53. False Claims Act, 31 U.S.C. §§ 3729–3733.

54. Vermont Agency of Nat. Res. v. United States ex rel. Stevens, 529 US 765, 769 (2000).

55. Press Release, US Dep't of Just., Bank of America to Pay $16.65 Billion in Historic Justice Department Settlement for Financial Fraud Leading Up to and During the Financial Crisis (Aug. 21, 2014), https://www.justice.gov/archives/opa/pr/bank-america-pay-1665-billion-historic-justice-department-settlement-financial-fraud-leading.

56. Christina Rexrode & Timothy W. Martin, *Whistleblowers Score a Big Payday: Three Individuals, One Firm to Receive $170 Million in Bank of America Probe*, Wall St. J. (Dec. 19, 2014), https://www.wsj.com/articles/third-whistleblower-to-collect-reward-related-to-bank-of-america-settlement-1419014474.

57. Zambrano et al., *Private Enforcement in the States*, *supra* note 4, at 93–95.

58. *Id.*

59. Paula Hannaford-Agor, Scott Graves & Shelley Spacek Miller, Nat'l Ctr. for State Cts., The Landscape of Civil Litigation in State Courts 6 (2015).

60. *Id.*

61. Kevin Kish, Dep't of Fair Employment & Hous., 2018 Annual Report 9-13 (2019).

62. The Hous. Workshop, CEQA by the Numbers: Myths & Facts 11 (2023).

63. Fla. Off. of the State Cts. Adm'r, 2022–23 State Courts System Annual Report 3 (2023), https://www.flcourts.gov/content/download/1334569/file/2022-23-srg-chapter-4-circuit-civil-20231219.pdf.

64. Searle Civ. Just. Inst., State Consumer Protection Acts: An Empirical Investigation of Private Litigation, Preliminary Report xi (2009).

65. Colo. Rev. Stat. Ann. § 6-4-115 (West 2025).

66. Cal. Bus. & Prof. Code § 17200 (2025).

67. In re Lithium Ion Batteries Antitrust Litig., 996 F.3d 1013 (9th Cir. 2021).

68. 431 US 720 (1977).

69. *Lithium Ion Batteries Antitrust $113M Class-Action Settlement*, Hagens Berman, https://www.hbsslaw.com/cases/batteries-antitrust (last visited July 21, 2025).

70. In re: Automotive Parts Antitrust Litigation, 997 F.3d 677 (6th Cir. 2021).

71. *Automotive Parts Litigation: $1.2 Billion*, https://www.autopartsclass.com (last visited July 21, 2025).

72. United States v. Microsoft Corp., 84 F. Supp. 2d 9 (DDC 1999).

73. Jack Schofield, *Microsoft Settles with California for $1.1 Billion*, The Guardian (Jan. 11, 2003), https://www.theguardian.com/technology/blog/2003/jan/11/microsoftsettl.

74. Cal. Labor Code §§ 2698–2699.8 (West 2024).

75. California Labor & Workforce Development Agency, *Private Attorneys General Act (PAGA) Frequently Asked Questions*, https://www.labor.ca.gov/resources/paga/paga-faqs/ (last visited March 22, 2026).

76. Joyce E. Cutler, *Google Pays California, Workers Largest PAGA-Only Settlement*, Bloomberg L. News (Dec. 5, 2023), https://news.bloomberglaw.com/litigation/google-pays-california-workers-largest-paga-only-settlement.

77. Danielle Wiener-Bronner, *McDonald's Pays $26 Million to Settle Wage Theft Suit*, CNN (Nov. 25, 2019), https://edition.cnn.com/2019/11/25/business/mcdonalds-wage-theft-settlement/index.html.

78. Tracy Colman, *Security Guards Settle Claims of Violated California Work Break Laws*, Top Class Actions (Feb. 25, 2019), https://topclassactions.com/lawsuit-settlements/employment-labor/security-guards-settle-claims-of-violated-california-work-break-laws/.

79. See Minn. Stat. § 116B.03 (2021); *see also* Haw. Const. art. 11, § 9 ("Each person has the right to a clean and healthful environment . . . including control of pollution and conservation, protection and enhancement of natural resources. Any person may enforce this right against any party, public or private, through appropriate legal proceedings . . . .").

80. Ohio Rev. Code § 3734.101 (West 2025).

81. Tex. Nat. Res. Code Ann. § 134.018 (West 2025).

82. Nev. Rev. Stat. § 575.040 (2025).

83. N.Y. Env't Conserv. Law § 71-0709 (McKinney 2025).

84. Cal. Health & Safety Code § 108860 (West 2025).

85. N.J. Stat. Ann. § 2A:35A-4 (West 2021).

86. Gen. Assemb. 1245, 196th Leg., 1st Sess. (N.J. 1974), https://repo.njstatelib.org/bitstream/handle/10929.1/5886/L1974c169.pdf?sequence=1&isAllowed=y [https://perma.cc/Q6C5-564A].

87. Mich. Comp. Laws §§ 324.1701 (2021).

88. *Michigan Environmental Protection Act*, Mich. World, https://michiganintheworld.history.lsa.umich.edu/environmentalism/exhibits/show/main_exhibit/1970s_activism/mepa [https://perma.cc/84S4-QF7A] (last visited Jan. 16, 2023).

89. Matthew W. Sawchak & Troy D. Shelton, *Exposing the Fault Lines Under State UDAP Statutes*, 81 Antitrust L.J. 903, 904 (2017).

90. *See id.* at 903; *see also* James Cooper & Joanna Shepherd, *State Unfair and Deceptive Trade Practices Laws: An Economic and Empirical Analysis*, 81 Antitrust L.J. 947 (2017).

91. *See, e.g.*, Tenn. Code Ann. § 47-18-109 (West) (allowing potential treble damages and attorney's fees); Haw. Rev. Stat. Ann. § 480-13 (West) (same); Tex. Bus. & Com. Code Ann. § 17.50 (West) (same).

92. *See e.g.*, Tenn. Code Ann. § 47-18-109 (West) (allowing potential treble damages and attorney's fees); Haw. Rev. Stat. Ann. § 480-13 (West) (same); Tex. Bus. & Com. Code Ann. § 17.50 (West) (same).

93. Cal. Bus. & Prof. Code § 17200 (West) ("As used in this chapter, unfair competition shall mean and include any unlawful, unfair or fraudulent business act or practice and unfair, deceptive, untrue or misleading advertising and any act prohibited by Chapter 1 (commencing with Section 17500) of Part 3 of Division 7 of the Business and Professions Code.").

94. Tex. Bus. & Com. Code Ann. § 17.44.

95. N.Y. Gen. Bus. Law § 349 (McKinney).

96. *See, e.g., id.* (enabling both the state AG and private plaintiffs to bring suit against violators of the statute).

97. Blue Cross & Blue Shield of N.J., Inc. v. Philip Morris, Inc., 190 F. Supp. 2d 407, 423 (E.D.N.Y. 2002) (rev'd on other grounds).

98. Dee Pridgen, *Wrecking Ball Disguised As Law Reform: Alec's Model Act on Private Enforcement of Consumer Protection Statutes*, 39 N.Y.U. Rev. L. & Soc. Change 279, 284 (2015) ("[N]inety-five percent of all antitrust cases are brought by private plaintiffs.").

99. *Id.* ("[O]ne major goal of these state 'little FTC Acts' was to supplement the enforcement activities of the FTC by enlisting the help of a potentially large cohort of consumer victims or 'private attorneys general' empowered to bring their own cases by virtue of the private right of action under the state laws.").

100. Bell v. Publix Super Markets, Inc., 982 F.3d 468 (7th Cir. 2020).

101. Pelman v. McDonald's Corp., 237 F. Supp. 2d 512 (S.D.N.Y. 2003).

102. Kagan, *supra* note 12, at 3.

103. Kagan, *supra* note 12, at 3.

104. *Id.*

105. *Id.* at 7–8.

106. Tomer Zarchin, *Israel First in World for Lawyers per Capita, Study Finds*, Haaretz (August 03, 2011), https://www.haaretz.com/2011-08-03/ty-article/israel-first-in-world-for-lawyers-per-capita-study-finds/0000017f-e805-da9b-a1ff-ec6f4bfa0000.

107. Alon Klement & Robert Klonoff, *Class Actions in the United States and Israel: A Comparative Approach*, 19 Theoretical Inquiries L. 151 (2018).

108. Fernán Restrepo, *The Capital-Market Effects of Introducing Private Rights of Action in Securities Regulation: Evidence from the United Kingdom*, 66 J. L. & Econ. 183, 189 (2023).

109. *Id.*

110. Srinivas Mazumdaru, *Will Class-Action Lawsuits Come to Germans' Rescue?*, DW (June 14, 2018), https://www.dw.com/en/dieselgate-will-class-action-lawsuits-come-to-germans-rescue/a-44227778.

111. Consumer Protection Act, 2002, SO 2002, c 30, ss 18(8)-(9), 99–100 (Ontario).

112. *See generally* J. Randy Beck, *The False Claims Act and the English Eradication of Qui Tam Legislation*, 78 N.C. L. Rev. 539 (2000).

113. *Antitrust Damages Actions in Europe*, Eur. Comm'n (Apr. 2025), https://competition-policy.ec.europa.eu/antitrust-and-cartels/actions-damages_en.

114. *European Competition Network: Statistics (ECN Statistics Data from 2004 to 2024)*, Eur. Comm'n (Apr. 2024), https://competition-policy.ec.europa.eu/antitrust-and-cartels/european-competition-network/statistics_en.; Lesley Hannah, *Taking Stock: The Implementation of the European Damages Directive*, Hausfeld Competition Bull. (Feb. 25, 2021), https://www.hausfeld.com/what-we-think/competition-bulletin/taking-stock-the-implementation-of-the-european-damages-directive#:~:text=What%20is%20clear%20is%20that,to%20have%20increased%20during%202020.

115. Charles Whiddington, Yumiko Takahashi & Zanda Romata, *Antitrust/Competition: Key Considerations in the EU and the UK in 2024*, Steptoe & Johnson LLP (Jan. 22, 2024), https://www.steptoe.com/en/news-publications/antitrustcompetition.html.

116. Sabrina Lombardi & Chanèle Rioux-McCormick, *Canadian Competition Law and Class Actions: Assessing Regulatory Shifts and Their Implications*, McKenzie Lake Lawyers LLP (Apr. 4, 2024), https://www.mckenzielake.com/insights-articles/canadian-competition-law-and-class-actions-assessing-regulatory-shifts-and-their-implications/.

117. Jonathan Hood, David Kent & D. Martin Low, *Canada: Private Antitrust Litigation, in The Antitrust Review of the Americas 2010*, McMillan LLP (Jan. 1, 2010), https://globalcompetitionreview.com/review/the-antitrust-review-of-the-americas/the-antitrust-review-of-the-americas-2010/article/canada-private-antitrust-litigation.

118. J. P. Nettle, *The State as a Conceptual Variable*, 20 World Pol. 559, 585 (1968).

119. Marc Galanter, *Reading the Landscape of Disputes: What We Know and Don't Know (and Think We Know) About Our Allegedly Contentious and Litigious Society*, 31 UCLA L. Rev. 4 (1983).

120. P. S. Atiyah, *Tort Law and the Alternatives: Some Anglo-American Comparisons*, 1987 Duke L.J. 1002 (1987).

121. For example, Brazil's antitrust statute contains a private right of action, but private plaintiffs rarely file suit under the statute. *See, e.g.*, Decreto No. 8.884 de 6 de Junho de 1994, Diário Oficial da União [D.O.U.] de 6.13.1994 (Braz.).

122. 50 U.S.C. § 4042.

123. 50 U.S.C. § 1324.

124. 46 U.S.C. § 31304.

125. 52 U.S.C. § 20510.

126. 47 U.S.C. § 274.

127. Cal. Bus. & Prof. Code § 18897.8 (West 2025) (emphasis added).

128. Tex. Bus. & Com. Code Ann. § 108.003 (emphasis added).

129. Fla. Stat. § 485.005 (West 2025) (emphasis added).

130. Okla. Stat. Ann. tit. 4, § 507 (West 2025) (emphasis added).

131. N.H. Rev. Stat. Ann. § 265:41-a (2024) (emphasis added).

132. N.H. Rev. Stat. Ann. § 339-C:7 (2024) (emphasis added).

133. N.C. Gen. Stat. § 20-116 (2023) (emphasis added).

134. Tex. Transp. Code Ann. § 70.072 (2024) (emphasis added).

135. N.C. Gen. Stat. § 66-247 (2019) (emphasis added).

**Chapter 3**

1. Gilman M. Ostrander, *The Colonial Molasses Trade*, 30 Agric. Hist. 77 (1956).

2. *Id.*

3. Tariff of 1790, ch. 39, 1 Stat. 180; Act of Aug. 4, 1790, ch. 35, 1 Stat. 145.

4. Baronia, Lucky & Zambrano, *supra* note 22, at 5, 37.

5. *Id.* at 38.

6. *Id.*

7. 3 William Blackstone, Commentaries *159.

8. 2 William Blackstone, Commentaries *438.

9. J. W. Gordon, Monopolies by Patents and the Statutable Remedies Available to the Public 52 (1897).

10. Charles Davenant, An Essay Upon the Probable Methods of Making a People Gainers in the Balance of Trade 55 (1699).

11. 3 William Blackstone, Commentaries *160.

12. *See* Felix Frankfurter & Thomas G. Corcoran, *Petty Federal Offenses and Trial by Jury*, 39 Harv. L. Rev. 931 n.65 (1926) (discussing an excise and customs act that provided for "one half the penalty" to go to any unofficial informer).

13. Beck, *supra* note 112, at 566.

14. *Id.* at 568–70.

15. *Id.* at 567–68.

16. *Id.* at 572.

17. *Id.* at 573.

18. *Id.* (quoting G. R. Elton, *Informing for Profit: A Sidelight on Tudor Methods of Law-Enforcement*, 11 Cambridge Hist. J. 149,150 (1954)).

19. *Id.* at 588.

20. *Id.* at 578.

21. Jessica Warner & Frank Ivis, *'Damn You, You Informing Bitch': Vox Populi and the Unmaking of the Gin Act of 1736*, 33 J. Soc. Hist. 299, 303 (1999).

22. *Id.* at 303.

23. *Id.* at 303.

24. *Id.* at 304.

25. *Id.* at 307.

26. *Id.* at 299.

27. *See* Philip B. Kurland & D. W. M. Waters, *Public Prosecutions in England, 1854–79: An Essay in English Legislative History*, 1959 Duke L.J. 493, 550–562.

28. *See id.* at 502.

29. *See* Baronia, Lucky & Zambrano, *supra* note 22, at 6.

30. 2 William Blackstone, Commentaries *436.

31. 145 E.R. 778 (Parker 274) (1709).

32. Sung Yup Kim, *"In a Summary Way, with Expedition and at a Small Expence": Justices of the Peace and Small Debt Litigation in Late Colonial New York*, 57 Am. J. Legal Hist. 83, 101 (2017).

33. Gordon, *supra* note 9.

34. Thomas Tapping, The Law and practice of the High Prerogative Writ of Mandamus, As It Obtains Both in England, and in Ireland 5 (1848).

35. Harold Garrett-Goodyear, *The Tudor Revival of Quo Warranto and Local Contributions to State Building*, *in* On the Laws and Customs of England: Essays in Honor of Samuel E. Thorne 231, 231–95 (Morris S. Arnold et al. eds., 1981).

36. James E. Pfander & Jacob Wentzel, *The Common Law Origins of Ex Parte Young*, 72 Stan. L. Rev. 1269 (2020).

37. Pfander & Wentzel, *supra* note 36, at 1278 n. 33.

38. *Id.* at 1277.

39. *Id.* at 1278.

40. James Bagg's Case (1615) 77 Eng. Rep. 1271; 11 Co. Rep. 93b.

41. Pfander & Wentzel, *supra* note 36, at 1296–98.

42. Laura Phillips Sawyer, *US Antitrust Law and Policy in Historical Perspective* 5 (Harv. Bus. Sch., Working Paper, Paper No. 19-110, 2019), https://www.hbs.edu/ris/Publication%20Files/19-110_e21447ad-d98a-451f-8ef0-ba42209018e6.pdf.

43. William L. Letwin, *English Common Law Concerning Monopolies*, 21 U. Chi. L. Rev. 355 (1954).

44. W.H. Price, English Patents of Monopoly (1906) ([The] "important exceptions . . . authorized by the act . . . opened a new chapter in the history of monopoly.").

45. Matthew Fisher, *The Statute of Monopolies and Modern Patent Law: Foundation Or Elaborate Folly?*, Intell. Prop. Q. (2022), https://discovery.ucl.ac.uk/id/eprint/10154944/2/Fisher_Statute%20of%20Monopolies%20-%20Foundation%20or%20Folly%20-%20for%20submission.pdf.

46. Statute of Monopolies, 1624, 21 Jac. 1, c. 3 (Eng.), reprinted in Primary Sources on Copyright (1450–1900) (L. Bently & M. Kretschmer eds., 2008).

47. Adams v. Woods, 6 US (2 Cranch) 336 (1805) ("[a]lmost every fine or forfeiture under a penal statute, may be recovered by an action of debt as well as by information . . . .").

48. Gordon, *supra* note 9, at 52.

49. *Id.*

50. *Id.*

51. *Id.*

52. Fisher, *supra* note 45, at 47 n.195.

53. Baronia, Lucky & Zambrano, *supra* note 22.

54. See Jared Lucky, "The Colonial Origins of Consumer Protection Law" (forthcoming PhD dissertation at Yale University, on file with author).

55. *Id.*

56. Randy Beck, *Qui Tam Litigation Against Government Officials: Constitutional Implications of a Neglected History*, 93 Notre Dame L. Rev. 1235 (2018).

57. *Id.* at 1271–72.

58. *Id.* at 1279.

59. *Id.* at 1287.

60. Baronia, Lucky & Zambrano, *supra* note 22.

61. See Steven L. Winter, *The Metaphor of Standing and the Problem of Self-Governance*, 40 Stan. L. Rev. 1371, 1395 (1988).

62. James E. Pfander, *Public Law Litigation in Eighteenth Century America: Diffuse Law Enforcement in a Partisan World*, 92 Fordham L. Rev. 469, 471 (2023).

63. Act of Mar. 14, 1820, ch. 24, 3 Stat. 548 (1820).

64. Act of June 30, 1834, ch. 161, § 20, 4 Stat. 729, 732 (1834).

65. Act of Aug. 25, 1841, ch. 12, 5 Stat. 445, 449 (1841).

66. Baronia, Lucky & Zambrano, *supra* note 22.

67. Richard A. Bales, *A Constitutional Defense of Qui Tam*, 2001 Wis. L. Rev. 381, 387 (2001).

68. Ann Woolhandler & Caleb Nelson, *Does History Defeat Standing Doctrine?*, 102 MICH. L. REV. 711, 728 (2004).
69. TransUnion LLC v. Ramirez, 594 US 413, 428 n.1 (2021).
70. Manuscript, Common Informers, available on request.
71. TransUnion LLC v. Ramirez, 594 US 413, 428 n.1 (2021).
72. Chitty, Of the Forms of action 113
73. *See* Woolhandler & Nelson, *supra* note 68, at 728 n.183 (citing United States v. Wonson, 28 F. Cas. 745 (C.C.D. Mass. 1812) (No. 16,750); United States v. Allen, 24 F. Cas. 772 (C.C.D. Conn. 1810) (No. 14,431); *see also* Stockwell v. United States, 80 US 531, 542–43 (1871)).
74. Act of Mar. 14, 1820, ch. 24, 3 Stat. 548, 548–51 (1820).
75. Act of June 30, 1834, ch. 161, 4 Stat. 729 (1834).
76. *Id.*
77. Act of Aug. 25, 1841, ch. 12, 5 Stat. 445, 449 (1841).
78. *Id.* § 4, at 451.
79. *Id.*
80. Perrin v. Sikes, 1 Day 19, 1802 WL 311 (Conn. 1801)
81. Eastman v. Curtis, 1 Conn. 323, 324 (Conn. 1815).
82. Wilmot v. Monson, 4 Day 114, 116 (Conn. 1809) (discussing an informer action over a usurious contract); Williams v. Jackson, 5 Johns. 489 (NY1809) (discussing an adverse possession informer claim).
83. Perrin v. Sikes, 1 Day 19, 1802 WL 311 (Conn. 1801).
84. Eastman v. Curtis, 1 Conn. 323, 324 (Conn. 1815).
85. Cole v. Smith, 4 Johns. 193 (N.Y. Sup. Ct. 1809).
86. Williams v. Jackson, 5 Johns. 489 (NY1809)
87. Pfander, *supra* note 62, at 488; United States ex rel. Zafirov v. Fla. Med. Assocs., 751 F. Supp. 3d 1293, 1319 (M.D. Fla. 2024).
88. Black. Com. 4th Eng. Ed. (Kerr) 149.
89. U S v. Tilden, 28 F. Cas. 179, 180 (C.C.D. Mass. 1859).
90. United States v. Morris, 26 F. Cas. 1321, 1322 (C.C.S.D. Ohio 1866)
91. Pollock v. The Laura, 5 F. 133, 141 (S.D.N.Y. 1880).
92. U S v. Tilden, 28 F. Cas. 179, 180 (C.C.D. Mass. 1859).
93. United States v. Morris, 26 F. Cas. 1321, 1322 (C.C.S.D. Ohio 1866).
94. Collection Act of 1789, § 36, 1 Stat. 29, 47 (1789).
95. Act of Apr. 7, 1798, ch. 28, 1 Stat. 549 (1798).
96. *Id.* § 7, at 550 (emphasis added).
97. Act of Apr. 29, 1802, ch. 36, § 3, 2 Stat. 171, 172 (1802).
98. *Id.* § 4.
99. Act of Aug. 29, 1842, ch. 263, § 5, 5 Stat. 543, 544 (1842).
100. Patent Act of 1870, ch. 230, § 39, 16 Stat. 198, 203 (1870).
101. Copyright Act of 1790, Pub. L. No. 15-1, 1 Stat. 124 (current version at 17 U.S.C. §§ 1–8, 10–12); Copyright Act of 1856, ch. 169, 11 Stat. 138, 139.
102. Copyright Act of 1856, ch. 169, 11 Stat. 138, 139.

103. *The 18th Century*, US Copyright Office, https://www.copyright.gov/timeline/timeline_18th_century.html (last visited Aug. 1, 2025); *see* Diana C. Obradovich, Garcia v. Google*: Authorship in Copyright*, 31 Berkeley Tech. L.J. 785, 786–77 (2016).

104. *Id.*

105. Oren Bracha, *The Adventures of the Statute of Anne in the Land of Unlimited Possibilities: The Life of a Legal Transplant*, 25 Berkeley Tech. L.J. 1427, 1455 (2010).

106. *Id.*

107. 11 Annals of Cong. 202 (1801–1802).

108. Jason Lee Guthrie, *Entered According to Act of Congress: Copyright and Photography in 19th Century America*, 38 Mil. Images 72, 72 (2020).

109. Act of Apr. 29, 1802, ch. 36, § 3, 2 Stat. 171, 171–72 (1802) (repealed).

110. *Id.*

111. Act of Mar. 3, 1845, ch. 83, 5 Stat. 615, 617–18 (1845).

112. Act of Aug. 11, 1856, ch. 86, § 30, 11 Stat. 33, 41 (1856).

113. Act of Aug. 18, 1856, ch. 127, § 17, 11 Stat. 52, 58 (1856).

114. Jared Lucky's dissertation (on file with author).

115. Gary Potter, *The History of Policing in the United States*, E. Ky. U. Police Stud. Online 1, 1–3 (2013), https://drive.google.com/file/d/1HZP07TsrsW02GX_GbhCQdgtI436uY_GL/view.

116. *Id.* at 2.

117. Beck, *supra* note 112, at 601.

118. Thomas Grande, *The False Claims Act: A Consumer's Tool to Combat Fraud Against the Government*, 12 Loy. Consumer L. Rev. 129, 130 (2000).

119. H.R. Rep. No. 111–97, at 2 (2009) (citing Cong. Globe, 37th Cong., 3d Sess. 952 (1863)).

120. *Id.*

121. Act of March 2, 1863, ch. 67, 12 Stat. 696, 698 (1863); *see* Charles Doyle, Cong. Rsch. Serv., R30785, Qui Tam: The False Claims Act and Related Federal Statutes (2021).

122. Doyle, *supra* note 121.

123. Cong. Globe, 37th Cong., 3d Sess., 955–56 (1863).

124. Theodore Eisenberg, *Section 1983: Doctrinal Foundations and an Empirical Study*, 67 Cornell L. Rev. 482, 484 (1981).

125. Monroe v. Pape, 365 US 167, 174 (1961)

126. Cong. Globe, 42d Cong., 1st Sess. 505 (1871).

127. *Id.* at App'x 40.

128. *The Ku Klux Klan Act of 1871*, US House of Representatives, https://history.house.gov/Historical-Highlights/1851-1900/hh_1871_04_20_KKK_Act/#:~:text=On%20this%20date%2C%20the%20House,civil%20and%20political%20rights%20of (last visited July 23, 2025).

129. 2 Cong. Rec. 4677 (1874). Senator Sherman noted in response to a question from Senator Conkling that the moieties under the internal-revenue laws, steamboat-inspection law, and "passenger law" have already been repealed. *Id.* at 4678.

130. Act of June 22, 1874, ch. 391, 18 Stat. 186, 186 (1874).

131. 2 CONG. REC. 4678 (1874).

132. HISTORY OF THE COMMITTEE ON FINANCE: UNITED STATES SENATE, S. DOC. NO. 95-27, at 43 (1977), https://www.finance.senate.gov/imo/media/doc/Sdoc95-27.pdf (noting how John Sherman was "Finance Committee member for 33 of the 37 years from 1861 to 1897, and Chairman from 1867 to 1877.")

133. 2 CONG. REC. 4674 (1874).

134. *Id.* at 4678.

135. *Id.*

136. *Id.*

137. Act of June 22, 1874, ch. 391, 18 Stat. 186, 186–87 (1874).

138. *Id.*

139. Senator Cameron from Pennsylvania objected to this provision because it gave "so much power" to the Secretary of the Treasury, as he would have the "authority to spend $200,000 to employ spies and informers at his own pleasure." 2 CONG. REC. 4679 (1874). However, while he moved to reconsider giving the Secretary of the Treasury money to pay informers, the motion "was not agreed to." *Id.*

140. *Id.* at 4680 (emphasis added).

141. 2 CONG. REC. 4801 (1874).

142. *Id.*

143. *Id.* at 4801–02.

144. *Id.* at 4802.

145. 2 CONG. REC. 4680 (1874).

146. 116 US 616 (1886); *see* Donald A. Dripps, *"Dearest Property": Digital Evidence and the History of Private "Papers" as Special Objects of Search and Seizure*, 103 J. CRIM. L. & CRIMINOLOGY 49 (2013).

147. ANNUAL REPORT OF THE SECRETARY OF THE TREASURY ON THE STATE OF THE FINANCES FOR THE YEAR 1877.

148. *Id.* at XXVIII–XXIX.

149. *Id.* at XXIX.

150. *Id.* at XXIX–XXX.

151. US DEP'T OF THE TREASURY, *John Sherman (1877–1881)*, https://home.treasury.gov/about/history/prior-secretaries/john-sherman-1877-1881 (last visited July 20, 2025).

**Chapter 4**

1. *See, e.g.*, STEPHEN SKOWRONEK, BUILDING A NEW AMERICAN STATE (1982).

2. The Clayton Antitrust Act of 1914, 15 U.S.C. §§ 12–27.

3. 29 U.S.C. § 216.

4. 42 U.S.C. § 7604.

5. Wayne D. Collins, *Trusts and the Origins of Antitrust Legislation*, 81 FORDHAM L. REV. 2279, 2281–88 (2013).

6. *Id.* at 2315–23.

7. *Id.* at 2335.

8. *Id.* (citing Report of the Committee on General Laws on the Investigation Relative to Trusts, S. 111–50, at 5 (N.Y. 1888)).

9. *See id.* at 2322–29; James May, *Antitrust Practice and Procedure in the Formative Era: The Constitutional and Conceptual Reach of State Antitrust Law*, 1880–1918, 135 U. Pa L. Rev. 496, 498 (1987); Laura Phillips Sawyer, *US Antitrust Law and Policy in Historical Perspective* 5 (Harv. Bus. Sch., Working Paper No. 19-110, 2019), https://www.hbs.edu/ris/Publication%20Files/19-110_e21447ad-d98a-451f-8ef0-ba42209018e6.pdf.

10. Myriam Gilles, *The Private Attorney General in a Time of Hyper-Polarized Politics*, 65 Ariz. L. Rev. 337, 349 (2023).

11. May, *supra* note 9, at 520.

12. Hans B. Thorelli, The Federal Antitrust Policy: Origination of an American Tradition 156 (Johns Hopkins Press 1955).

13. Gilles, *supra* note 10.

14. *Id.* at 155.

15. Act of March 9, 1889, ch. 257, 1889 Kan. Sess. Laws 390.

16. Thorelli, *supra* note 12, at 156.

17. The Sherman Antitrust Act of 1890, 15 U.S.C. §§ 1–7.

18. *Id.* § 1.

19. *Id.* § 2.

20. 21 Cong. Rec. S2456 (March 21, 1890).

21. May, *supra* note 9, at 504 n.63; H.R. Rep. No. 51-1707 (1890).

22. *See* 21 Cong. Rec. 2456 (March 21, 1890).

23. *Id.*

24. *Sherman Anti-Trust Act (1890)*, Nat'l Archives, https://www.archives.gov/milestone-documents/sherman-anti-trust-act (last visited July 28, 2025).

25. 21 Cong. Rec. 2455 (1890).

26. *Id.* at 2456.

27. *Id.* at 2457.

28. Statute of Monopolies 1624, 21 & 22 Ja. 1 c. 3.

29. Thomas C. McConnell, *Antitrust Enforcement by Private Parties: Analysis of Developments in the Treble Damage Suit*, 61 Yale L.J. 1010 (1952).

30. 21 Cong. Rec. 2564 (1890).

31. *Id.*

32. 21 CONG. REC. 2461 (1890) ("[E]ven the United States is scarcely the equal of a powerful corporation in a suit where a single officer with insufficient pay is required to compete with the ablest lawyers encouraged with compensation far beyond the limits allowed to the highest government officer.").

33. *Id.* at 2456.

34. 21 Cong. Rec. 4090 (1890).

35. *Id.*

36. Kent Roach & Michael J. Trebilcock, *Private Enforcement of Competition Laws*, 34 Osgoode Hall L.J. 461, 465 (1996).

37. 15 U.S.C. §§ 1–2.

38. United States v. E. C. Knight Co., 156 US 1, 13–16 (1895).

39. *Id.* at 17.

40. *See generally* NAOMI R. LAMOREUX, THE GREAT MERGER MOVEMENT IN AMERICAN BUSINESS, 1895–1904 (1985).

41. Gilbert Holland Montague, *The Defects of the Sherman Anti-Trust Law*, 19 Yale L.J. 88, 92 (1909);

George Bittlingmayer, *The Stock Market and Early Antitrust Enforcement*, 36 J.L. & ECON. 1, 6 (1993).

42. Montague, *supra* note 41, at 92 (citing North Securities Co. v. United States, 193 US 197 (1904)).

43. Gilles, *supra* note 10, at 347.

44. *Id.* at 348.

45. *Id.* at 350.

46. *Id.* at 351.

47. Arthur M. Johnson, *Antitrust Policy in Transition, 1908: Ideal and Reality*, 48 MISS. VALLEY HIST. REV. 415 (1961).

48. *Id.* at 97.

49. *Id.* at 99.

50. Johnson, *supra* note 47, at 426.

51. Montague, *supra* note 41, at 99; Johnson, *supra* note 47, at 425.

52. Johnson, *supra* note 47, at 426.

53. *Id.* at 425.

54. *Id.*

55. Montague, *supra* note 41, at 100.

56. *Id.* at 99.

57. *Id.* at 100.

58. Daniel A. Crane, *All I Really Need to Know About Antitrust I Learned in 1912*, 100 IOWA L. REV. 2025, 2031 (2025) (citing WILLIAM LETWIN, LAW AND ECONOMIC POLICY IN AMERICA: THE EVOLUTION OF THE SHERMAN ANTITRUST ACT 269 (1965)).

59. *See* James C. Lang, *The Legislative History of the Federal Trade Commission Act*, 13 WASHBURN L.J. 6, 23 (1974).

60. *See* Clayton Antitrust Act of 1914, H.R. 15657, 63rd Cong. (1914).

61. *See* Federal Trade Commission Act of 1914, H.R. 15613, 63rd Cong. (1914); 51 CONG. REC. 9059 (1914).

62. Gilles, *supra* note 10, at 352.

63. 15 U.S.C. § 45.

64. 15 U.S.C. §§ 46, 49.

65. 15 U.S.C. § 45(b).

66. 15 U.S.C. § 46.

67. 15 U.S.C. §§ 41, 57c.

68. 15 U.S.C. § 13.

69. 15 U.S.C. § 19.

70. 15 U.S.C. § 18.

71. *See* 15 U.S.C. § 15.

72. The Clayton Antitrust Act of 1914, Pub. L. No. 63-212, § 4, 38 Stat. 730 (1914).

73. *See* 15 U.S.C. § 15(a).

74. 15 U.S.C. § 26.

75. 15 U.S.C. § 16.

76. *See, e.g.*, Zenith Radio Corp. v. Hazeltine Rsch., Inc., 395 US 100, 130–31 (1969) ("[T]he purpose of giving private parties treble-damage and injunctive remedies was not merely to provide private relief, but was to serve as well the high purpose of enforcing the antitrust laws.").

77. Comment, *Proof Requirements in Anti-Trust Suits: The Obstacles to Treble Damage Recovery*, 18 U. Chi. L. Rev. 130, 138 (1950).

78. *See* Peter Labuza, *Millionaires Against Billionaires: The Rise and Fall of the Private Plaintiff Antitrust Lawyer, 1946–1976*, 62 Am. J. Legal Hist. 88, 95 (2022) ("The government recorded thousands of cases through the first 50 years of antitrust, but private action had only led to a reported case 175 times—with only 13 in favor of the defendant. As one attorney explained, antitrust cases were difficult to prove without the time and resources the US government had.").

79. *Id.* at 96.

80. *Id.* at 99.

81. Hawaii v. Standard Oil Co. of Cal., 405 US 251, 262 (1972).

82. Zenith Radio Corp. v. Hazeltine Rsch., Inc., 395 US 100, 131, 133 (1969).

83. Perma Life Mufflers, Inc. v. Int'l Parts Corp., 392 US 134, 139 (1968), *overruled on other grounds by* Copperweld Corp. v. Indep. Tube Corp., 467 US 752 (1984).

84. Credit Suisse Sec. (USA) LLC v. Billing, 551 US 264, 279, 281, 285 (2007).

85. Bell Atl. Corp. v. Twombly, 550 US 544, 558–59 (2007).

86. Perma Life Mufflers, Inc., 392 US at 139.

87. Mitsubishi Motors Corp. v. Soler Chrysler-Plymouth, Inc., 473 US 614, 635–36 (1985).

88. Jonathan Grossman, *Fair Labor Standards Act of 1938: Maximum Struggle for a Minimum Wage*, Soc. Welfare Hist. Project, https://socialwelfare.library.vcu.edu/federal/fair-labor-standards-act-of-1938-2/#:~:text=During%20the%20constitutional%20crisis%20over,You%E2%80%99re%20pretty%20unconstitutional%2C%20aren%E2%80%99t%20you%3F%E2%80%9D17 (last visited July 29, 2025).

89. *Id.*

90. John S. Forsythe, *Legislative History of the Fair Labor Standards Act*, 6 Law & Contemp. Probls. 464, 465–66 (1939).

91. Grossman, *supra* note 88.

92. *See* Price v. Fishback & Andrew J. Seltzer, *The Rise of American Minimum Wages, 1912–1968*, 35 J. Econ. Persps. 73, 85 (2021).

93. Grossman, *supra* note 88.

94. *Id.* (quoting Record of the Discussion before the US Congress on the FLSA of 1938, at 20–21 (1938)).

95. *Id.*

96. *See* Forsythe, *supra* note 90, at 466.

97. James M. Landis, The Administrative Process 142–45 (1938) (7th prtg. 1966).

98. Reuel E. Schiller, *The Era of Deference: Courts, Expertise, and the Emergence of New Deal Administrative Law*, 106 Mich. L. Rev. 399, 406 (2007).

99. Forsythe, *supra* note 90, at 468–71.

100. Grossman, *supra* note 88.

101. Forsythe, *supra* note 90, at 476.

102. Fair Labor Standards Act of 1938, Pub. L. No. 75-718, § 16(b), 52 Stat. 1060, 1069 (1938).

103. *Id.*

104. H.R. Rep. No. 75-2738, at 33 (1938) (Conf. Rep.).

105. Brooklyn Sav. Bank v. O'Neil, 324 US 697, 705 n.16 (1945).

106. *Id.* at 699 n.1.

107. *Id.* at 705 n.16.

108. *Id.*

109. *Fair Labor Standards Act of 1937: Joint Hearings on S. 2475 and H.R. 7200 Before the S. Comm. on Educ. and Labor & the H. Comm. on Labor*, 75th Cong. 457–62 (1937) (statement of John M. Keating).

110. *Id.*

111. Mariano-Florentino Cuéllar, *Administrative War*, 82 Geo. Wash. L. Rev. 1343, 1355 (2014).

112. *Id.*

113. Alan Brinkley, The End of Reform: New Deal Liberalism in Recession and War 177–82 (1995).

114. Cuéllar, *supra* note 111, at 1405 ("This restrictive approach to administrative subpoenas probably reached its apogee in *Jones v. SEC* [in 1936].").

115. Brooklyn Sav. Bank v. O'Neil, 324 US 697, 705 n.16 (1945).

116. Beulah Amidon, *New Floors and Ceilings: The Wage and Hour Administration Reaches a Second Stage*, Survey Graphic (Dec. 1939), https://socialwelfare.library.vcu.edu/eras/great-depression/new-floors-ceilings-minimum-wage-1939.

117. *See* David Freeman Engstrom, *The Lost Origins of American Fair Employment Law: Regulatory Choice and the Making of Modern Civil Rights, 1943–1972*, 63 Stan. L. Rev. 1071 (2011).

118. *See Regulating the Recovery of Portal-to-Portal Pay, and for Other Purposes: Hearings Before Subcomm. No. 2 of the H. Comm. on the Judiciary*, 80th Cong. 166 (1947) (testimony of Lee Pressman, General Counsel, CIO).

119. Marc Linder, *Class Struggle at the Door: The Origins of the Portal-to-Portal Act of 1947*, 39 Buff. L. Rev. 53, 74 n.108, 137, 172 (1991).

120. 29 U.S.C. § 216(b).

121. *See, e.g.*, Tunstall v. Brotherhood of Locomotive Firemen, 323 US 210 (1944); Steele v. Louisville & Nashville & N.R. Co., 323 US 192 (1944); *see also* J.I. Case Co. v. Borak, 377 US 426 (1964).

122. Farhang, *supra* note 16, at 3.

123. *See* Engstrom, *The Lost Origins of American Fair Employment Law*, *supra* note 117, at 1084.

124. *Id.* at 1081.

125. Sean Farhang, *The Political Development of Job Discrimination Litigation, 1963–1976*, 23 STUD. AM. POL. DEV. 23, 36 (2009).

126. *Id.*

127. *Id.*

128. 42 U.S.C. § 2000e-5(f)(1).

129. Farhang, *The Political Development of Job Discrimination Litigation*, supra note 125, at 37.

130. *Id.*

131. J.I. Case Co. v. Borak, 377 US 426 (1964).

132. RALPH NADER, UNSAFE AT ANY SPEED: THE DESIGNED-IN DANGERS OF THE AMERICAN AUTOMOBILE (1965).

133. 25 N.Y.2d 560 (1970); Craig R. Whitney, *G.M. Settles Nader Suit on Privacy for $425,000*, N.Y. TIMES (Aug. 14, 1970).

134. Courtney Leatherman, *You Want Their Attention? Sue!*, CHRON. HIGHER EDUC. (Feb. 10, 1995), https://www.chronicle.com/article/you-want-their-attention-sue/.

135. *Id.*

136. *Id.*

137. Susan Gonzalez, *The Rise of Public Interest Advocacy — and the Attack on Big Government*, YALENEWS (Sept. 30, 2021), https://news.yale.edu/2021/09/30/rise-public-interest-advocacy-and-attack-big-government.

138. Nader v. Allegheny Airlines, 426 US 290 (1976).

139. Arthur Snow & Burton A. Weisbrod, *Consumer Interest Litigation: A Case Study of Nader* v. Allegheny Airlines, 16 J. CONSUMER AFFS. 1, 9 (1982).

140. 421 US 773, 791–92 (1975); *Victories*, PUB. CITIZEN, https://www.citizen.org/victories/ (last visited July 15, 2025).

141. *See, e.g.*, Pub. Citizen Health Rsch. Grp. v. Tyson, 796 F.2d 1479 (DC Cir. 1986); Pub. Citizen Health Rsch. Grp. v. Chao, 314 F.3d 143 (3d Cir. 2002); Pub. Citizen Health Rsch. Grp. v. US Dep't of Labor, 557 US 165 (3d Cir. 2009).

142. *See* David E. Craw, *The 'Freedom From Information' Act: A Look Back at Nader, FOIA, and What Went Wrong*, 126 YALE L.J.F. 232 (2016).

143. *Public Citizen's Role in Obtaining Nixon Watergate Tapes*, PUB. CITIZEN (June 3, 2005), https://www.citizen.org/news/public-citizens-role-in-obtaining-nixon-watergate-tapes/; Pub. Citizen v. Burke, 843 F.2d 1473 (DC Cir. 1988).

144. *See* Karen O'Connor & Lee Epstein, *Rebalancing the Scales of Justice: An Assessment of Public Interest Law*, 4 HARV. J. LAW PUB. POL'Y 483 (1984).

145. Memorandum from Lewis F. Powell, Jr. to Eugene B. Sydnor, Jr., Chairman, US Chamber of Com. Educ. Comm. (Aug. 23, 1971), https://scholarlycommons.law.wlu.edu/powellmemo/1/.

146. *Id.* at 6.

147. 42 U.S.C. §§ 7401–7671q.

148. 42 U.S.C. § 7604(a).

149. Adler, *supra* note 9, at 48.

150. Thompson, Jr., *supra* note 9, at 192.

151. Cong. Rsch. Serv., Env't Pol'y Div., 93-18, A Legislative History of the Clean Air Amendments of 1970, Together with a Section-by-Section Index 355 (1974).

152. Thompson, Jr., *supra* note 9, at 196.

153. *Id.*

154. *Id.*

155. Walker Newell, *The Legacy of Nixon, Reagan, and Horton: How the Tough on Crime Movement Enabled a New Regime of Race-Influenced Employment Discrimination*, 15 Berkeley J. Afr.-Am. L. & Pol'y 3, 14–15 (2013).

156. Gerard E. Lynch, *RICO: The Crime of Being a Criminal, Parts I & II*, 87 Colum. L. Rev. 661, 672 (1987).

157. 116 Cong. Rec. 585 (1970).

158. *See* Antonio J. Califa, *RICO Threatens Civil Liberties*, 43 Vand. L. Rev. 805, 807 (1990).

159. Organized Crime Control Act of 1970, Pub. L. No. 91-452, § 1, 84 Stat. 922, 923 (1970).

160. Califa, *supra* note 158, at 808.

161. *See Organized Crime Control: Hearings Before Subcomm. No. 5 of the H. Comm. on the Judiciary*, 91st Cong. 520 (1970).

162. *Id.* at 543–44.

163. *Id.* at 688.

164. 18 U.S.C. § 1964.

165. *See Organized Crime Control: Hearings Before Subcomm. No. 5 of the H. Comm. on the Judiciary*, 91st Cong. 520 (1970).

**Chapter 5**

1. *See* Sean Farhang, The Litigation State: Public Regulation and Private Lawsuits in the U.S. 57 (2010) ("Scholars have long recognized that private litigation plays an unusually pervasive and important role in the implementation of public policy in the United States as compared to industrial democratic countries with predominantly parliamentary systems."); Kagan, *supra* note 12, at 7–9 ("The United States has by far the world's largest cadre of politically-oriented cause lawyers who seek to influence public policy by means of innovative litigation.").

2. *See* Kagan, *supra* note 12, at 6–10 ("The very pervasiveness of American adversarial legalism, moreover, suggests that it is best viewed not merely as a method of solving legal disputes but as a mode of governance, embedded in the political culture and political structure of the United States.").

3. David Freeman Engstrom & David K. Hausman, *Rights, Redistribution, and the Rise of the "Litigation State": The Case of Disability Discrimination Laws*, 46 L. & Soc. Inquiry 788, 789 (2021).

4. *Id.* At 821.

5. Zambrano et al., *supra* note 4, at 62.

6. Kagan, *supra* note 12, at 16–21.

7. Farhang, *supra* note 16, at 3–6.

8. *See, e.g.*, KAGAN, *supra* note 12, at 16–21 (emphasizing other drivers of litigation, not legislative adoption of private rights of action, while holding statutory private rights of action to be an outgrowth of an adversarial legalist style).

9. Farhang, *supra* note 16, at 3.

10. *Id.* at 19–59.

11. *Id.* at 94–128.

12. *See id.* at 219–20.

13. *See id.* at 57–58.

14. *Id.* at 12.

15. *Id.* at 11–12.

16. *Id.* at 12.

17. *Id.*

18. *Id.* at 13.

19. *Id.* at 4.

20. *Id.* at 16.

21. *Id.* at 5, 17.

22. *Id.* At 5.

23. *Id.* at 16.

24. *Id.* at 5.

25. Zambrano et al., *supra* note 4, at 121.

26. *Id.* at 93.

27. *Id.* at 121.

28. *Id.* at 62.

29. *Id.*

30. *See generally* Baronia, Lucky & Zambrano, *supra* note 22.

31. Farhang, *supra* note 16, at 12.

32. Tunstall v. Brotherhood of Locomotive Firemen, 323 US 210, 213 (1944); *accord* Steele v. Louisville & Nashville R. Co., 323 US 192, 207 (1944).

33. J.I. Case Co. v. Borak, 377 US 426, 430–31 (1964).

34. US CONST. art. III; *see also* Diego A. Zambrano, *Federal Expansion and the Decay of State Courts*, 86 U. CHI. L. REV. 2101, 2113–14 (2019).

35. *Id.* at 2116–24.

36. 5 U.S.C. §§ 702, 703; 28 U.S.C. § 1331.

37. Michael D. Meuti, *Legalistic Individualism: An Alternative Analysis of Kagan's Adversarial Legalism*, 27 U.C. L. S.F. INT'L L. REV. 319, 342–43 (2004).

38. Daniel Polisar & Aaron Wildavsky, *From Individual to System Blame: A Cultural Analysis of Historical Change in the Law of Torts*, 1 J. POL'Y HIST. 129 (1989).

39. *See* MIRJAN DAMAŠKA, THE FACES OF JUSTICE AND STATE AUTHORITY: A COMPARATIVE APPROACH TO LEGAL PROCESS 44 (1986).

40. Farhang, *supra* note 16, at 13.

41. Farhang, *supra* note 16, at 13–14 (footnotes and citations omitted).

42. *See* MICHAEL SCHUDSON, THE GOOD CITIZEN: A HISTORY OF AMERICAN CIVIC LIFE (1999); SAMUEL WALKER, THE RIGHTS REVOLUTION: RIGHTS AND COMMUNITY IN MODERN AMERICA (1998); ERIC FONER, THE STORY OF AMERICAN FREEDOM 299–305 (1998).

43. Farhang, *supra* note 16, at 14–15.

44. John H. Langbein, *The German Advantage in Civil Procedure*, 52 U. Chi. L. Rev. 823, 855 (1985).

45. *See* Marc Galanter, *Reading the Landscape of Disputes: What We Know and Don't Know (and Think We Know) About Our Allegedly Contentious and Litigious Society*, 31 UCLA L. Rev. 4, 58 (1983).

46. *Id.*

47. Kagan, *supra* note 12, at 48.

48. *Id.*

49. *Id.* at 54.

50. *Id.* at 18.

51. *Id.* at 43.

52. *Id.* at 41.

53. *Id.*

54. *Id.*

55. *Id.* at 17; *see also* Daryl Levinson, Law for Leviathan: Constitutional Law, International Law, and the State 107–109 (2024).

56. Kagan, *supra* note 12, at 19.

57. *Id.* at 45.

58. *Id.* at 42.

59. *Id.*

60. *See* Erie Railroad Co. v. Tompkins, 304 US 64, 78–80 (1938).

61. *Id.* at 43.

62. *Id.* at 17.

63. An Act for the Prevention and Suppression of Combinations Formed in Restraint of Trade, S.C. 1889, c. 41.

64. Combines Investigation Act, S.C. 1923, c. 9, amended by S.C. 1976, c. 76.

**Chapter 6**

1. Paul Pierson, *Increasing Returns, Path Dependence, and the Study of Politics*, 94 Am. Pol. Sci. Rev. 251, 251 (2000).

2. Margaret Levi, *A Model, a Method, and a Map: Rational Choice in Comparative and Historical Analysis*, *in* Comparative Politics: Rationality, Culture, and Structure 28 (Mark I. Lichbach & Alan S. Zuckerman ed., 1st ed. 1997).

3. Pierson, *supra* note 1, at 252–53.

4. Chapter 3.

5. Act of June 30, 1834, Pub. L. No. 161-23, 4 Stat. 729, 732.

6. Sherman Act, Pub. L. No. 547-51, 26 Stat. 210 (current version at 15 U.S.C. § 15(a)).

7. Statute of Monopolies 1624, 21 & 22 Ja. 1 c. 3.

8. *The 18th Century*, US Copyright Office, https://www.copyright.gov/timeline/timeline_18th_century.html.

9. *Id.*

10. Oren Bracha, *The Adventures of the Statute of Anne in the Land of Unlimited Possibilities: The Life of a Legal Transplant*, 25 Berkeley Tech. L.J. 1427, 1428 (2010) (internal citations omitted).

11. Statute of Anne 1710, 8 & 9 Ann. 1 c. 19.
12. Copyright Act of 1790, ch. 15, 2 Stat. 124, 124.
13. Bracha, *supra* note 10, at 1448.
14. Statute of Anne 1710, 8 & 9 Ann. 1 c. 19, § 1 (emphasis added); *see also* Bracha, *supra* note 10, at 1448.
15. Bracha, *supra* note 10, at 1454.
16. *Id.* at 1455.
17. *Id.*
18. Giovanni Capoccia & R. Daniel Kelemen, *The Study of Critical Junctures: Theory, Narrative, and Counterfactuals in Historical Institutionalism*, 59 World Pol. 341, 341 (2007).
19. *Id.*
20. Beck, *supra* note 112, at 601–08.
21. James C. Lang, *The Legislative History of the Federal Trade Commission Act*, 13 Washburn L.J. 6, 23 (1974).
22. Gilbert Holland Montague, *The Defects of the Sherman Anti-Trust Law*, 19 Yale L.J. 88, 97 (1909).
23. *Id.* at 99 (emphasis added).
24. Arthur M. Johnson, *Antitrust Policy in Transition, 1908: Ideal and Reality*, 48 Miss. Valley Hist. Rev. 415, 426 (1961).
25. Montague, *supra* note 41, at 109; Johnson, *supra* note 47, at 425.
26. Johnson, *supra* note 47, at 426 n.41.
27. *Id.* at 425.
28. *Id.*
29. Montague, *supra* note 41, at 100.
30. *Id.* at 99 (internal citations and quotation marks omitted).
31. *Id.* at 100.
32. Jack M. Kress, *Progress and Prosecution*, 423 Annals Am. Acad. Pol. & Soc. Sci. 99, 100 (1976).
33. Joan E. Jacoby, *The American Prosecutor in Historical Context*, Minn. Cnty. Att'ys Ass'n 3, https://cdn.ymaws.com/mcaa-mn.org/resource/resmgr/Files/About_Us/AmericanProsecutorHistorical.pdf (citing Jack M. Kress, *Progress and Prosecution*, 423 Annals Am. Acad. Pol. & Soc. Sci. 99, 100 (1976)).
34. *Id.* at 6.
35. 42 U.S.C. § 7604; 33 U.S.C. § 1365.
36. Charles O. Jackson, Food and Drug Legislation in the New Deal (Princeton U. Press, 1970)
37. Federal Trade Commission Act of 1914, Pub. L. No. 63-203, § 5, 38 Stat. 717, 719 (codified as amended at 15 U.S.C. §§ 41–58); Fair Debt Collection Practices Act, Pub. L. No. 95-109, § 813, 91 Stat. 874, 881 (1977) (codified as amended at 15 U.S.C. §§ 1692–1692p).
38. Zambrano, *supra* note 5, at 139.
39. *See* Kagan, *supra* note 12, at 19.

40. Marc J. Dunkelman, Why Nothing Works: Who Killed Progress—and How to Bring It Back (2025) New York: PublicAffairs, first ed.

41. Miss. Code Ann. § 63-11-30(3)(g) (2010).

42. *See* Zambrano et al., *supra* note 4, at 71.

43. See Mancur Olson, The Logic of Collective Action: Public Goods and the Theory of Groups 23–36 (Harv. U. Press 1971).

44. Sean Farhang, *Congressional Mobilization of Private Litigants: Evidence from the Civil Rights Act of 1991*, 6 J. Empirical Stud. 1, 20–21 (2009).

45. Myriam Gilles, *The Private Attorney General in a Time of Hyper-Polarized Politics*, 65 Ariz. L. Rev. 337, 361–65 (2023).

46. *Id.* at 363–64.

47. United States v. Nixon, 418 US 683, 693 (1974).

48. *See, e.g.*, Ric Simmons, Private Criminal Justice 54 (2024) ("[L]aw enforcement functions have historically been a private function, and the government's involvement in deterring crime and apprehending criminals is a relatively recent phenomenon."); Emma Kaufman, *The Past and Persistence of Private Prosecution*, 173 U. Pa. L. Rev. 89, 123 (2024) (recognizing that "[t]here is an enormous body of writing on the private security industry").

49. *See* Kaufman, *supra* note 48, at 122–23.

50. *See id.* at 128–29.

51. *See id.*

52. *See id.* at 131–39.

53. *See generally* Kaufman, *supra* note 48.

54. *See* Simmons, *supra* note 48, at 33–34, 74 (noting that many victims choose to adjudicate crimes as civil proceedings and seek restitution, rather than report them to the criminal justice system).

55. *See id.* at 119–127.

56. *See id.* at 74–83.

57. *See* W. Scott Van Alstyne, Comment, *The District Attorney—A Historical Puzzle*, 1952 Wisc. L. Rev. 125, 128–34 (1952) (suggesting that the American public prosecutor descended from the Dutch *schout*). *But see* Jack M. Kress, *Progress and Prosecution*, 423 Annals Am. Acad. Pol. & Soc. Sci. 99, 103–04 (1976) (casting doubt on the explanatory power of Van Alstyne's thesis).

58. Loi du 1er juillet 1972 relative à la lutte contre le racisme [Law of July 1, 1972, relating to the fight against racism], Journal Officiel de la République Française [J.O.] [Official Gazette of France], July 1, 1972 (Fr.).

59. Julie C. Suk, *Procedural Path Dependence: Discrimination and the Civil-Criminal Divide*, 85 Wash. U. L. Rev. 1315, 1326–33 (2008).

60. *Id.* at 1337–41.

61. *See id.* at 1343–46.

62. *Id.* at 1327–28.

63. *Id.* at 1343–46.

64. *Id.* at 1327–29.

65. *See generally* Zambrano, *supra* note 5.

66. Amalia D. Kessler, *Our Inquisitorial Tradition: Equity Procedure, Due Process, and the Search for an Alternative to the Adversarial*, 90 CORN. L. REV. 1181, 1233 (2005). *See generally* Richard Marcus, *"Looking Backward" to 1938*, 162 U. PA. L. REV. 1712 (2014).

67. Cuéllar, *supra* note 111, at 1402.

68. *Id.*

69. *Id.* at 1405.

70. FED. R. CIV. P. 26(a).

71. FED. R. CIV. P 45.

72. FED. R. CIV. P. 26(b)(1).

73. Richard L. Marcus, *Retooling American Discovery for the Twenty-First Century: Toward a New World Order?*, 7 TUL. J. INT'L & COMPAR. L. 153, 154–57 (1999).

74. *See, e.g.*, Geoffrey C. Hazard Jr., *From Whom No Secrets Are Hid*, 76 TEX. L. REV. 1665, 1681 (1998).

75. Zambrano, *supra* note 5, at 75.

76. Joanna C. Schwartz, *Introspection Through Litigation*, 90 NOTRE DAME L. REV. 1055 (2015); Joanna C. Schwartz, *A Dose of Reality for Medical Malpractice Reform*, 88 N.Y.U. L. REV. 1224 (2013).

77. *See generally id.*

78. *See generally* Fed. R. Civ. P. 23.

79. *See* David Marcus, *The History of the Modern Class Action, Part I: Sturm Und Drang, 1953–1980*, 90 WASH. U. L. REV. 587, 588 (2013); David Marcus, *The History of the Modern Class Action, Part II: Litigation and Legitimacy, 1981–1994*, 86 FORDHAM L REV 1785, 1788 (2018).

80. *See* Deborah Hensler, *From Sea to Shining Sea: How and Why Class Actions Are Spreading Globally*, 65 KANS. L. REV. 965, 971–79 (2017).

81. FITZPATRICK, *supra* note 36, at 59.

82. *Id.* at 60.

83. *Id.* at 59.

84. *See id.* at 59.

85. Beck, *supra* note 112, at 539.

86. *Id.* at 601

87. *Id.* at 603–04 (quoting HC Deb (6 Nov. 1934) (293) c. 843–46).

88. *Id.* at 606 (quoting HC Deb (9 Feb. 1951) (483) c. 2097); *id.* (quoting HC Deb (9 Feb. 1951) (483) c. 2094, 2100).

89. *Id.* at 606 (quoting HC Deb (9 Feb. 1951) (483) c. 2159) (alteration in original).

90. Ann Woolhandler & Caleb Nelson, *Does History Defeat Standing Doctrine?*, 102 MICH. L. REV. 689, 729 (2004) (quoting Richard A. Bales, *A Constitutional Defense of Qui Tam*, 2001 WIS. L. REV. 381, 389 (2001)).

91. Beck, *supra* note 112, at 604 (quoting Gerald Hurst, *The Common Informer*, 147 CONTEMP. REV. 189, 189 (1935)).

92. *See generally* HADLEY CANTRIL & LLOYD A. FREE, THE POLITICAL BELIEFS OF AMERICANS (1967).

93. John P. Robinson & John A. Fleishman, *Ideological Identification: Trends and Interpretations of the Liberal-Conservative Balance*, 52 Pub. Opinion Q. 134, 135 (1988).

94. *See generally* Ruy Texeira, *The Public Opinion Paradox: An Anatomy of America's Love-Hate Relationship with Its Government*, Center for American Progress (2010).

**Chapter 7**

1. Engstrom, *supra* note 26, at 634.

2. Federal Trade Commission Act of 1914, Pub. L. No. 63-203, § 5, 38 Stat. 717, 719 (codified as amended at 15 U.S.C. §§ 41–58); Fair Debt Collection Practices Act, Pub. L. No. 95-109, § 813, 91 Stat 874, 881 (1977) (codified as amended at 15 U.S.C. §§ 1692–1692p).

3. Zambrano, *supra* note 5, at 139.

4. Baronia, Lucky & Zambrano, *supra* note 22, at i.

5. Merrell Dow Pharms. Inc. v. Thompson, 478 US 804, 830 (1986) (Brennan, J., dissenting) ("The enforcement scheme established by the FDCA is typical of other, similarly broad regulatory schemes. Primary responsibility for overseeing implementation of the Act has been conferred upon a specialized administrative agency, here the Food and Drug Administration (FDA).").

6. *See* Alexander v. Sandoval, 532 US 275, 286–87 (2001).

7. The comparative angle, too, suggests that private enforcement should not be seen as a default. Other countries routinely solve problems in every regulatory area that we care about via public enforcement. Yet they only rarely add private rights of action on top of that.

8. Nicholas Bagley & David Schleicher, *The* State *Capacity Crisis* 11 (Univ. of Mich. Pub. L. & Legal Theory, Rsch. Paper No. 24-057, 2025), https://ssrn.com/abstract=5188510 (citations omitted).

9. *Id.* at 12 (citing Luciana Cingolani, *The Role of State Capacity in Development Studies*, 2 J. Dev. Persps. 88, 105–06 (2018)).

10. Francis Fukuyama, *What Is Governance?* 7 (Ctr. for Glob. Dev., Working Paper No. 314, 2013), https://ssrn.com/abstract=2226592.

11. Bagley & Schleicher, *supra* note 8, at 17 (citing Daron Acemoglu & Thierry Verdier, *Property Rights, Corruption and the Allocation of Talent: A General Equilibrium Approach*, 108 Econ. J. 138, 138–41 (1998).

12. Brink Lindsey, *State Capacity: What Is It, How We Lost It, and How to Get It Back*, Niskanen Ctr. (2021), https://www.niskanencenter.org/wp-content/uploads/2021/11/brinkpaper.pdf.

13. Bagley & Schleicher, *supra* note 8, at 27.

14. Library of Congress, Environmental Policy Division, A Legislative History of the Clean Air Amendments of 1970, Together with a Section-by-Section Index 355 (1974).

15. Margaret H. Lemos, *State Enforcement of Federal Law*, 86 N.Y.U. L. Rev. 698, 707 (2011) (discussing how private plaintiffs cannot be "captured by industry

or controlled by politicians" and can therefore serve "as a failsafe mechanism by reducing the risk that entire classes of violations will go unremedied"); *see also* FITZPATRICK, *supra* note 36, at 37–40.

16. George J. Stigler, *The Theory of Economic Regulation*, 2 BELL J. ECON. & MGMT. SCI. 3, 3 (1971); Samuel P. Huntington, *The Marasmus of the ICC: The Commission, the Railroads and the Public Interest*, 61 YALE L.J. 467 (1953); MARVER H. BERNSTEIN, REGULATING BUSINESS BY INDEPENDENT COMMISSION (1955).

17. Daniel Carpenter, *Corrosive Capture? The Dueling Forces of Autonomy and Industry Influence in FDA Pharmaceutical Regulation*, *in* PREVENTING REGULATORY CAPTURE: SPECIAL INTEREST INFLUENCE AND HOW TO LIMIT IT 152, 152–72 (Daniel Carpenter & David A. Moss eds., 2014).

18. Philip Wallach, *What Is Regulatory Capture?: Review of Preventing Regulatory Capture: Special Interest Influence and How to Limit It*, NEW RAMBLER, https://newramblerreview.com/book-reviews/political-science/what-is-regulatory-capture (last visited Dec. 18, 2025).

19. Carpenter, *supra* note 17, at 152.

20. JAMES Q. WILSON, BUREAUCRACY: WHAT GOVERNMENT AGENCIES DO AND WHY THEY DO IT 70 (1989) ("Experience, professionalism, and ideology are likely to have their greatest influence when laws, rules, and circumstances do not precisely define operator tasks.").

21. Engstrom, *supra* note 26, at 677.

22. James D. Cox & Randall S. Thomas, *Revolving Elites: The Unexplored Risk of Capturing the SEC*, 107 GEO. L.J. 845, 848 (2019).

23. *Id.*

24. Nicholas Bagley, *The Procedural Fetish*, 118 MICH. L. REV. 345 (2019).

25. Claire Liu & Jared R. Stanfield, *Do Connections to the U.S. President Enable Regulatory Capture? Evidence from Antitrust Merger Reviews* (Sept. 2, 2025) (manuscript at 6), https://ssrn.com/abstract=4714228.

26. FITZPATRICK, *supra* note 36, at 29–47; *see also* William H. J. Hubbard, *A Fresh Look at Plausibility Pleading*, 83 U. CHI. L. REV. 693, 706–07 (2016).

27. REBECCA L. PERLMAN, REGULATING RISK: HOW PRIVATE INFORMATION SHAPES GLOBAL SAFETY STANDARDS 20 (2023) ("There can be no product safety regulation without accurate information about the product in question."); *see also* FITZPATRICK, *supra* note 36, at 40–44.

28. Gary S. Becker, *Crime and Punishment: An Economic Approach*, in ESSAYS IN THE ECONOMICS OF CRIME AND PUNISHMENT 1, 1–54 (Gary S. Becker & William M. Landes eds., 1974).

29. Stigler, *supra* note 16.

30. Cary Coglianese, Richard Zeckhauser & Edward A. Parson, *Seeking Truth for Power: Informational Strategy and Regulatory Policymaking*, 89 MINN. L. REV. 277, 277 (2004) ("Information is the lifeblood of regulatory policy.").

31. STEPHEN BREYER, REGULATION AND ITS REFORM 109 (1982).

32. Jeounghee Kim & Skye Allmang, *Wage Theft in the United States: A Critical Review* 10 (Rutgers Sch. of Soc. Work, Ctr. for Women & Work, Working Paper

No. 2020-1, 2020), https://smlr.rutgers.edu/sites/default/files/Documents/Centers/CWW/Publications/wage_theft_in_the_united_states_a_critical_review_june_2020.pdf.

33. Rebecca L. Reindel & Ayusha Shrestha, AFL-CIO, Death on the Job: The Toll of Neglect 4 (33rd ed. 2024), https://aflcio.org/sites/default/files/2024-04/2411%20DOTJ%202024%20DIG%20NB%20REV.pdf.

34. Env't Integrity Project, EPA Enforcement After 20 Years: Inspections, Investigations, Prosecutions Down by Half; 20-Year Decline Undermines Environmental Justice 3 (2022), https://environmentalintegrity.org/wp-content/uploads/2022/02/EPA-Enforcement_20-Year-Review_Final.pdf.

35. Zambrano, *supra* note 5, at 102.

36. Alexander Dyck, Adair Morse & Luigi Zingales, *Who Blows the Whistle on Corporate Fraud?*, Harv. L. Sch. F. Corp. Governance (Feb. 15, 2010), https://corpgov.law.harvard.edu/2010/02/15/who-blows-the-whistle-on-corporate-fraud.

37. Peter G. Bryant & E. Woodrow Eckard, *Price Fixing: The Probability of Getting Caught*, 73 Rev. Econ. & Stat. 531, 535 (1991).

38. Stephen J. Choi & Adam C. Pritchard, *SEC Investigations and Securities Class Actions: An Empirical Comparison*, 13 J. Empirical Legal Stud. 27 (2016), https://doi.org/10.1111/jels.12096.

39. Zambrano, *supra* note 5, at 74 n.9 (quoting Stephen B. Burbank & Sean Farhang, Rights and Retrenchment: The Counterrevolution Against Federal Litigation 70 (2017)).

40. Jack Goldsmith, *Trump's Continuing Illegal Refusal to Enforce the TikTok Ban*, Exec. Functions (June 19, 2025), https://executivefunctions.substack.com/p/trumps-continuing-illegal-refusal.

41. H.R. 7521, 118th Cong. (2024).

42. Exec. Order No. 14310, 90 Fed. Reg. 26913 (June 19, 2025).

43. Luke P. Norris, *The Promise and Perils of Private Enforcement*, 108 Va. L. Rev. 1483 (2022); David L. Noll & Luke Norris, *Federal Rules of Private Enforcement*, 108 Cornell L. Rev. 1639 (2023); *see also* Jon Michaels & David Noll, *Vigilante Federalism*, 108 Corn. L. Rev. 1187 (2023) (discussing similar themes).

44. Norris, *supra* note 43, at 1489.

45. *Id.* at 1509–12.

46. *Id.*

47. *Id.* at 1512–14.

48. *Id.* at 1514–16.

49. Matthew C. Stephenson, *Public Regulation of Private Enforcement: The Case for Expanding the Role of Administrative Agencies*, 91 Va. L. Rev. 93, 114 (2005).

50. *Id.*

51. William M. Landes & Richard A. Posner, *The Private Enforcement of Law*, 4 J. Legal Stud. 1 (1975).

52. A. Mitchell Polinsky & Steven Shavell, *The Economic Theory of Public Enforcement of Law*, 38 J. Econ. Literature 45 (2000).

53. *See also* John C. Coffee, Jr., *The Regulation of Entrepreneurial Litigation: Balancing Fairness and Efficiency in the Large Class Action*, 54 U. CHI. L. REV. 877, 882–83 (1987).

54. Stephenson, *supra* note 49.

55. Chad M. Oldfather, *Judging, Expertise, and the Rule of Law*, 89 WASH. U. L. REV. 847, 851–54 (2012).

56. Engstrom, *supra* note 26, at 634.

57. Zachary D. Clopton, *Redundant Public-Private Enforcement*, 69 VAND. L. REV. 285 (2016).

58. FITZPATRICK, *supra* note 36, at 35.

59. JON D. MICHAELS & DAVID L. NOLL, VIGILANTE NATION: HOW STATE-SPONSORED TERROR THREATENS OUR DEMOCRACY (2024).

**Chapter 8**

1. Chris Micheli, *Private Attorneys General Act Lawsuits in California: A Review of PAGA and Proposals for Reforming the "Sue Your Boss" Law*, 49 U. PAC. L. REV. 265 (2018).

2. CAL. LAB. CODE §§ 2698–2699.5 (West 2004).

3. Private Attorneys General Act, ADVOCACY – CAL. CHAMBER OF COM., https://advocacy.calchamber.com/policy/issues/private-attorneys-general-act/ (last visited Oct 16, 2024).

4. Ben Nicholson, Legislation Review, *Businesses Beware: Chapter 906 Deputizes 17 Million Private Attorneys General to Enforce the Labor Code*, 35 MCGEORGE L. REV. 581, 581 (2004) (citing TOM GALLAGHER, TOUGH ON CRIME? THE DECLINE OF LABOR LAW ENFORCEMENT IN CALIFORNIA 1970–2000, 6–9 (June 2001) (copy on file with the McGeorge Law Review)).

5. *Id.* at 582.

6. *Assembly Committee on Labor and Employment: Hearing on S.B. 796*, 2003–04 Reg. Sess., 3 (Cal. July 9, 2003).

7. *Id.* at 4.

8. *Center for Oral and Public History Records Biographies of Three OC Leaders*, CSUF NEWS (Mar. 10, 2020), https://news.fullerton.edu/2020/03/coph-recognizes-political-leaders/.

9. Cheryl Miller, *"Not Forthright" or a "Dreamer"? Dueling Images of Joe Dunn Emerge as Bar Court Trial Nears Close*, LAW.COM: THE RECORDER (Apr. 17, 2024), https://www.law.com/therecorder/2024/04/17/not-forthright-or-a-dreamer-dueling-images-of-joe-dunn-emerge-as-bar-court-trial-nears-close/.

10. *About Our Firm*, THE SENATORS FIRM, https://www.thesenatorsfirm.com/our-history/ (last visited Oct 16, 2024).

11. SB 796 passed the Labor and Industrial Relations Committee 5–3 and the Judiciary Committee 4–2. *See* Cal. S. Journal, 2003–2004 Reg. Sess., No. 132.

12. Telephone Interview with Senator Joseph Dunn.

13. S.B. 796, 2003 Leg., Reg. Sess. (Cal. 2003).

14. For a full list of organizations registered in support/opposition to SB 796, *see* CAL. SENATE JUDICIARY COMMITTEE, ANALYSIS OF SB 796, at 8–10 (April 29, 2003).

15. Cal. Assemb. Comm. on Lab. & Emp., Analysis of SB 796, at 5 (July 9, 2003).

16. Cal. Senate Judiciary Committee, *supra* note 14, at 5.

17. *Id.*

18. Cal. Assemb. Comm. on Lab. & Emp., *supra* note 15, at 7.

19. Randall S. Leff, *"Bounty Hunter" Bill Becomes Law*, Ervin Cohen & Jessup LLP: Employment Law Reporter (Dec. 19, 2003), https://www.ecjlaw.com/publication-bounty-hunter-bill-becomes-law.

20. Nicholson, *supra* note 4, at 584.

21. *See* CalChamber, *Nonprofits, Disability Advocates, Small Businesses Join Fix PAGA Coalition to Reform California's Broken Private Attorneys General Act*, Advocacy – Cal. Chamber of Commerce (Mar. 26, 2024), https://advocacy.calchamber.com/2024/03/26/nonprofits-disability-advocates-small-businesses-join-fix-paga-coalition-to-reform-californias-broken-private-attorneys-general-act/; Press Release, CalChamber, New Report Finds Private Attorneys General Act Is Too Slow to Resolve Claims, Too Little Compensation Goes to Workers (Feb. 22, 2024), https://advocacy.calchamber.com/2024/02/22/new-report-finds-private-attorneys-general-act-is-too-slow-to-resolve-claims-too-little-compensation-goes-to-workers/.

22. Micheli, *supra* note 1; Tia Koonse & Minsu Longiaru, *A Shrinking Toolbox: The Corporate Efforts to Eliminate PAGA and Limit California Workers' Rights*, UCLA Lab. Ctr. (2024), https://labor.ucla.edu/publications/paga-california-2024/; Jennifer Kramer, *Why PAGA Still Matters*, Advoc. Mag. (Mar. 2023), https://www.advocatemagazine.com/article/2023-march/why-paga-still-matters.

23. Micheli, *supra* note 1, at 266.

24. *Id.*

25. Michael J. Nader, Timothy Fox & Zachary V. Zagger, *The Data Is In—California Class Action and PAGA Filings to Hit New Highs*, Ogletree Deakins: Insights & Resources (Jan. 12, 2024), https://ogletree.com/insights-resources/blog-posts/the-data-is-in-california-class-action-and-paga-filings-to-hit-new-highs/.

26. Koonse & Longiaru, *supra* note 22.

27. Rachel Deutsch, Rey Fuentes & Tia Koonse, UCLA Lab. Ctr., California's Hero Labor Law: The Private Attorneys General Act Fights Wage Theft and Recovers Millions from Lawbreaking Corporations 2 (Feb. 2020), https://www.labor.ucla.edu/wp-content/uploads/2020/02/UCLA-Labor-Center-Report_WEB.pdf.

28. Cal. Chamber of Com., *Private Attorneys General Act: Business Community Secures Historic PAGA Reform* (updated Jan. 2024), https://advocacy.calchamber.com/policy/issues/private-attorneys-general-act/.

29. Deutsch, Fuentes & Koonse, *supra* note 27, at 2.

30. Cal. Chamber of Com., *supra* note 28.

31. *Id.*

32. *Id.*

33. *Id.*

34. *Id.*

35. Suhauna Hussain, *Ballot Battle Averted: Labor and Business Reach Deal on Law Addressing Workplace Abuses*, Los Angeles Times (June 18, 2024),

https://www.latimes.com/business/story/2024-06-18/labor-business-reach-deal-to-get-paga-off-the-california-ballot.

36. Denise Davis, *CalChamber Applauds Passage of PAGA Reform Measures; Bills Head to Governor's Desk*, Advocacy – Cal. Chamber of Com. (June 27, 2024), https://advocacy.calchamber.com/2024/06/27/calchamber-applauds-passage-of-paga-reform-measures-bills-head-to-governors-desk/.

37. *See* Press Release, Governor of Cal., Governor Newsom Signs PAGA Reform (July 1, 2024), https://www.gov.ca.gov/2024/07/01/governor-newsom-signs-paga-reform/.

38. AB 2288, 2024 Cal. State Assemb., 2023–2024 Reg. Sess. (Cal. 2024).

39. *Id.*

40. *Id.*

41. *Id.*

42. Garrett D. Kennedy, *US: Maine Passes Law Similar to California's PAGA*, Lexology (July 22, 2021), https://www.lexology.com/library/detail.aspx?g=2b73d553-1463-4613-a9c1-f03f327ebbf7.

43. LD 1711, 2021 House of Rep., 129th Sess. (Me. 2021).

44. S.B. 152, 2023 Gen. Assemb., Reg. Sess. (Conn. 2023).

45. S.B. 1178, 2023 Gen. Assemb. Reg. Sess. (Conn. 2023).

46. A1474/S511, 2022–2023 General Assemb., Reg. Sess. (N.J. 2023).

47. *Id.*

48. Int. 563-2022, codified at N.Y.C. Admin. Code § 20-924.

49. Jamie Haar & Zachary V. Zagger, *New York City Creates a Private Right of Action for Alleged Violations of the Earned Sick and Safe Time Act*, Ogletree Deakins (Jan. 23, 2024), https://ogletree.com/insights-resources/blog-posts/new-york-city-creates-a-private-right-of-action-for-alleged-violations-of-the-earned-sick-and-safe-time-act/.

50. Micheli, *supra* note 1; Kramer, *supra* note 2.

51. Garrett Brown, *Field Enforcement Inspectors (CSHOs)*, Inside Cal/OSHA (Nov. 1, 2023), https://insidecalosha.org/wp-content/uploads/2024/02/CSHO-Summary-Chart-November-1-2023.pdf.

52. Jeanne Kuang, *California Is Sitting on Millions That Could Boost Wage Theft Response*, CalMatters (June 10, 2024), https://calmatters.org/politics/capitol/2024/06/california-wage-theft-enforcement-fund/.

53. Deutsch, Fuentes & Koonse, *supra* note 27.

54. Koonse & Longiaru, *supra* note 22.

55. *Id.* at 27.

56. Gerald L. Maatman, Jr. & Jennifer A. Riley, *Trend #6 – PAGA Filings Reached an All-Time High*, Duane Morris (Jan. 22, 2024), https://blogs.duanemorris.com/classactiondefense/2024/01/22/trend-6-paga-filings-reached-an-all-time-high/.

57. Deutsch, Fuentes & Koonse, *supra* note 27.

58. Marie Burke Kenny, *PAGA Reform Deal Announced by Governor Newsom: Placebo Or Panacea?*, Procopio: Labor & Emp. L. Blog (June 20, 2024), https://www.procopio.com/resource/paga-reform-deal.

59. *Id.*

60. California Labor & Workforce Development Agency, *Private Attorneys General Act (PAGA) Frequently Asked Questions*, https://www.labor.ca.gov/resources/paga/paga-faqs/ (last visited July 24, 2025).

61. Superintendent of Ins. of N.Y. v. Bankers Life & Cas. Co., 404 US 6, 13 & n.9 (1971).

62. Edward Flores & Svetlana Starykh, *Recent Trends in Securities Class Action Litigation: 2024 Full-Year Review*, NERA (Jan. 22, 2025), https://www.nera.com/insights/publications/2025/recent-trends-in-securities-class-action-litigation--2024-full-y.html.

63. *Id.*

64. *Id.*

65. *Id.*

66. Gary Gensler et al., *Testimony of the Securities and Exchange Commission Before the United States House of Representatives Committee on Financial Services*, US Sec. & Exch. Comm'n (Sept. 24, 2024), https://www.sec.gov/newsroom/speeches-statements/testimony-securities-exchange-commission-united-states-house-representatives-committee-financial.

67. Press Release, Weil, Gotshal & Manges LLP, Weil Welcomes Former Senior SEC Enforcement Official Sanjay Wadhwa (Feb. 3, 2025), https://www.weil.com/articles/weil-welcomes-former-senior-sec-enforcement-official-sanjay-wadhwa.

68. Press Release, US Sec. & Exch. Comm'n, SEC Announces Enforcement Results for Fiscal Year 2024 (Nov. 22, 2024), https://www.sec.gov/newsroom/press-releases/2024-186.

69. Benzinga, *How Many Stocks Are There?* (Sept. 24, 2024), https://www.benzinga.com/money/how-many-stocks-are-there; Financial Industry Regulatory Authority (FINRA), *Market Activity*, in 2024 Industry Snapshot (2024), https://www.finra.org/media-center/reports-studies/2024-industry-snapshot/market-data.

70. Robert R. Henssler, Jr. & T. Alex B. Folkerth, *Newfound Appreciation for Private Securities-Fraud Rights of Action to Protect the Public*, Daily Journal (reprinted with permission, Apr. 21, 2025), https://www.rgrdlaw.com/news-item-Newfound-appreciation-for-private-securities-fraud-rights-of-action-to-protect-the-public.html; Giovanni P. Prezioso, Gen. Couns., US Sec. & Exch. Comm'n, Speech by SEC Staff: Remarks Before the American Bar Association Section of Business Law, General Counsel Forum (June 3, 2004), https://www.sec.gov/news/speech/spch060304gpp.htm, *see also* Brief for the United States as Amicus Curiae Supporting Respondent, Halliburton Co. v. Erica P. John Fund, Inc., 573 US 258 (2014) (No. 13-317).

71. Elisse Walter, *The Interrelationship Between Public and Private Securities Enforcement*, Harv. L. Sch. F. Corp. Governance (Dec. 11, 2011), https://corpgov.law.harvard.edu/2011/12/11/the-interrelationship-between-public-and-private-securities-enforcement/ (quoting J.I. Case Co. v. Borak, 377 US 426, 432 (1964)).

72. Choi & Pritchard, *supra* note 38.

73. Fernán Restrepo, *The Capital-Market Effects of Introducing Private Rights of Action in Securities Regulation: Evidence from the United Kingdom*, 66 J. L. & ECON. 183 (2023).

74. Ed deHaan, Kevin Koh, Simi Kedia & Shivaram Rajgopal, *Does the Revolving Door Affect the SEC's Enforcement Outcomes? Initial Evidence from Civil Litigation*, J. ACCT. & ECON., Nov.–Dec. 2015, at 65, 66 (citing Mary Schapiro, Testimony Before the US Senate, 2009, at 28).

75. Michael Smallberg, *Revolving Regulators: SEC Faces Ethics Challenges with Revolving Door*, PROJECT ON GOV'T OVERSIGHT (May 13, 2011), https://www.pogo.org/reports/revolving-regulators-sec-faces-ethics-challenges-with-revolving-door.

76. Cox & Thomas, *supra* note 22, at 848.

77. Michael Shen & Samuel T. Tan, *The SEC Revolving Door and Comment Letters* (Singapore Mgmt. Univ. Sch. of Acct., Research Paper, Paper No. 2025-204, 2025), https://ssrn.com/abstract=3096855.

78. Daniel M. Hawke & Christian D. H. Schultz, *Top Takeaways from the Annual Report on the SEC's Whistleblower Program*, ARNOLD & PORTER (Nov. 26, 2024), https://www.arnoldporter.com/en/perspectives/advisories/2024/11/top-takeaways-sec-whistleblower-annual-report.

79. Dyck, Morse & Zingales, *supra* note 36.

80. Choi & Pritchard, *supra* note 38.

81. Donald C. Langevoort, *Disasters and Disclosures*, 107 GEO. L.J. 967, 967 (2018).

82. James D. Cox & Randall Thomas (with Dana Kiku), *Public and Private Enforcement of the Securities Laws: Have Things Changed Since Enron?*, 80 NOTRE DAME L. REV. 893, 897 (2004)

83. William W. Bratton & Michael L. Wachter, *The Political Economy of Fraud on the Market*, 160 U. PA. L. REV. 69 (2011).

84. James D. Cox & Randall S. Thomas, *Mapping the American Shareholder Litigation Experience: A Survey of Empirical Studies of the Enforcement of the U.S. Securities Law*, 41–42 (Duke L. Sch. Working Paper, Paper No. 41, 2010), https://scholarship.law.duke.edu/faculty_scholarship/2329/.

85. Ryan Lewis, Comment, *What Happens in Delaware Need Not Stay in Delaware: How Trulia Can Strengthen Private Enforcement of the Federal Securities Laws*, 2017 BYU L. REV. 715, 715 (2018).

86. John C. Coffee, Jr., *Reforming the Securities Class Action: An Essay on Deterrence and Its Implementation* 2 (Columbia L. & Econ. Working Paper No. 293, 2006), https://ssrn.com/abstract=893833.

87. Walter, *supra* note 71.

88. SKADDEN, ARPS, SLATE, MEAGHER & FLOM, LLP, Christopher P. Malloy & Shaud G. Tavakoli, *Securities Litigation Under the Private Securities Litigation Reform Act (PSLRA)*, LEXISNEXIS: PRACTICAL GUIDANCE (2021).

## Chapter 9

1. Eric Goldwyn, Alon Levy, Elif Ensari & Marco Chitti, Transit Costs Project: Understanding Infrastructure Costs in American Cities 11–12, https://transitcosts.com/wp-content/uploads/TCP_Final_Report.pdf.

2. Levy, *supra* note 28, at 6.

3. Richard J. Lazarus, The Making of Environmental Law 50 (2004).

4. Mance, *supra* note 16, at 1505 (citing 116 Cong. Rec. 32927 (1970) (statement of Sen. Edmund Muskie)); S. Rep. No. 91-1196, at 36–37 (1970); see also Env't Pol'y Div., Cong. Rsch. Serv., A Legislative History of the Clean Air Amendments of 1970, at 127 (Comm. Print 1974).

5. Current Documents, President Nixon's Message on the Environment, 1970, 58 CURRENT HIST. 362, 364 (1970).

6. Nina M. Hart, Cong. Rsch. Serv., R47205, Judicial Review and the National Environmental Policy Act of 1969 1 (2022), https://www.congress.gov/crs_external_products/R/PDF/R47205/R47205.1.pdf.

7. Marsh v. Or. Nat. Res. Council, 490 US 360, 375 (1989); Citizens to Pres. Overton Park, Inc. v. Volpe, 401 US 402, 414 (1971); Ctr. for Biological Diversity v. Nat'l Highway Traffic Safety Admin., 538 F.3d 1172, 1193 (9th Cir. 2008).

8. Mance, *supra* note 16, at 1509 n.72 (quoting David E. Adelman & Jory Reilly-Diakun, *Environmental Citizen Suits and the Inequities of Races to the Top*, 92 U. Colo. L. Rev. 377, 390-91 (2021)).

9. Brink Lindsey & Samuel Hammond, Niskanen Ctr., Faster Growth, Fairer Growth 108–09 (2020), https://www.niskanencenter.org/wp-content/uploads/2020/09/FGFG-full-report_final.pdf.

10. Michelle Ouellette & Ali Tehrani, *"The Lord's Work": An Overview of CEQA's Judicial Remedies and Recommendations for Reform*, 25 Hastings Envtl. L.J. 85, 87 (2019).

11. Diego A. Zambrano, *Litigation Scar Tissue & Construction Costs*, in Research Handbook on Law and Time 165, 181 (Frank Fagan & Saul Levmore eds., 2025).

12. Leah Brooks & Zachary D. Liscow, *Infrastructure Costs*, 15 Am. Econ. J.: Applied Econ. 3, 4 (2023).

13. Adelman & Reilly-Diakun, *supra* note 8.

14. Mance, *supra* note 16, at 1511 (citing John C. Ruple & Kayla M. Race, *Measuring the NEPA Litigation Burden: A Review of 1,499 Federal Court Cases*, 50 Env't L. 479, 500 (2020)).

15. Brian Potter, *How NEPA Works*, Construction Physics (Aug. 19, 2022), https://www.construction-physics.com/p/how-nepa-works.

16. Brooks & Liscow, *supra* note 12, at 17.

17. Alastair Bland, *Weakling or Bully? The Battle Over CEQA, the State's Iconic Environmental Law*, CalMatters (May 13, 2019, updated Mar. 27, 2025), https://calmatters.org/economy/2019/05/weakling-or-bully-ceqa-environmental-law-california-development-battles/.

18. Zambrano, *supra* note 5, at 182.

19. Adelman & Reilly-Diakun, *supra* note 8, at 387.

20. 42 U.S.C. § 7604.

21. Mance, *supra* note 16, at 1497–98 (citing Matthew C. Stephenson, *Public Regulation of Private Enforcement: The Case for Expanding the Role of Administrative Agencies*, 91 VA. L. REV. 93, 99 (2005)).

22. Adler, *supra* note 9, at 39, 47, 50.

23. Roger A. Greenbaum & Anne S. Peterson, T*he Clean Air Act Amendments of 1990: Citizen Suits and How They Work*, 2 FORDHAM ENV'T L. REV. 79, 80 (2011).

24. US ENV'T PROT. AGENCY, OFFICE OF ENF'T & COMPLIANCE ASSURANCE, FISCAL YEAR 2019 EPA ENFORCEMENT AND COMPLIANCE ANNUAL RESULTS 12 (Feb. 13, 2020), https://www.epa.gov/sites/default/files/2020-02/documents/fy19-enforcement-annual-results-data-graphs.pdf.

25. *Id.* at 12.

26. *Id.* at 3.

27. Adelman & Reilly-Diakun, *supra* note 8, at 383.

28. Ben McIntosh, *Standing Alone: The Fight to Get Citizen Suits Under the Clean Water Act into the Courts. Ailor v. City of Maynardville*, 12 MO. ENVTL. L. & POL'Y REV. 171 (2005) (citing Michael S. Greve, *The Private Enforcement of Environmental Law*, 65 TUL. L. REV. 339, 353 (1990)).

29. Anna Berti Suman & Sven Schade, *The Formosa Case: A Step Forward on the Acceptance of Citizen-Collected Evidence in Environmental Litigation?*, 6 CITIZEN SCI.: THEORY & PRAC. at 7 (2021), https://doi.org/10.5334/cstp.367.

30. Mance, *supra* note 16.

31. LINDA LUTHER, CONG. RSCH. SERV., RL33152, THE NATIONAL ENVIRONMENTAL POLICY ACT: BACKGROUND AND IMPLEMENTATION 5 (2008), https://sgp.fas.org/crs/misc/RL33152.pdf.

32. US GOV'T ACCOUNTABILITY OFF., GAO-14-370, NATIONAL ENVIRONMENTAL POLICY ACT: LITTLE INFORMATION EXISTS ON NEPA ANALYSES 27 (2014), https://www.gao.gov/assets/gao-14-370.pdf.

33. US DEP'T OF TRANSP., ESTABLISHING A TRANSPORTATION LIAISON PROGRAM 27 (2021), https://www.environment.fhwa.dot.gov/env_initiatives/liaisonCOP/documents/Establishing_a_Transportation_Liaison_Program_Guidebook_UpdatedFinal.pdf.

34. Christian Langpap & Jay P. Shimshack, *Private Citizen Suits and Public Enforcement: Substitutes or Complements?*, 59 J. ENV'T ECON. & MGMT. 235, 238 (2010).

35. Zambrano et al., *supra* note 4, at 93–95.

36. Adelman & Reilly-Diakun, *supra* note 8, at 434–35.

37. Ben Tyson, *An Empirical Analysis of Sue-and-Settle in Environmental Litigation*, 100 VA. L. REV. 1545 (2014).

38. Mance, *supra* note 16, at 1493.

39. Ha Chung, *Moving CEQA Away from Judicial Enforcement: Proposal for a Dedicated CEQA Agency to Address Exclusionary Use of CEQA*, 93 S. CAL. L. REV. 307 (2020).

40. Philip Rossetti, R Street, Addressing Nepa-Related Infrastructure Delays 7 (2021), https://www.rstreet.org/wp-content/uploads/2021/07/FINAL_RSTREET234.pdf.

41. Brian Potter, *supra* note 15.

42. Michael Bennon & Devon Wilson, *NEPA Litigation Over Large Energy and Transport Infrastructure Projects*, 53 Env't L. Rep. 10,836 (2023).

43. Brian Potter, *supra* note 15.

44. Jennifer Hernandez, *California Environmental Quality Act Lawsuits and California's Housing Crisis*, 24 Hastings Env't L.J. 21, 32 (2018).

45. Bland, *supra* note 17.

46. *Id.*

47. Adelman & Reilly-Diakun, *supra* note 8.

48. Hernandez, *supra* note 44, at 66.

49. Christian Britschgi, *How California Environmental Law Makes It Easy for Labor Unions to Shake Down Developers*, Reason (Aug. 21, 2019 at 10:00 PDT), https://reason.com/2019/08/21/how-california-environmental-law-makes-it-easy-for-labor-unions-to-shake-down-developers/.

50. Giulia Gualco-Nelson, *Reversing Course in California: Moving CEQA Forward*, 44 Ecology L.Q. 155, 166 (2017).

51. Carolyn Schuk, *Construction Unions Make CEQA Work for Them*, The Silicon Valley Voice (Aug. 9, 2019, at 13:00 PDT), https://www.svvoice.com/construction-unions-make-ceqa-work-for-them/.

52. Robert Selna, Opinion, *How a Few Unions Are Hijacking California Environmental Law*, S.F. Chron. (Jul. 3, 2022), https://www.sfchronicle.com/opinion/openforum/article/california-unions-environmental-law-17279821.php.

53. Zambrano, *supra* note 5, at 167 (quoting Selna, *supra* note 52).

54. Zambrano, *supra* note 5, at 183 (citing Alon Levy, *Costs Are Rising, US Highway Edition*, Pedestrian Observations (July 15, 2019), https://pedestrianobservations.com/2019/07/15/costs-are-rising-us-highway-edition).

55. Kevin Dayton, *Mailers Expose Union CEQA "Greenmail" Against Solar Developers*, Cal. Pol'y Ctr. (Sept. 26, 2012), https://californiapolicycenter.org/mailers-expose-union-ceqa-greenmail-against-solar-developers/.

56. *Id.*

57. *Id.*

58. Jennifer Hernandez, David Friedman & Stephanie DeHerrera, Holland & Knight, In the Name of the Environment 21 (2015).

59. Thompson, Jr., *supra* note 40, at 190.

60. US Const. art. III, § 2; Lujan v. Defs. of Wildlife, 504 US 555, 560 (1992).

61. Chung, *supra* note 39, at 316–17.

62. Hernandez et al., *supra* note 58.

63. Canadian Environmental Protection Act, S.C. 1999, c. 33 (Can.).

**Chapter 10**

1. Farhang, *supra* note 16.

2. Zambrano et al., *supra* note 4, at 71.

3. Zachary D. Clopton, *The False Marking Gold Rush: A Case Study of the Private Enforcement of Public Laws*, 49 Law & Soc. Inquiry 2380 (2024).

4. Beck, *supra* note 112.

5. *Id.* at 606 (quoting 483 PARL. DEB., H.C. (5th ser.) 2097 (1951) (statement of Mr. Hughes)); *id.* (quoting 483 PARL. DEB., H.C. (5th ser.) 2094, 2100 (1951) (statements of Mr. Hollis)).

6. Farhang, *supra* note 16.

7. Nicholas Bagley, *The Puzzling Presumption of Reviewability*, 127 Harv. L. Rev. 1285, 1289–90 (2014) (citing 5 U.S.C. § 701(a) (2012)).

8. *Id.* at 1204 (citing 5 U.S.C. § 704).

9. 8 US Code § 1252.

10. 47 U.S.C. § 159a(a).

11. Sharkey v. Quarantillo, 541 F.3d 75, 85 (2d Cir. 2008); COMSAT Corp. v. FCC, 114 F.3d 223, 226–27 (DC Cir. 1997).

12. Ben Makuch, *Elon Musk's Gutting of US Agencies Is Illegal, Experts Say. How Do You Muzzle Doge?* The Guardian (Feb. 10, 2025 at 6:00 EST), https://www.theguardian.com/us-news/2025/feb/10/elon-musk-doge-agency-illegal.

13. 5 U.S.C. § 552a(g)(4) (2022).

14. Protecting Our Constitution and Communities Act, H.R. 3454, 119th Cong. § 1101 (2025).

15. Farhang, *supra* note 16.

16. Zambrano, *supra* note 5.

17. *Id.*

18. *Id.*

19. *Lujan*, 504 US at 560.

20. Zachary D. Clopton, *Civil Justice and the (Green) New Deal*, 69 DePaul L. Rev. 334 (2020).

21. Rachel Bayefsky, *Public-Law Litigation at a Crossroads: Article III Standing and "Tester" Plaintiffs*, 99 N.Y.U. L. Rev. ONLINE 128 (2024).

22. *Lujan*, 504 US at 566.

23. Arthur F. Coon, *CEQA Standing Reform: Could Statutory Standing Requirements Feasibly Be Tightened to Bar Anti-Competitive Lawsuits Motivated By Economic Rather Than Environmental Concerns?*, Miller Starr Regalia (Dec. 12, 2012).

24. *Id.*

25. Shady Grove Orthopedic Assocs., P.A. v. Allstate Ins. Co., 559 US 393, 420 (2010) (Stevens, J. concurring in part and concurring in the judgment).

26. 1945 N.J. Laws 487 (codified at C. 131 14:3–15).

27. Cohen v. Beneficial Indus. Loan Corp., 337 US 541, 552 (1949).

28. Franklin S. Wood, Survey and Report Regarding Stockholders' Derivative Suits 59 (1944).

29. N.Y. Bus. Corp. Law § 627 (McKinney 2005).

30. Cal. Civ. Proc. Code § 1030 (West 2007).

31. Miriam R. Albert, *Security for Expense Statutes for LLCs and Limited Partnerships: Adding Value or Simply Adding to the Owners' Hopelessness?*, 23 U. Pa. J. Bus. L. 626, 678 (2021).

32. Cal. Civ. Proc. Code § 391.1 (West 2023).

33. Tyler T. Ochoa & Andrew Wistrich, *The Puzzling Purposes of Statutes of Limitation*, 28 Pac. L.J. 453, 454–55 (1997).

34. *Id.* at 454 (citing Oliver W. Holmes, Jr., *The Path of the Law*, 10 Harv. L. Rev. 457, 476 (1897)).

35. Susan K. Hori, *Court Sets Strict Rules for Calculating Limitations on CEQA Challenges*, Manatt, Phelps & Phillips LLP (July 4, 2011), https://www.manatt.com/insights/newsletters/real-estate-and-land-use/_real-estate-07-05-11.

36. *90-Day Limitations Period in Government Code § 65009 Applied to Political Reform Act Challenge to Land-Use Permits*, Perkins Coie LLP: California Land Use & Development Law Report (Dec. 22, 2022), https://perkinscoie.com/insights/blog/90-day-limitations-period-government-code-ss-65009-applied-political-reform-act.

37. Anna Lisa Knafo, *The Rule of Six When Suing a California Public or Governmental Entity*, Advoc. Mag., Nov. 2016, https://www.advocatemagazine.com/article/2016-november/the-rule-of-six-when-suing-a-california-public-or-governmental-entity.

38. Vu v. Prudential Prop. & Cas. Ins. Co., 26 Cal. 4th 1142, 1147–48 (2001) (discussing Cal. Ins. Code § 2071).

39. N.Y. C.P.L.R. 217 (McKinney 2025).

40. Schmidt v. S. Cal. Rapid Transit Dist., 14 Cal. App. 4th 23, 29–30 (1993).

41. Maureen Carroll, *Fee-Shifting Shortcuts*, 60 Harv. C.R.-C.L. L. Rev. 47 (2025).

42. Ron De Arakal, Opinion, *Five Ways to Reform California's Landmark Environmental Law Without Ruining the Earth or the Middle Class*, L.A. Times (Sept. 14, 2017, 5:00 AM PT), https://www.latimes.com/opinion/op-ed/la-oe-de-arakal-ceqa-reform-20170914-story.html.

43. Andreas Borgeas, *When It Comes to California Environmental Review, Legislation Is Better Than Lawsuits*, Fresno Bee (Jan. 17, 2020), https://www.fresnobee.com/opinion/readers-opinion/article239377963.html.

44. Chung, *supra* note 39.

45. Ouellette & Tehrani, *supra* note 10.

46. Hernandez, *supra* note 44, at 78–80.

**Conclusion**

1. *See, e.g.*, David Freeman Engstrom, *Agencies as Litigation Gatekeepers*, 123 Yale L.J. 616 (2013).

# INDEX

Printed and bound by CPI Group (UK) Ltd, Croydon, CR0 4YY
21/09/2026
14966018-0001